Found in Translation

Found in Translation: Itinerant French Epics in Medieval Scandinavia contains English translations of three Old Norse–Icelandic renderings of French *chansons de geste*: *Elis saga ok Rósamundu*, *Bevers saga*, and *Flóvents saga*, as well as *Bærings saga*, an Icelandic chivalric romance. Unlike the courtly romances, such as the Arthurian narratives of Chrétien de Troyes, the French epics were anonymous; the earliest is the eleventh-century *Chanson de Roland* (Song of Roland), dated to around 1100. The epic poems were recited by *jongleurs*, itinerant storytellers, who performed, for example, at markets on feast days in exchange for payment. The French epics translated into Old Norse–Icelandic were composed a couple of centuries later, under the influence of courtly romance, and are commonly designated "romance epics." They introduced the motif of the love of a beautiful Saracen maiden, *la bele Sarrasine*, for a Christian knight in Scandinavia. The romance epics are anonymous, unattributed narratives, which were subject to revision and to recreation. Each epic, *Élie de Saint-Gilles*, *Boeve de Haumtone*, and *Floovant*, has been transmitted in only one manuscript. Comparison of the Old Norse–Icelandic translations with the French epics reveals that the translations are renderings of variant versions of these narratives. At times the translations provide more information or less than the French epics; leave out entire passages or figures; or add new matter and conflicting facts. These translations resulted in the creation of a new Icelandic genre, the *riddarasaga* (pl. *riddarasögur*), or chivalric saga. Found in the oldest manuscript containing translations of French epics, *Bærings saga* stands at the head of this tradition, the first *riddarasaga* and a thoroughly original Icelandic narrative, despite a plot heavily indebted to *Bevers saga*.

Mediaeval Sources in Translation 64

Found in Translation

Itinerant French Epics in Medieval Scandinavia

Translated by
MARIANNE KALINKE

Toronto
PIMS
PONTIFICAL INSTITUTE OF MEDIAEVAL STUDIES

Acknowledgements

This publication is made possible in part by generous support from the Program in Medieval Studies at the University of Illinois Urbana-Champaign.

Library and Archives Canada Cataloguing in Publication

Title: Found in translation : itinerant French epics in medieval Scandinavia / translated by Marianne Kalinke.

Other titles: Container of (expression): Elis saga ok Rósamundu. English. | Container of (expression): Bevers saga. English. | Container of (expression): Flóvents saga. English. | Container of (expression): Bærings saga. English.

Names: Kalinke, Marianne E., author, translator | Pontifical Institute of Mediaeval Studies, publisher.

Series: Mediaeval sources in translation ; 64.

Description: Series statement: Mediaeval sources in translation ; 64 | Includes bibliographical references and index.

Identifiers: Canadiana (print) 20240424018 | Canadiana (ebook) 20240424026 | ISBN 9780888443144 (softcover) | ISBN 9781771104418 (PDF)

Subjects: LCSH: Sagas – Translations into English. | LCSH: Old Norse literature – Translations into English. | LCSH: Lays – Translations into Old Norse. | LCSH: French poetry – To 1500 – Translations into Old Norse. | LCSH: Chivalry in literature.

Classification: LCC PT7294 .K35 2024 | DDC 839/.63008–dc23

ON THE TITLE PAGE Illuminated initial (detail) from the opening of *Elye de Saint-Gilles*, Paris, BnF, MS fr. 25516, fol. 76r. Photograph courtesy Bibliothèque nationale de France; reproduced by permission.

© Pontifical Institute of Mediaeval Studies 2024

Pontifical Institute of Mediaeval Studies
59 Queen's Park Crescent East
Toronto, Ontario M5S 2C4
Canada
pims.ca

PRINTED IN CANADA

Contents

Preface • vii
Abbreviations and Conventions • ix

Introduction • 1
    Heroic Epic and Courtly Romance in the Germanic Realm • 1
    Translating French Epics and Romances • 2
    The Creation of a New Literary Genre in Iceland • 10
    Four Old Norse–Icelandic Epics • 14
    Rendering Old Norse–Icelandic Sagas into English • 46

The Romance Epic of Elis and Rosamunda • 52
The Romance Epic of Flovent • 110
The Romance Epic of Bevers • 159
The Romance Epic of Baering • 210

Bibliography • 246
Index • 252

Preface

The Old Norse–Icelandic sagas translated here took root during my studies at Indiana University more than half a century ago, when I entered the graduate program in Germanic Philology in the Department of Germanic Studies. To my surprise, a two-semester course in Old Norse–Icelandic was a requirement. The professor, Foster W. Blaisdell, who eventually became my *doktorvater*, had published a diplomatic edition of *Erex saga*, an Old Icelandic translation of Chrétien de Troyes' courtly romance *Erec et Enide* in 1965. Subsequently, he had begun to edit *Ívens saga*, a translation of Chrétien's *Yvain*. My doctoral dissertation came to be a comparative study of *Erex saga* and *Erec et Enide*, which meant I also had to learn Old French. This opened up the world of courtly French romance in Old Norse–Icelandic translation. During the decades that followed I concentrated on the chivalric romances, especially *Tristrams saga*, *Ívens saga*, and *Möttuls saga*, which were rendered from French at the behest of King Hákon Hákonarson of Norway (r. 1217–63). He had also commissioned the translation of one *chanson de geste*, the epic *Élie de Saint-Gilles*, which was translated as *Elis saga ok Rósamundu* by a certain Abbot Robert, identical with Brother Robert, who had earlier rendered *Tristrams saga*. The Old Norse–Icelandic translations of the French romances vary in their fidelity to the French sources, chiefly because most are extant only in later Icelandic copies, which were subject to the abilities and proclivities of Icelandic copyists. Comparison of the thirteenth-century *Elis saga* and *Élie de Saint-Gilles* revealed, however, that the French source of the Norwegian translation was not the single French manuscript that transmits *Élie de Saint-Gilles*. The case is the same with two other French epics, namely *Floovant* and *Boeve de Haumtone*. The Icelandic translations, *Flóvents saga* and *Bevers saga*, are not of the two French epics, each transmitted solely in a single manuscript. Like *Elis saga*, they are translations of variant versions of these epic poems. Distinctive for the French *chansons de geste* is that unlike Chrétien de Troyes's romances, they are authorless, composed by anonymous *jongleurs*, who might reinvent an epic with each performance.

In the course of my research on the four Old Norse–Icelandic sagas offered here in translation, I have become greatly indebted to a number of scholars, espe-

viii • *Preface*

cially to Kirsten Wolf, Professor and Torger Thompson Chair at the University of Wisconsin-Madison, and to Þorbjörg Helgadóttir, editor at the *Dictionary of Old Norse Prose* at the Arnamagnæan Institute in Copenhagen, for assistance with Old Norse–Icelandic vocabulary as well as recalcitrant and intractable expressions and phraseology. I have very much profited from helpful criticism of my approaches to *Bærings saga* and its role in the origin of the indigenous Icelandic *riddarasögur* by Ralph O'Connor, Professor in the Literature and Culture of Britain, Ireland & Iceland at the University of Aberdeen.

I thank the anonymous external readers for their enthusiasm for *Found in Translation*, and at the same time their recommendations for improving and correcting my translations, as well as enhancing the introduction. Thanks also to John Schechtman-Marko for his splendid editing of my manuscript and for saving me from many a stylistic infelicity and aberration. I am indebted to Megan Jones for her meticulous care and editorial rigor in seeing my book to completion and into print. Above all, I am profoundly grateful to Fred Unwalla, sometime Editor in Chief and now Director of Publications at the Institute, for the role he has played in bringing my project to fruition. Long before the possibility of publication ever arose, he had already pondered in correspondence the authority of authorless medieval texts, when anonymity causes the author to cease and become text. This had an impact on my own reflections and understanding of the variant versions of the anonymous itinerant epics translated here. Throughout, he encouraged me in my endeavor, and was generous with thoughtful criticism, searching questions, and constructive advice. Without his support and steady guidance my translations would not have found their way into print.

Abbreviations and Conventions

DONP   *Dictionary of Old Norse Prose: Indices.* Copenhagen: Arnamagnæanske Kommission, 1989.

LMA   *Lexikon des Mittelalters.* 10 vols. Munich: Artemis, 1977–99.

MGL   *Medieval German Literature: A Companion.* New York: Routledge, 1997.

MSE   *Medieval Scandinavia: An Encyclopedia.* New York: Routledge, 1993.

Full details about the editions and translations of the original Old French epics and the four Old Norse–Icelandic epics translated here can be found in the bibliography. A short title is used after the first reference in the notes. References to Old French texts provide the relevant verse number(s) followed by the edition or translation used, as well as page numbers. Citations of Old Norse–Icelandic texts follow the usual pattern, citing the edition or translation used, followed by page or line number as appropriate. Numbers preceded by a section symbol (§) refer to chapters in Old Norse–Icelandic texts; thus *Elis saga* § 32 refers to the saga's thirty-second chapter.

Introduction

Heroic Epic and Courtly Romance in the Germanic Realm

Prior to the Christianization of medieval Norway and Iceland literature was oral, not written, as the word *literature* would etymologically suggest. Christianity was introduced during the reign of King Óláfr Tryggvason of Norway (995–1000), and subsequently adopted by public consent at Iceland's Althing in either 999 or 1000.[1] Book learning came to Iceland with Christianization and the translation of Latin homilies and saints' lives. Whereas these cannot be said to be the best or most compelling texts of Icelandic literature, one scholar has nevertheless noted that "the sagas of kings and of Icelanders, or even the sagas of ancient heroes, would not have developed as they did unless several generations of Icelanders had been trained in hagiographic narrative."[2]

The situation was different in Germany, and especially France, where Christianity had long been established, and written literature flourished. Yet in France, alongside both sacred and secular literature, oral literature was also practiced by professional story tellers called *jongleurs*. One of these, Jean Bodel (ca. 1165–1210), a *jongleur*, epic poet, author of fabliaux, and a dramatist, identified in his *La chanson des Saisnes* (Song of the Saxons) three types of French narrative: the matter of France, the matter of Britain, and the matter of Rome.[3] He declared that the narratives concerning Britain are solely entertaining; the matter of Rome is wise and instructive; and the matter of France is fact, not fiction, for it deals with historical events.[4] The last refers to the *chansons de geste*, French epic poems, the earliest of which is the eleventh-century *Chanson de Roland* (Song of Roland), dated to around 1100, which is based on the Frankish military leader at the battle of Roncevaux Pass in 778, during the reign of

1. See Gunnar Karlsson, *Iceland's 1100 Years: The History of a Marginal Society* (Reykjavík, 2000), 33.
2. Gabriel Turville-Petre, *Origins of Icelandic Literature* (London, 1967), 142.
3. On Jean Bodel's oeuvre, see L. Gnädinger, "Bodel, Jean," *LMA*, 2: 306.
4. Henning Krauß, "Romanische Heldenepik," in *Europäisches Hochmittelalter*, ed. Henning Krauß (Wiesbaden, 1981), 145.

2 • INTRODUCTION

Charlemagne.[5] These epic poems were performed by *jongleurs* and only later set down in manuscript. The oldest complete manuscript of the *Song of Roland* is Oxford, Bodleian Library, MS Digby 23. It is dated between 1129 and 1165 and was written in Anglo-Norman some three centuries after the battle of Roncevaux Pass.[6] Bodel's reference to the matter of Britain signifies the *roman courtois* (courtly romance), chiefly the late twelfth-century Arthurian romances of Chrétien de Troyes[7] and also Thomas d'Angleterre's *Tristran*, the greatest of medieval love stories, with an impact on literature and the arts in succeeding centuries. The courtly romances differ from the *chansons de geste* in that they were written by a known author and subsequently transmitted by anonymous copyists. The differences in the creation and transmission of *chansons de geste* and chivalric romances is significant, since the former were created orally by an anonymous author.

Translating French Epics and Romances

Twelfth-century French literature played a decisive role in the introduction of two foreign and previously unknown literary genres in the Germanic realm, heroic epic and courtly romance. Early Middle High German literature included historiography in the form of the chronicle. The most impressive and expansive work is the *Kaiserchronik* (Chronicle of the Emperors), which is an account of Roman and German emperors and kings in more than 17,000 verses. The chronicle concludes with the twelfth-century Emperor Conrad III.[8] But Germany did not know epic poetry until the *Chanson de Roland* was translated into German under the patronage of Heinrich III the Lion (1129/1130–95), duke of Saxony and Bavaria, by the Pfaffe Konrad in his *Rolandslied* (The Song of Roland), which is dated ca. 1170.[9] Oddly enough, the cleric Konrad reveals in an epilogue that he first translated the French source into Latin and only then into German.[10] One

---

5. See the discussion of *chansons de geste* in Krauß, "Romanische Heldenepik," 145–59, especially 145–50; see also W.D. Lange, *Chanson de geste, LMA*, 2: 1703–7.

6. Rudolf Weigand, "Rolandslied," *LMA*, 7: 959–62.

7. Regarding Chrétien de Troyes and his Arthurian romances, see Norris J. Lacy, "Chrétien de Troyes," in *The New Arthurian Encyclopedia*, ed. Norris J. Lacy (New York & London, 1996), 88–91.

8. The *Kaiserchronik* is discussed by Marion E. Gibbs and Sidney M. Johnson at *MGL*, 92–93.

9. On the Pfaffe Konrad, see Eberhard Nellmann, "Konrad, Pfaffe," *LMA*, 5: 1363–64. Regarding the *Rolandslied*, see *MGL*, 94–96. On the relationship of the *Rolandslied* to the *Chanson de Roland*, see Jessie Crosland, *The Old French Epic* (New York, 1971), 242–47.

10. *MGL*, 94.

supposes that this was because of the close linguistic relationship of French and Latin, which might have made translation into Latin by a cleric easier than direct translation into German from French. Also notable is the fact that Konrad mentions that his patron is Heinrich the Lion, whose English wife, Mathilde, had encouraged the translation. In this case, royal patronage in the German area foreshadows the same in Norway in the next century.

Three Arthurian romances by Chrétien de Troyes were transmitted in German: his *Erec et Enide* and *Yvain*, the latter also known as *Le Chevalier au Lion* (The Knight of the Lion), were translated by Hartmann von Aue in *Erek* and *Iwein*,[11] while Wolfram von Eschenbach rendered Chrétien's *Perceval* in *Parzival*.[12] Finally, Gottfried von Strassburg translated Thomas d'Angleterre's *Tristran* in his German *Tristan*.[13] The German *Tristan* is incomplete, however, for Gottfried died when he had translated no more than five-sixth of the romance. Thomas's *Tristran* has been transmitted only fragmentarily, and that is the conclusion of the romance.[14] The only complete version of Thomas's *Tristran* is the Old Norse translation in *Tristrams saga ok Ísöndar*, as will be seen. The German translations are dated to the end of the twelfth and the beginning of the thirteenth centuries.

French literature also migrated to Scandinavia in the early thirteenth century, where courtly romances, lays, and epic poems were translated into Old Norse at the behest of King Hákon IV, that is, Hákon Hákonarson, of Norway (r. 1217–63). The Norwegian king charged a certain Brother Robert with translating Thomas d'Angleterre's *Tristran* into Old Norse. His rendition of *Tristrams saga ok Ísöndar* (The Saga of Tristram and Ísönd) in 1226 was followed, again by order of the king, by *Ívens saga* (The Saga of Íven), a translation of Chrétien de Troyes's *Yvain*, and a number of anonymous lays: the *Lay du cort mantel* (Lay of the Short Mantle) and twenty-one Breton lays that are transmitted in an anthology known as

11. For Hartmann's *Erek* and *Iwein*, see *MGL*, 135–43.

12. Wolfram von Eschenbach's *Parzival* is discussed at *MGL*, 180–88.

13. For Gottfried von Strassburg's *Tristan*, see *MGL*, 157–69. Strictly speaking, *Tristran* is not an Arthurian romance, but it is drawn into the Arthurian realm inasmuch as *Tristrams saga* relates two episodes in which King Arthur battles giants, the beard-collecting giant from Africa (*Tristrams saga* § 71) and the giant of Mont-Saint-Michel (§ 78). See *Tristrams saga ok Ísöndar*, ed. and trans. Peter Jorgensen, in *Norse Romance*, vol. 1: *The Tristan Legend*, ed. Marianne E. Kalinke (Cambridge, 1999), 171, 173, 183, 185. One fragment of Thomas's *Tristran* (Oxford, Bodleian Library, MS. Fr. 16) transmits the story of King Arthur and Orguillus, the beard-collecting giant. See *Thomas's Tristran* 720–81, ed. and trans. Stewart Gregory, in *Early French Tristan Poems*, vol. 2, ed. Norris J. Lacy (Cambridge, 1998), 45–47.

14. For Gottfried's and Thomas's *Tristan*, see Gottfried von Strassburg, *Tristan: With the 'Tristran' of Thomas*, ed. and trans. A.T. Hatto (London, 1960), 9–10, 301–53. Regarding the fragments of Thomas d'Angleterre's *Tristran*, see *Thomas's Tristran*, ed. Gregory, 3–4.

4 • INTRODUCTION

Strengleikar, that is, Stringed Instruments. The Prologue to the *Strengleikar* states: "This book, which the esteemed King Hákon had translated into Norse from the French language, may be called 'Book of Lais,' because from the stories which this book makes known, poets in Brittany – which is in France – composed *lais* which are performed on harps, fiddles, hurdy-gurdies, lyres, dulcimers, psalteries, rotes and other stringed instruments of all kinds which men make to amuse themselves and others in this world."[15] The mention in the Prologue that the *lais* were performed on musical instruments attests that unlike most medieval vernacular verse, which was intended for recitation aloud, "the lai has a particular connection with the lyric in so far as it is traditionally associated with a musical performance."[16]

Half a century after the death of King Hákon, another Scandinavian monarch was responsible for a second translation of Chrétien's *Yvain*, namely Eufemia, queen of Norway (1300–1312), at whose behest *Hærra Ivan* was translated into Old Swedish. Unlike the Old Norse translation, *Ívens saga*, which was written in prose, the Swedish translation was rendered in verse, in the so-called *Knittelvers* (doggerel verse), imported from Germany. *Hærra Ivan* was the first major work of fiction in Swedish.[17]

Finally, King Hákon also commissioned Abbot Robert, presumably an older Brother Robert who had advanced in the monastic hierarchy, to translate a *chanson de geste*, the epic poem *Élie de Saint-Gilles* into Old Norse, which is known as *Elis saga ok Rósamundu* (The Saga of Elis and Rosamunda).[18] Another *chanson de geste, Floovant*, was rendered from French either in Norway or Iceland by an anonymous translator and is known as *Flóvents saga*. Finally, the Anglo-Norman *Boeve de Haumtone*, dated to the last decade of the twelfth century,[19] is transmitted in the fourteenth-century Icelandic *Bevers saga*. These three *chansons de geste* are known as romance epics, since they were composed under the influence

15. *Strengleikar: An Old Norse Translation of Twenty-one Old French Lais*, ed. and trans. Robert Cook and Mattias Tveitane (Oslo, 1979), 5, 7.

16. Glyn S. Burgess and Keith Busby, introduction to Marie de France, *The Lais of Marie de France*, ed. and trans. Glyn S. Burgess and Keith Busby, 2nd ed. (London, 1999), 25.

17. *Hærra Ivan*, ed. and trans. Henrik Williams and Karin Palmgren, in *Norse Romance*, vol. 3: *Hærra Ivan*, ed. Marianne Kalinke (Cambridge, 1999), 3–5; see also Sofia Lodén, "Laudine and Lunete Moving North," in *Medieval Romances Across European Borders*, ed. Miriam Edlich-Muth (Turnhout, 2018), 95–96; and also Sofia Lodén, *French Romance, Medieval Sweden and the Europeanisation of Culture* (Cambridge, 2021), 4–5.

18. Regarding the French narratives translated by order of the Norwegian king, see Marianne Kalinke, "Norse Romance (*Riddarasögur*)," in *Old Norse–Icelandic Literature: A Critical Guide*, ed. Carol J. Clover and John Lindow (Toronto, 1985), 320–22, 332–33.

19. For a discussion of the dating, see *Boeve de Haumtone and Gui de Warewic: Two Anglo-Norman Romances*, trans. Judith Weiss (Tempe, 2008), 3; see also Christopher Sanders, ed., *Bevers saga: With the Text of the Anglo-Norman Boeve de Haumtone* (Reykjavík, 2001), cxliii.

INTRODUCTION · 5

of the courtly romances. The texts refer to themselves as *romans* or *estoires*, that is, "romances" or "stories."

Why, we might well ask, did King Hákon have the French narratives translated into Norwegian? At the beginning of the twentieth century one scholar used the introductory representation of King Arthur in *Möttuls saga* (Saga of the Mantle), which is the most encomiastic portrayal of a Scandinavian monarch in Scandinavian literature, to suggest that the Norwegian king had French literature rendered for the edification and emulation of his courtiers.[20] The first French text the Norwegian king ordered translated was Thomas d'Angleterre's *Tristran*, a romance that features an adulterous relationship. This would hardly represent an endeavor on Hákon's part to edify his court or a call for his courtiers to go and do likewise. As Sif Rikhardsdottir has pointed out, however, the translations commissioned by King Hákon "formed part of an introduction and institution of the courtly tradition of the French and Anglo-Norman rulers" at his court.[21] That included the foreign literature, in its various genres and of high quality, which he imported from abroad. Translations of Old French and Anglo-Norman *chansons de geste* and romances were being made, first in Norway, subsequently in Iceland, and by around 1300 in Sweden. Romance in general and romance themes became an integral part of the Old Norse–Icelandic generic system.[22]

A question arises concerning the early fourteenth-century translators of *Floovant* and *Boeve de Haumtone*. There is no evidence that these epic poems were rendered in Norway, and it is assumed that they were translated by Icelanders. As Gottskálk Jensson has pointed out, a considerable number of Icelanders had a clerical education and had fluency in Latin and Old French.[23] The most renowned was Jón Halldórsson, a Dominican friar, and bishop of Skálholt in the years 1322–1339.[24] Evidence suggests that in his youth Jón Halldórsson

20. Rudolf Meissner, *Die Strengleikar: Ein Beitrag zur Geschichte der altnordischen Prosaliteratur* (Halle a.S., 1902), 119.

21. Sif Rikhardsdottir, *Medieval Translations and Cultural Discourse: The Movement of Texts in England, France and Scandinavia* (Cambridge, 2012), 29.

22. See Jürg Glauser, "Romance – A Case Study," in *A Critical Companion to Old Norse Literary Genre*, ed. Massimiliano Bampi, Carolyne Larrington, and Sif Rikhardsdottir (Cambridge, 2020), 301–3.

23. Gottskálk Jensson, "Bishop Jón Halldórsson and 14th-Century Innovations in Saga Narrative: The Case of *Egils saga Einhenda ok Ásmundar berserkjabana*," in *Dominican Resonances in Medieval Iceland: The Legacy of Bishop Jón Halldórsson of Skálholt,* ed. Gunnar Harðarson and Karl G. Johansson (Leiden and Boston, 2021), 67 n10.

24. It is possible that Jón Halldórsson was a Norwegian, not an Icelander, but there is no certain evidence of this. See Christian Etheridge, "Canon, Dominican and Brother: The Life and Times of Jón Halldórsson in Bergen," in *Dominican Resonances in Medieval Iceland,* ed. Gunnar Harðarson and Karl G. Johansson, 11–12.

6 · INTRODUCTION

studied at the Faculty of Arts at the University of Paris before he entered the Dominican Order. His studies probably began when he was fourteen years of age and continued for several years, during which time he presumably also learned French.[25] Jón was known as a fluent speaker of Latin and "was said to be a great preacher and a wonderful storyteller," and he is famed for the translation of a collection of Latin exempla by French *jongleurs*.[26] The bishop also wrote *Klári saga*, a bridal-quest romance, which, according to its introduction, he found in France composed in Latin metre.[27] While scholars have generally accepted the Latin origin of the tale, this has recently been questioned, and the thesis has been advanced that *Klári saga* is not a translation but rather an original composition by Jón Halldórsson.[28] Be that as it may, the prolific raconteur might in fact also have been the translator of *Floovant* and/or *Boeve de Haumtone*.

Elis saga, *Flóvents saga*, and *Bevers saga* are translations of *chansons de geste* that engaged in a dialectic with the *romans courtois*, the courtly romances.[29] They are so-called romance epics, for under the impact of contemporary courtly romances, love plays an important role in these late *chansons de geste*. As will be seen, the authors also borrowed motifs from the Arthurian romances of Chrétien de Troyes, who is thought to have composed his romances between the late 1150s and ca. 1190.[30] These three narratives, however, are not the only *chansons de geste* to be translated in the North. Antedating them is the monumental *Karlamagnús saga*, a thirteenth-century compilation of *chansons de geste* relating to Charlemagne, which contains such epics as the *Chanson de Roland*, *Chanson d'Aspremont*, *Otinel*, *Moniage de Guillaume*, and *Pèlerinage de Charle-*

25. Etheridge, "Canon, Dominican and Brother," 17–21.

26. Jensson, "Bishop Jón Halldórsson," 68. For the collection of exempla, see *Islendzk Æventyri: Isländische Legenden, Novellen und Märchen*, ed. Hugo Gering, 2 vols. (Halle a. S., 1882–83). See also Jonas Wellendorf, "Homilies and Christian Instruction," in *The Cambridge History of Old Norse–Icelandic Literature*, ed. Heather O'Donoghue and Eleanor Parker (Cambridge, 2024), 370–71.

27. Concerning the origin of *Klári saga*, see Marianne Kalinke, "Table Decorum and the Quest for a Bride in *Clári saga*," in *At the Table: Metaphorical and Material Culture of Food in Medieval and Early Modern Europe*, ed. Timothy J. Tomasik and Juliann M. Vitullo (Turnhout, 2007), 71–72.

28. Shaun F.D. Hughes, "*Klári saga* as an Indigenous Romance," in *Romance and Love in Late Medieval and Early Modern Iceland*, ed. Kirsten Wolf and Johanna Denzin (Ithaca, 2008), 135–63. See also Sif Rikhardsdottir, "The Phantom of Romance: Traces of Romance Transmission and the Question of Originality," in *Medieval Romances Across European Borders*, ed. Miriam Edlich-Muth (Turnhout, 2018), 133–51.

29. Simon Gaunt, "Romance and Other Genres," in *The Cambridge Companion to Medieval Romance* (Cambridge, 2000), 48. See also Glauser, "Romance – A Case Study," 306–7.

30. See Lacy, "Chrétien de Troyes," 88–89.

magne.[31] The oldest manuscript of *Karlamagnús saga* is the fragmentary Oslo, Riksarkivet, NRA 61, dated ca. 1250–75.[32] The translator rendered the epics so faithfully that, in the words of one scholar, the translations "can sometimes be used as an aid to a critical reconstruction of French texts."[33]

Beginning in the early fourteenth century Icelanders started copying the Norwegian translations of French literature that were commissioned by King Hákon Hákonarson.[34] The earliest Icelandic copy of *Elis saga ok Rósamundu* is preserved solely in a single vellum fragment: Copenhagen, Den Arnamagnæanske Samling, AM 580 4°, dated ca. 1300–1325.[35] *Möttuls saga*, the Norse translation of the *Lay du cort mantel*, also has been transmitted, albeit fragmentarily, in one leaf: Copenhagen, Den Arnamagnæanske Samling, AM 598 I ß 4°, from ca. 1300–1350.[36] The complete text of *Tristrams saga ok Ísöndar*, the Old Norse translation of *Tristran*, is alone preserved in seventeenth-century Icelandic paper manuscripts; three vellum fragments, each a single leaf, date to the fifteenth century.[37] The case is similar with the translation of Chrétien's *Yvain*, that is, *Ívens saga*, the two oldest Icelandic copies of which date to the fifteenth century.[38] Despite this relatively sparse record of early manuscript transmission in Iceland, the Norwegian translations of French literature were well known by the end of the thirteenth and the beginning of the fourteenth century, to judge by their influence on the composition of indigenous Icelandic romances, called *riddarasögur* (chivalric sagas).[39] *Tristrams saga* inspired the composition, presumably in the fourteenth century, of a Tristanian saga, *Tristrams saga ok Ísoddar* (Saga of Tristram and Ísodd).[40] At the same time, the various motifs of the French romance, such as the ambiguous oath and the hall

31. See Povl Skårup, "Karlamagnús saga," *MSE*, 349–50. On the Carolingian *chansons de geste* translated into Old Norse, see Henry Goddard Leach, *Angevin Britain and Scandinavia* (Cambridge, MA, 1921), 236–54.

32. See "Karlamagnúss saga," *DONP*, 312–14.

33. Crosland, *The Old French Epic*, 268.

34. On the copying of the Norwegian translations, see Marianne Kalinke, "Scribes, Editors, and the *riddarasögur*," *Arkiv för Nordisk Filologi* 97 (1982): 36–38.

35. See *DONP*, 236.

36. See *DONP*, 338.

37. See *DONP*, 404–5.

38. See *DONP*, 292.

39. On the composition of indigenous Icelandic romances, see Marianne Kalinke, *Stories Set Forth with Fair Words: The Evolution of Medieval Romance in Iceland* (Cardiff, 2017), 114–41. See also Kalinke, "The Genesis of Courtly Romance in Iceland," *Journal of English and Germanic Philology* 123 (2024): 271–94.

40. See Joyce Hill, "Tristrams saga ok Ísoddar," *MSE*, 657–58. The oldest manuscript is Copenhagen, Den Arnamagnæanske Samling, AM 489 4°, dated ca. 1450. See *DONP*, 405.

8 • INTRODUCTION

of statues, entered the *Íslendinga sögur*, that is, the Sagas of Icelanders, and the indigenous Icelandic romances.[41]

Brother Robert's translation of the French *Tristran* in *Tristrams saga* is of extraordinary importance, since the French romance is extant in a mere ten fragments containing six narrative episodes from the last third of the romance.[42] The very beginning of the romance, the forestory of Tristran's parents as well as Tristran's proxy wooing of Iseut and slaying of the dragon, are lacking, as is the account of the sea voyage during which the couple consume the love potion. The only complete text of the French *Tristran* is the Old Norse translation.[43] The Old Norse–Icelandic renderings of French *chansons de geste* in *Elis saga*, *Flóvents saga*, and *Bevers saga* are similarly significant, since they transmit translations of variant versions of the French epics that are no longer extant.[44] In other words, the translations bear witness to the existence of deviating versions of the three French epic poems in the thirteenth century.[45] The romance epics are anonymous, unattributed narratives and were subject to revision and recreation. They were composed by *jongleurs* who addressed their audiences, such as in the first *laisse* of *Élie de Saint-Gilles*, where the poet says: "Now be silent lords; may God bless you, / The glorious one of heaven, the son of Saint Mary! / Would it please you to hear three tales of noble knights?"[46] And the epic *Floovant* concludes with

41. Marianne Kalinke, "Arthurian Echoes in Indigenous Icelandic Sagas," in *The Arthur of the North: The Arthurian Legend in the Norse and Rus' Realms*, ed. Marianne E. Kalinke (Cardiff, 2011), 145–59.

42. On the extant French fragments, see *Thomas's Tristran*, ed. Gregory, 3–4.

43. Aside from the shift to prose in translation and some reduction of text, *Tristrams saga ok Ísöndar* faithfully reproduces Thomas d'Angleterre's *Tristran*. Scholars have demonstrated that the saga faithfully transmits the content of Thomas's romance. See the magisterial study by Álfrún Gunnlaugsdóttir, *Tristán en el Norte* (Reykjavík, 1978). Unfortunately, this important monograph has not been translated into English and is therefore unknown to many scholars.

44. A note on the term "Old Norse–Icelandic": this is properly used for the language of the translations. Whereas Old Norse was the language of Norway, and we know that *Tristran* was translated in Norway, the translations considered here, with the exception of *Elis saga*, are transmitted solely in Icelandic copies; hence the term Old Norse–Icelandic.

45. The existence of French variant versions of the *chansons de geste* was already noted by Leach, *Angevin Britain and Scandinavia*, 235, 255–61. In the Introduction to his edition of the Old French text, Sven Andolf provides a summary of the Icelandic saga and points out that it does not correspond to *Floovant* but rather to the story of Fiovo in *Storie di Fioravante*. See *Floovant: Chanson de geste du XIIe siècle*, ed. Sven Andolf (Uppsala, 1941), lviii–lxv.

46. *Élie de Saint-Gilles* 1–3. For the edited text, see *Élie de Saint-Gilles: Nouvelle édition par Bernard Guidot d'après le manuscrit BnF no. 25516*, ed. Bernard Guidot (Paris, 2013), 3. The translation is taken from *Elye of Saint-Gilles: A Chanson de Geste*, ed. and trans. A. Richard Hartmann and Sandra Malicote (New York, 2011), 3; see also Krauß, "Romanische Heldenepik," 146–47.

the voice of the *jongleur*: "May God protect all those who have listened to me, and do not forget what I have recited for you."[47]

When Jean Bodel, cited previously, declared the matter of France to be fact, not fiction, since it deals with historical events, he was referring to the oldest *chansons de geste*, which are devoted to historical figures, such as Charlemagne, Roland, and William of Orange.[48] These oldest *chansons de geste* are the ones translated in the *Karlamagnus saga* compilation. Jean Bodel would have approved of them on account of their historicity. The three *chansons de geste* that were translated into Old Norse–Icelandic starting in the reign of King Hákon Hákonarson, however, were composed at a time when courtly romance had become fashionable, and they were greatly influenced by the new literary genre popularized by Chrétien de Troyes. They were composed by anonymous itinerant storytellers known as *jongleurs*, who performed, for example, at markets on feast days in exchange for payment. No other medieval narrative genre had as close a relationship between an author and his public as the *chanson de geste*.[49] It is noteworthy that each of the *chansons de geste* – *Élie de Saint-Gilles*, *Floovant*, and *Boeve de Hamtoun* – is extant in only one manuscript today.[50] The Old Norse–Icelandic translations bear witness, however, to the one-time existence of variant versions of the three epics in thirteenth-century French manuscripts. To judge by the transmission of other Old French texts, for example, the Arthurian romances of Chrétien de Troyes, it becomes clear that authored texts did not generate variant versions. The seven complete manuscripts of Chrétien's *Yvain*, for example, transmit the same text, albeit with copyist's errors, such as a missing word, or a misreading or misspelling, or different word order.[51] Throughout, however, the various copies of *Yvain* trans-

47. *Floovant* 2533–34, ed. Andolf, 78.

48. See Crosland, *The Old French Epic*, 2.

49. On the relation between the *jongleur* and his public, see Krauß, "Romanische Heldenepik," 146–47.

50. *Élie de Saint-Gilles* is extant in the mid-thirteenth century manuscript Paris, BnF n° 25516; *Floovant* is preserved in the twelfth-century manuscript Montpellier, Bibliothèque de la Faculté de Médecine, nr. 441; *Boeve de Haumton* is transmitted in two thirteenth- and fourteenth-century fragments (Paris, BnF, nouv. acqu. 4532; and Paris, private property of Firmin Didot) which together constitute a complete text.

51. On Chrétien de Troyes's attempts to protect his romances from alteration by continuators, rewriters, and storytellers like *jongleurs*, see Keith Busby and Leah Tether, "'Que nus contes de ce n'amende': Chrétien de Troyes and the Assertion of Copyright," *Journal of the International Arthurian Society* 11 (2023): 1–18; also Sofia Lodén and Leah Tether, "Translating Copyright: *Herr Ivan* and the Impediment of Chrétien de Troyes," in *Authorial Publishing in the Middle Ages from Late Antiquity to the Renaissance*, ed. Samu Niskanen and Valentina Rovere (Turnhout, forthcoming).

10 • INTRODUCTION

mit only one version of the romance, the narrative composed by Chrétien de Troyes.[52]

The three Old Norse–Icelandic translations of *chansons de geste* differ from each other in their style and the nature of their narrative. *Elis saga ok Rósamundu* transmits high points of the metrical assonanced stanzas in *Élie de Saint-Gilles* in occasional euphoniously alliterating prose. The French manuscript that Abbot Robert was translating was fragmentary, however, and lacked the denouement of the *chanson de geste*. Subsequently an anonymous Icelander appended a conclusion in a style completely at odds with Robert's translation. The epic poem relates the story of warring between Christians and Saracens and introduces the motif of the love of a beautiful Saracen maiden, *la bele Sarrasine*, for a Christian knight in Scandinavia.

The source of *Flóvents saga* was not the extant *Floovant*, with its assonanced stanzas, but a variant version of the epic.[53] In any case, the translator was not familiar with the alliterative courtly style favored by Abbot Robert. *Flóvents saga* is distinctive for its narratorial interventions and the repeated intrusion of the alleged author with commentary on the plot. The motif of a Saracen maiden's love for the Christian protagonist is doubled, inasmuch as two women vie for the love of the same knight.

In many respects, *Bevers saga* is unusual, for although here too a Saracen maiden successfully woos the Christian protagonist, but unlike *Elis saga* and *Flóvents saga*, the narrative does not conclude with the wedding of the happy couple, but rather late in life with their joint death after an illness. *Bevers saga* is the biography of the protagonist, commencing in his childhood. The two significant themes of the saga are the recovery of the protagonist's misappropriated patrimony and the preservation of his marriage to Josvena, who bears him three children.

The Creation of a New Literary Genre in Iceland

The Old Norse–Icelandic translations of French courtly romances and *chansons de geste* provoked the creation of a new literary genre in Iceland, namely the *riddarasaga* (pl. *riddarasögur*), that is, chivalric romance. All throughout the period in which the translations were copied, which lasted into the nineteenth century,[54]

---

52. For the nature of the copies of Chrétien's *Yvain* in the manuscripts, see the editor's notes in Chrétien de Troyes, *Der Löwenritter Yvain von Chrétien de Troyes*, ed. Wendelin Foerster (Amsterdam, 1965), 273–327.

53. See Leach, *Angevin Britain and Scandinavia*, 255–57; *Floovant*, ed. Andolf, lviii.

54. The dates of the manuscripts transmitting the translations are found in Marianne Kalinke and P.M. Mitchell, *Bibliography of Old Norse–Icelandic Romances* (Ithaca and London, 1985).

INTRODUCTION • 11

Icelanders themselves composed chivalric romances in the wake of the translations of the French romances and epics. Scholars have dated the oldest of the Icelandic *riddarasögur* to the end of the thirteenth century, and the earliest Icelandic manuscripts transmit copies of these compositions.[55]

The oldest Icelandic manuscript containing translations of French *chansons de geste* is AM 580 4°, which contains a fragment of *Elis saga ok Rósamundu* and the entirety of *Flóvents saga*.[56] This manuscript also contains *Bærings saga* (Saga of Baering), the plot of which is largely indebted to *Bevers saga*. The protagonist of *Bærings saga*, like the protagonist of *Bevers saga*, attempts to regain a murdered ruler's purloined patrimony. At the same time, Baering, like the protagonists of the translations of the French romance epics, is repeatedly wooed by women while engaged in military confrontations, including with Saracen armies.[57]

Scholarship is divided on both the literary merits of *Bærings saga* and its provenance, that is, whether it is a translation or an indigenous Icelandic romance inspired by the translated French romance epics. The saga is unique for the geographic area traversed by the protagonist in the narrative. The plot takes us from northern Germany through France and Italy to Greece and then back to northern Germany, and this is accompanied by the names of cities and towns in the region. Indeed, *Bærings saga* might be characterized as a medieval *Baedeker*, the popular travel guide.[58] Gustaf Cederschiöld, who edited *Bærings saga*, was of the opinion that the work was doubtless a translation and that its author was neither a Norwegian nor an Icelander, although here and there one finds passages that might have been added by an Icelandic scribe.[59] In his history of Old Norse and Old Icelandic literature, however, Finnur Jónsson declared *Bærings saga* to be an original Icelandic composition, which contains foreign narrative matter that

55. On the dating of the oldest Icelandic romances, see Jürg Glauser, *Isländische Märchensagas: Studien zur Prosaliteratur im spätmittelalterlichen Island* (Basel and Frankfurt am Main, 1983), 22–23.

56. See *DONP*, 41, 236, 246.

57. For a discussion of the motifs in *Bærings saga*, see Kalinke, *Stories Set Forth with Fair Words*, 115–21.

58. *Bærings saga* bears comparison with *Leiðarvísir*, a twelfth-century Icelandic itinerary by Abbot Nikulás Bergsson of the Benedictine monastery of Þverá. It is a guidebook for pilgrims from Northern Europe to Rome and Jerusalem, and includes the names of towns in Denmark, Germany, France, Switzerland, Italy, Greece, and the Holy Land. See Joyce Hill, "Leiðarvísir," *MSE*, 390–91; also Guðrún Nordal, "Learned Literature," in *The Cambridge History of Old Norse–Icelandic Literature*, ed. Heather O'Donoghue and Eleanor Parker (Cambridge, 2024), 518–36.

59. Gustaf Cederschiöld, introduction to *Fornsögur Suðrlanda*, ed. Gustaf Cederschiöld (Lund, 1884), clxxxvi–clxxxvii.

12 • INTRODUCTION

derives most likely from oral tales of German merchants.[60] Henry Goddard Leach, like Cederschiöld, believed that the source of *Bærings saga* was foreign, imported in the fourteenth century by Hanseatic traders, and he classified the saga under the "Matter of Germany."[61] I deem *Bærings saga* to be an indigenous *riddarasaga*, indeed the first composition of this new Icelandic genre. *Bærings saga* is modeled on the Old Norse–Icelandic translations of *chansons de geste*, and contains motifs popularized by the French romance epics, such as the armed conflicts between Christians and Saracens, and the amorous interest of women in the male protagonist.[62] *Bærings saga* contains folkloristic motifs that are undoubtedly Icelandic, such as shapeshifters and giantesses,[63] and its author cites a most popular Icelandic proverb from *Gunnlaugs saga ormstungu*, one of the sagas of Icelandic poets: if a woman loves a man, her eyes won't hide it.[64] The surest indication that *Bærings saga* was composed by an Icelander is the author himself who refers to "Konstantinopolis, er ver kollvm Mikla garð" (Constantinople, which we call Miklagarðr).[65]

On the whole, scholars have criticized *Bærings saga*.[66] Jan de Vries characterized the saga as nothing but a tiring series of adventures and amatory relationships.[67] I do not concur. The author composed a narrative focused on the protagonist's efforts to regain his purloined patrimony, which is presaged at the very beginning of the saga by the antagonist's premonitory dream. Despite occasional narrative shortcomings, I include *Bærings saga* with the translations of *chansons de geste* because of its certain indebtedness to *Bevers saga*. Moreover, *Bærings saga* demonstrates how Icelanders adapted foreign models for the *riddarasögur*, a new genre, while at the same time incorporating indigenous motifs.

The oldest Icelandic *riddarasaga*, to judge by the manuscript in which it is transmitted, namely AM 580 4° (ca. 1300–1325), is *Bærings saga*. The manuscript lacks one leaf, and the edition draws for this on the manuscript AM 567 II 4°, which is dated ca. 1350.[68] The manuscript AM 580 4° also contains the old-

---

60. Finnur Jónsson, *Den oldnorske og oldislandske Litteraturs Historie* (Copenhagen, 1920–24), 3: 104.

61. Leach, *Angevin Britain and Scandinavia*, 165, 383.

62. On *Bærings saga* in general and a bibliography, see Jürg Glauser, *MSE*, 60.

63. See Margaret Schlauch, *Romance in Iceland* (Princeton and New York, 1934), "Magic and the Supernatural," 119–48.

64. *The Saga of Gunnlaug Serpent-Tongue*, trans. Katrina C. Attwood, in *Sagas of Warrior-Poets*, ed. Diana Whaley (London, 2002), 137.

65. *Bærings saga* 31–32, in *Fornsögur Suðrlanda*, ed. Cederschiöld, 98. All translations of Old Norse–Icelandic texts are my own unless otherwise noted.

66. For scholarly criticism of *Bærings saga*, see Glauser, *Isländische Märchensagas*, 241.

67. Jan de Vries, *Altnordische Literaturgeschichte*, 2nd ed. (Berlin, 1967), 535.

68. See *Fornsögur Suðrlanda*, ed. Cederschiöld, 89 n1.

INTRODUCTION • 13

est Icelandic copy of the Norwegian translation of *Elis saga ok Rósamundu* (only one leaf is extant), and of *Flóvents saga,* which is defective in that it lacks one chapter in the middle of the saga and the two concluding chapters. The slightly younger manuscript of *Bærings saga,* AM 567 II 4°, contains two leaves of *Elis saga* and one leaf of *Bevers saga,* and this would seem to confirm not only the indebtedness of *Bærings saga* to the translation of *chansons de geste,* but also that it presumably is the first *riddarasaga* to have been composed by an Icelander.

The four *riddarasögur* that are here presented in translation are diverse texts in respect to their origin and transmission. *Elis saga ok Rósamundu* is a hybrid text relating to its authorship. It is partly a Norse translation of a French manuscript by a known translator, partly a text authored by an anonymous Icelander. The French manuscript that Abbot Robert was translating was fragmentary and the narrative ended inconclusively. Therefore an anonymous Icelander picked up the narrative where Abbot Robert left off. *Flóvents saga* derives from a *chanson de geste,* but one that was transmitted in an unknown Franco-Italian version, and not in the French epic poem *Floovant.* The anonymous author of *Flóvents saga,* presumed to be an Icelander, translated a text that is no longer extant in the original language. *Bevers saga* is a translation, presumably by an Icelander, of a variant version of the epic poem *Boeve de Haumtone.* Finally, *Bærings saga* is an original composition by an anonymous Icelander, one inspired by and based on the translated *riddarasögur,* chiefly *Bevers saga.*

The study of translation from Old French into Old Norse–Icelandic has a long history. In 1876, Eugen Kölbing, editor of *Elis saga ok Rósamundu,* conducted a verse-by-verse comparison of *Élie de Saint-Gilles* and Abbot Robert's translation in *Elis saga ok Rósamundu.* He demonstrated that the saga is a translation of an unknown variant version of the *chanson de geste.*[69] In the early twentieth century, Leach published important chapters on the movement of courtly romance and the *chanson de geste* from France into the West Norse (Iceland and Norway) and East Norse (Sweden) language areas. Like Kölbing before him, who proved that *Elis saga* derives from a variant version of the French *chanson de geste,* Leach determined that the French source of *Flóvents saga* has not been transmitted.[70] More recently, the last decade saw the publication of a notable monograph by Sif Rikhardsdottir[71] dealing with the transmission of Marie de

---

69. Eugen Kölbing. See "Die nordische Elissaga ok Rosamundu und ihre quelle," in *Beiträge zur Vergleichenden Geschichte der Romantischen Poesie und Prosa des Mittelalters* (Breslau, 1876), 92–136.

70. Leach, *Angevin Britain and Scandinavia,* 256–57.

71. Sif Rikhardsdottir, *Medieval Translations and Cultural Discourse: The Movement of Texts in England, France and Scandinavia* (Cambridge, 2012). See also note 74 below.

14 • INTRODUCTION

France's *Lais*, the *Chanson de Roland*, and Chrétien de Troyes's *Yvain* into the Old Norse language area, as well as a volume including articles on the translation and transmission of Old French literature into the West Norse and East Norse language areas.[72] Jürg Glauser has also written articles on the subject of *riddarasögur* for two separate companion volumes to Old Norse literature, one on translated and one covering both translated and original Icelandic romances.[73] Another such survey, the most recent to be published, also includes an important chapter on the *riddarasögur*, in this case by Sif Rikhardsdottir.[74] Recent scholarship has also included a monograph by Sofia Lodén[75] studying a less well-known area of translation from French, namely the East Norse area of Sweden. Finally, "Romances (East and West Norse)" in the *Oxford Bibliographies in Medieval Studies* is an important tool for ascertaining the state of translation from the Old French language area in the Middle Ages.[76]

Four Old Norse–Icelandic Epics

The four epics translated in this volume are discussed in further detail below.

Elis saga ok Rósamundu

Elis saga ok Rósamundu is a translation of *Élie de Saint-Gilles*, a thirteenth-century epic that belongs to the so-called Guillaume cycle of *chansons de geste*.[77] The protagonist of this cycle is William of Orange, whose role model may have been William, Count of Toulouse (d. 812), who fought against the Saracens and founded a monastery at Gellone. The *Vita sancti Willelmi* (he was canonized in

---

72. Jürg Glauser and Susanne Kramarz-Bein, eds., *Rittersagas: Übersetzung, Überlieferung, Transmission* (Tübingen, 2014).

73. Glauser, "Romance – A Case Study," 299–311; Jürg Glauser, "Romance (Translated *riddarasögur*)," in *A Companion to Old Norse–Icelandic Literature*, ed. Rory McTurk (Oxford, 2004), 372–87.

74. Sif Rikhardsdottir, "Riddarasögur," in *The Cambridge History of Old Norse–Icelandic Literature*, ed. Heather O'Donoghue and Eleanor Parker (Cambridge, 2024), 435–51.

75. Sofia Lodén, *French Romance, Medieval Sweden and the Europeanization of Culture* (Cambridge, 2021).

76. Marianne Kalinke, "Romances (East and West Norse)," in *Oxford Bibliographies in Medieval Studies*, ed. Christopher Kleinhenz (New York, 2022).

77. For the cycle of epics devoted to William of Orange, see Crosland, *The Old French Epic*, 30–47, 92–111.

1066) may have been the catalyst for the William cycle of *chansons de geste*.[78] The French epics belonging to the cycle of William of Orange include *Élie de Saint-Gilles*, which relates the story of Count Julien of Saint-Gilles who became William's vassal and served King Louis the Pious of France (778–840).[79] The main focus of this *chanson de geste* is on Christian and Saracen mentalities and their faith, as it tells of military expeditions and mighty battles between opposing factions. But the motif of courtly love, *fin' amor*, intrudes on the martial reality of *Élie de Saint-Gilles* in its description of the love of a Saracen maiden for the Christian protagonist.[80]

Tristrams saga, as Thomas's romance is known in Old Norse, is of extreme importance for French literature. As was noted previously, it alone transmits the French romance in its entirety, the original of which survives solely as a set of nine fragments. *Elis saga*, transmitted in the Norwegian codex Uppsala, Uppsala universitetsbibliotek, De la Gardie 4–7, dated ca. 1270, is noteworthy for a similar reason, as it is a translation of a variant version of *Élie de Saint-Gilles* that has not been preserved. The Norse rendering deviates substantially from the sole extant French manuscript of the *chanson de geste*, namely the mid-thirteenth-century manuscript Paris, BnF, n° 25516. In their edition of *Élie de Saint-Gilles*, the editors and translators, A. Richard Hartman and Sandra C. Malicote, refer to *Elis saga ok Rósamundu* as an "Old Norse translation and adaptation" of the French text,[81] but that is wrong. *Elis saga* is neither a translation nor an adaptation of *Élie de Saint-Gilles*, but rather Abbot Robert's translation of a different version of the French epic. Moreover, it is a translation of a French manuscript that was a fragment: it lacked the conclusion of the epic poem. The narrative ends in midstream, and Abbot Robert explains: "But how Elis got out of these difficulties and how he came back home to France with Rósamunda is not written in this book."[82] Subsequently, in the fourteenth century, an anonymous Icelander appended a conclusion, the oldest manuscript of which, the fragment AM 567 II 4°, consisting of one leaf, is dated ca. 1350; the oldest complete manuscript, Stockholm, Kungliga biblioteket, Holm perg. 6 4°, is dated ca. 1400.[83]

78. See D. Boutet, "Wilhelmsepen," *LMA*, 9: 198–200.
79. See *Elye of Saint-Gilles*, ed. and trans. Hartman and Malicote, ix–xiii.
80. On the Saracen world and the courtly world, see *Élie de Saint-Gilles*, ed. Guidot, 134–40.
81. *Elye of Saint-Gilles*, ed. and trans. Hartman and Malicote, xvii.
82. *Elis saga ok Rósamundu*, in *Riddarasögur*, ed. Bjarni Vilhjálmsson ([Reykjavík]: Íslendingasagnaútgáfan, Haukadalsútgáfan, 1954–62), 4: 1–135, at 107. I cite the normalized Icelandic in Bjarni Vilhjálmsson's edition here and subsequently, rather than the diplomatic edition by Eugen Kölbing, *Elis saga ok Rósamundu* (Heilbronn, 1881), here 116.5–7. But I also provide the exact references to Kölbing's edition in order to orient the reader.
83. See *DONP*, 236.

16 • INTRODUCTION

Élie de Saint-Gilles is composed in assonanced stanzas that are called *laisses* and these are numbered. The Norse translation is in prose and divided into chapters, which, like the *laisses*, are numbered. The source of *Elis saga* was a variant version of the extant *chanson de geste*, which opens as follows: "Now be silent lords; may God bless you, / The glorious one of heaven, the son of Saint Mary! / Would it please you to hear three tales of noble knights?" Verse 4 of *laisse* I states that this is the story "of a count who was born in Saint-Gilles."[84] The count in question is Julien, Élie's father. *Elis saga ok Rósamundu* similarly opens with an exhortation: "Listen, wise men, to a delightful story about the glorious manliness, valiant chivalry, and splendid accomplishments of an honorable duke, who had the government and rule, power and administration and supervision over the land of Saint Egidius, in the southwestern quarter of the kingdom of the Franks."[85] The saga's reference to Saint Egidius (d. ca. 710), the Latin name of the saint, rather than the French form, and the discrepancy between Saint-Gilles as a place name in the French epic, but in the Norse translation as a reference to the area where St Egidius lived – the saint in fact founded a monastery in Provence, known as the *provincia sancti Egidii*[86]– demonstrates at the very outset that the source of the saga could not have been the extant French version.

The Norse translation provides evidence that its French source contained some stanzas that are longer, but others shorter than those in the extant French manuscript. An example of such discrepancies occurs at the very beginning of the epic poem, which portrays Count Julien as follows: " ... he lived so long his beard had grown white. / Never in all his life did he commit treason or do wrong. / Rather, he showed great love for Holy Mary's son, / And he generously supported churches and abbeys, / And he had good bridges built and large hospices."[87] While transmitting the above, *Elis saga* § 1 provides further information concerning the character of Elis's father:

> This duke was so old that his beard flourished with white locks. He was so blessed in his day that the fear of God and goodness of luck governed all his life with God's providence. When he was young and still in his childhood he

---

84. *Élie de Saint-Gilles* 1–4, ed. Guidot, 157; *Elye of Saint-Gilles*, trans. Hartman and Malicote, 3. Guidot numbers the *laisses* in Roman numerals, which is also the case with the chapters in Kölbing's diplomatic edition of *Elis saga*, which suggests that the French manuscript contained Roman numerals.

85. *Elis saga ok Rósamundu*, ed. Bjarni Vilhjálmsson, 4: 3; ed. Kölbing, 1.4.

86. See David Hugh Farmer, "Giles (Aegidius)," in *The Oxford Dictionary of Saints*, 3rd ed. (Oxford, 1992), 205–6; Günther Binding, "Aegidius," *LMA*, 1: 176.

87. *Élie de Saint-Gilles* 5–9, ed. Guidot, 157; *Elye of Saint-Gilles*, trans. Hartman and Malicote, 3.

was already proficient in good virtues and courtly manners and with such inborn goodness that never a maiden or widow or undeservedly helpless person was deprived of honor or possessions or inheritance or money because of his designs or unrighteousness; instead, his heart was always inclined to God's honor and to good works. At great expense he had many bridges built over rivers and impassable roads as an ever-present help for both rich and poor. He supported many magnificent hospices; his table was always available to anyone wanting to accept his hospitality; his alms were constant, as were his many generous and gracious disbursements.[88]

That the source of *Elis saga* was a version of the *chanson de geste* other than the one transmitted in the extant French manuscript, is evident not only in longer passages, like the one above, but also in narrative matter not found in *Élie de Saint-Gilles*. One of the individuals who plays an important role in the *chanson de geste* is William of Orange, chiefly known from the epic poem *Aliscans*, who is married to Guibourc, a Saracen princess. She is mentioned in *Elis saga* § 8. William, who has been captured by Saracens and is to be shipped out, calls to his fellow knights and says that it is deplorable to have to board the ships and be sent off with the accursed Saracens, thus not being able to receive help from any living being. And then he adds: "Guibourc, you courtly woman, I shall now be far apart from you. I do not know what is more fitting for me to say now, other than to ask Almighty God to have mercy on our souls in the time to come."[89] *Elis saga* § 8 corresponds to *laisse* XIX in *Élie de Saint-Gilles*, which lacks the foregoing address and merely states that William's companions "were lying under a tree, grieving and angry. / With silk cords and thick wool ropes, their hands were bound." And William asks: "Lord God ... by your most holy name / What have you done with the brave knight in anguish / Whom the scoundrels were chasing through the fields?"[90] He is referring to Élie.

A similar discrepancy concerns Rosamunda's first becoming aware of Elis. The beginning of *Elis saga* § 26 relates how King Malkabrez returns to Sobrie after Elis had escaped from his ship. The king is greeted by his wife, his son, and Rosamunda, and she says to her father: "You promised that when you came back from France, you would bring me a poor captive to teach me French." Her father

---

88. *Elis saga ok Rósamundu*, ed. Bjarni Vilhjálmsson, 4: 3–4; ed. Kölbing, 1.4–2.4.

89. *Elis saga ok Rósamundu*, ed. Bjarni Vilhjálmsson, 4: 20–21; ed. Kölbing, 22.4–7. On the "incomparable wife Guibourg" in the *chanson de geste*, see Crosland, *The Old French Epic*, 31–34.

90. *Élie de Saint-Gilles* 575–79, ed. Guidot, 177; *Elye of Saint-Gilles*, trans. Hartman and Malicote, 37.

18 • INTRODUCTION

tells her about the valiant Frank, without however naming him. When Rosamunda heard about this Frank, "her heart was inflamed with such great love for him that she could neither respond nor ask for leave, but instead she bowed down before her idols and with her whole heart asked them to protect that valiant young man from disgrace and death."[91] At this point the chapter concludes. The arrival of the Saracens in Sobrie is recounted in *laisse* XXIX of *Élie de Saint-Gilles*, in a single verse: "My lords, the pagans arrived below the walls of Sobrie."[92] There is no interaction between father and daughter, and Rosamonde does not become aware of Élie until some 300 verses later, yet the epic contains no information as to how she knows about him.

The first five chapters of *Elis saga* more or less match the broad outlines of the narrative in the first five *laisses* of *Élie*, but the conduct of the two principal characters, Count Julien and his son Elis, differs somewhat from that in the *chanson de geste*. The contentious relationship between Elis and his father is more pronounced in the saga and also more acrimonious. Count Julien accuses Elis, who has not yet been dubbed a knight, of leading a life more befitting a monk, and he states that he will disinherit him in favor of his daughter. He adds that he will have him tonsured like a monk or abbot and make him learn chants and lessons from the monks in the monastery, another detail absent from the corresponding *laisse* of *Élie*. *Elis saga* § 3 is much longer than the corresponding *laisse* III. In *Élie*, Julien responds to his wife's protest over his cruelty by simply telling her to be quiet, but in the saga he holds a long speech on the duty of a young man to travel to other lands, to get to know foreign customs, and to study others' laws and judgments. At the end of § 5, which corresponds to *laisse* V of *Elye*, he calls Elis a whore's son, whom he has raised from being a nobody, and says that he will incarcerate him for fourteen years, since he prefers to serve strangers rather than his own father.[93] In *Élie* the father also threatens to disinherit his son, but the tone in what follows is quite different. Although Élie nearly comes to blows as he is armed by his father, and mumbles "Old knight, you are very false and cruel and proud," he nonetheless adds under his breath, "But you are my father; I must not get angry."[94] In the end, when Julien tells him the inheritance he is willing to provide, Élie says that he is wasting his breath, and "I wouldn't remain if my limbs were torn off!"[95]

91. *Elis saga ok Rósamundu*, ed. Bjarni Vilhjálmsson, 4: 57; ed. Kölbing, 59.7–60.3.
92. *Élie de Saint-Gilles*, ed. Guidot, 192; *Elye of Saint-Gilles*, trans. Hartman and Malicote, 67.
93. *Elis saga ok Rósamundu*, ed. Bjarni Vilhjálmsson, 4: 14; ed. Kölbing, 14.13–15.1.
94. *Élie de Saint-Gilles* 111, ed. Guidot, 161; *Elye of Saint-Gilles*, trans. Hartman and Malicote, 9.
95. *Élie de Saint-Gilles* 158, ed. Guidot, 162; *Elye of Saint-Gilles*, trans. Hartman and Malicote, 11.

INTRODUCTION • 19

Starting with the saga's § 7, the *laisse* and chapter numbers no longer agree, for that section of the saga is still part of *laisse* VI. Henceforth there are discrepancies in numbering as well as in the length of the French *laisses* and the saga chapters. The French author frequently addresses the audience, as happens at the beginning of *laisse* XV, where he says: "Now listen, my lords, may God give you highest good, / the glorious heavenly One, through His most Holy Name! / I'll tell you about Elye, who had the heart of a noble knight."[96] Before § 16, which corresponds to *laisse* XV, the author of the saga inserted § 15, which consists solely of the poet's address to his audience: "Now listen quietly! A fine tale is better than a full belly; although one should sip while a story is told, one should not drink too much; it is an honor to tell a story if the listeners pay attention, but a lost cause if they refuse to do so."[97] The anonymous *jongleur*'s audience address above is a clear indication of the oral nature of this romance epic, but this particular address to the audience is not found in *Élie de Saint-Gilles*.

Throughout *Élie de Saint-Gilles* one finds that corresponding sections of *Elis saga* offer now more, now less information, as well as diverging facts. A case in point is the background of the little thief Galopin who is to become Élie's companion. In *laisse* XXXII Galopin states:

... I was born in the Ardennes. I'm the son of Count Tieri.
Berrars was my brother, the brave and noble.
At the hour I was born, this tragedy befell me:
Four fairies were present. When it came time to take leave,
One of them sought to keep me as her servant.
But the others wouldn't endure or bear it,
And they prayed to God, who never told a lie,
That I'd never grow any more; that I'd always remain small;
That I'd not reach more than three and one half feet in height,
And that I'd run faster than a warhorse or packhorse.
Believe me, I swear it's true.
Then my mother died, and my father as well,
My relatives held me in contempt because I was small,
They tried to drown me at sea, in the great current.[98]

---

96. *Élie de Saint-Gilles* 490–92, ed. Guidot, 174; *Elye of Saint-Gilles*, trans. Hartman and Malicote, 33.

97. *Elis saga ok Rósamundu*, ed. Bjarni Vilhjálmsson, 4: 31; ed. Kölbing, 33.11–13.

98. *Élie de Saint-Gilles* 1181–94, ed. Guidot, 197; *Elye of Saint-Gilles*, trans. Hartman and Malicote, 77.

20 • INTRODUCTION

Although *Elis saga* § 29 corresponds to *laisse* XXXII, the Norse translation contains a variant and abbreviated version of the above:

> You, noble lord, do not kill me, for I descend from good people and come from a wealthy land. I am the son of Earl Terri of the Southern realm. After my mother had given birth to me, four fairies took me in the night from the chamber in which I was lying, and one of them wanted to keep me and take me away with her. But two of them were displeased at this and said to one another that I should never grow and become tall, but that I should be able to run so fast that no warhorse should ever be able to catch me, for God never created an individual who could run as quickly.[99]

In this case, unlike in the introductory *laisse* I, the French source of the Norse translation contained an abbreviated variant stanza.

Elis saga often transmits a shortened text vis-à-vis *Élie*, and occasionally there are instances where the saga lacks an entire *laisse*. A prime example of this is the loss of almost the entirety of *laisse* XLVI, which comprised almost 150 verses. The context of this *laisse* is the invasion of Sobrie by the old King Lubien of Baghdad who demands of Macabre his daughter Rosamonde in marriage and also his entire land, or else that he send his son or another knight to engage him in a duel. Both his son Caifas and the knight Joshua refuse to duel with the old king. Macabre finally orders his daughter to be brought to him, to be given to Lubien, but Élie, who has been sheltered by Rosemond, offers to engage in combat with the old king. She refuses to let him do so and tells him to go instead to an inner room for safety, then to proceed past bowers, moats, and gardens to a room in the palace, which she describes in detail, where he will find 400 of his father's knights, whom she has hidden in her chamber, together with their ladies. And she goes on to describe the fantastic furnishings of the room, including her bed.[100] Bernard Guidot, who edited *Élie de Saint-Gilles*, refers to Rosamonde's domain as "a world of delicacy and refinement."[101] None of this is found in *Elis saga* § 40. Instead, the Old Norse version rejoins the narrative of the *chanson de geste* with the order that Rosamonde appear before her father. In *Élie*, Rosamonde says that she first has to dress, whereas in *Elis saga* the messenger says that "the king orders you to dress in your best clothes and go with me to the hall. I suspect that he wants to bestow

---

99. *Elis saga ok Rósamundu*, ed. Bjarni Vilhjálmsson, 4: 62–63; ed. Kölbing, 65.4–11.

100. For the above plot points, see *Élie de Saint-Gilles* 1690, ed. Guidot, 214; *Elye of Saint-Gilles*, trans. Hartman and Malicote, 109.

101. "[U]n monde de délicatesse et de raffinement." *Élie de Saint-Gilles*, ed. Guidot, 140.

INTRODUCTION • 21

honor on you and give you away in marriage."[102] The description of Rose-monde's garments and her own person extends to eighteen verses. Her mantle, the audience is told, "was a gift from a powerful emir. / It was seven years in the making before it was completed."[103] The description in the saga is similar, but differs, inasmuch as "three fairies wove that garment with threads made of the finest gold and with such great skill and such great care that they worked at this garment for nine years before it was completed."[104]

There are also instances where *Elis saga* contains information not found in *Élie*. A striking example occurs on a later occasion when Élie is to engage Lubien of Baghdad in combat, for which Rosamonde arms him: "She put on his hauberk, whose chainmail was made of gold; / Over it a tunic that reached all the way to the floor."[105] Corresponding to these two verses of Élie being armed, the scene in the saga contains additional information not only on the provenance of the hauberk, but also includes the helmet, which is not mentioned in *Élie*:

> She put a trusty hauberk on him, which Pharaon, the king of Biterna had owned; then she placed such a good helmet made of steel on him that no better could be found anywhere. Paris, the Trojan king, who took Helen, queen of Greece, lost this helmet on the day when King Menelaus knocked him out of his saddle and cut off his head on account of his beautiful wife, whom Paris had taken with treachery. Then Troy was totally destroyed and completely spoiled and laid waste.[106]

The above is one of the more striking instances of additional text in *Elis saga*, and further evidence that its French source was a variant version of *Élie de Saint-Gilles*.

The French *laisses* are rendered in the Norse translation in the distinctive "court prose," the so-called "courtly style," common to the thirteenth-century translations of French narratives.[107] At moments of heightened interest the prose

102. *Elis saga ok Rósamundu*, ed. Bjarni Vilhjálmsson, 4: 80; ed. Kölbing, 85.13–86.2.

103. For the relevant section, see *Élie de Saint-Gilles* 1698–99, ed. Guidot, 214; *Elye of Saint-Gilles*, trans. Hartman and Malicote, 111.

104. *Elis saga ok Rósamundu*, ed. Bjarni Vilhjálmsson, 4: 81; ed. Kölbing, 86.9–12.

105. *Élie de Saint-Gilles* 2085–86, ed. Guidot, 228; *Elye of Saint-Gilles*, trans. Hartman and Malicote, 137.

106. *Elis saga ok Rósamundu*, ed. Bjarni Vilhjálmsson, 4: 94; ed. Kölbing, 101.2–9.

107. On the "courtly style," see Thorkil Damsgaard Olsen, "Den høviske litteratur," in *Norrøn Fortællekunst: Kapitler af den norsk-islandske middelalderlitteraturs historie*, ed. Hans Bekker-Nielsen, Thorkil Damsgaard Olsen, and Ole Widding (Copenhagen, 1965), 109–11; Marianne Kalinke, "Sources, Translations, Redactions, Manuscript Transmission," in *The Arthur of the North*, 37–42.

22 • INTRODUCTION

is rendered in euphonious, rhythmic language, effected largely by synonymous, and occasionally also alliterating collocations. For example, in the *chanson de geste* Rosamonde steps to the window one morning "to hear the sweet sounds/ Of the little birds who were singing at break of dawn," and she is reminded of love.[108] The corresponding passage in *Elis saga* reads (with the alliteration italicized): "En *R*ósamunda var *s*nemma upp *r*isin, gekk út í *s*valir, og heyrði hún þá *s*íðan *s*máfogla *s*yngia með *f*ögrum söng, er *f*agnaði deginum, og kom *h*enni þegar í *h*ug *á*star*i*lmur" (But Rosamunda had risen early and gone out on the balcony, and heard little birds singing with beautiful song, rejoicing in the day, and at once love's fragrance entered her heart).[109] Adjectives, nouns, and verbs alliterate on the consonants *r*, *s*, and *f* and on the vowels *a* and *i*, given that vowels alliterate with one another in Old Norse. It is tempting to suggest that a Norwegian ear would also have caught the name of the female protagonist, *R*ósamunda, and the past participle *r*isin (risen) in the alliterating scheme. Another example of Abbot Robert's style corresponds to the first verse of *laisse* XXXVIII of *Élie*, which reads: "Rosamonde la bele ama molt le vasal" (Beautiful Rosamonde loved the knight very much). The text in Abbot Robert's French source was longer; it corresponded to the beginning of *Elis saga* § 34 in the saga: "Rósamunda hin kurteisa, hin *f*ríða og hin *f*ræga, hin *l*jósa og hin *l*ofsæla, *u*nni mjög hinum *l*ofsæla og hinum virðulega jarli *E*lisi við *á*kafri og hugfastri *á*st"(Rosamunda, the courtly, the beautiful and famous, the radiant and much praised, greatly loved the much praised and splendid earl Elis with a vehement and steadfast love).[110] The alliteration on *f* and *l* in the portrayal of Rosamunda is carried over to the object of her love, Elis, connected by the verb *u*nni which alliterates with his name *E*lis, thereby also linking the subject of the sentence to the object, whose name subsequently alliterates with the modifying adjective *á*kafri of her love.

The Norse translation of *Élie de Saint-Gilles* breaks off around *laisse* LXVIII, which tells of the extended continuing battle between Christian and Saracen forces. In *Elis saga* § 59, however, the protagonist is reunited with Rosamunda at this point, and the maiden embraces Elis and says: "The day has now come and the time for you to receive me as your wife; this should no longer be delayed."[111] Elis demurs, however, saying that this cannot be, since she believes in the wooden idols Mahomet and Tervagant. They decide to sequester in the highest tower and to send for Count Julien, Elis's father, and William of Orange for reinforce-

108. *Élie de Saint-Gilles* 1366–67, ed. Guidot, 203; *Elye of Saint-Gilles*, trans. Hartman and Malicote, 89.

109. *Elis saga ok Rósamundu*, ed. Bjarni Vilhjálmsson, 4: 69; ed. Kölbing, 72.3–5.

110. *Elis saga ok Rósamundu*, ed. Bjarni Vilhjálmsson, 4: 115; ed. Kölbing, 76.4–6.

111. *Elis saga ok Rósamundu*, ed. Bjarni Vilhjálmsson, 4: 106; ed. Kölbing, 115.5–7.

ments to engage the Saracens in combat. Elis predicts that they will then conquer the entire Saracen country and Rosamunda will become a Christian, to which she agrees. But the narrator intervenes a final time and states that "their troubles started up again."[112] This is where the French manuscript broke off (at *Élie de Saint-Gilles* 2476), and the Norwegian translator states:

> But how Elis got out of these difficulties, and how he came back to France with Rosamunda is not written in this book, which Abbot Robert translated and King Hákon Hákonarson had ordered translated into Norse for your enjoyment. May God give the one who translated and wrote this book grace in this world, and in his kingdom the glory of the saints. Amen.[113]

Abbot Robert's translation breaks off at the end of § 59; the concluding eleven chapters (60–70) were composed by an anonymous Icelander. This second author, however, did not emulate Abbot Robert's court style, eschewing alliterating collocations and instead making excessive use of the present participle to form the present and past tenses.[114] The continuator's penchant for employing the present or past tense of the verb *vera* plus the present participle where the simple present or past of the verb would have sufficed results in an inelegant, not to say clumsy, prose.[115] The very first sentence of the continuation reveals the remarkable stylistic shift from Abbot Robert's translation, which I in turn here translate as literally as possible, italicizing all present particles: "Elis og Rósamunda *voru sitjandi* í hæsta turn Sobrieborgar og það ráðs *takandi*, að þau *eru* Galopín burt *sendandi*" (Elis and Rosamunda *were sitting* in the highest tower of Sobrieborg and *were deciding* that they *are sending* Galopín off). Rosamunda then has a ship outfitted, and "*er* Elis bréf *skrifandi* og sínum kæra feður *sendandi* og frá sínum ferðum honum *segjandi*" (Elis *is writing* a letter and *is sending* it to his dear father and *is telling* him about his travels).[116] Evident here is also another stylis-

---

112. *Elis saga ok Rósamundu*, ed. Bjarni Vilhjálmsson, 4: 107; ed. Kölbing, 116.5.

113. *Elis saga ok Rósamundu*, ed. Bjarni Vilhjálmsson, 4: 107–8; ed. Kölbing, 116.5–11.

114. On Brother and Abbot Robert's style, see Paul Schach, "Some Observations on the Translations of Brother Róbert," in *Les relations littéraires Franco-Scandinaves au Moyen Âge: Actes du Colloque de Liège (avril 1972)* (Liège, 1975), 117–33; Kalinke, "Sources, Translations, Redactions, Manuscript Transmission," 37–39; Ingvil Brügger Budal, "A Translation and Its Continuation: The Use of the Present Participle in *Elíss saga ok Rósamundar*," in *Opuscula* 16, ed. Annette Lassen and Philip Lavender (Copenhagen, 2018), 63–89.

115. To be sure, Abbot Robert also used the construction finite verb plus present participle, but this was done to express durative action, which is not the case in the continuation.

116. *Elis saga ok Rósamundu*, ed. Bjarni Vilhjálmsson, 4: 108; ed. Kölbing, 116.13–15, 117.3–5.

24 • INTRODUCTION

tic quirk, namely that the continuator does not consistently use the narrative past, preferring to alternate between the present and past tenses. An egregious example of the continuator's paratactic style is found in the denouement, the wedding of Elis and Rosamunda (the participial constructions are again italicized):

> Eru þær nú í kirkju *gangandi* og á ágætum stólvm *sitjandi*; erkibiskup sjálfur messu *segjandi*, með ágætum klerkum *syngjandi*. Eru þessir jungu menn nú púsaðir með fagurlegri þjónustu. Síðan er Elis *offrandi* sínu góða sverði ... Eftir það *er* hertugi Júlíen *gefandi* sínum syni allt sitt ríki ...

> (they *are* now *going* into church and *sitting* on excellent chairs; the archbishop himself *saying* Mass, with excellent clerics *singing*. These young people *are* now *being married* in a beautiful ceremony. Afterwards Elis *is presenting* his good sword ... After this Count Julien *is giving* his son his entire realm ...)[117]

The continuator is a self-conscious writer who occasionally lets his own voice be heard. For example, § 61 depicts the expedition of the huge army of Count Julien and Earl William to Sobrie, which arrives in an excellent harbor at the foot of the castle. Here the author has the last word: "They now make land, cast anchor, and raid the coast – and the writer is now resting there comfortably." The continuator's Icelandic style differs substantially from that of my English translation: "*eru nú þar liggjandi og akkerum kastandi og strandhögg takandi; en skrifarinn sig þar hóflega hvílandi.*"[118] The single appropriate use of the present participle is the last verb, which thereby suggests duration. It has been noted that the Icelandic continuator's predilection for the present participle may possibly mirror contemporary stylistic preferences.[119] In the translation of *Tristrams saga*, Brother Robert also resorted to participles, but this was done for a specific effect, for example, to capture the enduring state of Tristram's emotional turmoil when he believes that Ísönd has not come to heal him. He laments:

> Nú *ertu*, Ísönd, mik *hatandi*. Ek *em* nú *syrgjandi*, er þú vill ekki til mín koma, en ek sakir þín *deyandi*, er þú vildir ekki miskunna sótt minni. Ek *em* nú *syrgjandi* sótt mína ok *harmandi*, er þú vildir ekki koma at hugga mik.

> (Ísönd, you hate me now. My heart aches, because you do not want to come to me, and because of you I will die, for you did not wish to take pity on me

---

117. *Elis saga ok Rósamundu*, ed. Bjarni Vilhjálmsson, 4: 133; ed. Kölbing, 137.19–138.2.
118. *Elis saga ok Rósamundu*, ed. Bjarni Vilhjálmsson, 4: 113; ed. Kölbing, 121.6–7.
119. Budal, "A Translation and Its Continuation," 86.

INTRODUCTION • 25

in my illness. Now I am suffering from my sickness and grieving, because you do not want to come to comfort me.)[120]

The translator, Peter Jorgensen, resorted to the present participle only in the concluding sentence, to suggest Tristram's enduring illness and grief.

The Icelandic continuator based the denouement of *Elis saga* on earlier passages in Abbot Robert's translation as well as on motifs found in contemporary indigenous romances. For example, when Count Julien hears that his son has been captured by the heathens, the court grieves, and the narrator states that "no one listened then to the harps or rebecs or hurdy-gurdies or other stringed instruments." The continuator injects this very motif into a passage depicting the joy of the court upon learning that Elis is alive: "Some play psalteries and hurdy-gurdies, some pump the organ, some beat drums and some blow trumpets." Subsequently, toward the end of the saga, the motif recurs, when Rosamunda and Elis's sister enter the hall at the wedding feast: "the organ was pumped and hurdy-gurdies and psalteries played and there was the sound of pipes with beautiful tones."[121]

The earlier *Elis saga* § 40 recounts that Rosamunda was to be married to the Saracen king Jubien the Old. Her father asks her to meet him in the hall, and a long description follows of the precious garments that Rosamunda wears:

She dressed in a precious garment made of the whitest fur that had such elegant trimming at the neck and arms that never was its like seen before. Thereupon she put on a gold-woven garment that was so valuable and excellent that its like was not found in all Saracendom. The little mantle that she put over this was sent from the western Saracen world where the sun sets, from the land called Occident. Three fairies had woven that garment with such great skill and such great care that they worked at this garment for nine years before it was finished. Woven into this mantle were large birds, all in gold, and set with the most precious gems. The merchant Samarien had sold the mantle's ties and their clasps to King Malkabrez for sixty pounds of pure Byzantine coins. The maiden then girded herself with a costly belt, which seemed to be a pure gold band with images of all kinds of animals. The most excellent goldsmiths had made it. Her hair was fairer than gold; it fell down to her shoulders in bright braids.[122]

120. *Tristrams saga ok Ísöndar*, ed. and trans. Jorgensen, 220–21.
121. The three quotations can be found in *Elis saga ok Rósamundu*, ed. Bjarni Vilhjálmsson, 4: 52, 110–11, 131; ed. Kölbing, 54.8–9, 119.2–4, 136.4–5.
122. *Elis saga ok Rósamundu*, ed. Bjarni Vilhjálmsson, 4: 80–81; ed. Kölbing, 86.4–87.4.

26 • INTRODUCTION

The striking feature is that her mantle was woven by three fairies. The author of the variant version of *Élie de Saint-Gilles* presumably was acquainted with Chrétien de Troyes's *Erec et Enide*, where four fairies designed the magnificent robe that Erec was to wear at his coronation.[123] Early in the romance, the queen presents Enide with a dress and mantle that she is to wear at her wedding to Erec. The garments are as opulent as those worn by Rosamunda, but fairies played no role here in their fashioning.[124]

It is noteworthy that in *laisse* XLVI of *Élie de Saint-Gilles* Rosemonde's mantle was also not produced by fairies. The French version in seven verses is as follows: "She put on a collared ermine robe/ With a golden cord she had bound the sides/ And wore rich hose and exquisitely painted slippers. / She put around her neck an envy-inspiring cloak / A gift from a powerful emir. / It was seven years in the making before it was completed. / Its expensive cloth was embroidered all around."[125]

Whereas the author of the French source of *Elis saga* most likely was inspired to introduce fairies as seamstresses by Chrétien de Troyes, the continuator drew on the passage quoted in the previous paragraph for his description of Rosamunda's apparel upon her entry into the hall in § 67:

> She dressed in a tunic woven in gold. She put around her waist a girdle, made with great artistry, which looked like fiery gold and was variably fashioned. Then she put on a mantle; none like it can be found in the entire world. This mantle had come from the land of the setting sun, which is called Occident. Four fairies had woven the mantle with the finest gold thread, and they were at this for four years before it was finished. The mantle was adorned with stars and many precious gems. The merchant Jon had sold the mantle clasps for forty pounds of pure gold.[126]

Eugen Kölbing, who edited *Elis saga*, notes that the continuator plagiarized much of this passage from Abbot Robert's translation.[127] Besides both being in the narrative past, the two passages exhibit unmistakable similarities in their content.

---

123. Chrétien de Troyes, *Erec and Enide*, in Chrétien de Troyes, *The Complete Romances of Chrétien de Troyes*, trans. David Staines (Bloomington, 1993), 84.

124. Ibid., 21.

125. *Élie de Saint-Gilles* 1694–1700, ed. Guidot, 214; *Elye of Saint-Gilles*, trans. Hartman and Malicote, 111.

126. *Elis saga ok Rósamundu*, ed. Bjarni Vilhjálmsson, 4: 128; ed. Kölbing, 133.7–16.

127. In the Introduction to his edition, Kölbing placed the two portrayals in columns facing each other and he commented that "der fortsetzer sogar ein plagiat an der saga selbst begangen hat" (*Elis saga ok Rósamundu*, ed. Kölbing, xxxii–xxxiii). See also Budal, "A Translation and Its Continuation," 63–88.

There is the gold-woven garment and the mantle, which came from the Occident, and it was woven by three, respectively four fairies, with gold thread. It took them nine, respectively four years to complete. A merchant named Jon had sold the mantle clasps for sixty, respectively forty pounds of pure gold.

The anonymous Icelander who took up the plot where Abbot Robert's manuscript broke off not only completed *Elis saga* in a completely different style from that of Robert. He also made up the plot based on and borrowed from the translation, as noted above. Furthermore, he described the armed conflicts between Christians and Saracens in great detail. Although they are based on the battles in the translation, his accounts are prolonged and more gruesome. He favored hand to hand combat with swords, spears, and lances; the resulting wounds are vividly depicted: heads roll, and bodies, even of horses, which end up split in half. Inevitably a Saracen is killed when the Christian knight hurls him, wounded, from his horse to death on the ground.

The most striking deviation from *Élie de Saint-Gilles* occurs in the ending. Not unexpectedly, the continuator has Elis and Rosamunda wed at the conclusion, and in the last chapter we are told, in good saga fashion, that the couple had many children, three sons and many daughters. That is not what happens in the French *chanson*: Élie cannot marry Rosamonde because at her baptism he "helped raise her / And bless her and sanctify her in the most holy font!"[128] In other words, Élie is Rosamonde's godfather, and she ends up marrying Galopin. In a note to verses 2675–76, two modern translators write: "The church forbade marriage on grounds of consanguinity; in the early thirteenth century this included ... also any relationship involving the godfather."[129] The problem is solved with Rosamonde marrying Galopin, who played a critical role in the greater part of the narrative. The question arises: if the French manuscript that Abbot Robert translated had been complete, would Rosamunda also have been prevented there from marrying Elis?

Flóvents saga

A second *chanson de geste* was rendered from Old French into Old Norse–Icelandic either in Norway or Iceland by an anonymous translator.[130] This is *Flóvents*

128. *Élie de Saint-Gilles* 2677–78, ed. Guidot, 247; *Elye of Saint-Gilles*, trans. Hartman and Malicote, 173.

129. *Elye of Saint-Gilles*, trans. Hartman and Malicote, 230.

130. Stefka Georgieva Eriksen erroneously writes that *Flóvents saga* "is probably not a translation ... but rather an adaptation of a lost *chanson de geste*, made during Hákon Hákonarson's

28 • INTRODUCTION

saga, which has been transmitted in two main Icelandic manuscripts, in AM 580 4°, dated ca. 1300–1325, and in the manuscript Stockholm, Kungliga biblioteket, perg 6 4°, dated a century later, to ca. 1400–1425.[131] The older manuscript (entitled *Flóvents saga I* by Gustaf Cederschiöld, the editor) has a defective ending; it lacks the last two chapters. Moreover, an entire leaf, which contained § 15, is missing in the middle of the saga. The younger manuscript (*Flóvents saga II*) has a defective first chapter. Overall, the two manuscripts diverge in that they differ in their chapter divisions and often also textually. As will subsequently be elaborated, because of the defective nature of the two manuscripts, the translation of *Flóvents saga* is a composite of the two texts.

Unlike *Elis saga ok Rósamundu*, *Flóvents saga* does not derive from an extant French *chanson de geste*. To be sure, the epic poem *Floovant*, transmitted in the single manuscript Montpellier, Bibliothèque de la Faculté de Médicine, nr. 441 and dated to the twelfth century,[132] resembles *Flóvents saga* in many respects, but this version is not the source of the Icelandic translation. Like *Elis saga ok Rósamundu*, which translates a variant version of *Élie de Saint-Gilles*, *Flóvents saga* represents a translation of a variant version of the French epic poem. A Norwegian, or possibly an Icelander, had access to a French manuscript of the *chanson de geste*, which he translated, but this translation, unlike that of *Elis saga*, is no longer extant. Transmitted are only two copies of the original translation, and they attest considerable scribal intervention.

In the introduction to *Flóvents saga*, Cederschiöld notes the inclusion of a French proverb toward the end of chapter 24 in *Flóvents saga*: "Ki tent sun pie plus que sa chape ne tient, (s'en repent) tost quant freid (li) vient."[133] This is fol-

---

reign. There is no connection, apart from the name, to the *Chanson de Floovant*." See Stefka Georgieva Eriksen, *Writing and Reading in Medieval Manuscript Culture: The Translation and Transmission of the Story of Elye in Old French and Old Norse Literary Contexts* (Turnhout, 2014), 174.

131. All references are to *Flóvents saga I* and *Flóvents saga II* in *Fornsögur Suðrlanda*, ed. Cederschiöld, 124–67, 168–208. Cederschiöld also takes the manuscript Copenhagen, Den Arnamagnæanske Samling, AM 152 fol. into consideration for his edition; it is his manuscript C (cxcv). This is notable, since it was "evidently produced at the behest of Björn Þorleifsson of Reykhólar in Breiðafjörður, one of the richest men in Iceland," who was also the translator of twenty-two legends from Low German in the *Reykjahólabók* (Jóhanna Katrín Friðriksdóttir, "Brothers in Arms," in *Manuscripts from the Arnamagnæan Collection*, ed. Matthew James Driscoll and Svanhildur Óskarsdóttir [Copenhagen, 2015], 80–81). See also Marianne Kalinke and Kirsten Wolf, *Pious Fictions and Pseudo-Saints in the Late Middle Ages: Selected Legends from an Icelandic Legendary* (Toronto, 2023), 1–3. On the dating of the manuscripts, see *Flóvents saga* at *DONP*, 246.

132. See *Floovant*, ed. Andolf, i–iii, 9–13.

133. *Fornsögur Suðrlanda*, ed. Cederschiöld, cxciv. For the quotation, see *Flóvents saga I*, ed. Cederschiöld, 164.63–165.1.

INTRODUCTION • 29

lowed by the statement that in "our" language (i.e. Old Norse–Icelandic) it means: "Whoever stretches his foot out from under his cloak, will regret it when coldness comes upon him."[134] The French text is found only in the oldest manuscript, AM 580 4°, and is quite garbled, and Cederschiöld provided an emended text.[135] The insertion of a French proverb in *Flóvents saga* would suggest that the source of the translation indeed was a French manuscript. The prologue to *Flóvents saga I* states that a certain teacher named Simon came across the tale in the French city of Sion, which he subsequently translated into French.[136] Cederschiöld accepts Arsène Darmesteter's 1877 thesis (in *De Floovante vetustiore gallico poemata*) that a Master Simon in Lyon[137] came across a Norman or Anglo-Norman manuscript, and that it is this manuscript which is the source of the Icelandic translation.[138] This is most unlikely, since the reference to Master Simon in the preface, and subsequently repeatedly throughout *Flóvents saga*, suggests that it is a rhetorical device, not an indication of the French source.

Flóvents saga derives from a *chanson de geste* the plot of which is set not in the Merovingian period, during the time of Clovis (ca. 466–511), as is the case with *Floovant*, but rather during the reign of Constantine the Great (306–337), that is, nearly one-and-a-half centuries earlier. This is found in the *Storie di Fioravante*, a prose narrative extant in two fifteenth-century Italian manuscripts.[139] The narrative, based on French sources, was composed by Andrea da Barberino (ca. 1370–1431), who included it in his collection *Reali di Francia* (The Royal House of France) along with a number of other *chansons de geste*.[140] The *Storie di Fioravante* is an Italian prose translation of a Franco-Italian *chanson de geste*,[141] from which *Flóvents saga* presumably derives.[142] In her magisterial study *Romance*

134. *Flóvents saga I*, ed. Cederschiöld, 162.2–5.

135. The emendation was suggested by V.E. Lindforss and F.A. Wulff; see *Fornsögur Suðrlanda*, ed. Cederschiöld, 165 n1.

136. *Flóvents saga I*, ed. Cederschiöld, 124.2–7.

137. The manuscript AM 580 4° (ca. 1300–1325) of *Flóvents saga* writes "Sion," but the manuscript AM 570 a 4° (ca. 1450–1500) has "Líon," and that is presumably Darmesteter's reason for placing Simon in Lyon, rather than in Sion.

138. *Fornsögur Suðrlanda*, ed. Cederschiöld, cxciv.

139. See Pio Rajna, *I Reali di Francia: Ricerche intorno Ai Reali di Francia*, vol. 1 (Bologna, 1872), viii–x; for Franco-Italian *chansons de geste*, see also Krauß, "Romanische Heldenepik," 171–73.

140. For a discussion of Old French epics in Italy, see Crosland, *The Old French Epic*, 259–67.

141. Rajna, *I Reali di Francia*, 41–42. For a survey of Italian versions, see *Floovant*, ed. Andolf, lv–lviii.

142. In the Introduction to his edition of *Floovant*, Andolf provides a summary of the Icelandic saga and points out that it does not correspond to *Floovant* but rather to the story of Fiovo in *Storie di Fioravante* (*Floovant*, ed. Andolf, lviii–lxv).

30 • INTRODUCTION

in Iceland, Margaret Schlauch surmised that "there must have been a lost French *chanson* as common ancestor of the saga and of *I Reali di Francia*."[143]

In addition to the discrepancy in the temporal setting of *Flóvents saga* and *Floovant*, the incident that triggers the plot is dissimilar in the two works. The protagonist of *Flóvents saga*, like Fiovo in the *Storie di Fioravante*, is Emperor Constantine's cupbearer who accidentally spills some wine on the mantle of a powerful nobleman. He assaults Flovent and calls him an illegitimate bastard, in reaction to which Flovent angrily strikes the nobleman so hard on his head with a pitcher that his brains spill out and he falls dead to the floor, at the feet of Constantine. Flovent flees from Rome.[144]

The plot of *Floovant*, the extant *chanson de geste*, is set at the court of King Clovis of France on the feast of Pentecost. Floovant, his oldest son, is to inherit the crown at his father's death, and Clovis asks the elderly Duke of Burgundy to take the young Floovant under his wing and guide his education. One day the duke falls asleep in a garden and Floovant mischievously cuts off his long white beard. As punishment for this deed Floovant is exiled from France.[145] In addition to the temporal and local differences in the setting and the deed that prompts the protagonist's exile in the two works, there are other disparities between *Floovant* and *Flóvents saga*, notably that in the saga both royal enemies, the Saxons and the Franks, are Saracens. Thus, Flovent, a Christian who identifies himself as a mercenary, serves the Saracen king of the Franks. In *Floovant*, however, the Frank, King Flore, although being a Saracen, has converted to Christianity, and that is why the Saracens are attacking him.[146] In *Flóvents saga* strife occurs between two Saracen forces, the Saxons and the Franks, and the conflict concerns land wrested from the Franks by the Saxons.

The distinguishing feature of *Flóvents saga*, compared to *Elis saga ok Rósamundu*, is that not one, but two female figures play the part of the *bele Sarrasine*: Florentia, the daughter of Florent, the king of the Franks, and Marsibilia, the daughter of the Saxon king Salatres. Not only do two Saracen maidens vie for the love of the Christian protagonist, but Marsibilia plays an unusually active role in attaining the love of Flovent who supports the Frankish king in his wars against the Saxons. In one of these battles, Otun, Flovent's squire and companion, is captured and thrown into a dungeon by Marsibilia's father. In a most dramatic and unusual episode, Marsibilia, accompanied by her foster-mother, seeks

143. Schlauch, *Romance in Iceland*, 181.
144. See "Il Libro delle Storie di Fioravante," ed. Pio Rajna, in Rajna, *I Reali di Francia*, 333–34.
145. *Floovant* 1–205, ed. Andolf, 9.
146. *Floovant* 229–55, ed. Andolf, 10.

to gain access to the dungeon in order to free Otun. Marsibilia and her foster-mother engage in a protracted and heated argument over Marsibilia's love of the foreign warrior, during which the foster-mother attempts to convince her to marry the Saracen king Almatur. The quarrel between the two women escalates and becomes so heated that the foster-mother threatens to report Marsibilia to her father and have her flogged. Only when the foster-mother realizes how terribly angry Marsibilia has become, does she relent and agree to help free Otun. Accompanied by two maidens, the two break into the dungeon and once there Marsibilia offers to set Otun free, on one condition: if he promises, on Flovent's behalf, that he will marry none other than her.

Flóvents saga is related to *Floovant*, inasmuch as two maidens also vie there for the love of the protagonist, namely, Florete, daughter of King Flore, and Maugalie, the daughter of Admiral Galien. King Flore offers his daughter to Floovant in marriage, but he rejects this. Jealous scenes between the two maidens occur, while Maugalie herself woos Floovant, and for love of him has herself baptized. On the whole, however, there are substantive differences not only in the development of plot in the French *chanson de geste* and the saga, but also in the character of the various personages who play vital roles in the epic poem.

There is a strong religious component in *Flóvents saga*. As noted previously, both the Saxons and Franks are Saracens, and Flovent serves the Frankish king. The relationship of the Saracens to their idols plays a greater role in *Flóvents saga* than in *Elis saga*. The Saxons also have close relations to their idols, which is reflected in their reaction when they suffer losses in battle. When Flovent captures their king, Salatres, his son berates Mahomet, calling him the vilest of gods. He storms at Tervagant, strikes the idol's head, and breaks off its nose. Then he continues by stabbing out the eyes of both idols and flinging the statues into a ditch. Throughout the narrative, the Saracens repeatedly invoke their gods, chiefly Mahomet, but occasionally also Tervagant.[147]

After one victorious rout of the Saxons, Flovent returns to Paris and at the urging of King Florent he visits the temple of the Franks to render thanks to Mahomet for his assistance in battle. To all appearances, Flovent seems to be worshipping the idol, as he lies prostrate on the floor, but instead he whispers a long prayer to God (over 200 words in the English translation) which covers the entirety of salvation history, from the birth of Christ to his death, resurrection, and the coming of the Holy Spirit. He concludes by asking God to free him from peril, so that he can live long enough to uphold Christendom and its holy laws.

147. Tervagant appears often in *Layamon's Brut*, where the Saxon leader Hengest lists Tervagant among the gods worshipped by the Saxons. See Layamon, *Layamon's Brut: A History of the Britons*, trans. Donald G. Bzdyl (Binghamton, 1989), 145.

Then Flovent leaves the temple, and now there occurs a strong earthquake, accompanied by loud claps of thunder. Fire falls from the heavens and the temple burns down altogether, including its idols.

Like the French version of the epic translated in *Elis saga*, the author of the variant epic translated in *Flóvents saga* seems to have been acquainted with Chrétien de Troyes' *Erec et Enide*. The magnificent garments given to Flovent by his host Hermet in Paris are depicted as follows:

> His tunic was of a costly fabric, with white fur underneath and a hood at the neck. Around this was a fashionable hands-broad border, made with wondrous skill and set with twelve precious stones ... Hermet placed the mantle over Flovent ... No one knew from where the furs that lined it came; they were sewn on with gold thread. People thought that they came from rare birds and were soft as skin. They were blue and brown, reddish with shifting colors. On the shoulders there were different kinds of stones continuing down the sleeves on both sides.[148]

Flovent's garments bear comparison with Enide's wedding apparel:

> The dress was trimmed with white ermine even along her sleeves; around the cuffs and the collar there was, to be precise, more than two hundred marks' worth of beaten gold enshrining exceptionally precious stones of indigo and green, of deep blue and dark brown ... the cloak was beautiful and of fine quality. Around the neck were two sable furs with clasps that contained more than an ounce of gold: on one side there was a hyacinth, on the other a ruby brighter than a flaming carbuncle.[149]

Flóvents saga opens with the statement: "This saga is not a compilation of nonsense, for it is true. Master Simon found it in writing in the city of Sion, where he maintained a school, and he translated it into French in agreeable fashion."[150] While there is a city called Sion in the Occitanie region of France, the introductory statement of *Flóvents saga* presumably is a cliché, similar to others in the *riddarasögur*, such as the concluding statement of *Konráðs saga keisarasonar* (Saga of Konrad, the Emperor's son): "A cleric found this saga written on a street in the

---

148. *Flóvents saga I*, ed. Cederschiöld, 142.6–16; *Flóvents saga II*, ed. Cederschiöld, 188.1–13.

149. *Erec and Enide*, in Chrétien de Troyes, *The Complete Romances of Chrétien de Troyes*, trans. Staines, 21.

150. *Flóvents saga I*, ed. Cederschiöld, 124.2–8.

style that learned men are wont to tell."[151] The plot of *Flóvents saga* commences by introducing Emperor Constantine: "This saga concerns the first emperor who ruled and worshipped the true God, utterly and strictly keeping his commandments. The great King Constantine, whom Pope Sylvester had baptized, ruled over Rome." And the protagonist is announced in the following sentence: "The son of his sister is called Flovent."[152]

Flóvents saga is characterized by the repeated intrusions of the aforementioned schoolmaster Simon, who claims to be the author of *Flóvents saga*. For example, when Flovent rejects an offer of marriage to Florentia, the daughter of King Florent, Master Simon interrupts: "'if it had been up to her,' says Master Simon, 'she would have been promptly married to Flovent.'"[153] Another time, Master Simon himself comments on the plot, when he says: "'But I think,' says Master Simon who composed this saga, 'even if Flovent were with Hermet for four years, together with a company of many thousands, he would not lack for money to support them, for he had more property than twenty camels could carry.'"[154] The author again interjects, though this time only in *Flóvents saga I*, during the description of Flovent's tunic, which is sumptuously adorned with jewels: "'Anyone who says that these are not the names of the precious stones that have been listed,' says Master Simon, 'lies about the legend of John the apostle; he is wrong who says that.'"[155] The reference to the apostle John is to Rev. 21:19–20, which lists the twelve precious stones adorning the foundations of the wall of the city of Jerusalem: jasper, sapphire, agate, emerald, onyx, carnelian, chrysolite, beryl, topaz, chrysoprase, jacinth, and amethyst. *Flóvents saga I* lists all twelve precious stones, but *Flóvents saga II* has only ten. In a later scene, Flovent is depicted riding to war against the Saracens, and Master Simon again interjects by saying: "'May God,' says Master Simon, 'who rescued the three innocent boys in the burning oven and Susanna from slander and Daniel from seven lions in their den, now help Flovent on this journey, so that he will not be wounded and captured.'"[156] At the start of the battle between the Franks and Saxons, Master Simon again speaks up: "'Whoever was there,' says Master Simon, 'could hear the loud clashing of spear shafts and the wondrous strokes of their glinting swords. One could see many a saddled horse and many a knight bend-

---

151. *Konráðs saga keisarasonar*, ed. Bjarni Vilhjálmsson, in *Riddarasögur*, 3: 269–344, at 344.

152. *Flóvents saga I*, ed. Cederschiöld, 124.9–16.

153. *Flóvents saga I*, ed. Cederschiöld, 155.51–53.

154. *Flóvents saga I*, ed. Cederschiöld, 185.5–11.

155. *Flóvents saga I*, ed. Cederschiöld, 142.18–21.

156. *Flóvents saga I*, ed. Cederschiöld, 144.28–34.

34 · INTRODUCTION

ing low and slashing hauberks into small pieces.'" The battle continues and toward the end of the battle between the Saxons and the Franks, Master Simon comments: "'And whoever saw the Franks,' says Master Simon, 'would regard it a wonder how many hauberks were slashed and how many helmets were split.'"[157] In all, the nominal author intervenes sixteen times in *Flóvents saga I* with a statement announcing that "meistari Simon segir" (Master Simon says), but only once in *Flóvents saga II*.

In addition to Master Simon, the anonymous narrator also lets his voice be heard throughout the saga in such a manner as to suggest that he controls the plot. He makes his presence known during shifts of scene such as the one between the end of chapter 1, where Emperor Constantine vows to have Flovent killed, and the beginning of chapter 2, when the narrator comments: "Now there is to be told about Flovent."[158] Later in the same chapter, the scene shifts back to the emperor when the narrator announces: "Now there is to be told about the Emperor and his men."[159] One of the more striking instances of narratorial intervention occurs when Flovent, on horseback, is engaged in hand-to-hand combat with a Saxon warrior, and his horse stumbles into a ditch. Flovent manages to leap off the horse and to continue fighting on foot. The plot now shifts to the horse as the narrator speaks up: "Now there is to be told of Magrimon, Flovent's horse."[160] The riderless horse returns to the city of Paris and the populace believes Flovent either to have been killed or captured. There is general mourning and the king's daughter is grief-stricken; her maidens unsuccessfully attempt to console her. The scene concludes with the narrator's comment: "Let her be comforted now, if she will, and now tell about Flovent and the Saxon king."[161] The author has introduced a shift of scene into his translation: the Old Norse "en segjum nú frá Flovent ok Saxa konungi" is reminiscent of "nú er at segja" (now there is to be told), a standard formula in the *Íslendingasögur*, the Sagas of Icelanders. In one instance, the narrator's comment declares that a scene has ended and a shift of place occurs in the next: "Let us now permit Flovent to go to a splendid chamber with Hermet, his host, to rest up in his exhaustion, and instead tell about the Saxons who had fled."[162]

Flóvents saga ends with the death of King Florent and the capture of King Salatres, who asks that his life be spared, and Flovent agrees, provided the lands

157. *Flóvents saga I*, ed. Cederschiöld, 144.63–145.5, 145.46–50.
158. *Flóvents saga I*, ed. Cederschiöld, 125.34.
159. *Flóvents saga I*, ed. Cederschiöld, 125.59–60.
160. *Flóvents saga I*, ed. Cederschiöld, 147.9–10.
161. *Flóvents saga I*, ed. Cederschiöld, 147.53–55.
162. *Flóvents saga I*, ed. Cederschiöld, 185.12–16.

INTRODUCTION · 35

and kingdom the Saxon king had appropriated be given to him, and also that he be given his daughter Marsibilia in marriage. The Saracen maiden is baptized and the wedding takes place.

Bevers saga

Bevers saga is a translation of the Anglo-Norman epic poem *Boeve de Haumtone*, presumably dating from the last decade of the twelfth century.[163] A manuscript of *Bevers saga* is mentioned in a Norwegian document dated 1366, which might suggest that *Bevers saga* had been translated in Norway, rather than in Iceland.[164] Christopher Sanders, who edited the saga, notes, however, that the Old Norse translation of *Boeve de Haumtone* was "probably made at some point in the period 1250–1350, certainly not later, and perhaps as an Icelandic rather than as a Norwegian venture."[165] The saga has been transmitted solely in Icelandic manuscripts. Gustaf Cederschiöld edited the saga in his *Fornsögur Suðrlanda* based on the manuscript Stockholm perg 6 4° dated ca. 1400–1425, which also contains *Flóvents saga II*. Bjarni Vilhjálmsson used Cederschiöld's edition as the basis of his popular edition of 1954, which is the source of my translation.[166]

Scholars disagree concerning the genre of *Boeve de Haumtone*. The *laisse* form is used in the work, something which, as Marianne Ailes has pointed out, is a generic marker of the *chansons de geste*.[167] Judith Weiss, however, who translated *Boeve de Haumtone*, refers to the work as an Anglo-Norman romance in the title of her translation.[168] Despite its metrical form, *Boeve de Haumtone* diverges occasionally from the type of narrative associated with French epic poems. To be sure, the conflict between individual Saracens and the armies they command

163. See Christopher Sanders, introduction to *Bevers saga*, ed. Christopher Sanders (Reykjavík, 2001), cxliii.

164. See Bjarni Vilhjálmsson, ed., *Riddarasögur*, 1: xxi; *Fornsögur Suðrlanda*, ed. Cederschiöld, ccxxxviii.

165. Christopher Sanders, "A Typology of the Primary Texts of *Bevers saga*," in *Rittersagas: Übersetzung, Überlieferung, Transmission*, ed. Jürg Glauser and Susanne Kramarz-Bein (Tübingen, 2014), 133.

166. *Bevers saga*, in *Riddarasögur*, ed. Bjarni Vilhjálmsson, 1: 285–398. See also *Bevers saga*, in *Fornsögur Suðrlanda*, ed. Cederschiöld, 209–67.

167. See Marianne Ailes, "The Anglo-Norman *Boeve de Haumtone* as a *chanson de geste*," in *Sir Bevis of Hampton in Literary Tradition*, ed. Jennifer Fellows and Ivana Djordjevic (Cambridge, 2008), 14.

168. *Boeve de Haumtone and Gui de Warewic: Two Anglo-Norman Romances*, trans. Weiss.

36 · INTRODUCTION

looms large in *Bevers saga*, just as in *Elis saga* and *Flóvents saga*, but there are major differences in both the focus and development of the plot, which takes us from England to Egypt, Damascus, Jerusalem, Germany, France, and back to England.

The protagonist of *Bevers saga* is the son of the powerful Earl Gujon in England, and the plot of the saga is triggered by the violent death of the earl, engineered by his wife who remains nameless throughout, and her subsequent heinous deed of selling their son Bevers into Saracen slavery. The plot opens with a bridal quest: the daughter of the Scottish king is wooed by two men: the old Earl Gujon of Hampton and an unnamed German emperor. Her father decides to marry her to the older of the two suitors, and Bevers, the protagonist of the saga, is their son. The mother is dissatisfied at being married to such an old man, and when Bevers is eleven years of age she asks the German emperor, her former suitor, to come to Hampton and kill her husband, which he does. In a battle he decapitates Gujon and has his head sent to Bevers's mother. Bevers in turn assaults the German emperor in front of his mother and in an act of vengeance she has him sold to Saracens who take him to Egypt, which is ruled by the Saracen king Erminrik.

The catalyst of the plot in *Bevers saga* is the killing of the protagonist's father and the subsequent loss of his patrimony. At the same time a large part of the narrative is given to the love of a Saracen maiden, Josvena, for the Christian protagonist; their repeated separations both before and after their eventual marriage; the preservation of that marriage; and her giving birth to two sons. She is seriatim forcibly married to a Saracen king and to a Saracen earl, but she retains her virginity, in the first instance by means of a chastity belt, and in the other through an ingenious device by means of which the husband is strangled as he gets into bed on the wedding night. Bevers suffers imprisonment, Josvena is abducted, and they are separated on two occasions, each time for seven years, during which they continue to search for one another.

Bevers saga repeatedly depicts the confrontations of Christians and Saracens, but most of the plot is dedicated to the love of the Saracen princess, Josvena, for the Christian knight Bevers, in Egypt. She falls in love with him as she observes him grappling with a wild boar and subsequently defending himself in an attack by a group of his enemies, all of whom he slays. Unlike Marsibilia in *Flóvents saga*, who employs an intermediary to attain Flovent's love, Josvena herself confronts Bevers after he is victorious in a battle against Saracens and declares her love for him. He rejects her advances, since she is a heathen, but in the end she declares that she will reject idolatry and believe in the one true God. Thus commences their loving relationship, but the narrative that follows consists of repeated separations instigated by Saracen enemies both before and after their marriage, and

INTRODUCTION • 37

it is only at the denouement that they are finally reunited. That the copyist of the oldest manuscript of *Bevers saga* understood the saga to be of the couple is evident from the incipit: "Here begins the saga of the courteous Bevers and the Lady Josvena," and the excipit: "There now ends here the saga of Bevers and the Lady Josvena."[169]

Two unusual figures play an important role in advancing the plot of *Bevers saga*, a giant named Eskopart and Bevers's remarkable horse, called Arundele. The former is Bevers's helpful companion early in the plot, but he subsequently deserts him and abducts Josvena for the Saracen king against whom she had earlier used a chastity belt. The latter aids Bevers not only in battle against Eskopart, but also in a fierce encounter with two lions. It is also the reason why Bevers is subsequently banished from England: the English king's son is killed when the horse rears in the midst of his attempt to steal it. This occurs about two-thirds of the way into the plot, after Bevers and Josvena are married, and precipitates a renewed long separation of the couple, engineered by Eskopart in the service of the Saracen king.

The relationship of the Saracens to their idols, chiefly Mahomet, in *Bevers saga* is similar to that in *Flóvents saga*. On more than one occasion they attack an idol, in one case smashing it to bits, for permitting Bevers to escape from the dungeon where he had been held for seven years. At the denouement of *Bevers saga* a tremendous battle between Christians and Saracens takes place, the latter led by the king of Damascus, the son of Brandamon, who had earlier wooed Josvena and had later captured and imprisoned Bevers. In this battle Bevers, together with his two sons, by now young adults, overcome the Saracens, who upon realizing that they cannot win, surrender and convert to Christianity. At the climax the idol of Tervagant is broken, and when a bishop throws holy water on it, the fiend escapes in the form of a dog which cries out: "Wretched is anyone who believes in me, and everyone who trusts in me is lost."[170]

Bevers saga contains some motifs popularized by the courtly romances. During one of their separations, Bevers searches for information concerning Josvena's whereabouts, and learns that King Ivorius had married her. He manages to find her and escape with her while Ivorius is out hunting. The couple come upon a huge giant, the aforementioned Eskopart, who serves King Ivorius. He is fifteen feet tall and is standing on the stump of a tree, holding a club that was so heavy that ten peasants couldn't carry more. His skin is black as coal;[171] the space

169. See *Bevers saga*, ed. Sanders, 3, 367.
170. *Bevers saga*, ed. Cederschiöld, 264.28–30.
171. On black Saracens, see Geraldine Heng, *The Invention of Race in the European Middle Ages* (Cambridge, 2018), 214–19.

38 • INTRODUCTION

between his eyes extends to three feet. His nose ends in a hook, and he has a voice that sounds like ten dogs barking. His teeth, in a very wide mouth, were like those of a wild boar.[172] The portrayal of the giant in *Bevers saga* corresponds more or less to that in the Anglo-Norman *Boeve de Haumtone*.[173] Arthurian motifs were extremely popular and appeared sporadically in the later epic poems which are sometimes referred to as *chansons d'aventure*, in which epic and romance merge.[174] At the beginning of Chrétien's *Yvain* there is a scene in which the Arthurian knight Calogrenant encounters a giant of a man who bears resemblance to the one in *Boeve de Haumtone*:

> A churl, who looked like a Moor, was sitting on a stump with a large club in his hand. He was exceedingly ugly and repulsive; in fact, no words could possibly describe such a hideous creature. I moved closer to the churl and saw that his head was larger than that of a packhorse or any other beast. His hair was in tufts, and his bare forehead was nearly two spans wide. He had big hairy ears like those of an elephant, heavy eyebrows and a flat face, the eyes of an owl and the nose of a cat, a mouth stretching wide like a wolf's, the sharp and yellowed teeth of a wild boar, and a red beard and twisted whiskers. His chin merged into his chest, and he had a large backbone, twisted and hunched.[175]

That Chrétien's *Yvain* may have been known by the author of the source of *Bevers saga* is also suggested by the motif of a magic ring that permits its owner to see what is happening elsewhere. In the Arthurian romance, however, the ring bestows invisibility on its wearer, namely Yvain, who pursues the fatally wounded lord of a castle through the palace gate, but is then trapped between two portcullises. He is saved from discovery by a maiden who gives him a little ring with a stone, which if worn with the stone facing the palm bestows invisibility on its wearer.[176] In *Bevers saga* the magic ring enables its wearer to see what happens elsewhere. When the king, who had been entrusted with guarding Josvena in *Bevers saga*, discovers that she is gone, he looks at his ring with its magic stone,[177] and now sees where Josvena has fled.

172. *Bevers saga*, ed. Sanders, 336–37.

173. *Boeve de Haumtone* 1744–62, trans. Weiss, 58.

174. See Jane H.M. Taylor et al., "Late Medieval Arthurian Literature," in *The Arthur of the French: The Arthurian Legend in Medieval French and Occitan Literature*, ed. Glyn S. Burgess and Karen Pratt (Cardiff, 2006), 515.

175. *The Knight with the Lion*, in Chrétien de Troyes, *The Complete Romances of Chrétien de Troyes*, trans. Staines, 260.

176. Ibid., 268–69.

177. On precious and magic stones in the indigenous *riddarasögur*, the chivalric sagas, see Schlauch, *Romance in Iceland*, 42–43.

INTRODUCTION • 39

Another motif in *Bevers saga* that would seem more at home in romance than epic is the motif of a man being wooed by a woman. To be sure, the motif is found in *Flóvents saga*, but there it is the specific motif of the *bele Sarrasine* who falls in love with a Christian knight. That is not the case in a noteworthy episode in *Bevers saga*, however, for the wooing woman is no Saracen maiden, but rather the Christian ruler of a kingdom. The motif is known from Arthurian literature, the most prominent example of which is found in the Breton lay *Lanval* by Marie de France. There a knight named Lanval, a member of King Arthur's court, encounters a lady who tells him that she has sought him out for love of him, and over an extended period of time they are lovers.[178] The situation is rather different in *Bevers saga*, yet the protagonist is also wooed by a powerful woman, the ruler of a city named Civile. Bevers comes to the city, which is under siege by a Saracen army, and he comes to its defense. The ruler of Civile watches the progress of the battle and sees the unknown knight strike down one after another of her enemies. She falls in love with him, and when he informs her that he is searching for his wife who has been abducted, she responds imperiously: "You are going to take me as your wife, and I shall give you dominion over my entire kingdom."[179] When Bevers refuses the offer, she becomes exceedingly angry and threatens to behead him. In response, Bevers agrees that he will marry her if after seven years Josvena has not been found. They repeatedly haggle over the number of years that have passed and during this time Bevers is chief of the knights in her kingdom. Finally, in the seventh year of his sojourn in Civile, Josvena, who has been searching for Bevers, comes to the town and is reunited with her husband.

One characteristic of *Bevers saga* that is found neither in *Elis saga* nor *Flóvents saga* is a subtle and odd sense of humor which obtains in a couple of episodes. In one rather serious scene, Bevers is in danger of being killed by King Brandamon from whose dungeon he has escaped. Brandamon learns that Bevers has escaped, and he becomes so angry that he picks up a staff and runs at the idol of Mahomet and strikes it. He calls up an army, pursues Bevers, and attacks him. Bevers draws his sword, strikes Brandamon's head, and the Saracen falls dead off his horse. In an instance of faint gallows humor, Bevers comments: "You can thank me for having ordained you a bishop, and now you resemble other bishops with your tonsure."[180] When a second Saracen attacks him, he urges him to turn back, unless he wants to meet the same end as his master and be ordained a deacon

178. On this scene, see Marie de France, *Lanval* 110–16, in *The Lais of Marie de France*, trans. Robert Hanning and Joan Ferrante (New York, 1978), 108. For a discussion of the place of *Lanval* in Arthurian literature, see Matilda Tomaryn Bruckner and Glyn S. Burgess, "Arthur in the Narrative Lay," in *The Arthur of the French*, ed. Burgess and Pratt, 190–94.

179. *Bevers saga*, ed. Cederschiöld, 249.58–61.

180. *Bevers saga*, ed. Cederschiöld, 228.8–10.

40 · INTRODUCTION

with his sword.[181] Another droll episode is the baptism of the giant Eskopart, which becomes somewhat of a parody because of his enormous size. The baptismal font is too small for him, and a huge tub had to be found, into which he has to lower himself, since he is so heavy that the entire populace is incapable of lifting him into the tub. The episode is somewhat longer in *Boeve de Haumtone* and more amusing. There the water was so cold that it chilled Escopart, and he jumped out of the tub and accused the bishop of trying to drown him, and he said: "Let me go; I've had enough of being a Christian." The narrator comments: "Whoever could see him jumping about, naked, would think – I won't deny it – he was a hungry devil."[182]

An odd type of humor also plays out when Bevers learns that King Ivorius of Munbrak has married his wife Josvena. He arrives while the king is out hunting and hears his wife lamenting at having lost Bevers. Appearing as a pilgrim, Bevers enters the hall and asks Josvena for some food. When she inquires where he was born, he responds that it was England. Whereupon she asks whether he knows a man from Hampton named Bevers, and he replies that he does, and that he is now back in his kingdom, having avenged his father and honorably married a beautiful woman. At this Josvena faints, but then she laments and looks closely at Bevers and says that he resembles him, except for a scar on his brow. But Bevers brazenly denies his true identity. It is only when Bevers's horse Arundele, which refuses to let anyone mount it except Bevers, recognizes him and runs toward him that he confesses his identity.[183] The motivation for his lie to Josvena that Bevers has married in Hampton may be his way of testing her fidelity to him; nonetheless the scene is odd. There are also other such occasions, when Bevers refuses to reveal his identity, yet for no discernible reason. A striking example occurs in chapter 9, when Bevers encounters a pilgrim who invites him to share a meal with him. Bevers asks him who he is and the pilgrim reveals that he comes from Hampton and is the son of Sabaoth – who happens to be Bevers's foster-father. Sabaoth had asked him to look for a child named Bevers who had been sold to Saracens. The pilgrim asks whether Bevers knows anything about his whereabouts, and Bevers responds that he saw the child being hanged.[184] In the

181. *Bevers saga*, ed. Cederschiöld, 228.18. *Boeve de Haumtone* has a variant of the exchange. "By God!" Boeve states to the first Saracen, "it's turned out well for you that you've been ordained by such a good bishop: you certainly look like a learned chaplain." To the second Saracen Boeve says: "I advise you to turn back and gather up your uncle; carry him home, for he's newly ordained priest" (*Boeve de Haumtone* 1210–18, trans. Weiss, 48).

182. *Boeve de Haumtone* 1977, trans. Weiss, 62.

183. *Boeve de Haumtone* 1402–68, trans. Weiss, 53.

184. *Boeve de Haumtone* has a nearly identical statement: "'Palmer,' said Boeve, "'you're talking nonsense, for the child I hear you mention has been hanged'" (*Boeve de Haumtone* 847, trans. Weiss, 39).

INTRODUCTION • 41

saga, but not in *Boeve de Haumtone*, Bevers does not want to give the pilgrim his name. The episode is rather puzzling and Bevers's lie is baffling.

After the protagonist of *Bevers saga* has regained his patrimony, England, at the saga's denouement, he sails back to Munbrak and finds Josvena seriously ill in bed and she tells him that she does not have long to live. Aware of his wife's mortal illness, Bevers prays to God to let both of them leave this world together, and "he was immediately stricken with a deadly illness and he lay down next to Josvena in the bed .... They embraced each other as was fitting and they gave up their ghost."[185] Not to be outdone, the horse Arundele also dies.

Though *Bevers saga* is a translation of *Boeve de Haumtone*, it is based on a different version of the text than that preserved in the Anglo-Norman manuscript. The first *laisse* of *Boeve* addresses the audience directly: "My lords, now pay attention to me. I shall tell you tales – I know different ones – about Boeve of Hampton, the courteous knight, who defeated so many good kings by dint of his sword. If you wish to hear, I will tell you; I believe you never heard anything better." The second *laisse* similarly addresses the audience, but also introduces "the good count, named Gui," who lived at Hampton.[186] This corresponds to the beginning of *Bevers saga*: "Gujon was the name of a powerful earl in England."[187] There follows the introduction of the old count and his decision to marry the daughter of the Scottish king. Throughout the saga it is evident that it is not a translation of the version transmitted in the two extant fragmentary Anglo-Norman manuscripts, which fortuitously complement each other, thereby constituting a complete text.[188]

A prime example of the textual discrepancies between *Bevers saga* and *Boeve de Haumtone* is the reunion of Sabaoth, Bevers's foster father, and Josvena in France at the shrine of St Gilles. The saga briefly relates that "Lord Sabaoth now took charge of Josvena, and they traveled everywhere, looking for Bevers and Terri, and they came to the city of Abbaport."[189] The corresponding passage in *laisse* CLXXV of *Boeve*, which is far longer and full of digressions, is as follows:

> ... Sabaoth speedily took charge of the lady. "My lord," she said, "by God, who never lies, how can you take me through the land?" "My lady," said Sabaoth, "don't be frightened; I will dress you like a man." And the lady said:

185. *Bevers saga*, ed. Sanders, 397–98.
186. *Boeve de Haumtone* 1–12, trans. Weiss, 25. The quoted text is verses 10–11.
187. *Bevers saga*, ed. Sanders, 285.
188. On the manuscripts of *Boeve*, see Albert Stimming, introduction to *Der anglonormannische Boeve de Haumtone*, ed. Albert Stimming (Halle, 1899), iii–viii.
189. *Bevers saga*, ed. Cederschiöld, 248.3–5.

42 • INTRODUCTION

"We are in great need." Sabaoth stayed behind, the pilgrims departed, and he dressed the lady and they went straight off to the market. She bought a herb – you never saw a better – and with it she dyed all her body and her face. Then they went looking for Boeve and Terri.[190]

Thus ends *laisse* CLXXV, and *laisse* CLXXVI commences with the statement: "They did not stop till they reached Abreford."

That *Bevers saga* is a translation of a version other than the one transmitted in the extant Anglo-Norman manuscript is nowhere more evident than in its conclusion. The saga ends with the simple statement: "Here there now ends the saga of Bevers and his wife Josvena." This is unlike the *jongleur*, whose voice is heard at the beginning of *Boeve de Haumtone*, who asks for attention while he tells his tales,[191] and at its conclusion, where he steps forward for a last time to state: "Our song is ended, it lasts no longer; I will tell you no more in words or in song. Thus finishes the tale, properly told, of Boeve of Hampton with the fearless face. I have read it to you and you have heard it. It would be courteous to give me my reward."[192] The saga's source was thus a variant version of *Boeve de Haumtone*. In other words, *Bevers saga*, like *Elis saga* and *Flóvents saga*, transmits a version of the *chanson de geste* that exists only in the Old Norse–Icelandic translation.

Bærings saga

The Icelandic codex AM 580 4°, dated ca. 1300–1325, contains translations of two *chansons de geste*, *Elis saga ok Rósamundu* (only a fragment of one leaf is extant) and *Flóvents saga*, as well as *Bærings saga*, the "Saga of Baering." Despite the belief of some scholars[193] that *Bærings saga* is a translation of a foreign text, it is more likely that it is an original Icelandic narrative, albeit one heavily indebted to *Bevers saga*. In the context of medieval Icelandic literary genres, *Bærings saga* is a *riddarasaga*, that is, a chivalric saga. Given that the manuscript in which *Bærings saga* is found is the oldest Icelandic manuscript to transmit translations of French romance epics, it is reasonable to consider *Bærings saga* the earliest indigenous Icelandic romance,[194] and given its indebtedness to *Bevers saga*, a

190. *Boeve de Haumtone* 2770–81, trans. Weiss, 76–77.
191. *Boeve de Haumtone* 1–12, trans. Weiss, 25.
192. *Boeve de Haumtone* 3846–50, trans. Weiss, 95. Notable is the fact that the "author" has read the story, rather than told it, as is the wont of *jongleurs*.
193. Gustaf Cederschiöld and Henry Goddard Leach; see above.
194. See Kalinke, "The Genesis of Courtly Romance in Iceland."

INTRODUCTION · 43

translation of a French romance epic, in my translation I classify *Bærings saga* as a romance epic.

Like *Bevers saga*, whose action begins in England, the plot of *Bærings saga* commences in northern Europe, specifically in Holstein, northern Germany. The plots of both sagas begin with the murder of the protagonist's father and the loss of the protagonist's patrimony. In both sagas the protagonist is a child, in the case of *Bærings saga* still a baby. And in both narratives the child ends up in foreign countries, where, once he reaches maturity, he endeavors to recover his patrimony. *Bærings saga* differs from *Bevers saga*, however, inasmuch as it is somewhat less concerned with the confrontation of the protagonist, a Christian, with Saracens and their forces. Moreover, whereas in *Bevers saga*, as also in *Elis saga* and *Flóvents saga*, the protagonist wins the love of a Saracen maiden, in *Bærings saga* the various women encountered by the protagonist are Christian.

The plot of *Bærings saga* is triggered by the death of Baering's father and the murder of the Duke of Holstein, the protagonist's uncle and namesake, and his mother's brother. The mother and her baby flee to the safety of the English court. Once Baering has reached maturity, events take him to Flanders, France, Greece, Constantinople, Italy, Switzerland, and finally Saxony and Holstein, in pursuit of regaining his patrimony. *Bærings saga* concludes with the protagonist becoming ruler of the entire Roman empire.

For the greater part of the narrative, Baering's identity remains unknown to others, and given his extraordinary beauty, he earns the cognomen *inn fagri riddari*, that is, the Fair Knight. Baering distinguishes himself in tournaments as well as in battles against both Christians and Saracens. As happens in the *chansons de geste*, women vie for the love of young Baering, among others the daughters of a king and an emperor. Unlike many courtly romances, where the woman is the object of the male gaze, in *Bærings saga* it is the protagonist who is subject to the female gaze. When Baering, the Fair Knight, enters the hall of King Pippin of France, Wilfrida, his daughter, "was intensely staring at Baering."[195] A similar reaction occurs in the palace of the Roman emperor Lucius, where everyone stared at Baering, because no one had ever seen such a handsome man before, and the nobles comment that Lucinia, the emperor's daughter, "stares at this handsome man."[196]

Wilfrida, King Pippin's daughter, is to be married to Emanuel, the Greek emperor, but once she has seen Baering she declares that she intends to enter a convent and dedicate her life to God. Subsequently she sends a letter to Baering in which she tells him that she has rejected her betrothed, the Greek emperor, on

195. *Bærings saga*, ed. Cederschiöld, 97.28.
196. *Bærings saga*, ed. Cederschiöld, 106.17–18.

44 • INTRODUCTION

Baering's account, and that she loves him with all her heart. Furthermore, she states that if he wishes to receive lands and riches from her father, he should come to her and she will firmly support their marriage. Lucinia, the Roman emperor's daughter is more aggressive. She confronts Baering and tells him that he has been on her mind both day and night and that she wants to marry him. She states, however, that he should first make love to her in secret. Should he reject her, she will see to it that he loses his life. And Lucinia attacks Baering, rips his clothes off him, and then tells her father that he had attempted to rape her.

Bærings saga contains two other incidents in which the protagonist's beauty motivates a woman to offer herself in marriage to him. On one occasion, while Baering is in Normandy, he is challenged to combat by a certain Count Samuel. The town's populace as well as the count's wife observe the duel, in which the count is slain. The count's wife catches sight of Baering during the funeral procession, sees how handsome he is, and instantly falls in love with him. The narrator comments that she did not much mourn the death of her husband. She sends him a message offering herself in marriage to him, together with much wealth and property.[197]

Baering's encounter with another widow has farcical aspects. Baering and his two companions take lodging with the wealthy widow of a count and her daughter. She offers the three one bed in the loft, but then both mother and daughter invite Baering to join each in her bed, to which he curiously agrees. But Baering instead sends one of his companions to the widow's bed and the other to the daughter's bed, while he sleeps in solitary splendor in the loft. Before daybreak Baering's two companions return to his bed. The widow believes that she has slept with Baering and offers herself to him in marriage.

The extraordinary and supernatural play a significant role in *Bærings saga*. There are angels, giants, and sorcerers, reflecting both Christian beliefs and pagan witchcraft. Baering is troubled that his beauty should attract the attention of women, but one night an angel appears to him in his sleep and tells him that God has bestowed great beauty on him and does not want him to hide this gift. After Baering has been accused of raping Lucinia, her father intends to kill Baering and has him thrown into a large waterfall. The divine intervenes, however, in the person of an angel who transports Baering on his wings and flies with him onto dry land.

197. On this episode, see Kalinke, *Stories Set Forth with Fair Words*, 118, 120. The motif of the easily consoled widow may have been inspired by the same in *Ívens saga*, whose protagonist kills a knight, yet whose widow is swiftly talked into marrying the killer. See *Ívens saga*, ed. and trans. Marianne Kalinke, in Marianne Kalinke, ed., *Norse Romance*, vol. 2: *The Knights of the Round Table* (Cambridge, 1999), 51–61.

INTRODUCTION • 45

Giants are significant figures in *Bærings saga*. In the battle of Constantinople, the Saracen chieftain, named Livorius, is an evil giant, who is described as being eight ells tall, and who, according to the narrator, resembles more the devil than a human being. His idols have given him frightful strength through the power of unclean spirits, and any Christian who looks at him loses his mind; many a Christian has died as a result. He has a face that is black like the bottom of a kettle, and his nose is crooked with two hooks at its end. The author of *Bærings saga* has lifted this depiction from *Bevers saga*, where, however, the portrayal is considerably longer.[198]

The Fraudster Heinrek, who has deprived Baering of his patrimony, has sired one son, named Skadevald, with a giantess living under a waterfall in the Elbe river.[199] In his army Heinrek had two dozen Russian knights who were taller and stronger than men who lived earlier. Their swords were tempered with poison and they themselves were filled with poison. Skadevald, Heinrek's son, is a sorcerer who engages in witchcraft and occasionally takes on the form of a dragon that spews poison at its enemies. At the denouement of *Bærings saga*, Heinrek's and Baering's forces confront each other, and Skadevald challenges Baering to a holmgang, that is, a duel on an island. Baering blesses himself upon reaching the island, but at this the island suddenly disappears, and he suggests to Skadevald that they confront one another from their boats, which they tie together. As they fight, Skadevald turns into a dragon, then back into a human, then, after Baering strikes down on him, into a bellowing ox, at which point two serpents slide over the side of the boat and spew poison at Baering. Thus it continues, until Baering finally delivers the death blow to Skadevald, now in the form of a serpent, and the river runs red from the blood of the monsters. The figure of Skadevald is clearly modeled on the shapeshifters of Icelandic folklore, and provides further evidence that *Bærings saga* was composed by an Icelander rather than that the saga is a foreign import.[200]

Bærings saga might be considered a medieval *Bildungsroman* (novel of character development), which takes the protagonist from childhood to maturity and marks not only his physical development but also his spiritual and ethical progress. Just before the narrative concludes with Baering's coronation and wedding, Emperor Lucinius, King Pippin of France, and King Richard of England, along with their bishops, meet with Baering and declare:

198. *Bevers saga*, ed. Cederschiöld, 336–37.
199. The name Skadevald means "wielder of harm."
200. On magic and shapeshifting in medieval Icelandic literature, see Schlauch, *Romance in Iceland*, 122–31.

46 • INTRODUCTION

Baering had comported himself well in face of the sexual desire of two kings' daughters, Lucinia and Wilfrida; the latter had rejected her betrothed, the emperor of Constantinople, while the former lost her father's empire. They were unable to refrain from love's passion, but Baering firmly resisted sexual desire and did not dishonor them; instead, he preserved his chastity and did not let himself be governed by lust. And all agreed that Baering was innocent and guileless in respect to the women and their guardians.[201]

By naming Lucinia and Wilfrida as sources of temptation, and citing Baering's resistance to them, the extraordinary judgment of three crowned heads and episcopal authorities suggests that the author intended the moral progress of the protagonist to be a theme of his narrative.[202]

Rendering Old Norse–Icelandic Sagas into English

The Old Norse–Icelandic translations of three French *chansons de geste* and the Old Icelandic *riddarasaga* are here presented in English translation. The translations from the French are of anonymous versions of epic poems other than those transmitted in the extant French manuscripts. *Elis saga ok Rósamunda* is a translation of a manuscript of *Élie de Saint-Gilles* that no longer exists, which moreover was fragmentary, for it lacked the denouement of the French epic. Some decades later an anonymous Icelander penned a conclusion to the saga in a style at odds with the Norse translation. He made excessive use of the present participle to form the present and past tenses. That is, he employed the present or past tense of the verb *vera* (to be) plus the present participle in constructions that serve no purpose, but which resulted in an inelegant and clumsy prose. Abbot Robert tended to employ euphonious alliterating collocations to convey drama or emotion in *Elis saga ok Rósamundu*. No effort has been made to emulate his style in the English translation, which strives for accuracy of content. The Icelandic continuator's participial style has been transmitted in straightforward English prose. The translation is based on Bjarni Vilhjálmsson's popular edition in *Riddarasögur* rather than on Eugen Kölbing's diplomatic edition of *Elis saga ok Rósamundu*.

201. *Bærings saga*, ed. Cederschiöld, 121.35–43.
202. One scholar observes that "Constantinople is configured as the *locus* of royal female virtue, while the negative example is the competition of Vilfríðr and Lucinia ... the unprincipled princesses of France and Rome." See Geraldine Barnes, *The Bookish Riddarasögur: Writing Romance in Late Medieval Iceland* (Odense, 2014), 167.

INTRODUCTION · 47

The translation of *Flóvents saga* presents a unique problem. Unlike Abbot Robert's translation of *Elis saga ok Rósamundu*, which is extant in a contemporary manuscript, *Flóvents saga* is not transmitted in the translator's manuscript, but solely in two copies of that translation. The saga is preserved in two primary manuscripts, in AM 580 4°, dated ca. 1300–1325, and in Holm perg 6 4°, dated ca. 1400–1425. The older manuscript lacks the last two chapters, while an entire leaf is missing in the middle of the saga. The younger manuscript commences with a slightly defective first chapter, consisting of some illegible words in the first few lines of the narrative, and it also lacks the attribution of *Flóvents saga* to a school master named Simon in the introductory lines of the saga.[203]

The two manuscripts differ in their chapter divisions and often also diverge textually. The editor of the diplomatic edition, Gustaf Cederschiöld, published the two manuscripts as *Flóvents saga I* and *Flóvents saga II*. The chapters in *Flóvents saga II* in the manuscript Holm perg 6 4° carry titles composed by the copyist, and in my translation I use this manuscript's chapter divisions rather than those of the older manuscript. Not all titles are legible, however, in the manuscript, thus Cederschiöld's edition, and I have provided titles for those chapters. My translation of *Flóvents saga* is a composite of the two redactions, based on the assumption that copies of an Icelandic manuscript – here, the source of both copies of *Flóvents saga* – generally do not add, but rather omit text.[204] An example of this is the depiction of Flovent's tunic, which is adorned with twelve gems that derive from the description of Jerusalem in the *Book of Revelation*. *Flóvents saga I* records all twelve, while *Flóvents saga II* lists only ten. Hence, the longer version in this passage is given preference in my translation.

One of the idiosyncrasies of *Flóvents saga* is its ascription to a Master Simon, who repeatedly comments on the plot throughout the saga. The introductory phrase is *meistari Simon segir*, that is, "Master Simon says," and it occurs sixteen times in *Flóvents saga I*, yet only once in *Flóvents saga II*. This suggests that the original translation included these references, and that *Flóvents saga* in the manuscript AM 580 4°, if not the original translation itself, is a relatively accurate copy of that translation. *Flóvents saga II* is presumably a copy of a manuscript that had excised all but one authorial comment, unless it was the copy-

203. *Flóvents saga I*, ed. Cederschiöld, 168.1–29, 124.5–8.

204. *Ívens saga*, a translation of Chrétien de Troyes's *Yvain*, commissioned, like *Elis saga*, by King Hákon Hákonarson, provides ample evidence that reduction of text occurs in the copying of manuscripts. See *Ívens saga*, ed. Kalinke, 35–36. On the translation and transmission of French romances in Iceland, see Marianne Kalinke, *King Arthur, North-by-Northwest: The* matière de Bretagne *in Old Norse–Icelandic Romances* (Copenhagen, 1981), 178–98.

48 • INTRODUCTION

ist of the saga in AM 580 4° himself who carelessly or willfully left out the authorial references.

Nonetheless, the above scenario is also problematic. Already at the very beginning of the saga the portrayal of Flovent differs in the two manuscripts, partly in word order. In *Flóvents saga I* Flovent is depicted as follows:

> Flovent then stood up, the emperor's nephew, and took off his mantle. He was in a tunic shot through with gold. He was keen-eyed, broad-shouldered, and slender-waisted, pleasingly shaped in every way. There was no man handsomer or fairer than he.[205]

The text in *Flóvents saga II* is somewhat longer, varied, and is structured slightly differently:

> Flovent then stood up, the son of the emperor's sister. He was in a tunic shot through with gold and was the handsomest of men. His face was white like a lily, and his cheeks red like a rose; his hair was like straw with .... He was hardy and strong, broad in the shoulders and at the chest; and his entire body was wondrously well shaped.[206]

The eight dots above indicate illegible letters; thus Cederschiöld. Striking are the three similes, and in the introduction to his edition of five *riddarasögur* in his *Fornsögur Suðrlanda* Cederschiöld included a list of such similes that are found in both translated and indigenous *riddarasögur*.[207] My "translation" attempts to include what I consider the best of both versions and it arrives at the following:

> Flovent stood up, the son of the emperor's sister. He took off his mantle and he was dressed in a tunic shot through with gold, and he was the handsomest of men. His face was white as a lily, and his cheeks were red as a rose; his hair was flaxen like straw. He was hardy and strong, broad in the shoulders and chest; and his entire body was wondrously well shaped. There was no man handsomer or fairer than he.

One major discrepancy between the two redactions of *Flóvents saga* is the inclusion of a French proverb in *Flóvents saga I*. Near the denouement of the saga

205. *Flóvents saga I*, ed. Cederschiöld, 124.29–34.
206. *Flóvents saga II*, ed. Cederschiöld, 168.30–38.
207. *Fornsögur Suðrlanda*, ed. Cederschiöld, xxiii.

INTRODUCTION · **49**

there occurs a flyting, that is, an exchange of insults hurled at one another by the Saracen kings Salatres and Florent. The latter accuses Salatres:

"With your corrupt avarice you have despoiled my kingdom and have repeatedly been most wicked and inimical, and for that reason you deserve to die." King Salatres said: "I do not fear you, most horrible of kings, you who does not dare to oppose me." The king of the Franks replied: "You greatest whore's son; for a long time you have worked your wickedness, and through your words you reveal your foolish intentions. And the old French proverb holds true: "Ki tent sun pie plus que sa chape ne tient, (s'en repent) tost quant freid (li) vient." In our language this states: 'whoever stretches his foot out from under his cloak, will regret it when the cold comes upon him.' You have many treasures, but a heart full of wickedness and unrighteousness; you have managed to fall into my hands, and I shall cure you of your wickedness rather than let you get away. And if you perish today, you will be hung on the tallest tree in France." King Salatres said: "Shut up, you cowardly and worthless fellow, I have been in your country for thirty months and have captured cities and castles, but I have never seen you demonstrate any prowess."

The above translation combines the texts of the two versions of *Flóvents saga*, and this is also the manner in which I proceed throughout my translation, focusing on what makes narrative sense in producing a more or less complete rendering of *Flóvents saga*. In sum, my translation is of neither manuscript, but rather a combination of the two texts in an attempt to arrive at an acceptable and reasonable facsimile of what might have been the original translation.

Stylistically *Flóvents saga*, *Bevers saga*, and *Bærings saga* are unlike *Elis saga ok Rósamundu*, a Norwegian translation. Abbot Robert's translation of the *chanson de geste* uses the narrative past, and his style is hypotactic. When his translation breaks off, because of his fragmentary French source, and the Icelandic continuator takes over, there is a drastic change of style. The Icelander favors clumsy participial constructions for verbs. The style of the Icelandic continuation of *Elis saga* is chiefly paratactic and the narrative past is avoided, yet now and then the continuator switches tenses in midstream. For example, in § 67 Rósamunda watches as "Elis *drap* bróður hennar, og *þótti* henni það gott. *Gengur* hún nú heim til skemmu sinnar. *Byr* hún sig með hinum bezta búnaði með snjóhvítum silkiserk ... engi *mátti* finnast betri, þó at leitað *væri* um alla veröldina" (Elis *killed* her brother, and she *approved* of that. She *goes* back to her bed chamber. She *dresses* in outstanding garments, in a snow-white silken chemise ... no better *could* be

50 • INTRODUCTION

found, even if one *searched* the entire world").[208] The shift between the present and past tenses is also common in the other sagas. For example, in *Bevers saga* we read: "Eftir það *hleypur* jarlinn að keisaranum og *dró* út sitt sverð"[209] (Then the earl *rushes* at the emperor and *drew* his sword). In *Flóvents saga* similar tense shifting occurs: "Keisari *er* hryggr eptir dráp hertogans ok *mælti* við sína menn"[210] (The emperor *is* sad at the duke's killing and *spoke* to his men). And a final example from *Bærings saga*: "Nú *sat* konungr ok *sá* um höllina ok *lítr* Bæring ok *sér* lengi á hann ok *mælti* við Ferant jarl"[211] (The king *sat* now and *looked* around the hall and he *notices* Baering and *looks* long at him, and he *spoke* to Earl Ferant). My translation uses the narrative past for the four sagas.

Overall, the style of *Flóvents saga*, is paratactic, like that of the Icelandic continuation of *Elis saga*, and contains a gratuitous overabundance of the coordinating conjunction *ok* (and) and the adverbs *nú* (now) and *þá* (then). Many adverbs have been deleted in translation. In *Flóvents saga*, however, the adverb *nú* is also used as a stylistic device to announce a shift of scene or the start of a new episode. As noted previously, the phrase is "nú er at segja" (now there is to be told), a standard formulation familiar from the *Íslendingasögur*, the Sagas of Icelanders.

Bevers saga is the least problematic of the four translations. It is based on Bjarni Vilhjálmsson's popular edition.[212] The saga is a translation of a version of the *chanson de geste* other than that of the two Anglo-Norman manuscript fragments, which in combination transmit the complete text of *Boeve de Haumtone*. In one instance *Bevers saga* deviates from a reading in the French manuscript, which indicates that the translator misunderstood the French syntax, and this has been corrected in my translation. However, the Icelandic translation also proves the French text to be in error on another occasion, when that text does not make narrative sense. Such errors are pointed out in notes to my translation. The rendering of *Bevers saga* has benefited from reference to Judith Weiss's translation of *Boeve de Haumtone* and her copious notes on the text.

As is common in translations from Old Icelandic, the spelling of proper nouns has been simplified, both by the elimination of non-English letters and by the reduction of inflections. Thus *Erminrikr* is Erminrik in the translation; *Bæringr* loses the digraph *æ* and is Baering, and *Geirarðr* becomes Geirard. References to historical personages are to their customary names, such as "Hlöðvir konungr,"

208. *Elis saga ok Rósamundu*, ed. Cederschiöld, 133.5–11.
209. *Bevers saga*, ed. Bjarni Vilhjálmsson, 1: 289.
210. *Flóvents saga I*, ed. Cederschiöld, 125.60–61.
211. *Bærings saga*, ed. Cederschiöld, 95.40–43.
212. *Bevers saga*, ed. Bjarni Vilhjálmsson, 1: 285–398.

INTRODUCTION • 51

who is identified as "King Louis," that is, the son of Charlemagne. Similarly, place names are identified in their English form; thus, Earl Gujon "í Hamtún" is identified as "of Hampton." And "pílagrímsferð í Kolni" is a "pilgrimage to Cologne." Place names in *Elis saga* are frequently corrupt and Hartman and Malicote's translation of *Élie de Saint-Gilles* has been a guide for contemporary French place names. Yet there are many place names in *Elis saga* the identification of which has been impossible for me, and I have let the Icelandic name stand. Of the four sagas, *Bærings saga* contains the largest number of place names and names of rivers. I have given them in the standard form. Thus the Saxelfr, literally "Sax river," is identified as the Elbe in Germany. Holsetaland and Saxland are identified as Holstein and Saxony. A few places, especially in the Italian region, could not be identified and were left in the form given in the manuscript, leaving it up to the reader to guess what the actual name might be. There are references to saints, such as to "heilagr Egidius," who is identified as St Giles, and to "Ioan postoli," who is the Evangelist John. Three pagan gods are invoked in the sagas: Apollo, Mahomet, and Tervagant, but reference to Mahomet occurs most frequently.

Elis saga and *Bevers saga* consistently refer to the Saracens as *heiðingjar* (heathens, pagans), but I regularly transmit this as "Saracens," as in the French epics. The reason for this is that in the European Middle Ages the non-Christian Other (no matter the persuasion) is always a Saracen.[213] In translating *Flóvents saga*, however, I translate *heiðingi* with "pagan," since the original translation no longer exists, only two copies of this. Furthermore, the French source of *Flóvents saga* was a Franco-Italian *chanson de geste* that is not extant, and thus it is impossible to know whether the word *Sarrasin* "Saracen" occurred in the epic. The word does occur in the Icelandic translations of other *chansons de geste*, and presumably for the first time in *Karlamagnús saga*, the oldest translation of a *chanson de geste*, in a reference to St James the Great, that is, Santiago de Compostela: "i Galicia landi, þar sem Saracinar hafa háðuligt vald yfir" (in Galicia, where the Saracens wield appalling power).[214] Why the Old Norse–Icelandic translations of the romance epics transmit the French *Sarrasins* (Saracens) as *heiðingjar* (pagans) remains a mystery to me, since the Icelandic loan word *Saracinar* did exist.

---

213. See Heng, *The Invention of Race in the European Middle Ages*, 110–18.

214. C.R. Unger, ed., *Karlamagnus saga ok kappa hans: Fortællinger om Keiser Karl Magnus og hans Jævninger* (Kristiania [Oslo], 1860), 265.9–10.

The Romance Epic of Elis and Rosamunda

1. *Elis saga* **begins.**

Listen, wise men, to a fine tale of the glorious righteousness, valiant chivalry, and splendid accomplishments of an honorable duke, who had the government and rule, power, administration, and supervision over the land of Saint Egidius[1] in the southwestern realm of the king of the Franks. This duke was so old that his beard flourished with white locks. He was so blessed in his day that the fear of God and his goodness directed his entire life with God's providence. When he was young and still in his childhood he already demonstrated every righteous virtue and all courtly manners, and did this with such inborn goodness that he never deprived a maiden or widow or an undeservedly helpless person of honor, possessions, inheritance, or money through scheming or unrighteousness; instead, his heart was always inclined to God's honor and good works. At great expense he had many stone bridges built over rivers and impassable roads as assistance for both the rich and the poor. He supported many magnificent hospices, along with monasteries and churches. His table was always available to anyone wanting to accept his hospitality, while his alms were unceasing and were large, liberal, and gracious.

Now it happened on the feast of St Dionysius[2] that this powerful duke sat in his palace, which was entirely built of marble in every kind of color, blue and brown, green and yellow, red, black, white, and blended, and carved with all the skill of which human hands are capable. The duke sat among his powerful barons and other gentry whom he had gathered for a great banquet on this feast, and he addressed them with loving words.

2. **The conversation between the duke and Elis, his son.**

"Listen, lords," he said, "to my words and give me sound and honest advice. Consider what is best and most appropriate and useful for providing for my heirs and

1. The reference is to the city of Saint-Gilles in southern France. *Egidius* is the Latin form of the saint's name.

2. This is St Dennis, bishop of Paris, and patron of France, who died ca. 250.

THE ROMANCE EPIC OF ELIS AND ROSAMUNDA · 53

heritors. Sixty years have passed since I first took up knightly weapons, but I am now so weak that I am no longer able to bear arms, and it behooves me to stay at home now and prepare myself appropriately for God and the joys of the afterlife through holy prayer, by furthering the church and offering alms, so that in my old age I will make amends for my youth. My wife gave birth to my two children, a splendid son whom God has given into my keeping, and a beautiful daughter, the gracious Ozible, whom Lord Gerin of Porfrettiborg seeks in marriage, but she is still too young to be married. But he has sworn on the body of St Hilary[3] that he would marry her before she was fifteen years old and honorably take her home with him to Blevesborg. I now want my son to appear before you here in this palace. He has become valiant and is accomplished in respect to intelligence and exemplary conduct. He is a tall man, broad-shouldered and strong-limbed, but I do not understand and think it strange why he is not the most stout-hearted person, given that physically he has developed so as to be able to pursue valorous and mighty accomplishments. But it has now been more than twelve months since he could bear arms and become a knight, and thus I wonder why he wants to lead a life of ease like a battle horse in its stall or a monk in his monastery. It would be more appropriate for him to be in Paris at Easter and to serve King Louis,[4] the son of King Charlemagne, so as to gain assets for his legacy and patrimony. For when I was young and at his age, I achieved so much with my weapons and prowess that I still possess thirty castles and six cities and another twenty-five.

"But now I want to declare one thing," he said, "here, before all of you, that my son should know he is to earn with weapons what I myself have earned, that is, property, inheritance, and assets, because he will never get from me anything I own, not a single penny, because my daughter and I shall live in this realm, which I attained, and when I die she shall be my heir and owner of all that I have acquired."

When Elis, his son, understood what he was saying, he got angry and extremely enraged, and he got up from his seat, vaulted over the table and onto the floor, intending to leave, but his father called out to him:

"Stand still, you scoundrel," he said, "you're not going anywhere. I do not want you to bring charges against me nor to censure me. If you now leave as things stand, penniless and alone, people will soon say in Paris and in Chartres: 'Look now at the son of old Julien, whose father has driven him from his realm out of anger and on false charges.' I do not want this, not for all the gold in Jacob's land.[5]

3. St Hilary (died ca. 367) was bishop of Poitiers, France.
4. This is Louis the Pious (778–840), who upon Charlemagne's death became king of the Franks.
5. The reference is to Spain and Santiago de Compostela.

54 • THE ROMANCE EPIC OF ELIS AND ROSAMUNDA

I shall instead give you my best battle horse and all my armor, my hauberk, which is brighter than silver, and my leaf-gilt helmet, my trusty shield, my stout spear with its gold-laced standard, and you are going to ride before us onto our wide and level plain. There I shall have an oaken tilt pole raised for you to attack, and shall fasten to it two good shields and a sound hauberk, and you are going to charge at it as would a knight, as fast as the horse can carry you, and you are going to attack it with the spear with all your might. If you pierce both shields and spoil and slash the hauberk, I shall reward you, insofar as I see your prowess and valor, your courage and your capabilities. I shall give you a company of twenty knights, fully armed, and enough gold and silver as your allowance, so that no one will consider you a worthless member of a noble family. But should I see that in your tilting you bring dishonor on your family and prove to be useless in handling weapons, then may the apostle of the Lord know, to whom people in all Christian lands go on pilgrimage seeking his mercy,[6] I'll take your horse and all your armor away, your white hauberk and the leaf-gilt helmet, your good shield and gilt standard, and I shall tonsure you above your ears like a monk or an abbot and have you learn chants and lessons, so that you will become a priest who is going to chant and read lessons with the monks here in our monastery."

3. Elis is dubbed a knight.

"Lord," said Elis, "you greatly reproach me. Let me instead depart with your leave. God, who created me through his mercy, knows that I do not ask for horses or knights to accompany me, for I shall travel alone and on foot. I thought I would be a rich man, with a good chance of great honors and power and wealth, but you have denied me everything now, so that I do not have a single penny of what I thought I possessed. Because you have now disowned me, may Jesus Christ be merciful to me."

With these words he left, and when he had come to the bottom of the palace's staircase, his father came running after him, grabbed his surcoat, stopped him, and spoke: "Scoundrel," he said, "I swear by my head that you are in no way going to leave like this. I shall give you armor and good chargers and the best weapons that can be found, and my dearest knights to accompany you, and suf-

6. This corresponds to *Élie de Saint-Gilles* 84 and refers to the martyrdom of St Peter; see *Élie de Saint-Gilles: Nouvelle édition par Bernard Guidot d'après le manuscrit BnF no.25516*, ed. Bernard Guidot (Paris, 2013), 160. When the *chanson de geste* was composed, Rome was the second most popular pilgrimage site, after Jerusalem. See *Elye of Saint-Gilles: A Chanson de Geste*, ed. and trans. A. Richard Hartman and Sandra C. Malicote (New York, 2011), 185 n84.

THE ROMANCE EPIC OF ELIS AND ROSAMUNDA • 55

ficient funds, so that you can live in high style, for it has been said and also proven that we judge someone by his appearance."

"Lord," said Elis, "since you are willing to do this, get me a horse at once and armor, and have a tilt pole with shields and hauberks raised out on the meadow, and I shall ride at it and attempt to see what I can achieve with one strike, be it to my honor or my disgrace, and I swear by the holy apostle of Our Lord, to whom people go on pilgrimage, that I shall no longer sleep in your dwelling, because you have denied me the entire inheritance I was expecting and made of me, a rich man, a poor one. For he is poor who has nothing, and also whoever cannot claim anything."

He had spoken this in the presence of all the powerful nobles assembled there, and they were all distraught at his words and sighed with great anguish. And the noble wife of the duke, the mother of the young man, cried sadly, and called the duke over to her, and spoke:

"Lord," she said, "for God's sake, we have no son or heir other than this one, who is quite accomplished. You do not know what might happen to yourself or what danger you might encounter in war against powerful nobles who are your equals. If this were to happen, our son would go to war against our enemies and be a protection, shield, and shelter, a defense and support against what could harm us. Furthermore, it is appropriate to consider not only what might be necessary, but also what seems of little worth, but is likely more promising."

Then the duke responded: "What are you saying, foolish woman?" he said. "How long might a young man lead a life of ease, when it behooves every valiant man to further his abilities and renown, to travel to other lands and get to know foreign men, to demonstrate his prowess, study the law and justice, valid decisions, proper judgments, and good precedents, and to convey both threat and love, threats to his enemies, but to his helpful friends humility, courteousness, and a sense of duty, for thereby valiant men become famous, and a valiant man of perfect rectitude becomes the head and blessed spirit of all generations of his family for their honor and blessing and noble beginning. By St Peter, the apostle of Rome, I shall straightaway dub him a knight."

Thereupon the duke called to Salatres, his squire, and said:

"Bring me my best weapon and apparel, because I now want to dub my son a knight, and have a tilt-pole raised on the meadows near Darbes, our fortress, and attach to it the shield and hauberk. There I shall test my son in front of all the nobles and knights and the town's entire population, women and men, to see whether he can demonstrate his prowess as a man of action.

When the duke had said this, more than a hundred knights ran up, all dressed in most precious cloth, and they raised the tilt-pole with two shields

56 • THE ROMANCE EPIC OF ELIS AND ROSAMUNDA

and a white hauberk. In the palace, where he was standing, Elis put on a four-fold hauberk and a gilt helmet. Then the old duke came and girded him with a good sword, but then struck such a hard blow on his neck that he staggered and nearly fell to the ground. And the entire court laughed at such a hard blow, but Elis thought it vile, yet did not want to react; instead, he muttered between his teeth:

"You are harsh and wicked, you old-timer. By the faith I owe God, I would repay this vicious blow fiercely if another had done it, and if you were not my father, you would pay dearly for this."

4. Elis breaks the tilt-pole.

It is known to all, and everyone has heard, that when a knight takes up weapons for the first time, young men grow bold and enjoy watching his conduct. All who had come that day did so. When Elis mounted his horse, everyone ran to watch him, since none of them had seen him before. Everyone who saw him asked God to protect him from harm and danger. But all their prayers served him little, for on the very same day, before evensong ended, he suffered such great anxiety and extreme agony that if God had not been merciful, he would not have come away with his life.

When the tilt-pole had been raised and well secured and the entire city's populace was standing around it, there were more than a hundred knights, powerful and outstanding men from the city of St Egidius, who for the love of Elis had armed and mounted their horses on the meadows for fun and sport. Count Julien was foremost in the group and cried out in a loud voice:

"May God protect you, good lords," he said; "ride out of the way and take place while this young man tests his riding and prowess. This will let us see how he will behave in desperate circumstances, for a little thing can foreshadow something greater."

The group rode to a spot and gathered as the duke was speaking.

The young man then went on the attack and held the spear in striking position, spurring the horse on to run as fast as it could. And when he ceased goading the horse, he raised his spear so that the wind riffled his standard.

When he had rested for a while, he spurred on the horse and galloped toward the pole and thrust his spear with such force through both shields and the double hauberk that the pole broke in two and fell to the ground.

When Lord Julien, the duke, observed the great thrust achieved by Elis, his son, he laughed and cried out loud to Elis:

"You are my son," he said, "a valiant lord! You shall now remain with me and respond to my every need."

THE ROMANCE EPIC OF ELIS AND ROSAMUNDA • 57

5. Elis rejects his father's offer.

Lord Julien was exceedingly happy, for his son Elis had afforded him great joy when he saw the broken pole lying on the ground. Laughing, he called the young man over to him and spoke lovingly to him:

"Knight," he said, "you are a valiant youth, strong and courageous. I know now what I have truly observed, that you will be strong and tough in face of your enemies. You shall now remain with me and take possession of my land and realm, for it does not behoove you to leave me in my old age to serve strangers."

"Lord," said the young man, "what you are saying is strange. You swore and took an oath that I would not sleep in your residence for many a winter to come. By the holy apostle to whom people go on pilgrimage, even if I were to be given all the gold of St Martin,[7] I would not serve you, as I have firmly sworn."

When Lord Julien grasped what he had said, he came running at him and spoke:

"You vile whore's son," he said, "you are my servant. I made you a man out of nothing. Now I am going to have you seized and thrown into the dungeon. You will lie there for fourteen years, since you would rather serve strangers than me. You bring on your own troubles. You'll never reach a land or country where you will be able to attain any honor worth a penny.[8] That is what my wits tell me. Be off now to wherever you please."

6. Elis leaves his father.

Thereupon Elis left, angry and distressed. When the old man saw him depart, he sighed wholeheartedly and asked the all-powerful God to keep and safeguard him. Then he summoned Emers and Terri and Earl Agamers, and spoke affably to them:

"Men," he said, "follow him; I kindly ask you to be his protectors, for he is still young and childlike, although once he matures, he will achieve much that is good, if he is as valiant as befits him and as he is disposed to be. Take with you Gillimer of Corinsborg and Agamer of Lesamborg and the brave Akleri. Once all of you have gathered, if one of you fails, he will be disgraced, for you are sworn brothers, comrades at court, and colleagues."

Elis now rode on his way alone, angry and distraught, until noon, and he spoke:

"Almighty God," he said, "look upon me, now that I have left alone, penniless and poor, my land and my relatives. God, you who have never lied, Father and

---

7. I have been unable to determine to what this refers. The reference to St Martin does not occur in the corresponding *laisse* V.

8. *Laisse* V of *Élie de Saint-Gilles* does not have a corresponding threat.

58 • THE ROMANCE EPIC OF ELIS AND ROSAMUNDA

Lord of all creatures, have mercy on me in this appalling condition without even a squire to serve me. I shall now have to suffer hardship and deprivation, unless you console me in your mercy, as you have done for me from before I was born."

When he had said this, he looked at the road before him and in the shadow of a tree by the road he saw a man lying with three spears in his body; his face had been struck so hard that the brain was visible through his eyebrows. He was lying on his belly, begging God for mercy and beating his breast, for he feared death. When Elis saw him, he rode toward him and spoke caringly:

"Who are you, knight?" he asked. "May God have mercy on you. Tell me, who it is who has so terribly wounded and disgraced you. I shall most certainly avenge you, let there be no doubt."

When the man heard this, he answered in a few words: "Why should I tell you this, noble friend and knight? Are you a scholar or a cleric to whom I might confess and acknowledge my sins? The kind of people who have injured me, would immediately kill and dishonor you, if they were to come here. But you swore by the God who created me, and therefore I want you to know that I am the son of Almauri, the glorious and valiant earl, and I was born in Poitiers. Lord Julien, the duke of Saint-Gilles,[9] is a very close relative of mine. My father is now his retainer and is in charge of his courts. I was in France and in the service of King Louis when he was crowned in the abbey of St Dennis.[10] Knights rode on good Arabian horses in a great tournament. While we were there, amusing and enjoying ourselves, a messenger came with the news that the Saracens had arrived in the kingdom with a large force. We hurried at once, not waiting for support, and immediately left with the forces we had, passing over Auvergne and Berri, and met the Saracens in the vicinity of Brittany, and we won a great victory in the first attack, and the next time we slew some thousands of them. The third time, when nearly all were vanquished, killed, wounded, and captured, a force of fifteen thousand Saracens arrived in support, and they pursued us all the way to Angers. There they captured William and Bertram, his nephew, and Bernard and Arnald the Fair. Now they have conquered all the cities along the coast, and their advance ceases neither by night nor day. They intend to seize and conquer Pellier and the city of Saint-Gilles. And the king asked me to bring this news to Lord Julien, his relative. When I left the king, the Saracens became aware of me: they found me, inflicting four wounds, three on my body and one on my face. I now suggest that you take care, for they have killed me."

9. *Elis saga* has: "the duke of the land of St Egidius."

10. St Dennis was a third-century Christian martyr. In the French original the coronation takes place "Up on the hill of Montmartre, near the city of Paris" (*Élie de Saint-Gilles* 202, ed. Guidot, 15).

When Elis heard this, he laughed at his words, and said:

"I am sorry, knight," he said, "for you are a close relative of mine. But the apostle, to whom people go on pilgrimage, knows that for love of you this is going to be avenged, I believe. Before this very evening I intend to kill seven of those hellish dogs with my spear."

Then he quickly mounted his horse, and was properly and splendidly armed, yet he behaved like a fool, reckless and audacious: without forethought he dared to ride alone to undertake an attack on such a large number of Saracens.

7. Elis comes upon a Saracen army.

Elis now rode on his way, but the messenger stayed behind. He rode for a long time through woods and over plains, while the Saracens rode as fast as they could with a large armed force. Malkabrez was its lord, with Josi as the leader.

"Lord," said Malkabrez, "by my white beard, Mahomet has now assisted us nobly in forcing the Christians to take flight in their own land and in our carrying off much booty. We are foolish if we do not guard our captives. We have William of Orange and the knight Bertram, his nephew, a famous hero. Let us now follow a plan I have thought of: let us send these men down to the beach and have them board our ships. If the Christians arm and want to do battle with us, we are better protected on the ships than on land."

Then the evil Malpriant spoke: "That is the shrewdest and most suitable plan. That is what we shall do. It is good to make secure arrangements now."

Malkabrez then called Rodoan of Calabria, Kursant of Tabarie, and Gradusa of Orcle, the false Salatre, and the wily Malpriant – may God bring shame on his white beard. They led William and Bertram onto the field. Then they tied them up and set them on mules, with both hands and feet tied, since they feared that they would escape. They then led them away from the army and rode down to the beach. Five rode along in front of them to guard the captives.

They now met Elis as he rode out of the woods, and it is expected that he will break his spear shaft before he gets away.

May God, who by his grace protects everyone, now protect him here and wherever he goes.

8. Concerning Rodeant's dealings with William and Elis.

Five lords now rode in front of those who had been captured, those who had tied up the knights sitting on the mules. William of Orange often sighed out of grief and sorrow, and he called out to his nephew Bertram and his other companions:

"Worthy friends," he said, "mightiest of knights, it is troubling for us that we are to board ships and sail out to sea with this accursed folk. We shall never receive help from any living being. Gibourc," he said, "you gracious woman, I shall now be far away from you. I don't know what is more fitting for me to say now, other than to ask you, Almighty God, to have mercy on our souls in the future."

"You evil wretch," said Rodeant, "your lamentation displeases us, that you should call upon your laws and idols to protect you. For the sake of your God, in whom you believe, you shall now receive a great and heavy whack from me," and he lifted a large club and struck him on the head, so that his blood spurted out all over.

When Bernard saw how he treated his relative William, he shook his head and bit into his beard:

"You evil dog," he said, "it is distressing what has now happened to us, that we are tied up and you strike us. God grant that I may yet see you humiliated."

When Rodeant got ready to strike him again, they saw Elis come riding from behind a woody vine, arrayed in fine and noble armor. The evil Rodeant addressed him first:

"What kind of a knight are you," he said, "that you should be riding all alone? You are a troublemaker and an idiot that you dare to ride toward me. I shall take your fleet horse away from you and also your hauberk and gilt helmet, your shield and sword, and everything you have on you."

"Friend," Elis said, "you're speaking childishly. Before you've gotten my shield and hauberk and helmet and sword, you will have been harmed so badly that you have never experienced the like in your life."

9. Elis kills Rodeant.

"Friend," said Elis, "you asked me about my family and what kind of man I am. Did you see," he said, "the large wooden fence by the meadow where you were riding? I am the son of the provost of this county; he is a very rich man with much property and many assets, and he bought me the knight's armor today and had me dubbed a knight, and I rode here for my amusement and to test my horse. And I know now, after having put it to the test, that my horse is the fastest, and there is no one alive who, if he wanted to attack and fight would not find it here, where I am, even though he might come from a most powerful family and be a most accomplished person. I want to know," he said, "since you are armed, where did you seize the captives who are tied up so shamefully behind you? Are they merchants or city dwellers or peasants?"

"No," said the evil Rodeant, "they are genteel vassals. One of them is William of Orange, together with his nephew Bertram, a most valiant knight, and also Bernard and Arnald."

When Elis heard what he was saying, he sighed wholeheartedly and in great sorrow:

"What are you saying," he spoke, "you devil incarnate? Is it true that this is Lord William together with Bertram his nephew, and Bernard and Arnald, their companions? You damn dog, unprovoked you seized them. I swear by the holy faith I owe God that you will have paid dearly for this before we part," and he immediately spurred his fleet horse on toward him. And when they met, Elis thrust his spear into his shield and hauberk and through his very body and cast him dead from his horse, and he spoke:

"This is the reward for your service!"

10. **Kursant of Tabarie is slain.**

When Kursant of Tabarie saw Rodeant lying dead on the ground, and neither remedy nor medicine could help him, he cried out to Elis with a loud voice:

"You lewd conceited man," he said, "may Mahomet shield my eyes, for in an evil hour you have killed this man. You shall pay dearly for this before evening falls."

When Elis heard this he was greatly enraged at the threats and the obscene language of the Saracen, and he immediately jumped on his horse, which galloped as fast as he wanted. When he reached the Saracen, he thrust his spear through his white hauberk and breast, and cast him dead out of the saddle, and spoke:

"Down with you, you damn dog, and don't stop until you've reached hell."

11. **Concerning the Saracen plan.**

Elis had now killed Rodeant of Kalabre and Kursant of Tabarie, and both were lying dead on the ground. When the other three, who were left, saw that their companions had fallen, they were clearly infuriated in their anguish and rushed all at once at Elis, but they were unable to bring him down off his horse, for he defended himself extremely valiantly, since God protected him in his mercy and might. After Elis's spearshaft broke, he hewed with his sword, and the one who received the first strike will never be able to tell the tale. And with the next strike he sliced the other armed man in half, but the third one he grabbed with his hands and hung him there on a woody vine. Then he hurried to those who had been captured and were looking to him for help, and it would be most fortunate if he could free them. But now his difficulties and troubles grew greatly, since the five Saracens, who had been left behind eating, soon became aware of him. When they saw him, each pointed him out to the other. Tiatres then spoke to his companions:

62 • THE ROMANCE EPIC OF ELIS AND ROSAMUNDA

"Knights, look," he said, "a young man is riding down the hill, but he carries no shield on account of his bravery and pride. The horse he is riding is quite fleet. If you permit me, I'll ride at him and hurl him off his horse."

"By my troth," said Malatries, "you intend to do something very foolish. So help me Mahomet, you shall not have the horse. Early today," he said, "when we left our army, we agreed on companionship and camaraderie. Whoever spoils that is a fool. We should all ride together at him and hurl him off his horse. Then we should divide the horse and his weapons as equally among us as possible, so that everyone receives an equal part."

"By my head," said Tiatres, "it would be utter cowardice for the five of us to ride together to kill one Frank. That would be cowardice, and not an accomplishment. Disgraced and dishonored is anyone who wants us to attack him in a group rather than one of us alone."

12. Elis slays Tiatres.

Tiatres now rode off from his companions and approached Elis. When he reached the plain, he asked:

"What kind of a man are you, knight?" he said. "Do you believe in Mahomet, who rules the entire world?"

"Certainly not," said Elis, "nor anyone who serves him. I am the son of Julien, the superb duke. Early today he dubbed me a knight and gave me this armor, and I set out to amuse and test myself against enemies, for Saracens have come into our land, and I set out to see if I could find them. I intend to hassle them greatly before nightfall."

"Mahomet knows," said Tiatres, "you should expect nothing but woeful anguish. You will have to leave your horse to me and you yourself will be thrown, greatly dishonored, off your saddle, with your feet in the air and head on the ground."

When Elis heard his furious and foolish words, he spurred his horse forward at great speed and thrust his spear into the Saracen's shield, into his hauberk and body, and cast him dead out of his saddle and to the ground. And when he had fallen, Elis cried out with a loud voice:

"You arrogant and wretched dog, I am still seated in the saddle on my horse, but I now hold your horse by the reins, and I shall hang your leaf-gilt helmet on my left shoulder, for I suspect that I shall need it before evening falls."

13. The duel of Elis and Malatries.

When the other four Saracens saw the fall and fate of Tiatres, they were disturbed and exceedingly distraught at his death.

THE ROMANCE EPIC OF ELIS AND ROSAMUNDA · 63

"See, lord," said Malatries, "the sad and unbearable harm wrought by this young man, barely fifteen years old, who killed this noble and mighty lord and with his weapons and bravery he overcame and dishonored him. May no one have honor who does not want to watch our battle now."

Thereupon he spurred his horse on and gave him rein while Elis turned his horse toward him with tremendous speed. And when they met, each levelled such powerful blows at the other's shield that both of their shields broke and each of them fell onto the ground. Then they jumped up and drew their swords, and Malatries rushed at Elis and struck him on the helmet so that all the leaves flew to the ground and at his feet together with all the straps on the helmet, and he struck the horse on the neck and clove it so that its head flew off.

"People know," said Elis, "that you are doing me great harm now. You have a good sword, and it is a shame that it is not well cared for. If I possessed it, I would not give it to my own brother, even for the most magnificent city in France."

"By my troth," said Malatries, "you're spouting ridiculous nonsense, since the sword is the best and is well cared for, where it now is. Your neck will be struck so hard with this sword, that it will end your life."

"Yes," said Elis, "that's what you think, but I am holding the other sword, and you will learn right now whether it can bite," and he struck the Saracen's helmet with the sword so that all the leaves and straps flew far off onto the ground, and the right arm with which he ought to defend himself he struck off at the shoulder, so that the hand holding the sword fell at the feet of Elis, who seized the sword. "Praise be to you, my omnipotent Lord, for having given me this good sword, having taken it away from my enemy, thereby lessening my struggle." Then he spoke to the Saracen: "You evil and unbelieving Saracen and doubting infidel. Now you can see how much greater the might and mercy of the omnipotent God is than your false faith and heathenism. You have now felt how my sword bites, and now I shall oblige you with your own sword!" And he struck down on his shoulders by the neck and sliced him from top to bottom, so that each half fell down.

Thereupon he jumped on the Saracen's horse. Anyone who now picks a fight with him, will be in for a tough battle.

14. Josi and Salatre are slain. Malpriant's flight.
When Josi saw his nephew Malatries lying there dead, he spoke:

"The one who killed you, fair kinsman," he said, "has done me great harm!"

He then sped on his horse as fast as possible toward Elis and thrust his spear into his shield so that it flew in pieces over his head.

64 • THE ROMANCE EPIC OF ELIS AND ROSAMUNDA

"Everyone knows," said Elis, "you are a doughty man and valiant knight. You truly wanted to have killed me now, had God permitted it, but my God, Jesus Christ, ever protects me in his mercy."

And with these words he drew his sword, with its Saracen emblems, and struck down on the Saracen's helmet, so that the head flew off his body and onto the grass on the ground, and then Elis took hold of the swift horse's bridle.

"This horse," he said, "I'll give to William or to Bertram, his nephew."

Then Old Salatre spoke: "This man is a sorcerer, if such valiant knights were not able to be his match."

"Yes," said Malpriant, "by the faith owed Mahomet, I know that. Let us allow him to go free, but we ought to flee as fast as possible, for he intends the same for you and me, should he get ahold of us."

But Old Salatre spoke: "Why are you speaking such disgraceful words? May Mahomet be enraged and my body damned, if I turn away before I find out what he is doing."

They then found Elis in the shadow of a tree called laurel, next to those who had been captured and who very much needed his help. If he could free them, he would escape death. But the Saracens came from behind him and called out to him:

"You evil dog," they said, "you have unwisely laid hands on them; they are our captives."

When Elis heard them, he jumped on his horse, but Salatre came and struck a mighty blow on his shield. Elis, however, returned the blow, striking the Saracen's chest behind his shield and cleaving it, so that his innards fell out. When Malpriant saw this mighty blow, he took flight, but Elis pursued him as fast as he could. Malpriant rode on such a good horse that if it were to run sixty quarter miles and swim across a large fjord, Elis would not come near it, whether on mountainous or flat terrain. It is to be feared now that Elis will pursue him too far, for he does not know how large an enemy force he will have to confront.

15. To those who are listening.

Listen quietly now! A good tale is better than a full stomach, though one ought to sip while listening to a story, but not drink too much. It is an honor to tell a story, if the audience listens, but a lost effort if they stop listening.

16. Malpriant tricks Elis.

Elis now pursued Malpriant so far that he had nearly caught up with him in a valley, and he called out to him:

"You evil Saracen," he said, "turn back; may God curse you for having me bound about so long."

Malpriant answered: "You are very foolish and wicked! Don't you see," he said, "that the ground is so rough where we are now standing, that no warhorse can run across it, but ahead of us are fair meadows with beautiful grassy fields. That's where we should attack each other to test our mettle. The horse which I am riding is fleet and very fast. Should I fall off the saddle, then you can take it away with you."

Elis responded: "Lord God, give me this gift for which I long so much, this good horse, that I might get it from this Saracen."

Malpriant then took off, and Elis pursued him for five miles, but then Elis's horse tired and fell into the sand under him. In great anger Elis called out to the Saracen:

"Woe to you, you cowardly Saracen," he said, "turn back; God curse you."

"Malpriant responded: "You speak too foolishly," he said, "and do not know how to take care of yourself. You undertook this pursuit carelessly and followed me so far, but 7,000 of my companions have assembled before us, and there is not a one among them who would not want to kill you. People know," said Malpriant, "that you are foolish and imprudent. Today you have done us such great harm that there will be no amends for this. The time has now come for you to regret it."

They had been talking so long that the entire army arrived. When the Saracens saw them they ran at them immediately. May God now have mercy on the noble and courtly Elis, who is now close to death and to losing his life.

17. Elis obtains Malpriant's horse.

When Elis saw the Saracens running toward him on foot, while the entire army behind them charged at him on horses, he called on God with all his heart to have mercy on him. Then he saw that Malpriant had stopped and then rode slowly, for he did not fear him. Elis's horse, which had been tired before, recovered, because it got its breath back and had rested while Elis and Malpriant were speaking with one another. Thereupon Elis spurred his horse on against Malpriant and struck his spear into his shield, which at once split apart at the blow, and with his spear he struck Malpriant's chest and hurled him off his horse as far as his spear shaft reached, and he threw Malpriant into a creek that was by the road, so that his spear flew far out of his hands, and he landed face down. Malpriant now crawled out of the muddy creek onto the river bank. Elis then jumped on Malpriant's horse, as the whole army watched, and he now rode off. May God protect him! No living person could catch him or come near him, as he was fleeing, for his horse had no equal in speed and never tired.

66 • THE ROMANCE EPIC OF ELIS AND ROSAMUNDA

18. The Saracens pursue Elis.

Malpriant looked behind him and saw Elis sitting on his horse, the man whom he hated above all others, and he saw that he was holding his spear in position, as though he were ready to attack and fight, and he cried out with a loud voice:

"Saracens," he said, "valiant champions and best of warriors, if he gets away, all of us will be disgraced."

When Elis realized their folly, he continued on his way. He sat on that good horse which could run so fast that he could get as far away as he wanted. A large crowd of Saracens pursued him, but he did not think they would be able to catch him. He would turn around to fight with those who came closest, because he thought it amusing to slay, kill, and mock them, to wound and humiliate them.

19. William and his companions are set free by a field hand.

It is now time to tell about the earls who had been captured and were lying tied up in great distress and anguish after Elis had left. Then William of Orange spoke:

"Glorious Lord, Almighty God, what have you done with the noble youth who had come here to help us? I fear that he has pursued the arrogant Saracens. If he lured them after him all the way to the main part of the Saracen army, help will be slow in reaching us. Almighty God and Lord of all creatures, gentle consoler of all in need, loving Savior of those in trouble and misery, grant us mercy and freedom and help. If we were free now, nothing would harm us, for we would get on these good warhorses and save ourselves."

As he was saying this, a field hand came out of the woods and walked past them with a wood axe hanging from his shoulder, with which he had worked the whole day. When he saw the Saracens lying dead on the ground, he got quite frightened and started to run away, but Lord William called most kindly out to him:

"Friend," he said, "do not be afraid and come over to us, and you will hear what will please you, and you will have compassion for us in our misery and difficulties, if you believe in God and his saints. We are from France and far from our friends. Today a month has passed since those accursed and unbelieving Saracens captured us, and no day has passed since then that we have not endured trouble and misery. Come over and cut these bonds off us to set us free."

"Noble lord," he said, "what can I do? I have to raise seven children, and I am so poor and destitute, and my oldest child doesn't have the wits to take care of and nurture the youngest."

When Lord William heard this, he pitied his poverty. "Go," he said, "and take the good silk and the white fur surcoat that the arrogant Saracen lying dead next

THE ROMANCE EPIC OF ELIS AND ROSAMUNDA • 67

to us is wearing, and sell it at the market for thirty shillings, and use this for your children, and then sell the four mules which we will give you."

When the field hand heard his words, he became happy and glad, and he took his knife out of its sheath and cut all of them loose.

20. William and his companions plan revenge.

When Lord William, Earl of Orange, realized he was free, he jumped up and spoke: "Almighty God, heavenly king, you know that I would rather receive twenty wounds and be pierced by hundred spears before the Saracens again place me in fetters or capture me."

Then Bertram, his nephew, spoke: "Woe to the Saracens, now that I am free; if I find them, I shall never take ransom from them other than their head and their body."

Bernard of Bruskam spoke: "Saracens," he said, "you accursed dogs, may God permit us to avenge the misery you have caused us."

And Arnald the Bearded answered: "I don't want to say anything other than that we take and use the armor that is lying here and these good horses and that we ride to assist the noble youth who killed our enemies and delivered us from our fatal troubles."

21. William and his companions meet up with Elis.

These noble lords have now been released and freed from their difficulties, and they were delighted and very happy. They were most courtly men and the most valiant of knights among Franks in their day. They ran for their weapons and got armed. Then they walked up the slope and climbed up a woody vine and looked around. They recognized the Saracens immediately and soon saw Elis, the good knight, as he rode ahead of the Saracens. But every once in a while he turned back and killed those who were in the lead. He now came to a deep and nearly impassable ford. The Saracens were so close to him that some were ahead of him, so that he could not spur his horse on, for they could have prevailed and captured him. But Lord William of Orange and his men came galloping through the valley, and when they reached the Saracens one could see their attack, how they threw Saracens off their horses and killed them and how they overcame their arrogance. They killed so many that their blood ran just like a river. And one could see there Lord Bernard, Earl of Bruskam, as he bit into his beard and twisted his whiskers, and the Saracens who came near his weapons were never cured. Then Josi of Alexandria, a Saracen, spoke:

"I see a surprising folk now," he said. "King Arthur of Britain, the famous and victorious king, has come here, and with him are Gawain the Strong[11] and

11. *Elis saga* writes "Gafer," but this is certainly a scribal error. *Élie de Saint-Gilles* 654 has *Gavain*. See *Élie de Saint-Gilles* 654, ed. Guidot, 179.

68 • THE ROMANCE EPIC OF ELIS AND ROSAMUNDA

Margant the Hot-headed, and Gulafri,[12] the Mad, who eats five or six men at a time. Let us return as fast as possible to our army for help, for no men alive can hold out against them. These valiant men are Christians, who were long dead, and who have now risen from the dead in order to kill us and defend their kingdom against us."

22. Julien's knights come to the aid of Elis.

Just as a lion puts a flock of sheep to flight when unawares it comes running out of its den to choose the sheep that is the largest in the entire flock, that is how Lord William, Earl of Orange, charged. When he came into the flock of accursed Saracens, whom he had to repay for their wickedness, he killed them and drove them apart, so that everyone who saw his conduct became frantic, and no one, on whom his blows rained, ever received wages again. The same was the fate of their companions. The Saracens now fled back to the army, but the Franks raced after them, killing them with their spears, and they did not stop until they had driven them into the midst of their army. But it was very imprudent and foolhardy to follow them so far. Then Josi of Alexandria spoke:

"Mahomet," he said, "and Apollo, woe to the necks and shoulders of those who should honor you more often and submit to you both by day and night, if you let those escape who have caused such great dishonor, shame, and harm, those few men against our many."

Then they attacked them from all sides and they would have overcome the earls and wounded them, had they not received help sent by God: twenty knights, whom Lord Julien had sent after Elis, now came riding on another route out of the woods. When Elis saw them and recognized them, he was so overcome with joy that he spurred his horse on toward Tunabes, a mighty noble from Alexandria, and with his sword he struck such a mighty blow on his neck, with its helmet and coif, that he plummeted far down onto the ground. And the twenty knights hurried there and joined battle with sharp spears and good swords.

23. Julien's knights are slain.

The twenty knights who had come now joined the five who were already there. When Elis saw this he thanked God that they had come, and they now played such a rough game with the 7,000 Saracens that none of them got away without wounds or disgrace. If there hadn't been more Saracens, matters would have gone well, but now the entire main army arrived, with Malkabrez at its head, and now it is not surprising that our men were worried. In the end it happened that none

12. At *Élie de Saint-Gilles* 655 the cannibal is identified as *Mordrant*. See *Élie de Saint-Gilles* 655, ed. Guidot, 179.

THE ROMANCE EPIC OF ELIS AND ROSAMUNDA · 69

of the twenty knights who had come to their assistance got away alive. But Lord William, Earl of Orange, and Bernard, his brother, who never tired or failed to kill Saracens, called out loudly to Elis:

"Good knight," they said, "join us and let us all fight together. Anyone who wants to harm you will pay dearly for that." And Elis immediately did as they said. As soon as he heard that a Saracen wanted to attack, he immediately turned his swift horse toward him, for he would rather die than be called a coward.

24. The Saracens capture Elis.
Elis felt great distress and anguish over his men having fallen, and he often lamented, saying:

"Your fate, noble champions, is distressing for having accompanied me only to have the Saracens overcome, kill, and capture you."

At this an infidel came running out of the army. He was strong and big. From the loins up he measured four and a half ells. Woe on account of his legs, which were powerful and had carried him very long. His sword was extraordinarily large and his shield so big and heavy that the strongest ploughman would not be able to lift it up. In a loud voice he called hotheadedly to Elis:

"So help me Mahomet, you, knight, have defended yourself against us too greatly, and the time has now come for you to be vanquished. I now advise you to give up your faith and your God and to believe in Tervagant, who works miracles for us, and in Mahomet, who gives trees their leaves and flowers and fruit."

But Elis responded: "You are the greatest fool among fools. The Lord, my Creator, knows that I would be worse than all scoundrels and resemble the miserable Jew who denied St Martin on account of a hall in which he was sitting,[13] if I were to deny and forsake the Lord of the whole world and all its creatures on behalf of your idols. Instead, I am ready to demonstrate with my weapons the power of God and that Mahomet and Tervagant and Apollo, your gods, are not worth a piece of straw next to God's saints who dwell in heaven."

When the Saracen heard Elis's answer, he was furious in his great contempt and zeal, for he believed there was no one his equal in strength and courage and valor in the whole world.

Both spurred on their horses, and because their horses were extremely fast, they came at each other riding so rapidly and vehemently, and they went at each other with such great blows and strikes that they cast each other off their horses. When both had fallen off, Elis ran at him and was faster to strike, and he raised his sword with both hands and as high above him as he could, and his blow came

13. It has not been possible to ascertain the incident to which this refers. See above, note 7, on St Martin.

70 • THE ROMANCE EPIC OF ELIS AND ROSAMUNDA

down in the middle of the shield on the Saracen's chest, so that the entire hauberk was torn off him, all his innards fell out, his hands and feet were cut off, and the sword did not come to rest until it hit the ground. The Saracen fell down so hard that the entire ground shook when his accursed body crashed down.

Elis spoke: "Mahomet and Apollo have now protected you poorly."

And when the Saracens saw that their greatest warrior had fallen and was dead, the entire army let out such a loud scream as though all the devils in hell had been let loose. More than 1,000 Saracens rushed forward, all with weapons and swords drawn, with Malpriant at the fore, and when he saw his horse, he quickly grabbed the bridle, rode off and handed it to a Saracen to watch. But all the others rushed at Elis from every side and bore their shields against him, and they captured him and bound him so hard that his skin and flesh were torn off his hands all the way down to the bone, with a great loss of blood.

When Lord William and his companions saw this tragic incident, they rode at once to the spot of the greatest turmoil and struck out on both sides, so that within a short time they had killed 100 Saracens. But then more than 300 Saracens attacked them.

When Elis saw that they would be captured, he called out to them:

"Good lords," he said, "save yourselves and leave this battle, for I have been seized and captured, and neither my prospects nor pain will be for the better, if you are killed along with me."

When William and his men heard Elis's words, they realized it was good advice, and they turned immediately away from the battle, and the Saracens pursued them for more than two miles yet were not able to catch any of them.

Josi of Alexandria then spoke to the other Saracens: "Misfortune has befallen us, since those who got away are great and powerful nobles and valiant knights, for no one living can withstand them or their blows. Before two days have passed they will come after us with 20,000 knights, and when they meet us not a single man in our entire army will get away, because one of them is better in battle than twenty of our own men."

The entire army then rushed to the ships and boarded, but Elis they threw below deck amidst the horses' hooves and shackled him there.

When the Saracens had boarded the ships, they raised the sails, and with a good wind sailed out to sea. They talked a great deal about the earls who had escaped, what valiant men they were and how courageous, but they praised the superb Elis most, far more than all the others. King Malkabrez then ordered Elis to be brought before him, and this was done.

When Elis appeared before him, the king thought this man most handsome, strong limbed and yet terrible, handsome and attractive, fair and valiant. The king then spoke to Elis:

THE ROMANCE EPIC OF ELIS AND ROSAMUNDA · 71

"Swear to Mahomet that you will forsake your faith and deny your Christ, and I shall then have you crowned in Sobrie and married to Rosamunda, my daughter."

The king then had him set free.

Let us now leave Elis and his troubles and tell a bit about the earls who had fled from battle. They rode their way along the beach and greatly mourned Elis.

Arnald spoke: "We must now speed on our journey to be able to reach the city of St Egidius, for we are in great need of good hospitality and lodging."

So they took the road to the left, past the town of Alles, and rode over the river named Tove, and arrived at the city of St Egidius before evenfall. When the citizens saw them riding on the street on sweaty horses with their hauberks slit, their splintered shields and broken spears, they wondered at this and did not know who the men were, and from where they had come with broken trappings. They rode to the castle and wanted to enter, but they met an evil and foolish man who turned them away and spoke quite foolishly:

"Evil men," he said, "what do you want here? You are certainly looking for great trouble, since you reveal your foolhardiness and foolishness by riding in armor to our castle like enemies."

William answered: "You have done wrong by greeting us so foolishly. Good friend," he said, "we are from France and are ambassadors of King Louis, who has sent us here with messages for Duke Julien, who is in charge of this castle. It is dishonorable for a valiant man on a mission not to bear weapons or armor to protect himself against miscreants, for it is vile to end up in the hands of those whom it is not appropriate to serve."

But the guard at the castle gateway answered: "By my troth," he said, "you won't get in by cajoling me and with sweet talk, and you will neither dress an altar nor celebrate Mass. If you insist on riding on, you behave like evil and foolish ruffians, for I intend to deliver such a mighty blow with the heavy, thick club I am holding that you will end up close to death." And then he dealt William four blows, as mighty as he could. But William protected himself with his shield, and it split from the handle on down.

When William saw the folly of this man, how harshly he had received him, he realized that it was unacceptable for a lord to be dealt a blow by a serf and not to retaliate. He drew his sword and struck this evil man down from the top of his head, thereby splitting his entire body, and he fell in two pieces at the feet of William. Then he flung him into the deep moat that was below the castle. When the son of the castle guard saw that his father had fallen and was dead, he immediately fled, terrified, to tell Lord Julien everything that had happened between his father and the newcomers. The son of the castle guard came into the palace and cried out in a loud voice:

72 • THE ROMANCE EPIC OF ELIS AND ROSAMUNDA

"Lord Julien," he said, "what are you doing? My father has served you for more than fourteen years, yet he has never received as much as a horse or a mule for his service. Now, however, he has been paid quite cruelly for his service, for I saw him being cast into the moat with a broken neck. God help you, if you do not mete out punishment for this."

When Duke Julien heard what he said, he became very angry and swore by his white beard that there is no man in his land who has committed such a disgraceful deed who will not be hanged at once.

At this moment the earls, fully armed, came riding into the palace. Lord William had the byname Hooknose, and he spoke:

"May Almighty God, who created heaven and earth, and who is more praiseworthy and glorious than anyone else, bless and protect you, Lord Julien, and your domain. Lord," he said, "I do not want to conceal from you who I am: some men call me William Hooknose; and this is Bertram, my nephew, who is close to me in stature; the third is Bernard of Bruskam, and the fourth Arnald, my other nephew. A month has passed, since the Saracens captured us, but early this morning we were freed, and since then we have ridden long so as to arrive here now. At the castle gateway, however, I encountered a foolish and ill-natured man. Four times he struck my shield, and at the fifth I got angry and gave him a tiny whack with my sword, and then I flung him into the moat below the castle. We are prepared to pledge our honor to you and to pass judgment in our own case, rather than for you to be angry at us for this."

When Lord Julien heard this, he approached them, embracing Lord William and the others, and he spoke:

"God knows, I think it would have been better if you had hanged him."

Then he said to his men: "Stand up, knights, and remove their armor. They are lords and nobles. Let us thank God that they have come here."

25. Elis regains his horse and gallops off.

The earls were now with this gracious lord, and twenty young men took their horses and armor. Then baths were prepared for them, and afterwards they sat down to eat. And when they were finished, Lord William spoke to Duke Julien:

"You have a handsome and valiant retinue. Lord Louis, the emperor, wonders why you have not visited him, and he has complained to the highest nobles and his vassals. He was also told that you have a son who is old and strong enough to be armed. Tell me, is he among the young and attractive men who are sitting here? If he is not here, then send for him, for we would like to see him and take him with us to Paris, where he will be well treated among the powerful and finest royal retainers."

Duke Julien then responded with great sorrow: "God knows, good lords," he said, "you have come too late, for early today I dubbed him a knight, and as soon as he was dressed he took off and left me, but I did not want to use force in face of his foolishness and instead sent twenty knights, the mightiest here, to serve as his retinue. But now I do not know where they were headed or in which land they ended up."

When the earls heard this, they looked at one another. And Arnald the Bearded asked:

"Is it true lord," he said, "that your son rode a dapple-grey horse and was wearing reddish-brown silk with white fur? Early today, as we were riding out of a wood, he demonstrated such great valor that within a short time he had killed nine knights. One got away, however, and he did not pause, but followed him over a ford all the way to where he encountered 700 Saracens. They would have seized and overcome him, if twenty knights had not come to his help, those twenty knights whom you sent him, such valiant and good warriors that not a single one can be reproached. But the evil Saracens confronted them with such a large number of men that not one of them got away alive. And they thronged against Elis in a gulch and seized and tied him up and took him away with them. His friends may certainly mourn such a man."

When Julien heard this, he lamented it very much, and the mother of the young man and sister cried over Elis's misery, that he should have been so harshly captured by the Saracens. Now great grief broke out in the palace, and all their previous pleasure changed into silent grief and distress. No one listened then to the harps or rebecs or hurdy-gurdies or other stringed instruments.

The duke then called a man named Thomas to him. He was a rich merchant who knew all the seas. Julien spoke to him:

"You are to equip my largest longship as quickly as possible with sufficient supplies, and you are to take with you twenty horse loads of gold, and goshawks and everything else you will need, and hurry as fast as you can, and do not let up until you find out into which land the Saracens have taken my son. You, Salatres, shall also sail with him. Make all the preparations today, for tomorrow you are to set sail." There is nothing else told about them in this story.

Lord William and his companions had risen early and asked for leave to depart, and Lord Julien treated them honorably. He gave them the best warhorses, and to each 100 shillings, as well as squires to carry their weapons and to serve them. And they parted in friendship.

The account now leaves off here to report that when the Saracens set sail they were at sea for five days and arrived in the country called Hungary. When they had cast anchor at the foot of an escarpment at the castle of Sobrie, King

74 • THE ROMANCE EPIC OF ELIS AND ROSAMUNDA

Malkabrez called for the Franks who had been captured, including Elis, and they were led before the king. The king then spoke to Josi, who was the ruler of Alexandria:

"Take these men with you and punish them as you like, but this handsome man who is so noble and valiant shall stay with me, and if he worships Mahomet I shall give my daughter Rosamunda in marriage to him."

Thereupon the king had Mahomet placed on a column that consisted entirely of gold and jewels. Then he spoke to Elis:

"Frank, swear by your troth: have you ever seen as handsome a god as this one is? He grants me whatever I want. He brought me from Africa, whenever I wanted, and took me north to Scotland, and from there to the harbor of Dalmaria. Know now for sure, if you ask for his mercy, I shall make you wealthy, both in respect to money and possessions."

"Lord," said Elis, "you are joking, speaking childish nonsense, when you say that you consider this accursed fiend to be god. This thing can't move and has neither life nor a body of flesh. And if someone were to come along now and slap it on its ear, it would topple over, for it has never been alive. Woe be to its might and also to those who serve it."

Malpriant was standing nearby and heard what Elis said. He became quite furious and ran toward Mahomet and spoke loudly:

"Oh, powerful god, do not charge me for these words. This Frank who has reviled you is a madman and does not have any sense. Accept my fidelity, for I shall avenge you, if I reach land alive, and I shall immediately have him hanged from this high rock."

When Elis heard this, he got very angry, and he immediately implored God the Almighty for help and mercy, for now he was very much afraid. Elis had been freed on the king's ship, and he now saw a sight that greatly excited him, for Malpriant had his horse led from below deck off the ship and onto land. It was saddled with its golden saddle and bridled and ready to be ridden. This horse was so good, as previously told, that no king had its equal. Elis then spoke in a low voice to himself:

"Help me, Lord Jesus Christ, son of the Virgin Mary. Six days have not yet passed since I still owned this horse. Now, God willing that I might sit on its back, armed as I want, for I would rather let myself be hewn to pieces than find myself once more in the Saracens' power."

Then he jumped high up and with such great force that no one was able to grab him, and upon landing he ran at once to the man who was leading the horse and hit him so sharply on the ear with his fist that his neck broke. Then Elis jumped on his horse, while everyone watched, and galloped off.

THE ROMANCE EPIC OF ELIS AND ROSAMUNDA · 75

When King Malkabrez saw this, he was infuriated and hurled vile oppro-brium at Mahomet:

"You evil god," he said, "what are you doing? Are you mad or are you sleep-ing? I have sworn fidelity to you, but woe be to your might and those who serve you. The Frank is now gone who reviled you so greatly."

Then he placed his foot against Mahomet and pushed the idol off the column and broke its nose and its right arm altogether. The Saracens then grabbed him and said:

"You evil king," they said, "what are you doing? You are full of malice, fool-ishness, and destruction, since you strike and break your god. Go to him now and bow before him and ask him to forgive you, otherwise you are doomed to die."

"I swear by my head," said King Malkabrez, "the man is foolish who serves him or believes in him, for all his might is gone and worth nothing, and he is noth-ing but a fraud and nonsense. He permitted the Frank who dishonored him and killed his men to escape. And I am truly filled with sorrow and shame that I freed him of his fetters, since that is the reason he escaped."

After the king had said this, everyone realized that he had spoken the truth. Then they left their ships. The king called for 700 knights, among them Josi of Alexandria and Hercoles and Guivers:

"You are to go to the ford at Dalbier and lie in wait for the Frank who escaped and deceived us. If Mahomet sends him back, he will have done well, and if the excellent Mahomet is benevolent, then I shall give him 400,000 marks of pure gold and make his head and shoulders, his hands and fingers, legs and calves, ankles and foot soles, his entire size bigger by half than he has been, and have him restored completely through excellent craftsmanship."

26. Concerning Rosamunda, the king's daughter.

All the Saracens had now left their ships and the king went home to his castle, Sobrie, the good. His entire family came to meet him, his wife and son and the radiant Rosamunda, his daughter, and she spoke at once to her father:

"You promised that when you came back from France, you would bring me a poor captive to teach me French."

"By my troth, fair daughter," said Malkabrez, "I had such a one with me, the likes of whom has never come into this kingdom since Mahomet created the world. He cowed Malpriant, your beloved, so much and brought down his great pride and arrogance with which for your sake he boasted, so that now, whenever the Frank is amidst those assembled on the fields, Malpriant does not dare to say a single word to him."

76 • THE ROMANCE EPIC OF ELIS AND ROSAMUNDA

When the maiden heard her father praise this valiant young man so much, her heart was inflamed with such great love for him that she could neither respond nor ask for leave, but instead she bowed down before her idols and asked them with her whole heart to protect that valiant young man from disgrace and death.

27. Concerning the dealings of Elis and three thieves.

Now it is time to tell about Elis. He rode along the beach and beseeched God in his goodness, and spoke, saying:

"Lord God, you mild and mighty king, lead me to a place and a shelter where I might obtain food, for I have suffered too long from lack of food. Five days have now passed, since I last ate, and my strength and energy have been greatly diminished."

Thereupon he rode down the hill, and when he came to a field, he saw three thieves sitting in a wood in the shadow of a large tree. They had much money which they had robbed and stolen, a large box full of pure gold from many a land. They had agreed to meet to decide what to do, and they had brought along a sumptuous meal: two peacocks and a well-peppered swan; a big pot full of beer blended with wine; and two large loaves of bread. When Elis saw that they were getting ready to eat a well provided meal, offering each other bread and wine and meat, he longed so much for food that he could not refrain, and gently dismounted. He asked for neither water nor a towel, but immediately sat down on the grass to eat with them. The three could not cut the food fast enough that he alone ate, and the leader of the thieves then spoke to him:

"You are audacious," he said, "you greedy glutton, to sit down and eat our food without asking for permission. Never have there been male hands like yours who have been so good at emptying dishes. And you will pay dearly for all of this before we part. The horse on which you came here you must leave behind with us, and if you annoy us any more in any way, you'll be beaten so hard with our fists, rods, and feet, that no doctor will ever be found who can help you."

"Good friend," said Elis, "it is unjust of you to say this. You are not considering the cost of this food and drink that we have enjoyed. Let's first find out what it truly cost and tell the truth; as far as I'm concerned, I shall gladly pay without objection."

"By my head," said the thief, "you shall know the cost: a hundred marks in pure gold were paid for this, and if you pay ten marks in pure silver, you'll get off scot-free."

"By my troth," said Elis, "I have never seen anything like this. If everything is so expensive in this country, it was much better where I was born. Take," he said, "five shillings of pure silver from me without my objecting and this silk garment with white fur, which cost me five marks of gold when it was bought."

"By my head," said the thief, "you will be singing a different tune. We shall take the horse on which you rode here. I have calculated that the bridle is worth twenty pounds of silver. You will be leaving us naked, on foot and carrying a staff like a beggar."

"Woe to you, you wicked vagabond," said Elis, "may God heap disgrace on you. I thought, when I saw you putting out food, that you were nobles or knights, townsmen or merchants, who knew how to greet gallant men properly. But now I see that you want to have my horse in exchange for your food and drink and you want to betray me, just like Judas who betrayed Our Lord at the supper table. But I swear by the same God and the holy apostle whom people visit on pilgrimage, if any one of you is so bold as to dare approach me, I shall lambaste him so that he will never cheer up again. And I won't give even one fake penny for the three of you. You would need more force before you got me to flee in fear of you."

28. Elis's dealings with the three thieves, cont'd.

"Woe to you, evil men," said Elis, "may God bring down misfortune on you. I truly see that you are thieves and wicked men. Where did you get the gold lying here? If you do not declare at once who the owner is, I shall hang you here," and with his foot he struck the neck of the one who was the leader of the thieves, and he pressed so hard that he could no longer answer, because his neck had been broken. With his hands he pulled the arm of the other thief so hard that the arm broke off at the shoulder, and his heart and innards fell out.

Galopin, however, the third thief, was small in size, and he approached Elis and got down on his knee and asked for peace, and spoke:

"Noble lord, do yourself a favor and don't kill me. Believe me, I never intended to harm you. If you want me to stay with you, you will be showing me great favor. No matter where you go, I shall always gladly accompany you. If you need money, I'll get you so much that you will never be wanting. I know of so much money that is hidden here in the woods that fourteen towns and twenty-two castles are not worth as much. I was a companion of these men for fourteen years and was often hunted in this wood, both night and day, and I was often captured and thrown into the dungeon and placed under hard guard. But I know so many tricks and ruses that even when I was guarded most carefully, I managed to escape. Therefore, I no longer want to steal, for it is a wicked skill to be a thief, and a thief is soon hanged if he is caught at thievery."

29. The Saracens come to blows with Elis and Galopin.

Elis saw Galopin on his knees before him, asking for mercy:

"You noble lord, do not kill me, for I descend from good people and come from a wealthy land. I am the son of Earl Terri of the Southern realm. After my mother had given birth to me, four elf women took me in the night from the chamber in which I was lying, and one of them wanted to keep me and take me away with her. But two of them were displeased at this and said to one another that I should never grow and become tall, but that I should be able to run so fast that no warhorse should ever be able to catch me, for God never created a being who could run as quickly."

As they were speaking, Josi of Alexandria, a wicked Saracen, came running, along with two other Saracens, his colleagues and companions, Hertori and Gunter. When Elis saw them, he was terrified of them, for he was without weapons, and expected to be struck. And Josi then came and struck at his shoulder blade, but Elis turned, dodging the spear, and it broke. When the other Saracen got ready to draw his sword, Galopin ran forward and with both hands he swung a big club of apple wood that was lying nearby and he struck the Saracen between the eyes so that his brain and blood stuck to the club, and he was thrown dead to the ground. When Elis saw this, he thought it strange and curious that the thief was so intrepid and bold as to attack an armed man and a Saracen. But when Josi drew his sword and wounded Elis again, Elis grabbed his hand and forcefully snatched his sword away. When the Saracen had lost his sword, he turned to flee, but then Hertori, the third Saracen, came and Elis struck him with his sword and hurled him dead to the ground. Then he seized the horse and said to Galopin:

"May God mercifully protect me," he said, "and deliver me from the accursed bunch of Saracens. I shall never leave you in the lurch, even in the face of death. Now take this horse, which you have well deserved."

But Galopin spoke: "Lord knight, revered friend, what should I do with the horse? I can neither ride a horse nor handle it. If I were on its back I would immediately fall off. You should take it instead, which is the best of these horses, and I shall take this gilded shield with the leaf-green strap that is lying behind me on the ground, and I shall lead the big Arabian horse by the bridle. If the horse does not want to follow me as quickly as I want, I shall kill it with my club, so that it can't be used by our enemies."

30. Elis and Galopin come to the city of Sobrie.

When Elis heard the thief saying that he was so fleet of foot that he did not want a horse, he let matters rest as they were. They then went their way, but they strayed off the road on which they should have continued, and it got so dark that

THE ROMANCE EPIC OF ELIS AND ROSAMUNDA • 79

they could not find the road they should be taking, and they got lost and finally came to Sobrie, the splendid capital city. It was unfortunate that they ended up there, because before evening they would experience much grief and danger, trouble and difficulty. Before them, at the city gate, stood Josi who on that very day had pursued Elis and wounded him, and as soon as he saw them, he hurried off and hid and ran as fast as he could to the king's hall. When he saw the king he spoke:

"Mahomet knows, lord king," he said, "that you have suffered great sorrow and disgrace, for Hertori, your best friend, has been killed, and also Gunter and King Malgant, whom you had crowned."

When the king heard this, he was extremely angry out of grief and sorrow, and he swore by Mahomet and all the other gods that Elis was to be banished from all castles and cities in his entire kingdom, and outlawed and killed if he was captured.

The wicked Josi answered: "Lord king," he said, "what you are saying is foolish. By my head, you need not put so much effort into looking for him, since he is very close by, and you can meet up with him in front of the city gate, if you want to find him."

31. Rosamunda learns of Elis's arrival.

Elis had now come to the city wall of Sobrie, and when he saw the towers and castles in the city, he spoke to Galopin, who had become his attendant and confidant:

"Tell me, friend," he said, "are you familiar with this land? Do you know who the lord of this land is?"

"Yes," he said, "I know everything about it. Those are the towers and castles of Sobrie. King Malkabrez, his son, and his daughter Rosamunda live in this city. In the whole world there is no woman equal to her in beauty. I was in this castle a short time ago in the company of the men whom you killed, and we robbed the castle of much money. If the king were to catch me, he would not fail for all the gold in Paris[14] to hang me today."

"You have betrayed me," said Elis, "and with your wiles have led me into the hands of my enemies."

"No, lord," he said, "the glorious Lord knows, to whom the most holy maiden Mary gave birth, that the darkness was deep and the way was not well known to me."

14. The lead manuscript writes *Paviborg*, but in his diplomatic edition, Eugen Kölbing suggests that *Paviborg* should be "Paris" in accordance with the reading in the manuscript AM 567 4to, dated ca. 1350. See Eugen Kölbing, *Elis saga ok Rósamundu* (Heilbronn, 1881), 70, 168.

As they were talking about this and other matters, the accursed Saracens came galloping along – may God disgrace, shame, and harm them – and killed Elis's good horse underneath him, which was worth more than seven hundred pounds of gold. But he drove them off with his sword and killed them on either side, while Galopin got a spear and helped him as much as he could, so that the two felled fifteen Saracens in a short time, while those who were left fled. Elis and his companion looked for a safe place, however, and continued along the city wall until they came to a garden that was below the city. No one had ever seen one equally beautiful and fine. The Saracens, however, who got away, hurried into the king's palace and told the king about their misfortune. When Rosamunda heard this, she rejoiced and spoke:

"Oho," she said, "my great lord Mahomet, promise me that I will live long enough to have this good man in my care. I would entrust both my life and my person to him!"

32. Rosamunda becomes aware of the whereabouts of Elis and Galopin.

Elis was in the garden below the towers the whole night, full of grief and anxiety, angry and distressed, and he often lost consciousness, lamenting his troubles, and he spoke:

"Oh, Lord Julien, my father, I was very foolish when I ran away from you without permission – my life is now worth nothing – and with your animosity. It is now certain that you will never again see me safe and sound. Galopin," he said, "go your own way now, for on this day we will be parted in great distress. Take care of yourself now, for all my strength is now gone."

"No, lord," said the thief, "I shall not leave for even a day, unless you accompany me. I would rather be killed here than leave you in such harsh circumstances."

When the night had passed and daybreak came, the Saracens jumped on their horses, those damned sons of dogs, and they now threatened that if they captured Elis they would maim or kill him.

Rosamunda had risen early and gone out on the balcony, and she heard little birds singing beautiful songs to greet the day, and the sweet scent of love entered her heart at once, and she spoke:

"Oh, my glorious lord Mahomet," she said, "you are so powerful and mighty, for you bring leaves and blooms and fruit forth from trees, free my Frank for me from the hands of the evil nobles and Saracens, so that they will not harm or kill him."

After she had said this, she looked down at the meadow below the tower and saw Elis lying in the garden by the tower. But the Franks who were in the dungeon kept bemoaning and lamenting Elis's misfortune. Now when Galopin heard their lamenting, he walked in that direction and listened, and then he took Elis and laid him on his back, for he wanted to leave with him, but then the maiden spoke to him from the tower:

"Friend," she said, "you little fellow, put that good man whom you are carrying on your back down. If you were to carry him any farther, you would be acting foolishly, because ahead of you sit thirty Saracens and there is none who does not have an axe or a spear, a staff or a stone, and they have sat in ambush since yesterday evening and kept watch over you the whole night, as they had been ordered, so that you would not escape."

33. The meeting of Elis and Rosamunda.

"Good friend," she said, "you little fellow, listen to me and follow my advice, lay him down carefully from your back. I want to greet him and find out what has happened to him. I have never been a friend of those who treated him in this way."

She then left her bedchamber and did not ask anyone to accompany her. She was dressed in a tunic of the best silk with white fur, which reached down to her feet, and had birds and gold woven into it. She then put on a little mantle of the most precious cloth. Her skin was whiter than newly fallen snow on a dry tree or the whitest blossom in the grass. Never was there a man so sorrowful and distressed in the world who would not smile and cheer up when he saw her. And she walked over to Elis where he was lying on the ground and placed her right hand under his neck. When the earl saw her, she seemed to him so charming and beautiful and lovely, so well-bred and becoming that he forgot all his grief and sat up in the grass, and the maiden then spoke to him:

"Knight," she said, "what kind of a person are you? Do you believe in Mahomet who rules the whole world?"

"No, God knows," said Elis, "I don't believe in anyone who serves Mahomet. I have come across the sea from the West, from the good land of Provence. The Saracens captured me—may God avenge this and humiliate them. Today I escaped them, when I came into this land, but then they pursued me and seriously wounded me. They assaulted me, giving me four wounds, which I believe are mortal, and it is my greatest worry that I might die without confessing my sins."

"By my troth," said the maiden, "I now know exactly what kind of person you are, and I know everything that has happened to you. Now don't worry about what will happen to you, and follow me as quickly as you can, and we'll walk silently, for I shall get you to a place where you'll feel quite different by evening, if you do as I say." And she took Elis by his right hand and led him behind her.

82 • THE ROMANCE EPIC OF ELIS AND ROSAMUNDA

Then they came into her bedchamber, which was decorated with all kinds of gold-enameled animal images, and she laid him in a bed the curtain of which was golden, while its sheets were of the finest silk and the coverlet was handsomely and magnificently fashioned, and all the other bed furnishings were handsome, so that even the greatest nobleman in the world could splendidly rest there. Then the maiden took out of her mead cask four herbs so potent that God had never created an animal or a person who, if he consumed the herbal mead that flowed down his throat into his chest, was not at once as healthy as a fish in water. The courtly maiden herself crushed the herbs with her hands and gave the potion to Elis, the bold and valiant knight, to drink. Once he had drunk and the potion reached his chest, he immediately felt well again, and he called at once to Galopin, and said:

"It is to paradise and heavenly glory that we have come! I never want to leave here, for I am enjoying such bliss here."

34. Concerning Elis's pleasures and Galopin's fear.
Rosamunda, the courtly, the beautiful and the famous, the radiant and the praiseworthy very much loved the praiseworthy and the noble Earl Elis with an intense and steadfast love, and she herself prepared the potion for him. When he had drunk and consumed the potion, he was restored to full health. And now he craved food, and immediately a meal, as he could only wish for, was prepared for him. Thereupon a bath was drawn for him and he stepped into it at once. After he got out of the bath and had lain for a while in the bed, clothes were brought to him. Never did a duke or a prince dress in finer garments. Then the maiden sat down next to him, and he embraced her and kissed her more than a hundred times.

"Galopin," said Elis, "see what a woman she is! In the entire Frankish king's realm none can be found like her. If only it were the will of the omnipotent God in heaven, that I had now with me in this tower William and Bernard, Arnald and Bertram. Before this maiden were to be given up, many a Saracen who is now hale and in good spirits would lie dead."

When Galopin heard this, he trembled all over with fear. "Noble lord," he said, "why are you saying that? I am so terrified that I hardly have my wits, for I know with certainty that if the king learns that both of us are here, we will be hanged this very day."

35. Jubien of Baldas asks for the hand of Rosamunda in marriage.
Elis now experienced four days of great joy with the maiden in the tower, while the wicked Saracens – may God impair and thwart them – were not aware of this.

THE ROMANCE EPIC OF ELIS AND ROSAMUNDA · 83

Malkabrez, the king of Sobrie, was sitting at table, but before he got up from the meal, he would become angry and irate, because Jubien, the king of Baldas, the white-haired and old, left his kingdom with 30,000 Saracens who pitched their tents unawares in the meadows surrounding Sobrie and set up catapults in order to break down the city wall. He then sent his capable and eloquent messenger on an errand, and in his letter he ordered Malkabrez to give him Rosamunda, his daughter, in marriage, and additionally half his kingdom, and he said that this would satisfy him.

Now while Malkabrez was sitting at table, the messenger turned up before him and spoke:

"Lord of Sobrie, let your retinue listen to us while we present our message to you. No messenger should hear a nasty response nor be injured on account of his message. My lord, King Jubien the White-haired, sends you the message that you should give him Rosamunda, your beautiful daughter, in marriage. He himself has come to demand tribute and to call in debts from your kingdom, for the oldest and wisest men and his counselors have told him that you owe him tribute. But if you refuse his demand, he challenges you to single combat here on the plain. If you are able to kill him and are victor, then you and your heirs will be forever free, and the entire army will depart without damage and loss on your part, and tribute will never be demanded from you again."

36. Malkabrez responds to the messenger.
Malkabrez was distraught, when he heard the news, and he answered Jubien's messenger in great anger and with acrimony:

"Friend," he said, "tell your lord, so help me Mahomet, that it is his great folly and arrogance that emboldens and eggs him on toward complete misfortune through such a message, for he shall meet me tomorrow in any case, or else someone in my stead, to oppose with weapons the payment of tribute. So help me, Mahomet, if you were not a messenger, I would immediately have you maimed or have both your eyes pierced and your beard burned off and send you disgraced back to a disgraceful ruler."

The messenger was frightened, when he heard that they would maim him for his service as messenger, and it is not surprising now that he left as fast as he could.

37. Kaifas, son of Malkabrez, shirks the duel.
The messenger, who had carried his errand out well, left, but Malkabrez sat there distraught and angry, and he spoke to his son, who was called Kaifas of Sobrie:

"You are to engage in this duel, son," he said, "for I have accepted this challenge on account of your accomplishments and courage."

84 • THE ROMANCE EPIC OF ELIS AND ROSAMUNDA

"Lord," said Kaifas, "you show great foolishness in what you say. Today it has been a month since I suffered from a fever, and I do not want to ride a charger for the sake of someone else. Give your daughter in marriage to him, for he loves and desires her so much. She could not be better married, since he is mighty and very powerful. May Mahomet, who governs everything, be angry with me if I were to fight for your or her sake."

38. Josi refuses to take on the king's case.

When the king gathered that his son feigned being sick, he realized that he was a coward and lacked courage, but he said little, since others were present. The king then spoke to Josi:

"Get armed," he said, "and undertake this duel for me."

"Lord," said that dog of a Saracen, "I would gladly undertake this if I had not been injured yesterday, when you sent me after the Frank who dealt me such a great wound that it is still bleeding. For that reason I cannot sit upright on a horse nor easily wear armor. May Mahomet bring down on me disgrace and ignominy, if I am wounded by fighting for your sake and endangering myself, who am so adept at weapons.

39. Malpriant tries to avoid the duel.

The king understood what Josi said, and that he pretended to be sick and did not dare go into battle, and he called on Malpriant and spoke:

"Good friend," he said, "come here! You are to fight with Jubien and you will be victorious in this duel out there on our fields, and you are to get armed with the intention of killing or overcoming or in some other way humiliating the obstinate and arrogant Jubien. Then you yourself shall receive my daughter in marriage, whom Jubien wants to obtain in his obstinacy and haughtiness, and you will obtain half my kingdom while I am still alive, and thereafter you will be named prince and lord, king and emperor of my entire realm."

Then the evil Malpriant responded: "King," he said, "what you are saying is childish and childish nonsense. You are dealing with me like a field hand with his dog, when he incites it to go where he himself does not dare go. But since you are a ruler and lord, a king and the elected of this kingdom, then defend the kingdom and your happiness, your rule and honor, your strength and your people, and the multitudes so that you will not be considered an outcast and a coward by confronting someone who is harassing your kingdom and even wants to overthrow you. So help me, mighty Mahomet, never to have to mount a charger to defend you or your kingdom."

When the king heard this, he became extraordinarily angry and spoke:

THE ROMANCE EPIC OF ELIS AND ROSAMUNDA · 85

"Woe to you, evil person," he said, "you immediately became pale because of your cowardice, and your dastardliness is ever the same, and it is to your disgrace that you put on armor. Everyone considers you an outcast. It was like this when we were to leave the ships, and you let the gallant man and noble hero, whom we captured in France, escape because of your cowardice and timidity. If he were safe now and with us, he would quickly save us and my kingdom with his weapons and through his valor from battle and this harassment."

40. Rosamunda enters the hall at her father's bidding.
"Kaifas," he said, "you behaved cruelly toward me when you refused to engage in a duel with Jubien. But now that it has become a matter of your ordeal and our need, your fear and cowardice has brought about our distress and harm, and for you it has brought slander and disgrace. I do not care a whit about your insignificance, and I am going to give my daughter in marriage to Jubien, and as dowry she will receive half of my entire kingdom, as he has demanded, and I shall make a special contract with him that I am to keep a fourth of this kingdom, free and unencumbered, in peace and freedom as long as I live."

Thereupon the king called Omer, his counselor, to him. "Go friend," he said, "go up to Rosamunda's loft and tell her to dress herself impeccably and elegantly. I shall marry her to Jubien.

And Omer replied: "Gladly lord, as you wish."

Now when they reached the loft, all the doors were locked and they took the door knocker and pounded four times. When Rosamunda heard this, she sighed wholeheartedly.

"By my troth, lord Elis," she said, "now we are in a bad spot, because I suspect we have been spied on and cruelly maligned."

"Maiden," said the earl, "do not fear. If I were armed now, you would see me delivering heavy blows and demonstrating my abilities."

"By my troth," said the maiden, "such should not be mentioned; don't talk about battle now. Both of you go up to the tower instead and hide there, but I'll go to the door and respond to those who have come. I'll manage to answer them appropriately."

"As you say, maiden," said Lord Elis, "it will be done as you wish."

When Elis and Galopin had concealed themselves in the tower, she went to the door and opened it, and Josi, the evil swindler, came in, and spoke:[15]

"Maiden," he said, "the king orders you to dress fittingly and go with me to the hall. I suspect that he wants to bestow honor on you and give you away in marriage."

15. The author has forgotten that Malkabrez had asked his counselor Omer to get Rosamunda.

86 • THE ROMANCE EPIC OF ELIS AND ROSAMUNDA

When she heard what her father had ordered and demanded, she dressed splendidly and becomingly, as was appropriate for her station and rank. She dressed in a precious garment made of the whitest fur with such elegant trimming at the neck and arms that never was its like seen before. Thereupon she put on a gold woven garment that was so valuable and excellent that its like was not found in all Saracendom. The little mantle that she put over this was sent from the western Saracen world where the sun sets, from the land called Occident. Three fairies had woven that garment with threads made of the finest gold and with such great skill and such great care that they worked at this garment for nine years before it was finished. Woven into this mantle were large birds, all in gold, and set with the most precious gems. The merchant Samarien had sold the mantle's ties and their clasps to King Malkabrez for sixty pounds of pure Byzantine coins. The maiden then girded herself with a costly belt, which seemed to be a pure gold band with images of all kinds of animals. The most excellent goldsmiths had made it. Her hair was fairer than gold; it fell down to her shoulders in bright braids. Her skin, where it was bare, shone whiter than flour or new-fallen snow. Never was any man born who, if he saw her, would not in truth say and certainly know that in all Christendom there was never anyone more beautiful.

41. Rosamunda refuses to marry Jubien.

When the maiden had come into the palace, the entire hall became radiant on account of her beauty and apparel. When the king saw her, he sighed from deep within his heart and said:

"My beautiful daughter," he said, "I am quite distraught and distressed that Jubien the Old and White-bearded, the evil and vile dogged lout, has come here from his kingdom with 30,000 Saracens because of the cowardice and arrogance of your brother Kaifas. He challenged him to a duel, but now your brother does not dare keep his promise or keep his word and engage in a duel with him. For this reason, I am forced to give you in marriage to Jubien, but in great sorrow and against my will."

"Good father," said the maiden, "I would have to be out of my mind and deranged or burned to cold ashes before Jubien the Old and White-bearded ever places his trembling hands on my body."

42. Rosamunda's suggestions.

"Good father," said the maiden, "you may praise yourself but little, and also my brother Kaifas, and Josi, who is considered a warrior and a berserkr, since none of you dares to face one strike by Jubien. All of you are afraid and cowed so much by a man and trembling churl that you all want to be rid of him by giving a woman up to him. But I swear to you by the great Mahomet, if you marry me to him by force, then you will have looked poorly after yourselves, because before twelve months have passed I shall have all your city walls, your castles and towers demolished, so that your living quarters become bleak and defiled, because you have embraced such a plan involving me. Now, since all of you are afraid, cowed, defeated, and overwhelmed by Jubien on account of your timidity and cowardly despicability, fall at my feet and ask me for mercy, and I shall come up with an outstanding knight who will deliver you and me from this battle.

43. Elis takes on the duel.

Then the maiden spoke: "Good knights" she said, "listen to what I say. If I can find a knight who is so good that he dares to charge at Jubien the Old and engage him in a duel on our fields, will you, lord, grant him safe passage in departing and returning, so that no one will dare harm, injure, or attack him?"

"Good daughter," said the king, "do not doubt that. See my fidelity and that of my kingdom which I owe to Mahomet, and he will not be harmed, inasmuch as we can offer him help. If he lacks money, we shall make him happy, wealthy, and powerful, and if you so desire we shall give him to you in marriage with honor, nobility, and generosity."

The maiden responded: "I ask for nothing else."

The king and all his nobles swore an oath to Mahomet, as she had asked.

Then she stood up and went into the loft to speak to Lord Elis.

"Mahomet knows, Lord," she said, "that I am grief stricken and terribly upset with worry. Old Jubien has come here, looking for a duel and a fight, and not one of our men dares to duel with him. And now we must say that our Saracens are afraid and cowardly, and all their pride in their heroic deeds is nothing but a travesty and vanity, disgrace and ignominy. They would rather lose their life here than that one of them dares to confront Jubien and kick him out of here. If you were so valiant and courageous in battle as to dare challenge him to a duel, then be assured that I will honor you so greatly as to have you crowned in this palace on the first holiday of the upcoming summer."

"Maiden," said the earl, "what you say is not fitting for me. I have no desire for power or riches, and I do not want to set out to prove this, and I do not want to have any wife unless she believes in the true God. But because of the Saracens' cowardice, about which you have told me, if you procure for me a charger and armor, I shall ride forth. And if I confront Jubien, then he gets into danger at the time we part. If he comes away with his life, he shall never again seek to charge against anyone born in France.

44. Galopin offers to get ahold of Jubien's horse.

"By my troth, maiden," said Lord Elis, "if your Saracens want to set out on an expedition, and the king orders it, then you have found someone who will not end up in the nether regions when he confronts Jubien, and I tell you the truth that God never created a Saracen so bold and mighty as to arrogantly demand something not to your liking or who arrogantly threatens you with battle, then he will here encounter in my person someone who will defend your honor and quickly avenge you."

When the maiden heard what he said, she joyfully thanked him and spoke:

"Glorious knight," she said, "and sweet bloom of lovely youth, do not forget my love when you strike with your spear, and do not fear the threats or nonsense of Jubien the Old. He owns such a good horse that it runs faster over mountains and crags and rough terrain than our fastest chargers on level ground. No greyhound can run so fast that it could catch up. The name of this horse is Primsant of Aragon, and it is so high spirited that it does not shy away from any hazard. When it comes into a battle where there is much jostling, it strikes with its feet and fetter bones so that no one comes away alive who is touched by its hooves; the horse bites with its teeth and tears into a person like a wolf or a lion."

When the maiden had said this, little Galopin jumped up and gesticulated joyfully and spoke:

"Lord Elis, by my troth, now we should be merry and happy and not fear. Carefully see to it that you are well armed, and I shall get ahold of this horse, no matter who gets upset."

45. Galopin visits King Jubien.

"Mahomet knows, Lord Earl," said the maiden, "it is the best horse and of great help in battle. It also has a habit that should greatly be praised, for it throws any man off its back who has not learned to ride well or bear arms. For this reason no incompetent knight can ride it, and the horse therefore always chooses the best knight.

Galopin now went his way and wanted to have neither attendants nor companions. He did not halt until he came to the tent of King Jubien, who was outside, and he greeted him courteously in accordance with Saracen custom.

"May Mahomet," he said, "who safeguards and rules the entire world, protect and honor the white-bearded Jubien."

"All the best to you, friend," he said, "who are you and from where do you come?"

"Lord," said the thief, "I come from Alexandria and am a wealthy merchant who sailed a precious merchant vessel, a more beautiful one has never been seen,

THE ROMANCE EPIC OF ELIS AND ROSAMUNDA · 89

and I was transporting ten warhorses and ten mules, the most comfortable riding horses, sent by your brother, who rules Alexandria and loves you above all. But King Malkabrez took the horses and mules away from me and had my ship broken apart and set on fire in order to humiliate you, because he had heard that you were moving against him with a large army. This is of great sorrow to me, but for you it is a great loss that I was robbed, for I expect that you do not have any horses as good as the ones he took from me, and he killed all my sailors, but I got away. I have now come to lament my difficulties and your dishonor, so that you take vengeance on him and punish him appropriately."

When King Jubien heard what he had to say, he placed his hand on his head and swore:

"On my head," he said, "I shall have you paid back twenty-fold from his possessions and give you just as good a ship at his expense, before this army rides out of his city."

46. Jubien shows Galopin the horse Primsant.

"Lord," said the thief, "I don't care about the possessions that I lost, but I am very sorry that he stole from you such good horses the likes of which you will not possess again."

"Friend," said Jubien, "don't worry about the horses. Even if you had collected thousands of chargers, the best you have seen or of which you have heard, I nonetheless have one that I will not give or exchange for all those, and even though I were offered all the gold in Araby, I would not sell that horse for it, and you will now go right away to look at it; there will be no delay."

The king then took him by the arm and led him to the horse. The stall was arranged for the comfort of the horse, which was fastened with a gold chain around its neck. Seven Saracens guarded it, each of whom bore a sword, so that in case any man were bold enough to lay hands on the horse, they would immediately kill him.

Jubien took the bridle off the horse, and its head and legs were whiter than snow, while its mane was golden like a most beautiful woman's, and it was interlaced in gold into beautiful braids.

"Tell me, friend," said Jubien, "were your horses just as beautiful?"

"No, Lord," he answered, "never before have I seen another like this one nor one so comfortably stabled."

Thereupon, he talked to himself in a low voice: "My noble Lord Elis and glorious knight, if I could get ahold of this horse, then you could truly say that no king in France had one its equal. But this horse is securely and too firmly guarded. May God help me, as I now attempt this, no matter what will happen."

90 · THE ROMANCE EPIC OF ELIS AND ROSAMUNDA

47. Galopin steals the horse.

Once Galopin had set eyes on this horse, he kept thinking about how he could get ahold of it. Now when he had eaten his fill at the king's table, the whole court went to sleep. When everyone had fallen asleep, Galopin got up but did not want company. All the folk were lying quietly asleep, because it occurred to no one that something other than rest might be afoot in such a large and fearsome crowd. Galopin now came to the stall where the horse was stabled. He had carefully checked out the door and the lock when the king brought him there. When he entered, the horse did not recognize him and became agitated, acting dreadfully, and it reared, intending to strike him. When one of the horse's guards awakened and stood up, he was struck by the horse's hooves, and the blow was so hard that he never moved again. When he fell, Galopin grabbed the sword that flew out of his hands, and he killed everyone there, so that none could ever utter another word. Then he went to the horse, intending to seize it, but the horse bit him, pulling him towards itself, and then it lifted him up and threw him far down, so that Galopin nearly ended up dead on the ground. Galopin fled and did not dare approach the horse again.

Nonetheless he thought it a poor idea to leave. When he had retrieved his sword, which had fallen down, he approached the horse and dealt three mighty blows with the hilt of the sword on the horse and thus cowed it into submission. The horse began to calm down then and Galopin put the bridle on the horse and removed the gold chain from around its neck. He took the saddle that was hanging there and put it on the horse's back, and he stepped into the stirrups and quickly jumped on the horse. When the horse began to gallop, he immediately fell off, and the horse nearly ran over his neck and head, but Galopin got angry. He grabbed the bridle and led the horse very quickly by the rein, cursing the individual who had raised him to believe as a child that he could not ride and would never learn to do so.

48. Galopin steals Jubien's sword.

Galopin now left, taking the horse with him, while Jubien, terribly betrayed, slept. By his bed hung his sword with the golden hilt. Galopin tied the horse up and hurried into Jubien's tent. When he came to the bed where Jubien was sleeping, he took the sword and hung it on his shoulder. Then he drew the sword halfway out of its sheath and considered killing Jubien, but it seemed to him that he ought not kill him in his sleep, and he let him lie there peacefully. Then he left with the horse and the sword. And even before Lord Elis awakened, he had come with the horse he so much desired to possess.

49. Jubien's men miss the horse.

The night had now passed and day had come, and there was a lot of noise in Jubien's army, for the men missed the horse, and they hurried to Jubien's tent with the news, and a Saracen then spoke:

THE ROMANCE EPIC OF ELIS AND ROSAMUNDA · 91

"By my troth, lord King, you will be very angry and distraught, for never again will you have Primsant of Aragon saddled."

"Mighty Mahomet," said the king, "who has done me this great wrong?"

"As I relish my life," said the Saracen, "that wicked ruffian who came here yesterday evening was neither a merchant nor a messenger from a foreign country, but rather a wicked thief and traitorous spy, who knew very well how to make up stories and nonsense. And he also has your sword, which King Gigant of Valternaland gave you, when you arranged that great feast at which Mahomet was carried out and placed on top of a crag to be venerated. See to getting yourself another charger as quickly as possible, for the time has now come to fight, if you want to get the maiden."

50. Jubien comes to Sobrie and challenges Malkabrez.

"Lord," said Jubien, "I am greatly angered and grief stricken, dishonored and disgraced that I have lost my horse, which was my greatest support in my feats and chivalric deeds, and it will turn out badly for me now if King Malkabrez finds out about this. Nonetheless, I shall get armed before he becomes aware of this." Four Saracen kings then dressed him in his hauberk. Maldras, king of Sorfreynt, girded him with his sword, and King Jodoan of Valduna brought his horse to him.

And when he had mounted the horse, he rode immediately out of the army and onto the field below Sobrie. When he came there he called out in a loud voice:

"You wicked Malkabrez," he said, "where are you with your nonsense? Come fight with me at once, for I have waited all day for you. But if in your cowardice you dare not fight, then hand your daughter over to me, who is the most beautiful of women."

51. Elis is armed.

Now I want to tell you about Rosamunda, the gracious, and Elis, the good knight, and how she placed his armor on him. She put a trusty hauberk on him, which Pharaon, the king of Biterna[16] had owned. It was bright as silver and fashioned of strong rings. Then she placed such a good helmet of steel on him that no better could be found anywhere. Paris, the Trojan king, who kidnapped Helen, Queen of Greece, lost this helmet on the day when King Menelaus knocked him out of his saddle and cut off his head on account of his beautiful wife, whom Paris had treacherously kidnapped. At that time Troy was totally destroyed and com-

16. The city of Biterne is mentioned twice at *Élie de Saint-Gilles* 1402 and 1872 and Bernard Guidot, the editor, points out that it is a city renowned for its silk (p. 371). At 1402 Rosemonde is dressed in a silk tunic from Biterne; the equivalent passage in *Elis saga* § 32, when Rosamunda first sees Elis, does not mention this.

pletely spoiled and laid waste. When the helmet was fastened on him and secured, Galopin came with a sword in his right hand which he gave him:

"You chivalrous lord," he said, "take this sword. There has never been a king who had a better one. Gird your sword on your left now and ask God to give you strength along with it and courage and victory."

The he went over to Primsant from the castle in Aragon and led him forward with all its trappings and the bridle. When Lord Elis saw the horse, he kissed Galopin more than a hundred times, and rejoicing he jumped off the ground and into the saddle. Primsant immediately ran forward, but the earl restrained the horse and turned it around, and said to Rosamunda:

"Let us proceed, maiden," he said, "the time and the day have now come for me to avenge you on Jubien when I meet him, thus bringing down his arrogance."

52. Elis rides into the palace.

Elis is now so well equipped with a horse and weapons that he is in good spirits: he has a good helmet, a good hauberk, the best sword, and the fastest horse. Jubien is out in the fields, however, waiting for him, and he calls out in a loud voice:

"What are you doing, Malkabrez, you crafty and wily flatterer? Come forward, if you dare. I challenge you to a duel; otherwise send me your daughter, or Kaifas, your son, or Josi, your champion, or Malpriant, your daughter's lover! Whoever comes, will never return, since he will lose his life and limbs here, know that for sure."

When the king heard his words, he nearly went mad with anguish and anger, and called out to a Saracen:

"Friend," he said, "go straight to my daughter, who said she would get ahold of a knight to defend her against Jubien and do battle out here in the fields. But if she hasn't gotten someone to defend her, then we will certainly hand her over to Jubien."

But he answered: "I shall gladly do what you said."

As they were speaking, Elis came into the palace, riding the horse through the long hall, and he turned the horse around in chivalric fashion and stopped in the middle of the floor. When the Saracens saw him, they all became afraid, and the king thought that neither he nor anybody else could hope to live, for he feared that Lord Elis would kill him and everyone else in the hall, and the king swore before those standing next to him that anyone trusting in a woman was a fool. Rosamunda, however, knew best what she had done, for Elis would defend her and certainly be victorious over her enemies.

53. Kaifas strikes his sister.

Then the maiden spoke: "Lord father," she said, "you and all the Saracens gave your word that this Frank should have safe passage everywhere and that you would protect him. Keep your word now so that your promise does not turn out to be a lie."

Then they opened the castle gate for him and he rode out. And all the people went up onto the ramparts of the castle to watch their duel. Many hundreds of Saracens, the king and Josi and Kaifas and Malpriant and Rosamunda were then on the ramparts. When Elis came out of the castle, he looked back and when he saw Rosamunda, he smiled in her direction and laughed lovingly, and he tested the horse now to see how fast it could run, and he galloped on it all along the field and the horse proved to be excellent and very swift. Then Kaifas, who was in the highest tower next to the king, spoke:

"Mahomet knows, lord king, you are now demonstrating your very great folly by letting the Frank engage in this duel. He has now escaped us and will flee, and in respect to my sister, what I think is worst is that he has dishonored her. For four days she has hidden him and had him in her bed. And almighty Mahomet knows, who rules over everything, if you, lord king, and our other men want, we shall right now burn her alive and not delay in doing so."

When Rosamunda heard his words, she got exceedingly angry:

"By my troth," she said, "you are the worst swindler and the filthiest whoremonger and the greatest liar with your lies about me. This knight, however, is a much more valiant young man than you are and much more dauntless. Wretched coward," she said, "you agreed to this duel, yet now do not dare to carry it out. He is now going to fight instead of you, and Mahomet, who protects us, knows that if the king and our Saracens follow my advice, then you shall never rule the kingdom because of your lack of manliness and cowardice."

When Kaifas heard this, he struck his fist with full force against her front teeth, so that her lips split and blood ran down. He foolishly laid hands on her and on account of the blow he gave her, he will be struck dead before evening.

54. The verbal exchange between Elis and Jubien.

Elis had now come onto the field across from Jubien, and he stopped. When Jubien saw him, he immediately recognized the horse, and he rode a short distance toward him and spoke to him in a friendly manner:

"Who are you, knight," he said, "and who gave you this horse? He was never my friend who gave the horse to you. Your handsome youthfulness, which foolishly brought you here, will soon cause your death. I think," he said, "that Mahomet is quite angry at me, for he allowed Malkabrez to betray me. He sent

94 • THE ROMANCE EPIC OF ELIS AND ROSAMUNDA

an evil man to me, who used duplicity and flattery toward me. Had I known this, I would have let him be hanged and then burned on the pyre. I am willing to withdraw from this duel, if you give me my horse. You shall accompany me to Domas, my capital city, and there I shall make you my cupbearer, and you shall pour wine for me, and I shall give you a troop of 400 Saracens, together with a kingdom."

"By my troth," said Elis, "you convey a futile proposal! I am a mercenary knight from France, and I shall support this king. He has a daughter who gave me this horse early today, and should I be lucky enough to be able to slay you, I will be rewarded by her with such resolute loving thanks, that she will never take another lover."

When Jubien heard this, he reacted with extreme fury: "You evil whore's son," he said, "and born of a thrall! Are you, a Christian, so audaciously impudent, as to dare to confront me and engage in a duel with me? By Mahomet," he said, "and all the gods in whom we believe, I shall never rejoice as long as I see you alive!"

55. Elis casts Jubien out of his saddle.

As soon as Jubien knew that he was a Christian, he spurred on his horse and struck a great blow on Elis's helmet. Lord Elis was a valiant knight, however, and most adroit at arms, and he did not yield; rather, as soon as his horse had turned around, he rode back at him, and when they came at each other once more, Elis thrust his spear into his shield and hauberk and even into Jubien himself, so that he cast him far off his horse. And when he pulled out the spear, Elis jumped at him and threw him head down onto the ground, so that his helmet got stuck in the sand and his neck was nearly broken. Then Primsant of Aragon, on which Elis was riding, leaped forward and wanted to stomp on him and kill him, but Elis reined the horse in. And Gundracle of Clisborg called out to King Malinge and to old Onabras and Scribas the Cheerful:

"By Mahomet, Saracens!" he said, "this is a madman; never before did our lord encounter a knight like this one. I do not know who he is, but he is an amazing rider who with his spear was able to throw our lord out of the saddle. And this Primsant of Aragon, on which he is riding, is going to kill our lord. Let's get armed as quickly as we can and give assistance to our lord, which he badly needs!"

May God now protect Lord Elis, for Jubien's entire army threatens to decapitate him.

56. Elis kills Jubien.

Jubien was distraught when he realized he had fallen off his horse and had come down so hard, and he saw how Primsant trampled and surely wanted to kill him. Then Jubien spoke:

THE ROMANCE EPIC OF ELIS AND ROSAMUNDA · 95

"Oh, you good Arabian horse," he said, "you are now threatening me and are menacing me with death. I have taken good care of you for many a day and covered you richly in your stall, and I have never allowed another animal into your stable. But now you want to repay me dearly, since you want to kill me and trample on me and crush my body. And you, knight," he said, "on account of your faith, listen to my words and fetch my horse from which I have fallen. If you can fell me once more, it will be a renowned feat!"

"Willingly," said Elis, "shall I do so for the sake of my faith and to prove my manliness!"

Thereupon Jubien drew his sword and charged at Elis and with both arms he struck his helmet so that all the leaf trimmings and helmet straps flew off far onto the field.

"By my troth," said Lord Elis, "you have a good sword, but I have one too, and we shall now find out, whether it can inflict damage on you." And he drew his sword and struck Jubien where the helmet and the hauberk meet, so that his head rolled far onto the field.

When Rosamunda saw that, she called out to Kaifas:

"You faint-hearted dolt," she said, "now you can see what this Frank can accomplish. Would to God, who rules the entire world, that you were armed there on the field, beside Lord Elis, and if he knew how disgracefully you have mistreated me, he would quickly cut off your head. And I swear to you by the faith we share, if he wants to have my friendship, then you shall pay dearly before evening draws near today, for your having struck me so hard."

57. Elis pursues the fleeing Saracens.

When Elis had killed King Jubien of Baldasborg, he took his horse by the bridle and led it along, and he planned to ride back to Sobrie. As he was riding, he saw ahead of him seven armed Saracens coming up from the valley. And when he saw them, he asked God with all his heart for help, and he turned his fleet horse toward them, and paid the one in front such a strong blow that he would never crave another again. And in his next assault he knocked two off their horses, and both were wounded and no longer able to fight. Then he drew his sword and struck Tanabraz on the helmet and down into his shoulder, and he could no longer utter a single word. But Kareld from Alfatt cried out with a loud voice:

"By Mahomet, Saracens," he said, "this man is a madman. He is the son of Letifer from Mount Garas, who killed Pharaon and Mars. If he comes near us, we shall all end up dead. Let us flee as fast as we can." And then Selebrant and Jonatre fled.

96 • THE ROMANCE EPIC OF ELIS AND ROSAMUNDA

Elis sat on his good horse, however, which was faster than a sparrow hawk, and he pursued them all the way to the camp. And Selebrant, whom Elis reached first, he clove in two from top to bottom and gave his horse a deadly wound. When Jubien's falcon, which was tied to the tent with a golden chain, saw Primsant, it wanted to fly there, for it recognized the horse and thought that Jubien was riding it, but it got nowhere, since the chain held the falcon back. When Elis saw the falcon, he rode there and took the bird on his arm, since he knew how to carry falcons gallantly, and he spoke:

"I shall give this bird to the maiden Rosamunda, who knighted me anew early this morning."

58. Elis strikes off Kaifas's right arm.

Elis, who could ride well, had now left the Saracens' din, and he returned. On his left arm he bore the falcon, and in his right hand a drawn sword. In the entire great army there was no one so bold or mighty as to dare utter or say that he had done something evil. When he rode out of the garden and came through the castle gate and to the door of the palace, he met the maiden and spoke to her:

"Look, fair one, this gift befits your graciousness."

But she was in distress and anguished, and did not respond. But Galopin went to him and told him what had happened.

"By my troth, Lord Elis," he said, "you are going to be displeased, for Kaifas has greatly humiliated her on your account: he beat and struck her, bloodying her, and if you don't avenge her, you are not worthy of being a knight."

When Elis heard this, he got angry and irate, and he went up into the palace with drawn sword. When he saw Kaifas, he ran at him and struck off his right arm at the shoulder, which meant that he would never again sit as a knight in the saddle. The Saracens now ran for their weapons, but Malkabrez spoke with a loud voice:

"Lord Elis," he said, "do not continue this scuffle. Accept my pledge, which I owe Mahomet, that you shall be at peace and not suffer any harm, and that we both agree, and you are willing to accept matters as they now stand."

"By my troth," said Elis, "gladly, as you wish, Lord King," and he went to take off his armor.

59. Concerning Elis's and Rosamunda's plan.

The Saracens now saw that the earl was very angry; in his hand he carried that terrible sword. In their entire army there was no one who dared speak to him except Malkabrez and Josi, who offered him a truce, saying that he was now out of danger. Elis then went to Rosamunda in the loft, where he took off his armor and his

THE ROMANCE EPIC OF ELIS AND ROSAMUNDA · 97

helmet, while Galopin removed his hauberk, and the maiden took his sword. The scabbard and sword-strap were of pure gold and inlaid with precious gems. The maiden then put her arms around his neck and spoke:

"Lord Elis of France," she said, "fortune has bestowed great bravery and strength on you. Never before have I seen a knight wield a weapon as well as you. The day has now come and the time for you to receive me as your wife; this shall not be put off any longer."

"Be silent, maiden," he said, "that cannot be: you are a Saracen who keeps Mahomet's laws and worships the wooden idols Mahomet and Tervagant. Even if I were given this entire valley filled with pure gold, I would never believe in them. Instead, we should make another plan I have thought of: let's get all the gold and silver and all kinds of riches and enough provisions to last for two months; we should not need more. And let's go up to the highest and sturdiest tower, and remain there. And let's get a trusty man to obtain an army to help me, and have Duke Julien of St Egidius come here together with William of Orange and a group of the best knights, and we shall then conquer this entire country. Then you will be baptized and become a Christian."

"Gladly," said the maiden, "provided you affirm your words to me by your faith."

This is what they were talking about, but it did not end there, for their troubles started anew. But how Elis got out of these difficulties, and how he came back to France with Rosamunda, is not written in this book.

Abbot Robert was the translator and King Hákon, son of King Hákon,[17] had this Norse book translated for your enjoyment.

May God give the one who translated and wrote this book grace in this world, and in his kingdom the glory of the saints. Amen.[18]

60. Galopin is sent with a letter to Julien.[19]

The entire army that had accompanied King Jubien now left and went back to Damascus. Elis and Rosamunda stayed in the highest tower of Sobrie, however, and decided that they should send Galopin on an errand. The maiden Rosamunda had a ship readied, without her father knowing this. She chose for it

17. This is King Hákon IV, that is, Hákon Hákonarson, of Norway (r. 1217–63), who in 1226 also had Thomas d'Angleterre's *Tristran* translated by the same Robert, who at the time was still a brother.

18. The passage "But how Elis got out of these difficulties ... the glory of the saints. Amen" indicates that Abbot Robert's French manuscript was incomplete. An unknown Icelandic continuator produced the conclusion of *Elis saga* but omitted Robert's epilogue above.

19. The oldest manuscript to transmit the Icelandic continuation is AM 567 II 4°, a fragment of two leaves, which are dated ca. 1350. See *DONP*, 236–37.

98 • THE ROMANCE EPIC OF ELIS AND ROSAMUNDA

friends whom she knew to be faithful and who had sailed before. She had the ship now outfitted with good provisions and chosen men in a secret bay. Elis then wrote a letter to his dear father, which he sent, and in which he told him about his travels. Along with this he asked his father to send him many ships, well outfitted, and with fine men. He sent a short letter to Lord William and to Bernard and Arnald as well, in which he asked them for their assistance, since he was under such a strict watch that he would not be able to escape without their help and support.

Galopin now put out to sea in his ship; he got a fair wind and arrived in France near where the duke resided. Galopin asked to meet him at once and he delivered a greeting and the letter from the young Lord Elis. He told him about everything that had happened in Elis's travels from the day he left his father's court to the time when "we parted," said Galopin.

The duke now became both anxious and angry, and yet happy. He was happy that Elis was alive, but anxious and angry that he had been captured by the Saracens. The lady, Elis's mother, and his sister wept copiously. The entire court was quite distressed, yet the duke was pleased to know where Elis had ended up. The duke now bid Galopin welcome, as did all his men. Now there was a most splendid celebration. Galopin sat next to the duke and they drank happily all day and into the night. Galopin told him all about Elis's travels. At daybreak, when the sun brightened the whole world, the duke arose, as did his entire court, and he sent word in all four directions and to every castle in the country, inviting everyone to come within half a month, that is, those who could ride and cast a spear, wield a sword, and cleave a hauberk. Those who remained behind were to be severely punished.

The duke now had horses with splendid trappings fetched, and they mounted their horses. Galopin mounted an excellent palfrey, and many local knights and all his own men followed him, bearing sharp swords and enameled helmets and ornate golden shields. They rode forth and did not let up until they saw a splendid city rise up before them with tall towers and strong walls. The admirable Earl William ruled there; he was more famous than all other men in France on account of his valiant accomplishments and chivalrous deeds. Galopin rode into the city and up to William's palace. Outside many servants took their horses and weapons and kept watch over them.

61. Julien and his knights sail to Sobrie.
The duke now walked toward them with his courtiers, all of whom were dressed in good woven cloth. They invited Galopin, together with all his men, to stay there as long as he wanted. Then they went into the hall and the duke had

THE ROMANCE EPIC OF ELIS AND ROSAMUNDA · 99

Galopin sit next to him. Galopin handed over the letters which Lord Elis and Duke Julien had sent to William. After he had read Elis's letter, he was very happy and said that he would gladly prepare for this journey. The duke feasted everyone with great splendor, excellent cheer, and entertainment. Some played psalteries and hurdy-gurdies; some played the organ; some beat drums; some blew trumpets; some played chess; and some cast dice. Afterwards everyone went to sleep.

In the morning, as soon as the sun had warmed the world with its bright rays of light, the duke was up with his mighty men and he sent a summons to the four corners of his realm, summoning all his best men to come to Engiborg within a week's time. He also made known to Bernard and Arnald that they should come to him with their chosen men within the time previously said.

William had the horses equipped and the swords readied and the helmets polished. Seven days now passed, and by the eighth day a multitude had arrived in Engiborg, and nearly all the lodgings in the city were full. Bertram and Arnald the Long-bearded came, and Bernard, the good knight. There was merriment and amusement, now that so many had come. People wondered most of all at Galopin and his petite stature, and how courtly he bore his small person, yet he was the equal of the strongest of men.

The men drank and were merry the entire day. But when morning came, Lord William had the entire army put on their coats of mail; in all there were 10,000 knights. William now rode off with his armed forces and he did not let up until he met Julien, the good duke, in his superb castle. So many men were there that one could scarcely count them. Duke Julien walked with his entire court, accompanied by music of all kinds of instruments, toward William, and welcomed him. They went into the hall and drank wine, which gallant youths poured for them with great skill and courtesy. The finest feast now took place. Galopin made the nature of his mission public to everyone there. Duke Julien asked everyone assembled to provide him with as many troops as they could, so as to rescue his son Elis, who was in straits, as was told earlier. All deplored his situation greatly and said that they would gladly provide him with all their troops, both young and old, rich and poor, in fact with higher as well as lower men.

The duke equipped his entire army with good horses and excellent weapons. One could now hear the neighing of horses and the clash of weapons. 5,000 knights had arrived, which King Louis, the son of Emperor Charlemagne, had sent, along with coats of mail and enameled shields, as well as excellent palfreys who were prancing splendidly. The duke then rode with the entire army, splendidly equipped, out of his castle. In all there were 30,000 knights and a large group of foot soldiers. The duke rode with his entire army, and he did not let up until

100 • THE ROMANCE EPIC OF ELIS AND ROSAMUNDA

he came to the harbor, where his ships were anchored with superb equipment and provisions galore. Galopin was to point the way for the ships, which were a great sight to behold, with all their fine men. The duke boarded the ship, as did Lord William, and the entire large army, the finest military force carrying superbly wrought banners. They now set sail with a fair wind, and one evening they arrived in an excellent harbor below the castle of Sobrie. They now lay there, cast anchor, and raided the coast – while the scribe was resting comfortably there.

62. Kaifas incites his father to kill Elis.

Now we must return to Elis and Rosamunda in the highest tower of Sobrie castle. They had been there for nearly twelve months and no one could get into their chambers during this whole time, as was reported earlier. King Malkabrez had a strong watch kept over Elis and his daughter, and forty armed men kept watch each night around this high tower. Kaifas kept urging his father to attack the tower with a large force and kill Elis, and to punish Rosamunda, his daughter, by torturing her. He said that she let herself be prostituted by Elis.

"And they will not stop until they have betrayed your country with their duplicities and deceptions, even going so far as to kill you and the doughty men who are with you. It is extraordinary that you tolerate such, considering your great ignominy to have your daughter dishonored right in front of you by a foreign churl and stranger. You will never be reckoned among brave men, if you do not avenge this."

There was great applause now at Kaifas's words, and all supported him, while they urged the king to attack Elis in the morning. The king became very angry at their inciting words, and he said that early the next morning they were to attack and not let up until they got hold of Elis and Rosamunda, and had demolished the tower. Immediately there was an uproar in the palace, but before there could happen what the king and his men had said, many a shield would first be cloven, many a coat of mail rent, many a helmet cracked and a spear shaft broken, before Elis would be captured by Malkabrez or his men. All of this happened on the same evening, as was told, when Sir Julien, the duke, and Earl William came to land. On this evening both parties engaged in lively drinking.

63. Rosamunda is promised in marriage to Ruben the Fat.

Very early in the morning, as the sun shone over the whole field with its bright rays, Duke Julien and Lord William were up early, together with the entire army. They sent eight handsome knights from their army to meet with King Malkabrez and to say that Duke Julien and Lord William of France had arrived and intended to lay waste his country and realm with fire and by force, and to despoil and defile everything. The knights arrived and walked into the hall and up to King Malkabrez. He was sitting at drink with all his men. They now delivered their message with great skill and courtesy. As soon as the king received this news, he became both distraught and angry, and said that it would be appropriate for the messengers to be hung from the highest tree, and that they should be happy if they got away with life and limb. Then the king spoke:

"It may be that you, my valiant men, get to fight with the knights who have arrived, while Elis meanwhile remains safe for the time being and is unable to harm us. Now will be proven, whether you are as brave in battle as you are with your feisty words against Elis. It may well be that you will now find out whether the Franks can fight or not. Behave like bold men now and dispatch this rabble with bravery and ruthlessness. There now is a great need for this, considering the great struggle in which we are engaged. Whoever fails now is both craven and fainthearted and will never be counted among admirable men."

Thus did the king end his speech and all his men were seized by fear and dread. The Saracens turned pale as bast on account of their cowardice and vile effeminacy.

When the king had concluded his speech, twelve men came into the palace, went up to King Malkabrez, and addressed him:

"King Ruben the Fat of Alexandria," they said, "has come and sends you his greetings. 12,000 knights accompany him and they send you the message that you are to give your daughter Rosamunda to him in marriage along with great riches. If you refuse to do so, he intends to harry your city and with might and main lay waste everything, and even kill you, and then marry your daughter and seize your entire kingdom. Ruben is tall and strong and such a good knight that there is no knight in the whole world who is his equal or whom he fears. He has slain twenty crowned kings in single combat. He is twelve ells tall and eight ells in girth. He is the brother of King Jubien, the White-haired, whom you had slain. King Ruben the Fat has learned this and therefore he has come here in order to avenge his brother. He has also learned that not one of you dared to fight with his brother, but that a foreigner overcame him in the duel. Now choose quickly, king, among the options you are offered, and do not detain us any longer, for we want to convey your answer to our king. And if you choose not to part with what the king wants, you and all your men will find a quick death, disgraced in this world, along with everlasting shame. And thus your disgrace will not last for a shorter time than the great victory won by Alexander the Great, which will never cease as long as the world exists!"

When King Malkabrez heard this message, he was silent for a long time and did not answer a single word. He thought he had been placed in a terrible position, yet did not know what he should decide. He thought his quandary was terrible and quite perplexing. The king now spoke to his men:

"You can now see, valiant men, what great obstacles we face in this situation. The messengers of King Ruben the Fat are now here and you heard what they said. Other messengers have also come, from Duke Julien of France, and they have challenged us to battle. Offer us advice now and consider what we should do."

They answered that they advise him to marry Rosamunda, his daughter, to King Ruben, on condition that he engage Duke Julien and Lord William in battle, "who have come to harry our land and kingdom, and even intend to kill him and abduct his daughter by force."

The messengers now went back and found King Ruben sitting in his tent. They told him how King Malkabrez had responded to his message and, moreover, "that you are to engage in battle in the morning."

King Ruben now had his good horse, named Piron, fetched. It was as fast at racing as a swallow in flight. He then armed four kings: One of them was named Maskalbret; the other, his brother Galinbert; the third Droim; the fourth Faliber. Two of the aforementioned kings held his stirrups, while the other two helped him into the saddle, and two of his knights placed his feet into the stirrups. After this he was handed his sword, together with the gold embroidered standard, which was very skillfully crafted.

King Ruben now rode at the head of his army to the city of Sobrie. When he arrived, King Malkabrez went to meet him with all his men and bowed before King Ruben. He took the horse by its bridle and in this manner led it into the city. He now submitted himself and his daughter to his authority, as well as his entire kingdom. King Ruben was pleased at his words and said that he accepted this and also that he did not consider it difficult to overcome Duke Julien and all the Franks. "I shall gladly engage the foreign knight who killed Jubien, my brother. You should now be glad, king, and in good spirits, and not fear, for victory is certain. There is not a man in the entire world whom I fear to encounter in a duel or in battle," said King Ruben, and he now ordered his entire army quickly to get ready.

King Malkabrez now ordered the trumpets to be blown to assemble his army, which now was armed, and all his warriors were splendidly equipped on this expedition. King Malkabrez now had his entire army charge out of Sobrie and onto the level field. Duke Julien also arrived with his army, which seemed to be ablaze from all the gold and jewels and excellent trimmings on their armor. King Ruben had also come with his entire army, and one could see there many a tall champion with terrible countenance and strong arms, with excellent armor and on large horses, who were well trained for war.

THE ROMANCE EPIC OF ELIS AND ROSAMUNDA · 103

64. The battle.

The fiercest of battles now commenced, with much din and clashing of weapons. Here one could see the brutal assault of the Franks as they attacked the Saracens, thrust their spears and brandished their swords, cleaved their shields, breaking many. They rent their hauberks, destroyed their helmets, and Saracens fell decapitated from their horses. Sir William was at the forefront of all his men, and now struck with both hands at men and horses, and felled one Saracen after another. Sir Arnald the Fair, Bernard the Long-bearded, and Bertram the third were not to be reproached, for not one of the Saracens who suffered their blows needed to worry about wine or food at Yuletide, since every one who encountered them and their blows ended up dead. These four champions led and rode at the forefront, and neither shield, nor hauberk, nor armor could protect the Saracens. King Ruben, however, rode forward on his good horse Piron and with his sword he struck the chest of an excellent knight, through his hauberk and into his chest, and with great energy he cast him dead to the ground. He ordered his men to press forward on their horses. He brandished his good sword, called Sarabit,[20] and struck the knight named Fabrin down on the helmet, splitting his skull, hauberk, and body, as well as the saddle and horse right down the middle. The Saracens then let out a great war roar, thinking that victory was assured. King Ruben now rode forward and into the middle of the Frankish army, striking two men with every blow of his sword, and now and then he thrust his sword and did both at once; he struck and thrust, as his horse stormed into the battle ranks. King Ruben now rode out of one rank and into another, and felled one man after another. Josi, however, advanced and hurled many a man off his horse, causing much injury to many a Frank. Malpriant also rode hard into the ranks and killed many a man.

The Saracens now saw someone riding forward, who was more excellent, more prominent and handsome, and in every way stronger and more valiant than those who had advanced previously, other than King Ruben, for no giant was stronger than he. This knight was arrayed in such a splendid outfit that its brilliance illumined the entire field. And he sat on such a splendid and fleet horse that sped no more slowly than a swift arrow shot from a crossbow. This very knight galloped at the head of the Franks' ranks and thrust his sword into the chest of a huge Saracen, which landed between his shoulders. He then hoisted him out of the saddle and cast him dead to the ground. Then he drew his good

---

20. King Ruben's sword is called *Sarabit* in the main manuscript, AM perg. 333, 4to, but in Holm perg 7 fol. the sword is called *Jarnbitr*, "Iron Biter," which makes better sense. See *Elis saga ok Rósamundu*, in *Riddarasögur*, ed. Bjarni Vilhjálmsson ([Reykjavík:] Íslendingasagnaútgáfan, Haukadalsútgáfan, 1954–62), 4: 1–135, at 120; *Elis saga ok Rósamundu*, ed. Kölbing, 127.7.

104 • THE ROMANCE EPIC OF ELIS AND ROSAMUNDA

sword, striking the chieftain named Gaddin, and the sword struck his right shoulder and sliced off the arm and that entire side, and he fell dead to the ground. After this the knight rode into the middle of the Saracen army and struck to his right and his left, both at men and horses, and hurled them down on one another. And thus he rode in and out of one battle rank after another. The Saracens now realized that this knight was Elis. The battle was fierce and intense now, and the slain covered the entire field. Blood rained down in streams, covering headless bodies. Riderless horses ran around neighing. One could now buy many a charger, even one well equipped, at a low price. Lord William and his four companions sought to meet up with this knight and thought that they recognized Elis. They rode now through the ranks of Saracens and within a short time had slain 500, each of them bigger and more accursed than the next.

65. Elis kills Ruben and captures Malkabrez.

King Ruben the Fat now saw this excellent knight and realized that he had killed King Jubien the White-haired, his brother, and that this same knight must now be protecting Rosamunda, the king's daughter and fair maiden. He believed that everything would now turn out well and that he would be able to avenge his brother and obtain the promised bride. He called out in a loud voice and told his men to clear the field, and this was done. King Ruben now rode forward, as did the four previously named kings. Elis and Lord William saw this and rode to confront them. These ten warriors now encountered each other, charging at each other while striking valiantly. Elis charged at King Ruben, and William at Malkabrez; Arnald charged at King Galinbert; Bernard at King Droim; Berard at King Faliber, the Old.

But first we shall tell how Elis and King Ruben attacked each other. They charged at each other with great vehemence and struck at each other with their swords, and they unhorsed each other, because the harnesses served them no better than might a blade of grass. Both were on their feet now and attacked each other with their swords. Elis struck King Ruben and sliced through his shield, while King Ruben struck at Elis and sliced off the handgrip of his shield. Each now attacked the other furiously and with such vigorous strokes that each was wounded. King Ruben then struck at Elis, seriously wounding him. Elis struck back and slashed the muscle of King Ruben's thigh. The king became very angry now and struck down on Elis's ornate helmet, but the helmet was not so much as dented. Yet the blow was so strong that Elis fell down on his knees. At this Primsant reared, lifting both legs and coming down so hard on King Ruben's thighs that he fell to the ground, and Elis, who was standing by, struck King Ruben's neck and lopped off his head.

THE ROMANCE EPIC OF ELIS AND ROSAMUNDA · 105

Galopin was nearby and handed Elis the well-saddled Primsant. Elis mounted the horse and stormed vehemently forward, while egging his men on. He now sought out King Malkabrez's men.

Now there is to be told that William charged at King Maskalbret and struck him with his sword, cutting the shield in two and wounding him greatly. King Maskalbret struck back and cut off a quarter of William's shield, seriously wounding him on his left thigh. At this William struck the Saracen king in great anger, so that the point of his sword stuck in his chest and he fell dead to the ground.

With his sword Arnald pierced the shield of King Galinbert, his hauberk, and his chest, ending up in his heart, and he fell dead to the ground.

Berard and King Droim joined in a fierce battle, which ended up with King Droim falling dead to the ground.

King Faliber saw his fallen comrades and rode in great anger at Bernard and struck him, delivering a great wound. Bernard struck back, and came down so hard on the helmet and the skull that his sword ended up in his teeth.

William and his men now rode through the army ranks and Ruben's entire army fled. Elis killed many a Saracen as he rode. He encountered Josi and intended to kill him. With his sword he struck down on the Saracen's helmet, splitting his skull, hauberk, his entire body, and he cut through the saddle and the horse, so that it all ended up on the ground. After this assault all the Saracens became frightened and were alarmed. They blanched and hesitated in their spinelessness. William rode toward one Saracen who was huge and of evil disposition, and he rammed the point of his sword into his chest and cast him dead to the ground. At this moment Lord Arnald and his companions slew six huge Saracens. There was such great carnage that Saracens fell by the hundreds.

Elis stormed toward the banner of King Malkabrez, and his four companions followed, striking down the entire rank, including its banner. Elis rode at the leader who had carried the banner and struck his chest, cutting it open so that his innards spilled out and he fell dead from his horse. At this moment Malpriant charged at Elis and struck his helmet, but did not cut it, and with his sword Elis now struck down on his back, cutting it straight through, and he fell dead to the ground.

King Malkabrez wanted to flee now and he headed for Sobrie, but Elis galloped after him on Primsant, spurring the horse on. He was able to reach the king, and took ahold of the knob on top of the helmet, and thus lifted him up and out of the saddle, and he rode back to his men. And Galopin, who was standing there, received the king, who was taken to the ships.

Elis now rode to meet his father, and there was a joyous reunion. The duke and also Sir William and his men as well as all the people were exceedingly happy.

106 • THE ROMANCE EPIC OF ELIS AND ROSAMUNDA

66. Sobrie is captured and Kaifas is killed.

They now rode with the entire army to the city and attacked it. There was a most fierce battle resulting in many deaths. Kaifas was at the forefront and egged the assault on, fighting now with his left hand. Elis and Lord William managed to destroy the city wall, and the five now rode around the city, slaying both men and horses. Elis unhorsed everyone he encountered, and the Saracens now fled to house and hearth.

Elis saw Kaifas riding away and he swiftly galloped after him on Primsant, raised his sword and slammed it down on his helmet. The blade sliced through his skull, hauberk, and body, right down the middle.

Following this great stroke, the Saracens surrendered to Elis. Thereupon he rode to the palace of King Malkabrez with the entire army of Franks. They dismounted and entered the hall, where they drank merrily and in good spirits. Duke Julien and Lord William were there, Bertram and Arnald the Fair, as well as Bernard Longbeard. Now there reigned pleasure and good cheer with all kinds of amusement and with great joy.

67. Malkabrez receives his kingdom back from Elis.

Now it is time to report what happened earlier, when Elis had left the maiden Rosamunda and had ridden off. She had gone up into the highest tower of Sobrie to watch the battle. There she observed everything that happened in the battle, and now saw how the Franks could fight, and that Elis killed her brother. She approved of this, and went back to her bed chamber. She dressed in elegant garments, a snow-white silken chemise, and over it a tunic woven in gold that was so exceptional that no better could be found, even if one were to search the entire world. She put around her waist a girdle, made with great artistry, which looked like fiery gold and was variably fashioned. Then she put on a mantle; none like it can be found in the entire world. This mantle had come from the land of the setting sun, which is called Occident. Four fairies had woven the mantle with the finest gold thread, and they were at this for four years before it was finished. The mantle was adorned with stars and many precious gems. The merchant Jon had sold the mantle clasps for forty pounds of pure gold. Her hair was fairer than gold; her skin was white like new-fallen snow. No more beautiful maiden was known at that time. Then she went into the hall, accompanied by thirty maidens, all in costly velvet. When she walked in, the entire hall was irradiated by her appearance. She now walked toward the throne and Elis stood up to greet her, as did all the others who were there. Elis set Rosamunda on his knee,[21] while the

---

21. This is a sign of affection; such a gesture occurs in many Sagas of Icelanders.

THE ROMANCE EPIC OF ELIS AND ROSAMUNDA · 107

maidens struck up for a dance and sang with splendid voices. Everyone looked at Rosamunda and admired her beauty. Now there was happiness and jubilation, with everyone greatly rejoicing at the overall gaiety. Rosamunda welcomed Lord Jubien and Lord William most of all, but also graciously all the Franks. Elis now told how Rosamunda had helped him many a time to escape death. And he told her that she should therefore now receive from him whatever she desired. And she chose for herself Elis as her beloved, and life for her father and the kingdom with every honor. Elis granted her wishes. He now sent Galopin for King Malkabrez and he swiftly returned with the king at his side. Elis greeted the king and had him sit on the throne beside him. He said that he would be granted his kingdom and be honored and continue to enjoy his daughter. At this King Malkabrez was extremely happy. Now there was much pleasure and diversion, as everyone rejoiced. Elis then revealed to everyone that he intended to go home with his father, and that Rosamunda and Galopin would accompany them.

68. Elis marries Rosamunda.

Elis's journey was now prepared at great expense; it included excellent provisions and vast financial resources. Elis rode out of Sobrie accompanied by a large group. Rosamunda accompanied him along with many maidens and an outstanding retinue. Elis boarded the ship with his entire retinue, and they brought along many superb possessions from Sobrie: pearls and precious gems, gold and silver, both wrought and unwrought. Now Elis set out to sea and they had a good wind. They arrived in their chosen harbor, and Elis and his retinue disembarked from the ships and rode home to Duke Julien's palace. Elis invited Lord William and his entire entourage to accompany him home to a superb feast, which William accepted. Elis sent many excellent knights ahead to report that he had arrived, and to ask that a feast be prepared with the best of provisions, and he bid his men to meet his retinue with great pomp and gallantry. Elis's mother was extremely happy, as was his sister and everyone else. They rode out of the city with both young men and old and met a short distance from the city, where there was a most joyous reunion of Elis, his mother and sister, and all his relatives and friends. The Lady, Elis's mother, and her daughter greeted the maiden Rosamunda graciously, and they rode into the city with great pomp, while all kinds of instruments were played as they approached. Priests and clerics walked, accompanied by pleasing music, in splendid procession, and in this manner Elis, Duke Julien, and Lord William were led to the church amidst great rejoicing. Afterwards they were led to the hall to take splendid seats.

Rosamunda was in a different chamber with her maidens on the first day. On the next day she was baptized at a divine service, as were all her maidens and

108 · THE ROMANCE EPIC OF ELIS AND ROSAMUNDA

her retinue. After the divine hours had been chanted and the service was over, the king's daughter was conducted to the grand hall with great pomp. In her retinue were the Lady, the mother of Elis, and also the maiden Ozible, his sister, and a large following of women in elegant dress. The organ was pumped, the hurdy-gurdies and psalteries were played, and there was the beautiful sound of pipes. The company then walked into the hall, which was tastefully decorated. The maiden Rosamunda sat on a splendid seat, dressed so elegantly and superbly, that no king, no matter how rich, would have been able to acquire her garments. As soon as she was seated, people could do nothing other than gaze at her beautiful countenance and the splendid garments she was wearing, for the mantle that enveloped her radiant body seemed to be ablaze from the red garnet that was set on it, together with other remarkable gems. There now was much joy and entertainment. Whoever so desired, gazed at Rosamunda and forgot about drinking, for no one thought ever to have seen a more beautiful maiden. Her cheeks looked as though the red rose were commingled with the white lily. The celebration lasted for three nights. Then Elis said that the celebration was to be extended: "I intend," he said, "to celebrate my wedding, and no one who is now here is to depart at this time, yet no one should come here uninvited, be he young or old, poor or wealthy.

69. Geirard, William's son, marries Ozible.

Elis now sent for his relatives and friends who had not yet come. The celebration was extended by every possible means. Lord William stepped forward and asked for the hand of Ozible, Elis's sister, on behalf of his son, the young lord Geirard. The count approved of this, and the young lord Elis wanted nothing other than that the maiden be married. This was now decided with the approval of the best men. She was the fairest and most courtly of maidens. Lord William sent his men back to Engiborg now, in order to present the young lord Geirard with a letter ordering him to come. He and all his men got ready with grandeur and gallantry, and they rode off with great pomp, accompanied by many musical instruments. They did not stop until they came to the city of St Egidius. William and the entire populace went to meet them with great honor and accompanied by musical instruments. The celebration now continued with a sumptuous feast. The day had now come for the young people to be married. Elis was led to church by his dear father and Lord William, while Bernard and Arnald led Geirard. Chairs of gold and pure silver were set up. One could see such a large party of fine persons that it was hard to count them. Amidst this party both maidens were led by remarkable ladies. Four men carried a canopy over the maidens, and they were accompanied by every type of instrument that could be played. They came into the church and sat down on splendid chairs. The archbishop himself celebrated the Mass, and excellent clerics chanted. These young people were now married in a beautiful ceremony. Afterwards Elis presented his good sword, but then redeemed it with thirty gold marks.

Duke Julien bestowed his entire duchy on his son, with its cities and towns, and all its wealth. He also bestowed the title of Duke on him. Rosamunda was seated on the throne next to the Lady, the mother of Elis. From now on Elis was to govern the duchy together with his wife Rosamunda.

Then the people went to the serving tables and drank merrily and cheerfully. This went on for half a month before the festivities concluded. Lord Elis bestowed great gifts, first on the archbishop and all the clerics, and then on Lord William, on Bertram, Arnald, and Bernard, and he thanked them in fine words for attending. Thereupon he gave Geirard, his kinsman, exceptional gifts, and his sister many castles together with their wealth. The celebration came to an end now and everyone honored Elis and his wife Rosamunda with speeches. The Duke then left for home, as did Geirard with his wife. They now ruled their kingdom and had many heirs.

70. The children of Elis and Rosamunda.

Lord Elis now resided most admirably in his kingdom, together with his wife. Galopin was well provided for by Elis, who gave him as wife the maiden who had accompanied Rosamunda. On this occasion there was a wonderful celebration. Furthermore, he gave him a castle with much property and bestowed on him the title of earl. At the conclusion of this celebration Lord Galopin rode home with his wife. He became a most exceptional man. He had two sons, handsome men.

Lord Elis and Lady Rosamunda had many children, three sons and many daughters. One son was named Julien, but the other two are not named. Julien resembled his father most. Elis ruled his kingdom together with Lady Rosamunda into old age. Their last day was good and their lives ended in fine manner. Their sons inherited the kingdom and all became outstanding men.

This saga has now come to an end. May Mary direct us to God, so that we may live eternally, without end, with God. Amen.

The saga has now ended.

The Romance Epic of Flovent

1. Flovent kills a duke at Christmas.

This saga is not a compilation of nonsense, for it is true. Master Simon found it written in the city of Sion in France, where he conducted a school, and he translated it into French in agreeable fashion.[1]

This story is about the first emperor who ruled and worshipped the true God and who fully and strictly kept his commandments. The great king Constantine ruled Rome, when this account took place, the same Constantine whom Pope Sylvester converted to Christianity.[2] The son of his sister was named Flovent. He was brought up in the city of Aube. He was young in years but mature in his fine conduct. He was fifteen years old when he went to Rome at the invitation of the emperor, and it was at Christmas. A large group of earls, barons, and other powerful men had assembled in countless number, in the hundreds. On the first day of Christmas the emperor sat at table with a large number of men. There was no lack of superb dishes, all kinds of drink, including spiced wine, absinthe, and claret.

Flovent stood up, the son of the emperor's sister. He took off his mantle and he was dressed in a tunic shot through with gold, and he was the handsomest of men. His face was as white as a lily, and his cheeks were red as a rose; his hair was flaxen like straw. He was hardy and strong, broad in the shoulders and chest, and his entire body was wondrously well shaped. There was no man handsomer or fairer than he.

He spoke to the emperor's cupbearer: "Fill a goblet for me, which I intend to serve meekly and humbly to the emperor."

---

1. The introductory sentence: "This saga is not a compilation of nonsense, for it is true," is a commonplace in the *riddarasögur*, such as the incipit of the saga *Af fru Olif ok Landres syni hennar*, one of the sagas in the monumental *Karlamagnus saga*, which states: "The saga that begins here is not nonsense, which men tell for entertainment; rather it is true." See *Karlamagnus saga ok kappa hans: Fortællinger om Kaiser Karl Magnus ok hans jævninger*, ed. C.R. Unger (Kristiania [Oslo], 1860), 50.

2. Constantine the Great ruled from 306 to 337. Pope St Sylvester died in 335; his feast day is celebrated on December 31.

THE ROMANCE EPIC OF FLOVENT · 111

The cupbearer filled the goblet too full, because he envied Flovent's good looks and courtly comportment which surpassed that of other men. Flovent took the goblet, but was unaware that it was too full, and walked to the emperor's table. In front of the emperor sat a powerful and arrogant duke, and when Flovent passed by him he accidentally spilled some drops of the wine on the duke's fur.

The duke got angry and struck Flovent on the neck and said: "You whore's son, so ignorant and ill-mannered; you show from where you come: 'a bitter tree bears bitter fruit.'[3] God knows, if it were not Christmas day and the emperor had not invited us here for a splendid banquet, I would chase you to the filthiest spot in Rome."

Now that we have heard the duke's abusive language, let us tell about Flovent's conduct. He slammed the goblet down on the table and did not care that its contents spilled, for he was exceedingly angry, though he was young. He turned to the duke, raised his fist and struck him so vehemently that his neck broke and his eyes popped out, and he fell dead to the ground. Then Flovent said: "Your abusive words have now been rewarded; you did not expect, did you, that I would tolerate such shame?"

Flovent headed for the door of the hall, but the emperor called out in a loud voice: "Stand up and seize this fool! I shall punish him for this misdeed as he deserves."

None of the emperor's men wanted to harm him, however, for Flovent was so popular and he came from the best of families. He left, but none of his friends or kinsmen dared to follow him. Then the emperor swore an oath by St Peter the apostle that he would have Flovent killed, if he were captured anywhere in Rome.

It is time now to tell about Flovent. He quickly went to the housemaster, with whom he had lodged before, and called his two squires, Otun and Jófrey, and said:

"Fetch me my horse and saddle your own horses. We shall ride away, for I would soon be killed were I to be seized."

The housemaster heard what Flovent said and asked: "What has happened, my lord?"

Flovent answered: "Something terrible has happened. I have committed a grave misdeed. I killed a man in front of the emperor, my uncle, and he has sworn an oath that he will have me killed if I am captured."

The housemaster was very sad at this and gave Flovent the horse called Baudan, and weapons and a bag full of money. "It seems to me," said the housemaster, "that you will have the need to defend yourself."

3. C.f. Matthew 7:17, "the bad tree bears evil fruit."

112 • THE ROMANCE EPIC OF FLOVENT

Flovent, armed, now mounted his horse, as did his two squires, and he thanked the housemaster profusely for his generosity. Then they headed north toward the mountains.

2. Flovent rides after the Emperor.

It is now time to tell about the emperor and his men. The emperor was mightily unhappy that such a misdeed had occurred in his hall, right in front of him and before his own eyes, and on Almighty God's great holy day.

He said to his men: "I shall neither eat nor drink until you deliver this hapless man to me."

They answered: "Lord, he rode out of the city long ago."

"Get armed," he said, "and follow Flovent; you shall pay with your lives if he gets away." And the emperor called out loudly: "Bring me my horse Magrimon and all my armor and get armed and follow me."

His horse was readied. No horse was faster; it never tired from spirited riding or by carrying heavy burdens. It was born on an island and was whiter than snow. The emperor now mounted the horse. He was girded with a sword, which was the best in Rome, and a heavy shield was fastened at his side. He was given a long lance with a beautiful standard. Then the emperor rode out of the city, along with a large number of knights, on the same road that Flovent had taken. The emperor rode so fast now that in a short time he was far ahead of all his men, for his horse was faster than any other.

The emperor now saw Flovent riding and called out to him in a loud voice, saying: "You evil character and cantankerous fellow. It will not avail you to flee now. Men will see, when we part this time, that you will never again kill a good fellow through recklessness and in front of my own eyes, and be shown mercy."

Flovent heard the emperor speak in great anger and saw him riding, and he was very much afraid and called out to God and prayed: "Almighty God and Ruler, protect me so that the emperor will not kill me for the great misdeed I have committed. I am a mere child and my mind and strength are untested. The emperor has condemned me to death. I now place my hope in the mercy of almighty God. You, holy Virgin Mary, be my defense and shield and support in all my troubles today."

Then he took heart and spurred his horse on and rode at his uncle, the emperor, with great impatience. They joined battle and each hewed at the other, but the emperor failed to strike Flovent. The latter struck at the emperor's shield, however, and cut through it and also his threefold hauberk. But God protected him and prevented his losing his life.

THE ROMANCE EPIC OF FLOVENT · 113

"But if Flovent had succeeded," says Master Simon, "there would be little need to make arrangements for the emperor's Christmas festivities."

With his lance Flovent managed to throw the emperor off his horse, but his sword flew out of its sheath, and he did not know where it had landed. Otun was nearby and grabbed the sword, while Flovent took the horse with its splendid tackle, and said to the emperor:

"God knows, you will not get the horse back, even if you were to give me twenty marks of pieces of gold. And if you were not my kinsman, you would lose both your helmet and hauberk, and lie naked on this plain."

Flovent now mounted the good horse Magrimon, which we mentioned earlier, and his squires had Baudan and accompanied him, and one hopes that they will not be captured in Rome.

The emperor was sitting on the ground as his men came, and he was in a foul mood.

They asked: "How could this have happened?"

"For God's sake," he answered, "do not mock me, good friends. I would have given much gold and silver, had I never come here. I have been greatly disgraced on this journey, for I have fallen before a young fellow. Let's go back to Rome. It would be better if Flovent had not vanished, for he has the two treasures that are the best in Rome, my horse and my sword, which never fails, whether confronted by stone or steel; and no better horse can be found in the entire world."

The knights cheered the emperor up, raised him from the ground and set him on the best horse in their party. They now rode back to Rome, where neither spiced wine nor claret were lacking. Let the emperor now celebrate Christmas, and tell instead about Flovent's troubles.

3. Flovent meets a hermit.

Now it is time to tell about Flovent and his squires. At evening they came to a town and found good lodging there. Early in the morning they rode with great difficulty to Mount Mundio, for they did not dare ride on a main road, and they encountered deep valleys and steep precipices and many dangerous passes. They were exceedingly exhausted.

When it got late in the evening, Otun looked around and spoke: "Lord Flovent, I see a little church ahead and a house next to it. We should get lodging there for the night."

"That may be," said Flovent; "let's ride there." A deep ditch was dug around the house, and the wall around the house was of stone. They now dismounted and Flovent went into the church to pray, while Jofrey guarded the horses. Otun knocked on the door.

114 • THE ROMANCE EPIC OF FLOVENT

This shelter belonged to a righteous hermit, and there were two men with him who fetched firewood for him. The hermit had been a most overbearing man, as pagan as a dog, who did not want to obey God's commandments. He had killed six holy men and greatly denigrated Christianity before Pope Silvester led him to the faith and out of heresy and christened him.[4] But now he had become so dear to God that the heavenly angels taught him the psalter and visited him every other day. Pagans often dropped in on him, but he had excellent weapons which he used to defend himself against them.

The hermit now went to the door and asked who was there and what he wanted.

Otun said: "Lodging, sir, for the night."

The hermit asked: "How many are you?"

Otun said: "A young man and the two of us who serve him."

The hermit asked: "Where is your lord?"

Otun answered: "See how he is on his knees, praying in the church."

The hermit now realized that they were Christians and spoke: "I will most certainly give you lodging for God's sake, as well as whatever hospitality is possible."

Jofrey now led the horses in and they were given oats. And Otun went over to Flovent and told him they were being granted lodging. He gave thanks to God for this and they went into the house. There was no place to sit except on an oak log. Then a fire was lit with dry wood.

And Flovent said: "If you give us food, we'll go to sleep afterwards." The table was set for them and three loaves of ash bread were placed before them, together with bowls of water.

Otun asked: "Lord Flovent, how are you going to be sated by this black bread?"

Flovent answered: "I am now going to eat enough to be sated." And the three ate no more than a quarter of a loaf each, before they were satisfied and could eat no more. Now they went to bed, but found neither down comforters nor pillows, but rather birch bark, and they lay down on this.

The hermit bade them sleep with God's peace, but he himself went to the church to pray. Immediately God's angel appeared to comfort him and spoke:

"The nephew of the Roman emperor has come. He has fled the country because he killed a man in the emperor's presence, which will cause him much anxiety. Brother," he said, "this young man is the nephew of the Roman emperor, and he has exiled Flovent because he killed a man right in front of the emperor's

4. Silvester was pope in the years 314–35.

THE ROMANCE EPIC OF FLOVENT · 115

table. Flovent will atone for this crime through much suffering. And Jesus Christ orders you to give him all your weapons, which you will henceforth no longer need. For he shall afflict many a pagan for the sake of God's commandments, which he will uphold. And if he firmly believes in God's mercy, he will in the end rule all of France."

The hermit replied: "I shall gladly provide him with these gifts." Then the angel disappeared and the hermit chanted the divine office and celebrated Mass in the morning.

Afterwards he went up into the loft of the church and fetched his weapons and called to Flovent, saying: "Son," he said, "you are truly a man and noble in comportment. I shall provide you with good and superb armor, and you need not fear any man if you have such weapons."

He then got a hauberk for Flovent, which was skillfully made and impervious, and was as bright as silver. He gave him a helmet, which was of pure gold, and along with this a shield with seven rivets on the boss. Then he gave him a sword with a golden hilt, its haft wound with gold.

The hermit then spoke: "Here is the sword I consider the best in the world. It was made by the smith Josef in the course of seven years and he used only iron for it. After he had wrought the sword, he struck the anvil with it, splitting the anvil and the sword ended up in the ground. This sword is called Jovis, which means 'joy',[5] because whoever bears this sword will always be victorious and rejoice."

Flovent accepted the weapon, bowed before the hermit, and wanted to kiss his feet, but he forbade this.

Otun and Jofrey came and said: "May God give you great luck and strength with the weapons you have received, and an army of good men."

But Flovent now asked: "Eminent and holy father, what advice do you have for me now?"

The hermit answered: "In the name of God I shall give you good advice. Go north to France, which is ruled by a king named Florent. He needs the help of good men, because Salatres, the king of the Saxons, has invaded France with an innumerable army. He is accompanied by four crowned kings and a large number of other excellent men. There have been many battles, and the king of the Franks has always been defeated. And his situation is now so straitened that he resides in Paris, but no longer possesses any of his land."

Flovent replied: "Would to God I were there now."

5. The Icelandic name is a defective version of the original French *Joieuse*, "joy." The name occurs in *Floovant: Chanson de geste du XIIe siècle*, ed. Sven Andolf (Uppsala, 1941), first at 911, and repeatedly thereafter.

116 • THE ROMANCE EPIC OF FLOVENT

The hermit spoke: "You should know that all the people north of here are pagans, as pagan as dogs. If they find out that you are a Christian, it will be your certain death. I now want to advise you that if you enter their temple you should bow down before their idols, but acknowledge in your heart that you are bowing down before Almighty God. And I can guarantee that God will look into your heart and regard your faith. You will endure much turmoil and trouble from the pagans for the sake of God, and that will be your penance for the killing you committed on the most solemn holy day of Almighty God. But God has told me that you shall rule the entire Frankish kingdom if you keep his commandments, and you will lead many a people onto God's path. Go now, in the name of the Lord."

Flovent answered: "Jesus Christ be praised." And now he called for his two squires, and when they came, they were pleased at the beautiful gifts Flovent had received, and they thanked God.

Flovent spoke: "Saddle our horses." And then he girded himself with his sword Jovis, and his horse was now saddled. The hermit held the stirrups as Flovent mounted, and he blessed Flovent.

He took the horse's bridle and turned the horse in the direction of France, and then said: "God, Father of all creation, strengthen this man, so that he will be victorious over his enemies and humble the accursed offspring of the Jews!"[6]

4. Flovent kills Fabrin and his men.

When Flovent had taken leave of the hermit, they rode down the mountain, and then another two miles.

Otun looked around and saw four armed knights on a bluff and said: "Lord Flovent, I see four knights on a bluff, all of them fully armed. Now that they see us approaching, they are hurrying to their horses and are preparing to attack us. What should we do now? These pagan knights bear no more love for us than a wolf does for sheep."

Flovent answered: "God, heavenly Father, humiliate them and strengthen our might against them." Then Flovent got armed and put on the hauberk which the hermit had given him, and placed the helmet on his head, and girded himself with the sword Jovis, and then he mounted his horse Magrimon.

The pagans galloped down from the bluff, but Flovent rode vigorously toward them. When they met, Flovent thrust his spear at the one closest to him, and it went through the shield, the boss, and the hauberk, so that the point of the spear came out through his back. Then he drew his sword and rode at another

6. As early as the seventh century, some Christians associated Jews with Muslims, that is, Saracens. See Geraldine Heng, *The Invention of Race in the European Middle Ages* (Cambridge, 2018), 96–97 n1.

pagan. With his sword he split the shield, severed the shoulder, and pierced the body, and it came to rest on the saddle. Both the pagan and the horse fell dead to the ground.

Then Flovent spoke: "Ride forward, Otun, and prove yourself. I don't want to have cowards tagging along with me."

Otun was sitting on Baudan and spurred the horse on. He rode vehemently at the pagan and struck him with the sword that had belonged to the emperor and cut the man in two through the middle.

At this Flovent spoke: "It seems to me that you are both strong and quite courageous, and you shall no longer be my servant, but rather my companion. The two of us will endure both good and ill together!"

Flovent asked: "Jofrey, my friend, what are you up to?"

Jofrey answered: "I am up to little, a weaponless man."

Flovent then rode at the remaining pagan and struck a wondrous blow on his helmet, and split his head, the armed body, and his horse in two.

Then Flovent spoke: "Thanks be to God, hermit, you have given me a good sword, which will never snap if a bold man wields it."

Flovent had now been victorious in this battle, and he dubbed Jofrey a knight, and gave him a white hauberk, a bright helmet, and a good sword.

Thereafter they rode their way, and after they had ridden about a mile, Otun looked around and saw a wondrously strong fortress in the valley. The man who was master of the fortress was named Fabrin. He was a great Viking who had settled in this fortress so as to be able to rob all wayfarers. A large crowd was with him.

Otun spoke: "Lord Flovent, do you see this fortress? Let's have our meal there."

And they now rode there and Jofrey bought food for them and they sat down to eat inside the building. Flovent blessed himself and the food, for he had forgotten the hermit's advice. A man in the fortress saw this and realized that they were Christians.

He ran out to Fabrin and spoke: "Lord Fabrin," he said, "you have suffered great humiliation today, for your lookout has been killed who was supposed to guard all your roads. Five of us rode out this morning to ward off your enemies, and as we were eating we saw three men riding toward us. They killed your steward and three other knights, and I barely made it out of the woods. These three Christian knights have now come here, and I recognize the harm their weapons did to our men."

Many pagans began to shout: "Let's get armed quickly and kill them." And Fabrin called out heatedly and asked for his horse and armor to be brought, and

118 • THE ROMANCE EPIC OF FLOVENT

it was done. He mounted his horse and 100 accursed men accompanied him, and they rode to where Flovent was staying.

Flovent heard a great din outside and looked out and saw a large group of armed men riding toward the building. He armed as quickly as possible and seized his sword Jovis.

At this Fabrin's men entered and spoke: "You evil men," they said, "this is now the end of your life."

But Flovent answered: "You are going to pay dearly for this," and he struck the pagan who was closest to him on his helmet, and he split his head as well as the whole body, together with its hauberk. When the pagans saw this great assault, they were stricken with fear. Flovent struck down one after another, until they all thought it better to be outside. Once the house was emptied of Fabrin's men, some were outside. Flovent's men got armed and prepared the tackle of their horses, and in the meantime locked the gate. The pagans attacked the building and blamed each other that three men should be able to kill so many, and then they raised the gate. At this moment Flovent came riding out; he protected the horse's head with his shield, while he had his sword in the other hand. And one can readily say that whoever was closest to him was certain of death. He cleared the path and felled many a pagan. His companions followed him out.

The pagans cried out with a loud voice, saying: "Lord Mahomet and Tervagant, express your ire at the one who made that sword and the one who wields it." And they rode, as fast as they could, toward the fortress.

Flovent spoke to his men: "Let's get out of here as fast as we can, for an ill wind blows here." They came to the gate of the fortress, but it was locked with stout bolts; Flovent broke them apart with his sword, and they rode out of the fortress.

5. Flovent meets Angseis, his kinsman.
Fabrin saw that his men had been slain, and at the head of his men he rode after Flovent and called out loudly: "Fleeing will not avail you now, you son of a whore, for I shall have you hung on the highest gallows like the worst thief."

Flovent heard Fabrin's vicious words, turned his horse around to face him, and split his helmet and head, slicing him all the way down to his waist, and he threw him dead to the ground and spoke: "I thought that you might be somewhat competent, pompous as you were, but it now seems that you are rather insignificant." Flovent took his horse by the silver bridle and rode after his companions. The pagans found their leader dead, and howled like wolves.

THE ROMANCE EPIC OF FLOVENT • 119

Flovent now rode his way, mocking the foul fate of Fabrin and his men. They rode all day until evening, but found neither town nor city, and they rode through the night until early morning,[7] when they came to the city called Besentum. Flovent sought to reassure his men and said: "Good friends, we must conceal that we are Christians in order to protect our lives. Remember the difficulties we encountered yesterday, when our host saw me making the sign of the cross, and he would have betrayed us, if God had permitted it. We should pray to God with our hearts and thank Him for our life and safety, but praise the idols by approaching them with pleasing words, yet evil intent."

Their host was courteous and had them be given water in silver hand basins. Then they sat down to eat and nothing was wanting.

When they were sated, the host asked: "From where do you come and what are you doing here?"

Flovent answered: "We are men who want to find a ruler whom we might serve and who would remunerate us for this. We have neither patrimony nor riches, only weapons and our horses, and we are seeking a lord, who might need the assistance of good men."

Their host spoke: "I can give you good advice: go to Florent, the king of the Franks, who needs assistance. The Saxon king Salatres, the Arrogant, is besieging the city of Paris with an innumerable army."[8]

Flovent answered: "That's where we'll go." Then they went to sleep.

They got up early the next morning and accompanied their host to the temple, where they prayed, but worshipped neither Mahomet nor Tervagant, only Almighty God and asked for His mercy, and prayed not to be killed or captured. And when they stood up, they did not dare make the sign of the cross. Then they saddled their horses and the host showed them the way.

They rode out of Besentum over many steep slopes and came to a deep forest. They began to speak about the wisdom of Solomon, the commandments of Moses, and the birth of Our Lord. A young fellow stood in a thicket by the path and heard what they were saying, and called out to them:

"For God's sake, good fellows, look upon me with merciful eyes. A half month ago I got out of a dungeon, where I had been shackled, and since then I have been living on wild vegetation."

Flovent asked: "From where do you come, and why have you come here."

7. The Icelandic reads *príma-mál*, "the liturgical hour of prime," that is, 6 a.m.

8. Here *Flóvents saga* corresponds exactly to the reading in *Storie di Fioravante*, where Fiovo is told to help the king of Paris, whose city King Salatres has seized, and who will not cede the city except through force. See "Il Libro delle Storie di Fioravante," ed. Pio Rajna, in Pio Rajna, *I Reali di Francia: Ricerche intorno Ai Reali di Francia*, vol. 1 (Bologna, 1872), 340.

"My lord," said the fellow, "I am the son of King William, who ruled Ange, the wealthy city. Do you remember the large army, when the Franks invaded Rome, after Emperor Constantine had become a Christian,[9] and they laid waste a great part of the empire and killed my father, and captured me and sold me to an earl? He forced me to worship Mahomet, but afterwards he gave me the same rights as the other servants. Later I ran away, but with great difficulty."

Flovent spoke: "I have heard of this, and I know that what you tell is true. Come, give me a kiss; you are my kinsman. I am the nephew of your father, the king. Come along with us, and ride the horse which belonged to the pagan Fabrin."

The young man mounted and the horse pleased him.

Flovent then asked: "What is your name?"

He answered: "My name is Angseis. But I would like to ask how many nephews there are." Flovent answered: "Philip, your brother is the oldest; he is king of the city of Ange and four other cities. But your youngest brother was dubbed a knight last spring and is at the side of the emperor."

6. Flovent kills Josez the Old.

They now rode on in the woods and the day waned. They saw a large castle with high towers rise before their eyes. Its ruler was a count named Josez the Old. At the time he was 300 years old; he was as tall as a giant and strong and he had often engaged in duels and had always won. Now there was no dauntless man who dared joust with him, for he aroused such great terror.

On this day his son had ridden out hunting, along with forty well-armed knights. That day they came upon a large and beautiful hart, and it ran off so swiftly that the animal fatigued them, as well as their horses and dogs, and they came near where Flovent and his companions were riding.

Jofrey said: "Look, lord, at the hart that is running toward us."

"God be praised," said Flovent, "for having sent us this animal." He spurred on Magrimon and rode after the hart and was able to reach it, and his sword struck into its body, all the way to its bloody innards. He dismounted and cut the hart up as would a superb hunter.

Then the man who had been chasing the hart the entire day rode up and spoke with a loud voice: "Let the hart be, man; you did not participate in the hunt, and you are not going to get the hart."

Flovent spoke: "You will have to give me one limb."

9. On the invasion of Franks during the reign of Constantine, see H.H. Anton, "Franken, Frankenreich. Allgemeine und politische Geschichte: Verfassungs- und Institutionsgeschichte," *LMA,* 4: 693–95.

He answered: "You will not get more than what you licked off your bloody hands. Get lost, you whore's son."

Flovent answered: "Now you have hurled abuse at me, and I shall repay you for that." He mounted his horse, very angrily, and galloped at the pagan and at once struck him a mighty blow, so that he fell dead to the ground. And God remembered his men, and in the first charge Otun and Jofrey killed three pagans with their spears and swords, and Flovent another three with his sword Jovis.

Otun and Jofrey then said: "God keep you, lord, you are now really angry." Then they rode toward the pagans and in a short time slew twenty knights, along with the son of Josez the Old, but another twenty fled.

Otun spoke: "Let's ride on our way and leave the hart." And they did so.

Now there was a man up on the castle ramparts who had seen the battle and how it ended, and he ran down as quickly as he could and cried out in a loud voice: "Oh, woe is me. Your son has suffered much harm, Josez, as have other brave men, who have been slain today. And some are fleeing, as fast as they can, to the castle."

Josez the Old became exceedingly angry at this news and called for his horse and armor. Then he rode out of the castle along with 100 knights, all armed, and they rode along the path Flovent had taken. They rode as fast as possible now, furious and angry. And matters did not bode well for Flovent and his companions.

Josez shouted with a loud and fierce voice: "Evil thralls and wicked thieves, it will not do now to ride off."

Flovent heard the pagan's voice and prayed: "God, eternal Father, be a shield for your men; protect me from pagans, more pagan than dogs and strong like giants. I think it better to die now than to flee any longer."

Then he turned his horse back and lunged at Josez the Old, and each aimed his spear at the other. Josez plunged his spear into Flovent's shield and through the shield into the hauberk, but it was so strong that it neither broke nor was rent. And Flovent sat so firm in his saddle before the giant, supported by God's mercy, that he did not yield. Then Josez's spear shaft broke. Flovent plunged his spear into and through Josez's shield and hauberk, yet at the edge, thereby not striking the body. Then Flovent reached for his sword and struck Josez the Old on the head in such a manner that his sword sliced all the way down to the saddle. But now the danger facing Flovent and his companions increased, for the 100 knights who had accompanied Josez came riding. One could now see a wondrous battle begin as four men fought against one hundred. But one can say that no man is ever alone when God is on his side. Flovent struck, using both arms, and felled many a pagan; and his companions also proved to be exceedingly good. The battle ended with their having slain thirty pagans. But the rest rode off.

122 • THE ROMANCE EPIC OF FLOVENT

Flovent and his men rode their way, and were both weary and wounded. They arrived in France and got good lodgings, and rested there for some nights.

Flovent spoke: "I suggest that we hire a guide to take us to Paris over unfamiliar secret paths, since the Saxons have control of the entire country and are on their guard, and they will kill us before we reach the Frankish king."

They did so and rode to Orleans and stayed there for the night. When the rooster crowed, they left and traveled by day and night until they arrived in Paris.

Florent, the king of the Franks, resided in this city. The Saxons had left him in such dire straits, however, that he no longer had control of France. He had one daughter named Florentia, but no son. Angseis rode to the city gate and asked that it be opened for them.

The guard answered: "The king has ordered us not to do so, and two months have passed since I dared open the city gate. Nor is there in the city of Paris a knight so keen that he would dare ride the length of an arrow-shot out of the city, because of King Salatres's men. He has four crowned kings with him: one is named Korsablin; another Kalive; the third Falsard; and the fourth Kanaber. They all vie for the love of Marsibilia the Fair, the daughter of Salatres, the sovereign king. And on his day, each rides toward the city, and we always get the worse lot. And our king swore that that none of his men would ride out until the end of April, this month.

"Brother," said Flovent, "we want to offer our assistance to the king. Open the city gate, and I shall give you a good horse."

But he set the horn to his mouth and blew it three times, and Flovent realized that there was no hope of getting into the city. They saw two little sheds outside the city, and rode there, and led their horses inside, and they stayed there for the night.

7. Flovent defeats King Korsablin.[10]

It is now time to tell about the Saxons. Salatres, the sovereign king, was in Corbeille, with a large army, as well as his son and daughter.

"Since God was tortured," says Master Simon, "there was no more beautiful a maiden than she."

With Salatres were four crowned kings: One was named Korsablin; another Kalive; the third Falsard; and the fourth Kanaber. These kings were hardy and great warriors, and they were all competing for the love of Marsibilia the Fair, the daughter of the sovereign king Salatres. The four kings had come to the out-

---

10. The chapter heading in the manuscript writes *drepr* (kills), to which the editor draws attention in a footnote (179 n3). I have corrected the heading in keeping with the plot. See *Flóvents saga II*, in *Fornsögur Suðrlanda*, ed. Gustaf Cederschiöld (Lund, 1884), 179.42.

THE ROMANCE EPIC OF FLOVENT · 123

skirts of Paris with 20,000 knights and had set up their camp and were guarding all the roads, so that nothing could be brought into Paris that might be to its advantage. It was a most lovely day now, and the sun shone on the entire world. King Korsablin had risen early, a tough man and the best of knights. He had armed himself with the best of weapons and girded himself with the sword that he called Ironbiter. It was sent to him from India. He mounted a good horse. The king's daughter had sent him, by messenger, a banner early in the day, with the request that he should demonstrate his prowess for her sake. The banner was mounted to the spear with four gold nails. He rode toward the city of Paris, resting on a slope, where he held up his spear, so that the banner glistened in the morning sun.

Otun had risen and saw the armed king, because the gold on his weapons glinted from afar.

He called to Flovent and spoke: "Lord Flovent, seldom does a sleeping man gain victory. Look at this noble king who is challenging you to a duel. That is where a young man can prove himself."

At Otun's words, Flovent greatly rejoiced and he asked Jofrey to fetch his hauberk; he armed himself quickly with his best weapons and mounted Magrimon. Thereupon he rode toward King Korsablin.

Florentia, the daughter of the king of the Franks, had gone up to the highest ramparts of the city to catch the breezes, and many maidens were with her.

She saw King Korsablin riding, and also Flovent, and she called out loudly to her father and asked: "My father," she said, "who is this man, who has disobeyed your orders, and has ridden out of the city for a duel with King Korsablin? They will soon attack each other now."

When King Florent heard what his daughter said, he called his trumpeter and asked him to sound the trumpet for everyone to go up onto the ramparts. He did so as well, and the entire population of the city joined him to watch the duel.

Flovent now rode to where Korsablin, who was some thirty feet tall, could see him.

He spoke: "Young man," he said, "what do you want? Are you a messenger, or do you bear news, and why are you armed?"

Flovent answered: "What I know is that I am not a messenger, but rather a knight. I intend to cause you such injury that you will regret it and will never again boast of the love of Marsibilia, the king's daughter."

King Korsablin answered: "What an exceedingly impudent and verbose young fellow you are. In no way could I fear you, even if I were weaponless. You are now going to go with me to the king's daughter and I shall present you to her in exchange for the banner that she sent me earlier in the day."

124 • THE ROMANCE EPIC OF FLOVENT

Flovent said: "You speak nonsense when you say that I should be your grudging messenger. My good advice to you is that you take care, otherwise I shall injure you and leave you so ugly that the king's daughter would never want to kiss you, not for all the gold in the world."

Now the pagan got angry and he spurred on his horse and galloped in great anger at Flovent, who did the same, and each attacked the other with his spear. Flovent's shield was so trusty, however, that the pagan's spear could not pierce it. But Flovent's spear broke in King Korsablin's shield. Then each drew his sword and they hewed at each other; the swords clashed in midair and sparks flew. The combat was now at its most heated. The pagan struck mightily, but Flovent was well protected by his trusty weapon, and with God eternal as his shield. Flovent was displeased at the prolonged combat and asked God to assist him, and he struck down onto the king's helmet across a quarter of his face on the left side and on his left hand. And his shield fell down.

The king then said to Flovent: "I surrender to you now. Take my sword and do with me what you want. Yet I ask you to let me live, and I shall give you as much money as you want."

Flovent took his sword then and held his horse's bridle and rode off the battle plain with him. The king now had no more people with him than a thief who was being led to the gallows, and he said not a word.

The citizens of Paris saw how their duel had played out, and they said to one another: "Now the arrogance of King Korsablin has plunged away. Where are his threats now and bragging? Now he has been shown that it is rude to brag too much."

Then Jofrey and Otun came running and spoke: "Lord, how long will you lead this dog by the reins, and why are you obligated to do so?" "God be praised," he said, "for we have parted well. To keep his life he has promised us a large share of money. Take him into your charge now. I would like to have many such pagan dogs." Flovent had him released on his own recognizance, provided he left his money in his custody. This was now a good and wise decision.

8. Flovent kills King Kanaber.

The pagans had spies now to ensure that the Franks did not come upon them unawares. One of these spies had seen the duel and its outcome.

He hurried to the camp and called out in a loud voice: "Your fellowship has now been severely damaged; you were excessively overconfident, and not lacking in arrogance. But Korsablin, your comrade, is worse than dead. You were arrogant, yet did not dare rescue him from the maltreatment of his enemies. I saw a Frank strike him in such a way as to cut off his hand, and he then surrendered to him, and rode with him to the city of Paris."

When the Saxons heard this news they were not at all pleased, and at once blew their trumpets and prepared for battle. Within a short time 20,000 knights were ready with shining helmets, white hauberks, and good swords, and the entire ground trembled as they vigorously galloped forward. Flovent heard the clashing noise of their weapons and the sound of their trumpets, and he prayed to Almighty God to help him, and he galloped off the field quickly, along with King Korsablin.

It is time to tell of Florent, king of the Franks. When he saw the great army that was pursuing Flovent and his companions, he called out to his men and said: "For the sake of Mahomet, get armed, good friends, as fast as possible, and aid the men who are fleeing, and have the trumpets sounded."

And in a short time 10,000 knights and 400 archers were ready, and there was no one who was not well equipped with weapons for going into battle. They now rode out of the city to assist Flovent, and the king himself was at the forefront.

When Flovent realized this, he spoke to his men: "Good companions," he said, "let us now remember our predicament: that we might not return home, and how awful it is to be nourished by others, unless a man owns something himself. Let us now prove ourselves in this battle, so that we shall be praised, when it ends. And we shall earn much honor and largesse from the Frankish king. And I promise that the Saxons are going to know my name and my sword before we part and not one of them will be happy afterwards."

Flovent now let King Korsablin ride off a free man, while he turned his horse back and galloped toward King Kanaber, and they charged at one another. Flovent struck the pagan and cut a quarter of his shield off, as well as his thigh on the saddle, and his gilet. And he hurled the king dead from his horse. Flovent's companions, Otun and Jofrey, did not want to delay giving him help, and one charged at King Falsard and the other at King Kalive, the Valiant, but both Otun and Jofrey fell off their horses in front of the pagans. Flovent saw his men fall and he grabbed the horse which King Kanaber had ridden and handed it to Jofrey, who mounted and was now as good as new. Angseis handed Flovent the spear that King Korsablin had, the one with the banner that the king's daughter had sent him. He rammed this into King Falsard, but his hauberk was so strong that it protected him, yet Flovent had struck him so forcefully that he fell off his horse and his helmet got stuck in the ground, all the way to the visor, and he was quite wounded, before he got back on his feet. Flovent then took his horse with the splendid tackle and said: "Otun, companion, your fall displeased me greatly, but now I have a good horse for you." Otun jumped on its back.

At this the Franks came riding, and whoever was there could see the start of a grand battle: one could hear the great and strong sound of the trumpets and

126 • THE ROMANCE EPIC OF FLOVENT

see there a brutal encounter and a deadly attack, with many a spearshaft broken and many a knight laid low. Flovent drew his sword Jovis and rode into the middle of the Saxon army and met up with no arrogant pagan who was not certain to be killed. Otun and Jofrey were next to him, giving him good support. The Saxons fought extremely well, but they discovered that Flovent was superior to them, for everyone who confronted him was quickly slain. The ranks of the army were so depleted that everyone avoided Flovent. Florent, the king of the Franks, and his knights fought extremely well, yet Flovent was easily recognized among them. The Franks then said: "Lord Mahomet, you have sent us a glorious fellow, who brings down the arrogance of the Saxons. You certainly have great love for him."

King Kalive, the Valiant, now saw many of his men slain. He was mounted on his horse named Aviment, which had been bought for the price of four castles, and it was more fleet than a swallow in flight, and all its tackle was splendid. He spurred his horse on and angrily rode into the midst of the Frankish army, where he caused much damage and slew many a superb fighter. Flovent was told what King Kalive, the Valiant, was doing, and he turned his horse toward him and one could see them approaching each other eagerly, and whoever was bold struck at the other even more aggressively. Then they rode with spears aimed at each other, tumbling from their horses, but they mounted again and used their swords and hewed at one another quite angrily. The pagan was displeased that Flovent should stand up to him so long and he struck him on the helmet, intending to kill him. Had God not been with him, he would surely have been slain, but his helmet was so strong that it did not break or crack. Yet the blow was so strong that Flovent felt faint and he came to rest on his saddlebow, and he spoke softly and said:

"God, the gracious and merciful, who always helps persons who love you, and who are a strong shield for those in need. As I believe that you were born of the holy maiden Mary, and suffered tortures and death at the hands of the Jews, and rose up from the dead on the third day, free me now from the power of these fiends through the power of your glorious name."

When he had uttered this prayer, he recovered and regained his strength and was no less able to fight or no more weary than in the morning when he got armed. He righted himself in the saddle and prepared to avenge himself. Flovent struck King Kalive the Valiant, on the helmet, splitting the helmet and the head and the mail-clad body all the way to the waist, and he hurled him dead out of the saddle.

Jofrey took hold of the horse and said: "You have obtained a good horse with your bravery; give it to me."

Flovent answered: "It is yours. If the battle continues in this manner, we shall obtain many good horses."

9. Victory of the Franks over the Saxons.

The pagans now saw that King Kalive the Valiant, had been slain. They cried out to each other: "Flee as fast as you can, for we are not fighting against a human being. May Mahomet let his anger loose upon him." All the Saxons now turned to flee and whoever had the best horse rode the fastest.

When Korsablin saw Flovent, he rode toward him and spoke: "Demand recompense from me now as you see fit, but let me ride away a free man; I do not intend to break my word of honor."

Flovent responded: "You surely are a trustworthy man, since you intend to keep your word. I am now going to give you good advice: take care that King Florent does not catch sight of you. His men have suffered great losses because of you, and he will repay you severely, if he meets up with you. For your ransom, however, you can send me whatever riches you see fit." King Korsablin then rode on his way.

Florent, the king of the Franks, now had the large booty of weapons, armor, and valuables collected.

Then he had Flovent summoned and spoke: "We owe you much gratitude for the victory we have achieved. And I want you now to take this booty, but later I shall gladly increase this if you stay with us."

Flovent answered: "May Mahomet reward you, lord, for your good offer, but I am not one of those men who are greedy, and therefore I want your men to divide the booty according to your customs."

Then the Franks said: "He is a gallant man and he must certainly be of royal birth. May you, Lord king, treat him well, for we do not fear the Saxons if this man is among us."

The king then asked Flovent from where he came, who his family might be, and what his name is.

Flovent responded: "My name is Flovent, and I come from Spain. King Galifrey has exiled me, but the men who are accompanying me did not want to leave me. We have come here because we heard about the great hostilities that you are experiencing. We are mercenaries and want to offer you our services."

The king replied: "I will gladly accept your service and bestow great honors upon you."

The Franks now rode to the city, and everyone praised Flovent and his prowess. Then the king called for the master of the house, whose name was Hermet. He was the wealthiest man in the city.

The king spoke to him: "I place this knight and his companions into your care. Do not let anything they desire be wanting."

Hermet answered: "I have the means to lodge them for three nights, though they are many."

128 • THE ROMANCE EPIC OF FLOVENT

"But I think," says Master Simon who wrote this saga, "even though Flovent were to stay three years with Hermet, with thousands of men, he would not lack the means to accommodate them, for he had more goods than twenty camels could carry."

Let us now permit Flovent to go to splendid quarters with his host Hermet and to rest up from his exhaustion, and tell of the Saxons who had fled. They came to their camp and set it afire, and the squires loaded up their horses, and they rode, as fast as they could, to Corbeille.

King Salatres was playing chess, when his son went up onto the ramparts to look around. He saw the kings' army fleeing and he hurried down to his father and spoke: "Have you sent for your kings who were to keep watch over the gates of Paris to make sure that your enemies would obtain neither food nor support? They must be getting assistance, before you can prevent it, and our troubles are now going to mount."

At this the king got angry and spoke: "Scoundrel," he said, "I did not send for them."

The king's son answered: "I know that you will soon see them." At this, King Falsard came in along with ten knights.

Salatres, the sovereign king, stood up and faced him, saying: "What are we now going to do, good fellows? Do not keep this from me. Why have you come here with your sweaty horses and your wounded and bloodied army?"

King Falsard told him about everything that had happened. When Salatres, the sovereign king, heard this, he became so angry that he nearly lost his mind, and he spoke: "Lord Mahomet, shall I live long enough to avenge myself on the man who has so wronged me?"

King Falsard spoke: "I know that you are going to see him, for he would like to meet you, but it will not make you happy."

Salatres, the sovereign king, asked: "From where does this man come?"

King Falsard answered: "I do not know this any more than you. And we do not want to fight any longer for any foreign kingdoms, for we ourselves will quickly be destroyed."

Then the king's son replied: "I've never seen greater cowardice than to be so afraid of a mercenary, and you are not worthy of being called a king on account of your faint-heartedness."

King Falsard then got angry and said: "I think that even if there were ten of you, and everyone were as overblown as you and as well armed as you want, if that mercenary were to fight with someone, and you saw one or two of his assaults, you would not want to have to confront him, not for all your gold."

The king's son was angered by his words and rushed at him, wanting to strike him. But King Salatres spoke: "I foresee that if you do not let up on your bickering it will end badly."

King Korsablin now entered; he was hemorrhaging so badly that he fell down unconscious. But Salatres, the sovereign king, raised him up, and he regained consciousness. All the pagans were distressed on his account.

King Salatres spoke: "Tell me, how you managed to escape from that wicked man who has caused me such harm." And Korsablin told him about their entire encounter and his parting.

The king's son said: "Mahomet knows, there will never be greater traitors than you two kings. You praise a man, yet are so afraid that you do not abide his presence." To this King Korsablin replied: "So help me, Mahomet, if I were healthy like other men, I would remember that you called me a traitor of my king."

At this, Marsibilia, the daughter of King Salatres, entered. She wore a mantle embroidered in gold and was wearing a tunic of precious cloth. It was said that since the Passion of Our Lord no woman was ever born who was fairer than she. And whoever saw her beauty said that her skin gave off light like sun beams, and her eyes resembled stars more than human eyes, while her hair was colored golden. King Salatres stood up at her entry and bade his daughter welcome. He then told her of the harm that the mercenary had inflicted.

The king's daughter responded: "Dear father," she said, "you must avenge this. Look at Korduban, my brother; if he were armed and God gave him good luck were he to encounter this man, he would never be able to report any news again."

King Korsablin then approached the sovereign king, bowed before him, and asked for money to keep his pledge to Flovent. And the king agreed to this and gave him an equal measure of gold pieces and many other treasures. Korsablin sent this with his kinsman, whose name was Gamelfin, and he had three camels loaded as best he could with reddish gold and pure silver and valuable treasures. He procured an additional ten men and bade them take these riches to Flovent, in keeping with his pledge.

They now rode on the most direct route to the city of Paris, bearing a white olive branch. When they came into the city, they asked where Flovent was lodged. Then they went in and Gamelfin spoke: "Be assured, Flovent, you most wicked man, that I have little love for you, who have deprived me of my uncle. Here are the riches he sends you to redeem his pledge."

Flovent responded: "Let him keep this for himself; I do not want it. But you can select three choice objects for yourself and one for each of your companions."

130 • THE ROMANCE EPIC OF FLOVENT

Gamelfin answered: "So help me God, none of us wants to accept your treasures. Keep this yourself, you miserable drifter."

Flovent responded: "If you were not a messenger, you would lose your life for your insulting words; nonetheless, we shall remember this another time."

Then they left, while Flovent considered the riches and gave them to Hermet, his host.

10. **Flovent meets with King Florent and the assembled court.**[11]

Florent, king of the Franks, sent for his nobles and mighty men, and all came. He addressed them: "I seek your advice, worthy nobles. You know that this knight who has come from Spain was victorious over two kings; the one he killed, while the other has fled, so that we need never fear them again. The knight who has come to us is known to everyone for his valor, and I promised him honors. I want to keep my pledge and ask for your advice."

His counselors responded: "We want you to keep your promise to the outstanding young man. If you do not do this, however, then you disregard our wishes and you will regret this greatly."

Once the king heard his counselors' response, he sent two men, Sinabat and Espanuel, to Flovent and said: "Give Flovent my greetings and ask him to meet with us, for I wish to honor my pledge to him."

When they met Flovent, they said: "The king sends you his greeting and asks you to come to him, since he wants to keep his promise to you."

Flovent now revealed his generosity, in which he resembled the Emperor Constantine, his uncle. He gave them precious fabrics for fashioning garments, and also to each a mantle.

Flovent then spoke: "Go now to the king and tell him that I shall soon come."

They met with the king and he asked them what they thought of Flovent, but "who has outfitted you so well?"

"Lord," they said, "Flovent is coming, and he selected the precious gifts for us."

Then the Parisians said: "Lord, never before has such a man come here; he must surely be of a noble family."

Now it is time to tell about Flovent and Hermet, who was a most gracious man. He called Flovent to him and spoke:

"Friend," he said, "the king has now sent for you. A large number of people will be there, all of them well dressed, and a poor man who comes there ill clad will quickly be derided. Now I don't want you to be disparaged. Let's go into my chambers."

11. I have supplied the chapter heading, which is illegible in the manuscript (*Flóvents saga II*, in *Fornsögur Suðrlanda*, ed. Gustaf Cederschiöld [Lund, 1884], 187 n3).

THE ROMANCE EPIC OF FLOVENT · 131

When they got there, Hermet removed Flovent's outer garments, for they were in poor condition because of the armor he usually bore. Then he took a tunic of a costly fabric, with white fur underneath and a hood at the neck. Around this was a fashionable hands-broad border, made with wondrous skill and set with twelve precious stones. There were crystal, emerald, jasper, and amethyst; these were around the neck like sequins. There were sapphire, ruby, sardius, and chrysolite; these went from the sequins down to the belt. Then there were topaz, chrysoprase, beryl, and jacinth; these were on the sleeves. Flovent was now well dressed in his tunic.

"Anyone who says that these are not the names of the chief stones that have been mentioned," says Master Simon, "lies about the Book of Revelation by John the Evangelist; he is wrong, who says that."[12] Hermet placed the mantle over Flovent; he had bought this from a thief for 1,000 marks of gold, which the thief had stolen from Salatres, the sovereign lord. If it had not been stolen, it would have been bought for 3,000 marks, and would have been a good buy. No one knew from where the furs that lined the mantle came; they were sewn on with gold thread. People thought that they came from rare birds and were soft as skin. They were blue and brown, reddish with shifting colors. On the shoulders there were different kinds of stones continuing down the sleeves on both sides. There is no clerk smart enough to discern the skill that wrought the mantle's bands, into which were woven all kinds of animals and birds and designs that people knew of. After this, Hermet gave Flovent a good mule; its tackle was worth no less than ten marks of gold. Flovent mounted but did not support himself either on the saddle or with the stirrups. Hermet provided good apparel for Otun and Jofrey.

When they had mounted, Hermet rode up to King Florent and they dismounted. Flovent then approached the king and spoke: "May Mahomet, who rules the entire world and governs all creatures, both in the heavens and on earth, bless you, Lord, and give you the power to crush your enemies."

The king accepted his words kindly. A servant then took a chair made of ivory, decorated with great skill, and placed it on the floor for the king. Then the servants spread silk cloth over the chairs, and Flovent sat on one and Hermet on the other. Otun and Jofrey sat at their feet.

12. C.f. the depiction of Jerusalem in Rev. 21:19–20: "The foundations of the wall of the city were adorned with every jewel; the first was jasper, the second sapphire, the third agate, the fourth emerald; the fifth onyx, the sixth carnelian, the seventh chrysolite, the eighth beryl, the ninth topaz, the tenth chrysoprase, the eleventh jacinth, the twelfth amethyst." Adèle Kraeger writes that the "twelve stones decorating an item of clothing" in *Flóvents saga* "reads as though it were directly lifted from a lapidary" (Adèle Kraeger, "Lapidaries and *lyfsteinar*: Health, Enhancement and Human-Lithic Relations in Medieval Iceland," *Gripla* 33 [2022]: 115–55, at 141). She errs; the saga itself states that the source is the Book of Revelation.

132 • THE ROMANCE EPIC OF FLOVENT

The Franks then said: "That man is handsome to look at and manly, and our king seems like an ordinary citizen next to him, who should be serving him."

Now the king's daughter entered the hall, led by two earls. She was sunny and pretty. She sat down on the seat of honor next to her father and at once caught sight of Flovent. The color of her face immediately drained and she became pale as death.

Then she spoke to herself: "Mahomet, the good! A woman would be fortunate to be married to such a man. He is handsome and becoming."

The king asked his daughter: "What has happened to your radiant appearance, why do you look so pale?"

She answered: "It is because of that knight," and the king sat her on his knee.[13] The Franks spoke: "Your daughter could not have a better husband. And if that were the case, the Saxons would get but little of our country and pay dearly for what they have conquered."

There was great applause among the courtiers of the Frankish king and everyone praised Flovent and his accomplishments.

The king asked for silence and then spoke: "The honors that I promised will now be bestowed on you Flovent. I shall make you my standard bearer and also give you 1,000 knights whom you may choose from my army. In addition you will obtain the city of Corbeille, which is in the hands of the Saxons. And if you win that back, I shall give you the whole of Vermund, including Flanders."

Then he added a gold ring to his gifts, which is worth mentioning, for it had a precious stone on it; if a person is in a crowded place and he places the ring in his mouth, he can't be seen unless he wants to be.[14]

Flovent then stood up and thanked the king with fine words for the honor he had bestowed on him. On that day the king entertained his court most lavishly; many dishes were served that were unknown in Northern lands.

Flovent took leave of the king and went back to his lodgings with Hermet. Flovent then said: "I fear reproaches from my men if they are so poorly clad and I don't do something about this. And I fear they will not have confidence in me, when there is need, for poor backing betrays many a man."

Hermet responded: "What do you want us to do now? By Mahomet, you know that you now have a good company of courageous and skilled men."

13. This gesture, a sign of affection, is found in many Sagas of Icelanders.

14. A ring which renders one invisible is known from Chrétien de Troyes's courtly romance *Yvain*, which was translated into Old Norse and entitled *Ívens saga*. See *Íven's saga*, ed. and trans. Marianne Kalinke, *Norse Romance* vol. 2: *The Knights of the Round Table*, ed. Marianne E. Kalinke (Cambridge, 1999), 48–49. The motif is subsequently found in many Icelandic *riddarasögur* that were inspired by the translated courtly romances. See Margaret Schlauch, *Romance in Iceland* (Princeton and New York, 1934), 41–43, 52–53.

THE ROMANCE EPIC OF FLOVENT • 133

Flovent said: "I am not possessive of my wealth, and I want to share it with everyone. I want you to buy weapons and attire for my men," and Hermet did as he was bidden.

Then Flovent behaved as a gracious man would: he gave each man a weapon, garments, and a horse. Then he entertained them lavishly all day. And after they had eaten the evening meal, Flovent asked for silence and spoke calmly to them:

"Good men! You are my retainers, and we must stand together like brothers. The devils have disgraced us greatly and have endangered our king's realm. He has given me the land of which they now have possession, and it is to be expected that they do not intend to return any of our possessions, unless we show them our swords and are prepared to place ourselves in danger. Let anyone who wants to accompany me, be armed by prime tomorrow morning." All said that they would gladly accompany him.

11. Flovent vanquishes the king's son at jousting.

In the morning 1,600 knights were ready to leave Paris. Flovent rode on his white horse Magrimon in the direction of Corbeille with his army, sure to be anxious about returning home.

"May God," says Master Simon, "who rescued three innocent young men from the burning oven, and delivered Susanna from slander, and Daniel from seven lions in their den, assist Flovent on this expedition so that he will not be wounded or captured."[15] Nonetheless, loss of his men will await him before he returns to Paris.

It is time to tell about Korduban, the son of Salatres, the sovereign king. He rose early in the morning and called to his steward and said: "Fetch my weapons and bid 10,000 men to get armed and accompany me."

And now 10,000 knights armed and rode out of Corbeille. When they had ridden a long time, they saw an army approaching.

The king's son spoke: "This is the army of the Franks; let's not ride any farther. Three of the most vigorous knights should ride back and tell my father of this, while we stand by with our army." They did so.

Flovent and his men now became aware of the army, and he spoke: "We shall prove to be competent in our first battle. Keep together, do not spread out, and aim for a hard onslaught."

At once a mighty battle took place. "And whoever was there," says Master Simon, "could hear the loud clang of spear shafts and the wondrous clash of glint-

15. The references to the three youths in the burning oven, Daniel in the lions' den, and the calumny of Susanna derive from the Bible, Daniel 3, 6, and 13.

134 • THE ROMANCE EPIC OF FLOVENT

ing swords. One could see there many a horse gallop with only its saddle and many a knight brought down and his hauberk cut to smithereens."

Flovent hewed at a nobleman's shield and his sword ended up deep in his body. Otun and Jofrey killed two noblemen. They used their swords as they valiantly followed Flovent. The Franks proved to fight exceptionally well, and in their first assault they killed 300 Saxons, and no matter how the battle ended, they comported themselves well in the first attack.

Korduban sat on an excellent pale horse. He saw his men slain, galloped forward, and thrust his sword through a Frank's shield and into his body and flung him dead onto the ground. The brother of the slain saw this and lunged at Korduban, wanting to avenge his brother, but did not succeed, because Korduban's shield was so stout. Korduban thrust his spear at him with such force, however, that he fell off his horse, landing with his head on a rock and his neck broke, thus ending his life.

Korduban then called out in a loud voice: "Let's strike, pagans, and avenge our kings." And they said that there would never be enough of vengeance.

The Saxons demonstrated such prowess, as though they could conquer the whole world, and they killed twenty knights in Flovent's army.

Flovent saw this and rode vehemently forward and said that the Franks should exert themselves more. When they heard Flovent's voice, they responded: "We have a leader who will repay the Saxons for their aggression."

Then Korduban assaulted a knight from Normandy and struck his shield, and his sword went through the hauberk and into his chest.

Flovent saw this and got angry and called out: "Let us avenge our men! The Saxons shall pay dearly with their lives." The Franks heard his words and attacked the Saxons vigorously.

"Anyone who saw the Franks," says Master Simon, "would think it a marvel, how many hauberks were rent and how many helmets were split."

Flovent then struck a nobleman, split his shield as well as his chain-mail protected body, and seriously wounded his horse.

Then the pagans became afraid and said: "Mahomet the Good, know that this man intends our swift death. Our kings told us about him. May Mahomet direct his anger at him. No one keeps his life who encounters him."

It is said that 300 Saxons fell in this battle, and many were mortally wounded. Flovent brandished his sword Jovis against his enemies and cleaved the chain-mail protected bodies of everyone he encountered, and no one dared face him. He had now killed 100 Saxons.

Korduban saw that his men were frightened, and he called out loudly: "Do not spare the Franks. May Mahomet's anger come down on anyone who spares them." He then struck a Frank who ended up dead on the ground. Then the Franks became frightened and called out to Flovent for help, and Flovent realized that his men feared the king's son.

He galloped toward him, and when Korduban saw him, he said: "You scoundrel, why have you killed my men?"

Flovent became infuriated and got ready to avenge himself. Korduban had a shield that was fashioned of ivory on the outside, but was lined with hide on the inside, and it was harder than marble. He used his shield to ward off Flovent's blows, whose sword neither broke nor cracked; instead, it split Korduban's shield in half, along with the hauberk, but did not cut the arm, which was worse.

Korduban then spoke: "This is a devil, not a human being, and if I suffer another blow, I'll soon lose my life."

In great fear he then turned toward Corbeille, and did not want to part with his horse for all the gold in the world. At this, all the Saxons fled and those who were foremost were the happiest, and they did not spare their horses. Flovent did not pursue them. The Franks chased after them and seized many knights for money. Flovent did not want any dead or wounded men, but instead pursued Korduban, the king's son, spurring his horse on. No one followed Flovent.

12. Otun is captured by the Saxons.

It is now time to tell about Salatres, the sovereign king. The sun shone brightly, and Salatres had gone up onto the ramparts to look around. He saw his men returning dejectedly. When he saw Flovent pursuing his son Korduban, and that he was gaining on him, he hurried down and had the trumpets blown, and his courtiers got armed. He had his chestnut horse, named Bodran, saddled and jumped on its back, and 1,000 knights accompanied him.

Flovent pursued Korduban, and let Magrimon feel the spurs, and he gained on Korduban, who saw this and was much afraid. At this moment Korduban's horse fell into a pit. But before he could get out, Flovent grabbed the helmet visor over his nose, brandished his sword and threatened to kill him.

But Korduban spoke: "For the sake of Mahomet and Tervagant, spare my life, and I shall give you one hundred times my weight in gold. And you can arrange all this with my father."

Then he surrendered and Flovent took his sword. Flovent gave him into the custody of Otun and Jofrey, who then headed home.

At this moment King Salatres came running and shouted in a loud voice: "Where are you taking him? I shall redeem him, and all of you are going to be killed."

Flovent got angry at the king's words and turned his horse around and galloped toward him, and each rode at the other. Flovent struck the king in such a

136 • THE ROMANCE EPIC OF FLOVENT

manner that he split his shield and wounded him seriously on his arm and thrust him, together with his shield, off his horse. At this moment Flovent's horse fell into a ditch. Flovent jumped off, holding his sword Jovis in one hand and his shield in the other.

It is now time to tell about Magrimon, Flovent's horse. It jumped nimbly out of the ditch and headed for Paris, and many a person will be sad at its coming. When the horse arrived at the city gate, through which it had galloped in the morning, and it was opened, it neighed so loudly that the entire city heard it. King Florent had gone up onto the ramparts with 15,000 knights.

The king recognized the horse and said: "Good men, something bad must have happened, for the horse to return riderless. Its master must have been killed or captured. It is a great pity that I did not know about Flovent's departure. I would have given him 15,000 knights."

Then he said to his men: "Fetch me the horse." This was done, and with his mantle the king dried the sweat off the horse's head and bridle, and he said: "Flovent, there is much grief over such a young man; no one equally chivalrous has been born in our time. You would have brought down the arrogance of the Saxons if you had lived."

"One could hear there," said Master Simon, "the grief of many, both men and women, over Flovent."

One could hear many sadly weeping, but the news affected Hermet, his host, and Anseis, Flovent's cousin, most of all, for they thought that he was dead.

The king's daughter heard the news, and she was so unhappy that she came close to fainting. She lay down on her bed and spoke:

"I am miserable now and wretched, and I shall never be happy again, for I have lost the man who was dearest to me in the world, and also the most beloved."

When she had said this with great sorrow, she cried bitterly and ripped off her clothes. Her handmaidens came and wanted to cheer her up, but could not do so because of her grief.

Let her be comforted now, if possible, and instead tell about Flovent and the Saxon king.

The Saxon king's men hurried as fast as they could to get him back on a horse. When he had mounted, he spoke: "Seize this noxious creature. I shall avenge myself on him and have him hanged like a thief, and also his men."

The king's men answered: "That will happen at once." Then they rode at Flovent, but he stood on a little boulder and protected himself with his shield and defended himself better against the pagans than a wild boar against small dogs. He wounded and killed many a man, whereas they could not attack him. Four pagans then dismounted and tried their best to seize Flovent and

THE ROMANCE EPIC OF FLOVENT · 137

shackle him, but their difficulties were such that their lives were worth but a few pennies.

Otun and Jofrey came to the aid of Flovent, and were forced to let Korduban go. Jofrey dismounted and stepped on the boulder and spoke: "Lord Flovent," he said, "mount the horse that you gave me; you ride it now."

Then Flovent jumped on his horse and rode toward a mighty nobleman and struck him so that his head flew far off. He took the pagan's well-equipped horse and gave it to Jofrey. When he had mounted, however, Otun's situation was dire, because riding out of the castle came 20,000 Saxons to assist their king. In the lead were two noblemen: Gamalfin, kinsman of Korsablin, and Tenebet. They rode ahead and attacked Otun simultaneously; one struck his shield and the other his helmet, quite dexterously, and he fell off the boulder. He leapt up lithely and quickly drew his shield to his chest to be better able to defend himself against the two men. But then forty knights advanced and he was captured and taken to the arrayed forces.

When Flovent saw how they treated him, he rode there exceedingly fast and struck wondrously, and with one blow he killed fourteen knights, but they had such strong support that Flovent had to turn back, and Jofrey did as well, but Otun remained behind.

When the Franks saw the Saxons, those who were last fled first. Flovent often turned around and attacked the Saxons, not fearing anyone he encountered.

Gamalfin then rode forward and spoke: "Flovent, return to me the money that you took from King Korsablin, my kinsman."

Flovent saw Gamalfin and turned toward him, with his sword Jovis in one hand and his shield in the other. When they met, Gamalfin attacked Flovent, but the shaft of his spear broke. He then struck at Flovent vigorously, but Flovent's shield neither bent nor broke. In return Flovent struck Gamalfin and severed the head from his neck.

Then Flovent spoke: "You have avenged King Korsablin shamefully, and the money you demanded makes little difference to me."

When the Saxons saw this, they said: "We have been pursuing them too long, and he will play us the same way if we wait for him. May Mahomet bestow his wrath on him." Then they fled to the castle. Flovent was unhappy that Otun had been left behind. The Franks attempted to cheer him up, but did not succeed.

13. The temple of the pagans burns down.

It is now time to tell about the Franks in Paris, who were grievously mourning Flovent. King Florent spoke to his men: "Protect the city gate well, so that the Saxons do not come in unawares, for now they will be eager to conquer Paris.

138 • THE ROMANCE EPIC OF FLOVENT

After the king had spoken, 100 men went up to the ramparts and saw the Frankish army.

Four knights went downstairs and told the king: "The Franks, whom we thought dead, are coming, but we do not know how they have fared."

The king then said: "Saddle my horse; I want to ride to meet them."

He rode out with many men, and one nobleman spoke: "Lord, have faith in Mahomet that you will retain your kingdom and all your men."

The king told twelve knights: "Go and polish our gods and make them shine, and take the censor there, for I shall later go to worship them."

When Flovent came into the city and dismounted at the palace door, he removed his weapon, and brought Anseis along. The king embraced Flovent and wanted to kiss him. But Flovent put his hand over his mouth and said:

"Do not come near me, for I have vowed to Mahomet that I shall not kiss anyone until I have avenged my loss, for Otun has been captured by the Saxons and will soon be killed." Then Flovent added these mournful words: "Otun, my good companion, if I am not able to help you, then your great love for me is poorly rewarded, you who forsook your native land for me, and whose keenness has often saved my life."

The king spoke: "Do not be sad, for I shall load twenty wagons with gold to ransom him, so that he will not be tortured. You have now been with us for a while and not yet visited our gods, and I fear that Mahomet will be angry with you. Let us go to the temple now and offer the gods ten marks of gold!"

Flovent answered: "As you wish, lord!"

The king and Flovent now came into the temple, along with a large number of others. When Flovent saw the idol and the many pagans around, he did not dare make the sign of the cross. The temple's interior had gold and silver everywhere, except on the floor, which was of blue and white marble. The temple was adorned with draperies woven with gold and with costly fabrics, and everything glittered when the sun shone through the windows. The king handed Flovent ten marks of gold and he laid this in front of Mahomet, yet with ill will, for he had to conceal his faith. Then he lay down on the ground, and the king thought that he was praying to Mahomet, but Flovent was praying to the true God with a righteous heart, and he prayed in this manner:

"God, Creator of all beings, the mercy of sinners, the glory and praise of the righteous, the assistance of the innocent! You came as Redeemer of the whole human race and chose as your vessel the most pure womb of the holy Virgin Mary. You were born in Bethlehem and washed the sins of all mankind in the Jordan river. You fasted for forty days and nights, and raised Lazarus from the dead, who had lain in the grave for four days, and for our sake you were tortured by the Jews on the cross. You were raised on the third day from the dead, and ascended into heaven, and you gave your twelve apostles the Holy Spirit to strengthen them against the wiles of the devil. Now Lord, since I believe everything I said is true, release me from my tortures and difficulties so that the accursed offspring of the Jews do not destroy me. And grant me in your great mercy that I might suppress the erroneous laws of the Jews and live long to uphold your Christendom and holy laws! In your mercy permit me to suppress the heresy of the pagans, so that I might uphold your commandments. *In nomini Patris et Filii et Spiritus sancti.*"

When he had finished praying, he left the temple. Divine miracles now occurred: there was a strong earthquake and there were loud claps of thunder, and so much fire fell down from heaven that the temple burned down altogether, along with the idols Mahomet and Tervagant. The pagans became frightened and ran away. The king had wise men called and asked them what these signs portended, and they said that there would come a king who would abolish the pagan laws and Christianize everyone, "but we do not know his name."

Flovent left, as the temple burned down, and went back to his host Hermet.

Let us permit Flovent to rest now, and instead tell of Otun's troubles.

14. Concerning Otun who killed Bellirus and Kassus.

The sovereign lord Salatres returned to Corbeille and sent for physicians to bind his wounds. Then Otun was led before him by ten pagans. The king asked: "How are you related to Flovent?"

"Lord," he said, "I am his companion, and not a relative, and I entreat your royal highness that you accept my ransom and release me."

"No," said the king, "by Mahomet and Tervagant, you shall not be exchanged for either gold or silver."

"Lord," said Otun, "I am now in your power, but you will pay dearly if you kill me, for Flovent will cause you to lose many an outstanding nobleman."

Then Korduban, the king's son, spoke: "I tell you, my father's entire kingdom will have to perish before he lets you live. Rather he shall have you hanged on the gallows like the vilest of thieves."

Otun responded: "Lord Korduban, what a tough man you are, and in appearance you seem to be a good knight, but it seemed to me that you quickly left your company, when you felt the first strike on your shield and dared not wait for another, even if your beloved were to offer you all the gold that Samson the strong possessed. And one would have expected that the one who pursued you would have overlooked your bragging words, if only you had asked him. But you fell down, as was fitting, and you were captured, and in exchange for your life you

140 • THE ROMANCE EPIC OF FLOVENT

offered more money and gold than all the kings have possessed from the time of Adam to this day. And that was on account of your fear."

The king's son was angry at his words and jumped up and delivered a great blow and pulled his hair. But Otun was quite courageous and not afraid, though he was in a dire situation. He preferred to die rather than not avenge himself, and he raised his fist and with great force struck the ears of the king's son, so that he fell on his knees in front of his father, and Otun uttered these words:

"I know, you worthless fellow, that you would be brutally repaid if Flovent were here."

But the king's son jumped up, grabbed a staff, and struck Otun's head and face, so that blood came streaming down, as he attempted to ward this off.

Salatres spoke to the wardens of the dungeon – one was called Marun, and his two sons, Bellirus, the faithless, and Kassus, the betrayer – "Guard this man until morning; then I shall have him tortured."

They took a rope and tied it around his middle, and led him to the dungeon like a thief. Otun was sure that he would be killed and wanted to take vengeance. He slammed Bellirus's head against the stone wall of the dungeon, breaking his skull and neck. And the head spoke: "Lord Mahomet and Tervagant, help my soul."

Then Otun grabbed Kassus's hair with both hands and slammed his head against the stone wall and killed him.

The evil Marun ran back into the hall shouting: "Help me; this fiend has killed both of my sons and I fear for myself."

Twenty pagans ran out and dragged the dead out of the dungeon, but left Otun there.

"Now if you, God, do not help him, Eternal Father, he will suffer a harsh fate."[16] But let us leave Otun in this predicament until God sets him free.

15. Marsibilia aids Otun.

Marsibilia, the beautiful, went to see her father and said: "I cannot be happy when I see that you are wounded, and whoever did this to you should be burned."

After she had said this, there arose in her breast such warm love for Flovent that she turned pale and began to sigh from the depths of her heart. The king looked at his daughter and spoke: "Do not be sad, daughter, for I am better now, since the doctors have bandaged my wound. And we seized Flovent's kinsman in the battle, and he is now in the dungeon and shall be killed before prime in the morning."

Marsibilia said under her breath: "By Mahomet, who made me so beautiful, I shall get him out of the dungeon, and he is not to be hurt by your men. He is to

16. The speaker is Master Simon.

THE ROMANCE EPIC OF FLOVENT • 141

acquaint me with the recently arrived mercenary, Flovent, and draw us together in love."

Marsibilia then bid her father a good day, and called for her foster-mother, who had taught her much and in whom she had great trust, and spoke: "How can you help me, foster-mother, to promote my love for Flovent? There is no man whom I desire more than him."

She answered: "Your words are foolish and make little sense, since you love the man whom you should hate. He has killed many of your father's knights. Do not trust in yourself, but take my advice. Here there is King Almatur, who loves you greatly and who rules over many large lands, and he is a mighty ruler. Marriage to him would be honorable. That mercenary, however, is a total wretch and not worth a single penny."

Marsibilia answered: "It avails you nothing to speak ill of him, for his keenness in battle and his beauty are superior to that of any sovereign king. And you know, mistress, that King Almatur is neither manly nor a good catch, and his gifts to you mean more than his comportment in battle. Look for another love than me for him; he shall not have mine."

"By Mahomet," said her foster-mother, "you are very foolish in your considerations."

Marsibilia answered: "Do not think my considerations foolish. I have showered you with good gifts and you must do what I want, namely to attain this man's love. With your charms you have the power to compel this to happen, for no man is so hard-hearted that you cannot compel his love, if you set your mind on this."

She answered: "By Mahomet, who has supported me in many matters, it is folly on your part to love the man whom you should kill, if you could seize him. Leave off this foolishness and become Almatur's beloved; he has a following of many thousands of good men. Take my advice and marry him. You cannot find a better husband than the wealthiest king in Ricialand."

Marsibilia answered: "By Mahomet, I would rather be thrown in the fire than not attain Flovent's love. Surely you would not want to hand me over as a bribe."

She answered: "By my troth, you want to be married to a man worse than King Almatur."

Marsibilia answered: "Good foster-mother, take pains now to obtain the love I want."

"What an imp you have become,"[17] said the foster-mother. "So help me, Mahomet, I shall report this to your father, and he will flog you so that you will

17. The word in Icelandic, *víxlingr* (changeling), refers to a child surreptitiously or unintentionally substituted for another. Changelings are found in European folktales and are thought to have been left by fairies in place of the real child. The Icelandic word was generally used as a derogatory term; hence my "imp."

142 • THE ROMANCE EPIC OF FLOVENT

not be able to move anymore." At this Marsibilia got so angry that she did not know how to respond.

"It is to be expected," said Master Simon, "that Marsibilia would have struck her foster-mother had they been alone."

When she realized that Marsibilia was angry, she spoke: "I would not have opposed you so much had I known that you would be angry, and I would rather cut my own throat than anger you. Now I shall see to it that Flovent will love you. Otun is in the dungeon guarded by the evil Marun. If we can remove four stones at the gable end of the wall, he will be able to escape, and he is to confirm that he will unite you in love with Flovent."

Then Marsibilia spoke: "I like your plan and I know now, foster-mother, that you are giving me wholesome advice."

When evening came, Marsibilia and her foster-mother went to the dungeon, along with two gracious maidens, each of whom carried a stonemason's hammer, and they intended to break into the dungeon. After they had broken in, they lit a large candle and carried it into the dungeon. Otun now saw that there was a light in the dungeon, and he prayed to God, and asked him for help, and he said: "God All Powerful and Ruler of all, you are the salvation of your people, and your might safeguards the hearts of everyone. I commit my life and limbs to your mercy so that I will not be killed by that accursed folk."

Then Marsibilia called out to him and spoke: "Good brother, you who are sitting in shackles, speak to me and save your life. Are you willing to see to it that Flovent, your kinsman, comes to love me?"

Otun responded: "It is rude to mock a man sitting in chains. If you knew who Flovent is, then you would not consider him a fool or a simpleton, for his equal cannot be found in the entire world. He is well suited to be king, and his zeal was evident when he came here."

Marsibilia spoke: "Do not be afraid of us, good man. What I am saying is not meant to harm you. Rather it will be quite different, if you promise me on Flovent's behalf that he will marry none other than me; and you will then leave here unharmed. Look on my beauty; many kings are with my father, all contesting to marry me, but I do not want any of them. If Flovent becomes my beloved, however, I shall give him gold and silver, towns and castles, and much wealth."

Otun answered: "I do not want to disagree, if you promise to keep your word."

She said: "I shall not break my promise and I shall give you a horse and weapons, if you can obtain on my behalf your relative Flovent's love for me. You will then be freed by my father."

THE ROMANCE EPIC OF FLOVENT • 143

Otun then swore that he would not break his promise, and he left the dungeon. "And it is to be expected," says Master Simon, "that the one who was to guard Otun, is going to lose his life."

Then he went up the stairs with the maidens and was happy to be freed of his troubles. They dressed him and offered him food.

Otun said: "I do not want to eat until I meet Flovent and give him the news."

Marsibilia took a good hauberk out of a chest and a knight's complete outfit and gave it to Otun and said there was none better in the entire court.

Otun thanked her for the gift, and put on the hauberk and girded on the sword, which had a hilt of gold.

The maiden Fauseta said to Marsibilia: "Otun shall have as his beloved the one who sets a helmet on his head. And I shall do so."

Then Marsibilia said: "Otun, choose a love among my maidens, for you are a courtly fellow."

Otun looked carefully at the maidens. "Yes, Lady," he said, "I choose Fauseta for myself and Florenta for my companion Jofrey."

"That is fine," said the king's daughter, "because both are daughters of kings; but tell me whether you maidens agree to this."

They said: "Gladly, considering your discretion, lady."

Then Otun spoke: "I shall marry Fauseta and Jofrey Florenta. He is a courtly man and a good warrior. We shall make many a pagan jealous of our love. I shall dip my sword into the heart of many a pagan for your love, Fauseta."

She embraced him and kissed him repeatedly on account of her great love. Marsibilia, the king's daughter, sent Flovent a ring and a standard embroidered in gold, and very skillfully made. When the sun shone on it, two dragons seemed to be biting each other with fire coming out of their jaws. Then Marsibilia took a gilded saddle and placed it on a good horse and gave it to Otun, and he said to her:

"I shall remember to woo my companion Jofrey for the maiden Florenta. He is a superb man who can support his lord in battle."

Florenta said: "I shall not refuse him, if he is as good as you say. And when you ride to Corbeille and meet up with our men, we shall exult in your affection, if you overcome them. And you shall tell Jofrey that if he becomes my beloved, I shall give him twenty castles with everything pertaining to them, and also 2,000 knights for his expeditions. Now I am going to give him a belt as a token of my love, and a precious banner, and ask you, Otun, to give it to him."

Otun said: "Never have I seen better or more glorious maidens than you, whom no brave man would scorn."

Otun now mounted an excellent horse, and took leave of the king's daughter, and she and the maidens accompanied him out through the gate of the cas-

144 • THE ROMANCE EPIC OF FLOVENT

tle, and he thanked them profusely for their kindness. Otun now rode his way, and it is expected that he will not be apprehended on his way to Paris.

16. Flovent kills King Falsard.

Otun now arrived at the city of Paris and the gate was immediately raised for him. He rode to Hermet's lodgings and arrived at the cock's crow. He knocked softly on the door. Flovent had been lying awake, however, worrying about Otun. When he recognized his voice, he embraced him and said:

"Otun, my companion, tell me who freed you. I owe him most who has given you the greatest help."

Otun spoke: "Lord Flovent, keep your word now." Then he delivered Marsibilia's message. Otun reported everything that had happened, and then said: "Lord Flovent, I am not going to keep anything from you. Salatres, the sovereign king, has a daughter who is wealthy and beautiful. She came to me and for your sake released me from my shackles. In return I swore an oath that you shall not marry any woman but her. And that is how I was freed from death. Look at the tokens that she sends you as a sign of her love: this golden ring with its stone is greatly to be cherished, for anyone who has this stone on him will not be harmed by poison or through treachery and malice.[18] She also sends you a standard, a more valuable kind of treasure cannot be found in all of France."

Flovent answered: "You need not fear, Otun, for I would sooner give up my life than betray her, since she freed you from danger for my sake."

Otun then spoke: "Jofrey, my companion, I have also found a good love for you, and also for myself." He then showed him the belt and token, which Florenta had sent him. Then they went to sleep.

May, the first month of summer, had now come. The days grow longer, the weather improves, plants become green, and herbs and woods break out in foliage. Flovent had risen early and went to look for the king, and he greeted him with these words:

"May he who rules the whole world protect you, king, and give you strength and steadfastness in all useful matters."

The king responded: "May the same manifest his good will toward you. I want to give my daughter to you in marriage and make you an earl, and after my day you shall inherit the entire kingdom."

18. Earlier King Florent had given Flovent a ring with a magic stone which, if placed in the mouth, enables a person to become invisible. Here the stone prevents one from being harmed by poison, treachery, or malice. Similar stones are found in the later indigenous Icelandic romances, the *riddarasögur*. On magic stones in the *riddarasögur*, see Schlauch, *Romance in Iceland*, 41–43, 52–53.

THE ROMANCE EPIC OF FLOVENT · 145

"That is too much for me, Lord," said Flovent. "I am a mere youth, and your daughter deserves a better and wealthier man than I, for I have neither lands nor a kingdom, and it is not fitting for her to give her love to someone like me."

Then the king's daughter spoke up. "I do not ask for a better man than you, if my father wishes this as I do, for you are both handsome and stout of heart."

"If it had been up to her," says Master Simon, "she would quickly have been married to Flovent."

But Flovent said: "Lord, I am very angry at the men who have deprived you of your kingdom. Where are your knights now? They should not be enjoying life as long as your situation has not been avenged. Let us now plan to take vengeance for the disgrace you have suffered for many years. Go now with 1,000 men to spy on Corbeille, and have our army follow you. But if the Saxons ride toward us, then our men should turn around in the direction of home. The Saxons will pursue them then and we shall come to the aid of our men. Then will be seen who fights best."

Everyone praised his suggestion. The king then had the trumpets blown, and all those with trumpets in the city responded. All the men able to fight got armed and rode out of Paris. They chose 1,000 of the most capable men from the troops, and Otun and Jofrey headed this army.

It is now time to tell about King Florent and Flovent, who stayed behind with the main army in an area of climbing vines. However, 1,000 men rode to Corbeille. Otun and Jofrey rode at the head of the army and did not let up until they got to the city gate of Corbeille. When they arrived at the city, the Saxons were up on the ramparts and did not fear the few men.

Otun called out: "Tell the sovereign king Salatres that we are asking for the return of our possessions and ancestral property which you Saxons laid waste in France and obtained through plunder. Hand over our land, Saxons, as is proper."

When the sovereign king heard their words, he called to his men and said: "Seize this fool and bring him to me!"

The Saxons heard this and quickly got armed and sounded the trumpets, and whoever was ready, rushed out of the city. But then Otun and his men turned around and the Saxons pursued them in their great arrogance and foolhardiness.

Marsibilia went onto the highest ramparts with her maidens to watch the Saxon expedition. Marsibilia saw Otun on the horse she had given him and said to Fauseta: "See how your love is riding on the pale horse I gave him. I recognize him from the weapons I gave him, and we can see that they have now come."

Florenta then spoke: "I think that Jofrey, my love, is riding next to him; his fine weapons become him. I don't desire any other man, if he wishes to be mine."[19]

19. The conversation of the two maidens is an example of *teichoscopy*, a stylistic device in drama, the reporting of offstage events.

146 • THE ROMANCE EPIC OF FLOVENT

"I think," said Fauseta to Marsibilia, "that your love must be asleep, for he has not come."

Marsibilia responded: "Stop it, he is not to be reproachecd, for he is both handsome and spirited and more praiseworthy than both of your men."

At this moment two noblemen rode out; one was called Esturin and the other Finabless, and 1,000 knights accompanied them. They were haughty and were not with the army, but rode far ahead, as did ten other knights, for they did not consider other knights their equals.

Otun and Jofrey saw them and said: "This is an example of the arrogance of the Saxons; may God bring about their downfall. Let's ride at them and gladden the hearts of our sweethearts on top of the ramparts, who are watching to see who fares better."

Then they galloped toward the pagans and when they met, they struck them on their helmets and cut through their mail-clad bodies. Then the ten knights rode forward.

When Marsibilia saw this, she prayed: "Mahomet, mighty lord, who rules over all, protect our men in your kindheartedness so that they will not be killed or captured!"

Then the citizens of Corbeille heard the shouting of the pagans, and Otun and Jofrey drew their swords and struck so vigorously that the lives of those they encountered became worthless. At this moment the main army arrived, and Otun and Jofrey turned back to their men.

The Franks now ran out from under the climbing vines and surrounded the Saxon army. Otun and Jofrey egged their men on and killed a large number of the pagans who had come. They heard their great battle cry now and the sound of trumpets. At this Salatres, the sovereign king, came riding, together with Korduban, his son, as well as King Falsard and Rudent, the valiant. He had come from Denmark with his army, accompanied by 20,000 knights and 10,000 citizens. Their frightful clamor could be heard. Rudent, the valiant, called in a loud voice and asked: "Where are you, mercenary? Ride toward me and join battle with me, if you dare."

Flovent answered: "Here is the man you are asking for."

They spurred on their horses and rode at each other with such great vehemence that their spear shafts broke. Then they drew their swords, and Flovent struck him with such great anger that he cut him in two from the shoulders on down.

Then Flovent said: "Praise be to you, eternal God and Creator! Our weapons are renowned because of your might." Then he addressed the dead man: "Down, you dog! This service I shall render all the kinsmen of Salatres, the sovereign king, without charge, because he wrongfully seized the kingdom that the King of the Franks gave me; and it would be too bad if I did not reward him myself."

THE ROMANCE EPIC OF FLOVENT · 147

It is time to tell about Salatres, the sovereign king. He was infuriated at the death of his kinsman and at Flovent's words. He now saw that his kinsman was slain, and he recognized Flovent by his bright weapons and powerful strokes. He lunged at him and thrust his spear at Flovent's shield.

"But God, who is a help to all his people, protected Flovent," says Master Simon, "so that his good hauberk did not break, and he was not wounded."

But when he felt the thrust, it was so powerful that the stirrups and saddle-girth broke, and he had to dismount. Anseis was nearby and seized the horse, saddled it, and led it to Flovent, who jumped on its back and said: "I shall not be happy until I have avenged this." Jofrey was nearby when the king struck Flovent and he ran at the king and struck the back of his helmet with all his might, cutting it off and also the chain mail at his elbow and the horse's saddle, but he did not get ahold of the king, who fell off his horse inmidst of the army. 100 knights ran forward and brought the king another horse, and he got ready to avenge himself. He blew his trumpet three times and his men rushed there as fast as they could, including Korduban, Kanaber, and King Falsard. Salatres then spoke: "Much disgrace has the newcomer mercenary brought on us. He has killed thirty men, whom I greatly cherished, before my very own eyes. But you are my kinsmen and sworn brothers and ought to avenge me." They answered: "They shall not get away."

King Falsard called four oustanding noblemen to him, and they all swore by Mahomet that none of them would leave there until Flovent had either been killed or captured.

The Saxons now attacked the Franks, and the onslaught was great. One could see many a shield cloven there and many a hauberk split and many a knight humiliated. King Florent now saw his men slain and he intended to flee, but at this moment Flovent came riding, holding the king's standard, along with 2,000 knights. Flovent attacked one Saxon nobleman and quickly killed him, and then he slew another four noblemen. The Franks attacked extremely well and killed more than 300 Saxons. Flovent, however, encountered no arrogant knight whom he did not slay, and Otun and Jofrey followed his good example.

"And one could see," says Master Simon, "that it was as though a man in the woods were cutting down all trees, both small and large."

Flovent now rode a distance of three arrow shots forward and confronted King Falsard and his army.

And Master Simon says that this was the greatest battle of peoples since Alexander the Great was betrayed.[20]

---

20. It is possible that this comment refers to the Battle of the Hydaspes in 326 BCE, in which Alexander's troops suffered severe casualties.

King Falsard saw Flovent's conduct and he rode up with four others who had pledged to kill Flovent. They attacked the soldiers from either side, and it is said that never had there been a more hard-fought battle. Flovent rode forward and killed four knights. King Falsard egged his men on and rode up and killed six knights, and Flovent saw this. Falsard and Flovent recognized each other and galloped toward one another, holding their swords in bruised and bloodied hands. The king struck Flovent with great force on his helmet, the helmet that the hermit had given him. The blow was mighty but did not damage the helmet, whereas the king's bright blade broke in two. Flovent rushed to avenge himself and struck the king with his sword, which never broke when struck, and he sliced through both his head and his shoulders, and Falsard plunged dead to the ground.

Flovent said: "Down you go, you accursed dog! You trusted too much in your own might. You won't be able to brag to the gracious Marsibilia that you have slain me!"

Those who had pledged to kill Flovent feared greatly. And God be praised that Flovent was not killed. The Franks then gave the Saxons the gift they liked best: few of them escaped death.

Salatres, the sovereign king, now saw that King Falsadr had been slain, and he spoke: "The loss through the death of such a fine man is great. Mahomet's wrath descend upon you, you malevolent Flovent. If I get ahold of you, I shall have you hanged and your skin and bones burned."

Flovent responded: "I claim the lands that you wrongfully seized from the king of the Franks, whose subject you ought to be and to whom you owe tribute every year."

The king answered: "If you are paid by him for your service, things will end poorly for you, since I have sent for my two sons and for King Almatur. They have an army of 6,000 fine men, and you will be killed. I shall possess France, however, as will my heirs, who are quite fit to wear a crown.

17. Flovent kills King Salatres's horse.

Otun and Jofrey said to Flovent: "Our king is in great danger, and he thinks that you have been captured, since you have not come. For God's sake, let us ride there and help him!"

Flovent said: "God, the Creator of all, knows that I shall not let the Saxons think that I am not at hand."

Then he rode there with his army. King Florent saw him and said: "Brother Flovent, our men are in a terrible spot. Korduban, the king's son, is attacking us fiercely. For Mahomet's sake, avenge our men on him. He has caused a great loss of lives, so that even those who are most courageous are ready to flee."

Flovent answered: "Lord, do not let cowardice overcome you. You are our chieftain and must speak well in this regard. Conflicts often end well. I promise you that I shall not flee as long as I can sit upright on my horse and wield my sword. Let us attack them now and not spare our enemies."

The Franks rejoiced at his words and said: "The Saxons will now pay dearly for our lives. Flovent will now properly repay them and bring down their arrogance."

Flovent assaulted the Saxons in the same manner as a hungry falcon swoops down for its prey, and he killed ten noblemen, outstanding men.

Then he called out: "Korduban, son of the king, ride here, if you dare, and fight with me. Never did your father, or his father, win the patrimony of other kings in battle. Rather he should be the vassal of the king of the Franks and pay him homage. But now I call him a traitor, who is waging war against his lord. But if you dare to defend his cause, you will not escape me."

Korduban recognized Flovent by his weapons and saw how bloodied his sword was. He was very much afraid of him and rode into the battle array, where it was deepest. Flovent galloped after him, but the ranks were so dense that he could not reach him. He was annoyed at this and expressed his anger at those closest, and killed many. Flovent's men backed him well, so that they quickly thinned the Saxon ranks and avenged their men. Flovent rode into the midst of the Saxon army and struck right and left in an attempt to reach the sovereign king Salatres. Anyone not doughty was ill protected by Mahomet.

King Salatres now saw that Flovent was looking for him and that he caused much damage, and that there was no one dexterous enough to prevent being slain. Weapons were a good bargain there, since the whole battlefield was strewn with the bodies of the pagans.

When Flovent saw the king fleeing, he called out to Salatres: "Why are you fleeing from a young man? It is a great disgrace to be killed as one is fleeing. Instead, turn around and face me, if you dare."

But the king did not want to wait for him. The Saxons did not let up until they came to Corbeille. The main part of the army came to where there were large climbing vines, which greatly obstructed them in their flight. The Saxons hastened to the city gate, but the throng trying to get in was so large that many were trodden under the horses' hooves, and got in only with difficulty. Flovent spurred his horse on, and gained quickly on the galloping king whose horse fell under him dead to the ground.

18. King Salatres is captured.

Marsibilia, the king's daughter, and her maidens were up on the ramparts and were casting large rocks down onto the Franks and they killed six knights. Otun

150 • THE ROMANCE EPIC OF FLOVENT

saw that and said to Marsibilia: "You are too angry now and have forgotten the conversation we had. Flovent is not going to love you if you kill his men."

Marsibilia answered: "We are not going to become enemies on this account, for I shall never cease loving him. I have experienced nothing but good behavior and excellent service from you, and if you had fled from us in Saxony, then I would have had to marry your squire, and I would be living in disgrace my entire life."

Otun spoke: "I do not think that you are right, my Queen, because I shall not break our agreement as long as you intend to keep your word in respect to Flovent."

Marsibilia answered: "I would rather kill myself than cease loving Flovent."

Then she walked from the highest tower to the one over the city gate and saw many of the Saxons dejectedly coming home. She took a sharp flint and with it struck the head of a Frank, whose brain fell out and he dropped dead to the ground. Then Marsibilia saw that her father was in a tough spot, because Flovent was attacking him hard, and each struck vehemently at the other.

She turned pale when she saw this and said: "Oh no, now I am disconsolate and miserable at seeing the two men attacking each other whom I love most on earth; no matter whom I lose, I will never recover from this. Hear me, Mahomet, you who have created and ordered everything, grant me your help, so that my white-bearded father is not overcome, and also, gracious lord, that I do not lose the man whom I love most, Flovent, for if I were to lose him, I would lose all my happiness in this world."

Then Fauseta came and said: "My queen, the day has now come when you will regret the burning love that was kindled when you heard of Flovent's prowess. Now the saying will prove true that 'sweet loves burn.' Flovent will now kill your father and your brothers, and thereby disgrace Saxony."

Now you have heard how Flovent pursued the fleeing horde. He managed to get Salatres, the sovereign king, off his horse outside the city, but he nimbly mounted again and drew his sword and defended himself bravely. He struck mightily on Flovent's helmet, but it was neither dented nor did it break. Then the king attacked Flovent again, but he was soon exhausted, and rested for a while, and spoke:

"You surely are a valiant fellow, Flovent, and your equal is not to be found as long as you live. But you must realize that the wretched king whom you serve is so poor that he can hardly support himself, and he will be but little able to reward you as you deserve. Come over to my side and become my nobleman. I shall give you a large kingdom to rule and a following of 30,000 knights. Otherwise, I shall have you killed. I have sent for my two sons, Gvinimer and Yssat, who are leading an innumerable army. They will soon reach Paris and conquer it."

THE ROMANCE EPIC OF FLOVENT • 151

But Flovent responded: "I am a knight serving the king of the Franks, and I have sworn allegiance to him. If I repudiate this, I shall never cease being reproached."

At this the king struck at Flovent, but he protected himself with his shield. Flovent then lunged at the king, cleaving his shield and striking his shoulder, thereby dealing him a serious wound. But then the king rushed at Flovent and took him in his arms as one might carry a child, since he was four feet taller than Flovent.

Then Flovent cried out loudly: "Hear me, my companions, aid me now. My foe is carrying me off, and things will end badly for me if he gets away with me."

Jofrey heard Flovent's cry and spurred his horse on and thrust his spear at the king, through the hauberk and into the chest, and in this way threw him off the horse so that he landed far down on the ground. And Flovent struck the king and split his helmet and cut off his right ear. Then the king spoke: "Why do you wish to kill me, Flovent? I shall give you much money for my life. I shall give you the kingdom that I promised you earlier, which Florent possesses; and you will be the chieftain over 100 men. And I shall give you Marsibilia, my daughter, in marriage; no one is considered to be her equal in beauty in the world. You will then be a great ruler." After this speech he raised his sword and gave himself up. Then Flovent mounted his horse and took his sword.

When Marsibilia saw this, she nearly fell unconscious. Florenta saw this and spoke to the fleeing Saxons: "Listen, good fellows; ride after the Franks and help our ruler who has been captured by Flovent. You are our king's men and ought to lay down your life for him. If he is killed, however, you will be unable to boast that you have won the kingdom of the Franks through your bravery. Instead, you will live in infamy for the rest of your lives." The Saxons were upset by her words, but none of them dared ride after the Franks.

When King Florent saw the sovereign king Salatres, he spoke with great joy: "You good god, Mahomet, and Tervagant, and the excellent Apollin, and Lord Jove: it is clear now that whoever serves you with good will shall earn victory and honor in all matters; those who say otherwise are wrong." The Franks now rode very happily back home, and they chattered a lot, and one could hear them from afar. "But I think," says Master Simon, "that all their joy will turn to grief, and the one who is most accomplished among them, will have to prove this even more."

19. The death of King Florent.

It is now time to tell of those who were back in Corbeille. They lamented and wept over the unfortunate fate of Salatres, their sovereign king. Then they went

152 • THE ROMANCE EPIC OF FLOVENT

to the temple and verbally blamed Mahomet and Tervagant and threatened to burn them. Marsibilia was much unhappier than the others. The son of King Korduban ran forward out of this crowd and spoke:

"Woe to you Mahomet, you vilest of gods, your might has now been overcome. Whoever believes in you is wretched, and your help is useless when needed. Salatres, my father, worshipped you with a good heart, and he had your likeness made of the most precious marble, and he complied with all your wishes. Now you have been truly undercut, since you have disappointed him."

Then he ran at Tervagant and struck his head with a staff and broke off his nose. Then he saw where Mahomet sat and he continued similarly with both of them, and he stabbed their eyes out and attacked their faces. After this he flung them in a ditch and said: "You are going to lie here forever, unless you return our king in good health out of the hands of the Frankish king."

The Saxons then spoke to Korduban: "You show little respect for our gods, when you treat them so wretchedly."

Some said: "They deserve this, since they failed our king. Work some miracles now," they said, "and have our king come back."

"But they believed wrongly," says Master Simon, "in thinking they could help the king, when they could not help themselves."

The time has come to tell about the kings Salatres and Florent. "You wicked man," said the king of the Franks, "I have to repay you greatly for your evil deeds, for you have seriously tarnished the reputation of the Franks. Neither grain nor wine has thrived in France during these thirty months while you have been here. On account of your iniquities, however, you are now in my hands. You are to go with me to Paris, where you will have the lodging that you deserve: a dungeon that is the filthiest in the city. There you will suffer greater hardship than any other person since the days of Noah. There you shall starve so much that you will be unable to mount a horse, even if three men were to support you. That will make you regret your impudence."

King Salatres responded: "Shut up! You are of little significance and are unworthy of being called a king. I have been in this kingdom that you are unworthy of ruling, and I have conquered cities and castles, but you never left Paris to engage in battle before that young man came to your rescue. I intended the worst death for you, and Flovent is unworthy of serving you, craven king that you are. He has killed three of my kings and many noblemen, but you I do not fear, cowardly and indolent king, who does not dare to defend your city. I have two sons who are courtly men and powerful. They are now in Normandy with 30,000 knights. Almatur, king of Rome, will soon come with 20,000 knights to assist me. No four days will pass before you will no longer dare to hold me captive, because

THE ROMANCE EPIC OF FLOVENT · 153

they will oppress you so greatly that you will no longer possess any part of your kingdom, or keep your head. Soon they will attack your city of Paris and burn it down with fire spewing devices for which I have sent to Finland."

The Frankish king responded: "Mahomet knows that I shall quash you before they come to Paris, and they will be of little help to you."

King Salatres spoke: "By my troth, I do not fear that you will dare rob me of life or limb. You are a most vile man and have never been known for prowess. France would be disgraced if you were to rule it, you who do not dare to help your people or your country, which will not be yours any longer. I have given your country to my sons on account of your cowardice and pusillanimity. One will possess France and the other Normandy. Then they will release me, happy and free, from your detention. You, however, will not remain here, but rather be sent to the country called Nubia to end your life there."

King Florent replied: "So help me, Mahomet, I have never heard of a more foolish plan. Your life and death are in my hands. Know that I have no love for you, for with your corrupt avarice you have despoiled my kingdom and have repeatedly been most wicked and inimical, and for that you deserve to die."

King Salatres said: "I do not fear you, most horrible of kings, you who does not dare to oppose me."

The king of the Franks replied: "You greatest whore's son; for a long time you have worked your wickedness, and through your words you reveal your foolish intentions. And the old French proverb holds true: 'Ki tent sun pie plus que sa chape ne tient, s'en repent tost quant freid li vient.' In our language this means: 'whoever stretches his foot out from under his cloak, will regret it when coldness comes upon him.' You have many treasures, and a heart full of wickedness and unrighteousness; you have managed to fall into my hands, and I shall cure you of your wickedness rather than let you get away. And if you perish today, then tomorrow you will be hung on the tallest tree in France."

King Salatres said: "Shut up, you cowardly and worthless fellow, I have been in your country for thirty months and have captured cities and castles, but I have never seen you demonstrate any prowess. And if that youth had not come, who slew three of my kings and many other valiant men, and attacked me on three occasions, I would have had you dragged by your hair out of Paris, attached to a horse's tail."

20. King Salatres is defeated by Flovent.[21]

The two sons of Salatres, the sovereign king, arrived in Paris with a large army, as well as King Almatur with his army of 30,000 knights. The brothers intended to

21. I have supplied the title, which is illegible in the manuscript.

154 • THE ROMANCE EPIC OF FLOVENT

arrange for the marriage of their sister Marsibilia. They had conquered all of Normandy and the Roman empire all the way to the Greek sea. And when they received the letter from the Saxon king, they turned with their entire army toward France.

"And whoever was in Paris," says Master Simon, "could see the large expedition."

Gernimer, the king's son, rode to the gate of the city, and called out in a loud voice and spoke: "Where are you, mercenary, the protector and support of the king of the Franks and his men? Ride here and fight with me, if you dare! You do not need to be afraid of my men."

One Parisian answered: "Keep riding and don't stop here! But if you are looking for Flovent, you can find him in Corbeille, along with the Franks and a large number of citizens from Paris. And the good god Tervagant knows that if you find Flovent he will not flee, but will instead cut off your arrogant head."

When Gernimer heard what he said, he quickly turned his army around and headed for Corbeille. The day waned now and the sun set, while the hills and dales glinted from the weapons of the pagans.

It is time to speak of the Franks, who had removed their armor, but when they reached a certain valley, they were confronted by a large army of Saxons who killed many Franks.

It is time to speak of Gernimer: he was as well armed as he pleased, and he sat on a good horse. He rode at a Frank now and struck at his head, splitting it, and also his chest with its hauberk, and he flung him dead to the ground.

Then he called out in a loud voice: "Where are you, Flovent? Are you afraid of me that you dare not ride forward? Your last day has come."

Flovent heard his abusive words and spurred his horse on, charging like a bolt of lightning at him with his spear. His hauberk was sturdy, however, and that saved his life, but he was thrown off his horse, landing far off on the ground. At this moment, Isaac, Gernimer's brother, struck Flovent in the chest with his spear, for he was not wearing a hauberk, and he was seriously wounded.

Salatres rode at once to Corbeille, as the battle was being waged in the valley, and the citizens rejoiced at his return.

Flovent realized that he was wounded and rode into the battle array and dismounted. Otun and Jofrey accompanied him, and he said to them:

"Good friends, I shall be disgraced, if I do not avenge myself. I now ask you to do what I want, namely make the pagans pay dearly for me."

Then, as fierce as a lion, he mounted his horse.

"Moreover, it is to be expected," says Master Simon, "that he will quickly avenge himself on his enemies."

THE ROMANCE EPIC OF FLOVENT • 155

Otun and Jofrey and 15,000 knights egged one another on to avenge Flovent, who then spoke:

"May God give us the strength and determination in the battle against our enemies. And if we should die, let us end our lives as valiant men, for it is better to die bravely than to live in shame."

Flovent now egged his men on, and they attacked well. The trumpets in Flovent's army blared, and the valleys resounded from the clash of weapons. The Saxons assaulted them now and a terrible battle took place. There were so many dead that they could not be counted. The king's sons fought brutally and whoever crossed their path met up with death. King Florent proved to be good, as were all the Franks. Flovent, however, had not lost heart in this respect, and it was as though he had awakened from sleep to do battle. No one in the army was superior to him. He struck the Saxons down as though they were twigs.

Otun said: "God watch over you, Lord; never before have I seen you this angry. Protect yourself!"

Flovent answered: "I cannot live anymore, unless I have freed the country that God has given me."

Isaac, the king's son, now attacked King Florent, and thrust his spear into his shield so that the spear shaft broke. He then drew his sword and struck the shoulder of the king and sliced all the way down to his hip on that side, and he cast him dead onto the ground. Then he raised his sword and boasted of his victory.

When the Franks saw that their king had been slain, flight broke out in their army. Otun then said to Flovent: "Lord, the news is bad; the king of the Franks has been slain, and nearly all the Franks are fleeing. No more than 15,000 are left, but the Saxons are so many that they are six to one of us. Let us now retreat."

But Flovent responded: "We should get one of their leaders in exchange for our king, or else be killed."

Flovent now rode at King Almatur and chopped his shield in two. Almatur struck Flovent's shield and aimed his spear at the horse's belly, but it reared and the spear shaft broke. Flovent then struck the king's head with his sword, splitting his body as he fell down dead, and he said: "You shall not be celebrating your wedding to the king's daughter tonight."

Then he spoke to his men: "Let's head for Paris now, not in flight, but rather in battle array, for we shall then be less easily attacked."

They headed for Paris in battle array, but the hostile Saxons pursued them. Flovent and his men often turned around to face them and killed many men. When they were approaching the city, the king's sons shouted to their army: "Let us return," they said, "after our fine victory, and not pursue them any longer."

156 • THE ROMANCE EPIC OF FLOVENT

They now turned back and met their father and said that they no longer wanted to stay in France. "We have lands enough as well as other kingdoms."

Salatres, the sovereign king, asked them to settle this among themselves, and he said that he would ride back to Corbeille to get his daughter and the money. "But you ride back to Saxony, and in another month I shall come to you." They now parted; the king's sons went back to Saxony, and the king to Corbeille, to have his wounds cared for.

21. King Salatres is defeated by Flovent.

It is time to tell about Flovent. He is in Paris, very much grief-stricken at the king's death, and he consulted the wisest men. After a week he convened a meeting in the city and said that he intended to go to Corbeille to arrange a settlement with King Salatres. All the Franks said that they would gladly accompany him. They mounted their horses, and 20,000 knights, as well as 20,000 citizens, left Paris.

They arrived in Corbeille at sunset. This fortress was so strong that it had never before been captured by anyone, for a high and strong stone wall surrounded it, and a broad and deep moat encircled this wall. While there were bridges across the moat by day, the fortress was locked at night. Flovent ordered the entire army to go into the woods, a short distance from the fortress, and they were to gather bundles of wood and fill the moat with them. And this was done. Then Flovent had the wood set on fire and there was a great blaze. When the wall heated up, the lime mortar weakened. Then catapults were used and the wall collapsed and fell into the water, cooling the stones, and Flovent and his men prepared to enter. Those in the fortress, however, had few soldiers for the defense. Flovent's men entered the fortress with shouting and the sound of trumpets.

King Salatres proffered strong resistance, but he was outmanned and thus captured, and he asked that his life be spared.

Flovent agreed, "If you keep the promise that you have made, that is, to give me the kingdom and its riches, and also your daughter Marsibilia in marriage, and that you swear an oath that you will never again come into France waging war, for it is God's will that I am to be the rightfully appointed ruler of France."

The king spoke: "I promise you that, for I agree that my daughter could never have a worthier husband than you. And as her dowry I give you the dominions of the three kings whom you slew, and you shall be my support in everything that befits you." Flovent agreed to this.

The truce was sworn and then the betrothal took place. The beautiful princess Marsibilia, the king's daughter, was led in. Since the Passion of Christ no equal to her in beauty has ever been born. Only one thing was wanting: that she live forever and never die.

THE ROMANCE EPIC OF FLOVENT • 157

Thereupon Flovent sent for bishops and other clerics in Rome. Most people believe that St Mark was pope at the time.[22] He sent an excellent bishop along with many clerics. Marsibilia was then christened along with many others. Flovent had a superb feast prepared in Paris. He issued a directive that everyone in France should support Christendom and the holy faith, and renounce pagan sacrifices. He had a public assembly convoked and summoned the entire population. Everyone there acclaimed him king and accepted all his mandates.

22. Flovent comes to the aid of Emperor Constantine against the pagans.
The date for the wedding of Flovent and Marsibilia, the king's daughter, was set, and the celebration took place with great enthusiasm and lasted as long as was the custom in the country. After the celebration, King Salatres returned to his kingdom with great honors that Flovent had bestowed on him.

Flovent Christianized all of France and had many churches built; he destroyed all the pagan temples or had them consecrated as churches.

Flovent now learned the news that King Ammiral of Spain had invaded Rome with an innumerable army of pagans. Emperor Constantine had repeatedly engaged in battle with him, but was not successful, and he had confined himself to the city. When King Flovent received news of this, he assembled an army in France and then rode to Rome. As soon as he approached the camp of the pagans, he had the trumpets sounded, and a fierce battle ensued. When the emperor learned that a large army had come to his aid, he had the city opened and he rode against the pagans himself. There were renewed massacres. Flovent was easy to recognize in the army, for he encountered no nobleman so haughty that he did not quickly bring him down to the ground. He had his sword in his hand and both arms were bloodied all the way up to his shoulders. As before, Otun and Jofrey accompanied him now with great prowess and courage. Finally, Flovent rode into the midst of the battle array of King Ammiral and killed him with one stroke of his sword. After this the pagans took flight, but the Christians pursued the fleeing pagans and struck them down like cattle. When they had pursued those fleeing, the emperor turned back and greeted Flovent, his nephew, most happily and kissed him and thanked God and Flovent for his victory.

Following this, Flovent stayed for a time in Rome and he was crowned king by Pope Mark on the Feast of the Annunciation of Mary.[23] After all these events he returned to France, having been greatly honored by the emperor, his uncle. When he came home, the queen was very happy, as was the entire country. Otun then married Fauseta and King Flovent gave him Corbeille and made him its

22. Pope St Mark died in the year 336.
23. March 25.

king. Jofrey married Florenta and Flovent gave him Normandy and made him its king. They thanked him graciously for his gifts now and then traveled to their kingdoms.

Flovent reigned as sovereign king over all of France now and was known for his countless outstanding accomplishments, which are too many to relate. He and Queen Marsibilia had sons who were excellent men. Flovent now ruled his kingdom for many years. He was powerful and righteous, honest and excellent. He finally died of illness in his old age and was interred near the church of God's mother Mary, which he had built for the salvation of his soul, and in honor of God, the Father and the Son and the Holy Spirit, who lives and reigns forever and ever.

The Romance Epic of Bevers

1. Concerning Earl Gujon of Hampton.

Gujon was a mighty earl in England, who resided in a place called Hampton. With his sword he had conquered many kingdoms. In his day there was no better knight than he in Christendom. He was an old man and there was no heir for the kingdom. His counsellors thought this would be disastrous, and they advised him to get married. Gujon therefore sent messengers with a letter to the king of Scotland, asking for the hand of his daughter in marriage; she was a most beautiful woman. The emperor of Germany had earlier asked for her hand in marriage, but the king did not want her to marry him. Although Gujon was old, he preferred to marry his daughter to the earl on account of his valor and chivalry, rather than to the emperor, despite his might, yet cowardice.

The maiden was now sent to England and Earl Gujon celebrated their marriage. When they had been married only a short time, they had a son, who was named Bevers. He was the fairest of children. He grew up at the court of his father, and when he was eleven years old, there was no fifteen-year-old in England who was his match in height and physical strength, in all chivalric deeds and accomplishments.

His mother was young and the fairest of women, as was written above. Yet although she was very beautiful, she was most devious and wicked. It vexed her that she should be married to such an old man. She thought it appalling not to be married to the emperor, and she thought both night and day about how she might betray her husband and have the emperor instead.

2. The Queen's betrayal.

It now happened one time, when the queen was in her chambers, that she called for a page whom she considered most devoted to her and spoke to him: "You are going to leave on a mission to the emperor in Germany with a letter from me. You must promise me that you will tell the English that you are going on a pilgrimage to Cologne. You shall give the emperor the letter and return as quickly as possible to me and tell me about your mission."

160 • THE ROMANCE EPIC OF BEVERS

The page left and did not stop until he met the emperor and delivered the queen's letter to him. The emperor immediately opened the letter and read it. It said that she sends her greetings, along with her burning love:

You should know that when you asked for me in marriage, my father did not want to give me in marriage to you, but that was not my doing, for I wanted to have you as much as I wanted to live. And I have loved you ever since that time. If you are willing to do something for my sake, then kill that accursed fellow whom I was forced to marry. But this has to be well planned, for it cannot be carried out if he suspects something. Therefore I ask you to come with a hundred men on the first day of May to the hunting woods that are but a short distance from Hampton. I shall have Earl Gujon go there alone, and I ask you to arrange matters so that he will never again come into my bed. And you will earn my love if you bring me his head.

When the emperor had read her letter, he was very happy and he had a horse given to the messenger, along with twenty gold coins. He stayed with the emperor for half a month, and then took leave of him and returned home. He gave his lady the letter the emperor sent her, in which he said that he would come for her sake, as she had asked. When the time came, the emperor secretly left Cologne and did not stop until he had crossed the sea and arrived in England and had come to the hunting woods on the day she had requested.

3. Earl Gujon is killed.

Now the tale turns to Earl Gujon: early on the first day of May, as they were lying in bed, his wife spoke to the earl and said that she was very sick. The earl asked about her illness and asked her to tell him if she craved a certain food. She said: "If I might have some wild boar meat, I expect that I would quickly be restored to health."

"God knows," said the earl, "I shall happily try to get some wild boar meat."

The earl now mounted his horse and took along a short sword and his shield. He wore neither his hauberk nor his helmet nor any knightly attire.

When the earl and his men came to the hunting ground that was mentioned earlier, the emperor and his men rushed out at them, and the emperor called out in a loud voice: "You, old man," he said, "come here. I swear that you shall lose your life here. I shall have your son Bevers hanged, and I shall marry your wife against your will and seize all of your possessions by force and also your earldom."

Earl Gujon responded: "Your conduct is evil and unjust, since you seek my life for no cause, and I swear by my God that if there were more of us and I had my hauberk and my helmet, I would never be afraid of you. And I pray to the Holy Spirit that were I to die here today that my sins will be forgiven."

Then the earl rushed at the emperor, drew his sword and struck him so hard that he was flung off his horse. And one hundred men immediately rushed at the earl, assaulting and striking him. He defended himself with such great prowess that in a short time he had killed sixty knights, yet he had received many wounds, all of which were mortal. When he realized he was terribly wounded and saw his three companions lying dead next to him, he was terribly worried and realized that his best chance was to surrender to the emperor, and he got down on his knee before him and said: "I ask for your mercy and present my sword to you, and additionally I surrender all my worldly possessions to you except for my child and wife and you will never have to fear me."

The emperor then answered: "That will never happen, as long as you live." And he quickly drew his sword and beheaded the earl. After this he called for one of his knights and said to him: "Take this head to the Lady of Hampton, my beloved, and greet her for me."

The knight left with the head of Earl Gujon. When he approached the lady, he greeted her on behalf of the emperor and spoke: "Lady," he said, "my lord has sent me here with evidence that he has killed your lord and husband, and he shall come to you if you so desire."

Then the lady said: "Sir knight," she said, "you should return as quickly as possible to the emperor. Greet him on my behalf and say that he should come here without delay, for our wedding shall take place tomorrow."

The knight returned now and told his lord, the emperor, the state of things.

4. Concerning Bevers and Sabaoth.

Now we shall report what the son of Earl Gujon, who is called Bevers of Hampton, did when he heard about the crime committed against his father. He cried pitifully over the death of his father and he went to his mother, angered deep in his heart, and said: "You evil whore, what was your reason for having my father killed? In an evil hour you were created so beautiful, you malevolent strumpet. I swear by the one born of the dear Virgin Mary, if I live long enough to be able to sit on a horse and bear weapons, I shall repay you for what I have learned has happened."

When his mother heard what he said, she became angry and struck him so hard that he fell on the ground in front of her.

Now an old knight jumped up, whose name was Sabaoth – he had long served Bevers's father – and quickly picked up the boy, intending to carry him to his room. He was the boy's foster-father and loved him very much.

When the Lady saw this, she called out to Sabaoth and said: "Sabaoth, you have to swear that you will have the boy killed by evening. In exchange you can have from me anything you desire."

162 • THE ROMANCE EPIC OF BEVERS

"My Lady," said Sabaoth, "I shall gladly do as you wish," and he took the boy home with him.

As soon as he came home, he had a pig killed and its blood collected. He smeared this blood on Bevers's garments and then had them hung in a mill as proof that the boy had been killed.

Then he called for Bevers and said: "You must now listen to my advice: you shall guard my lambs and dress shoddily for seven days. After that I shall send you to another kingdom, to an earl who is my best friend. You shall stay there until you are sixteen years old, when you will be allowed to bear weapons. Then you shall engage the emperor in a duel, and I shall help you as best I can."

The boy thanked him and now left to guard the lambs.

When he was on the heath with the lambs, he looked about and to his right he heard and saw the big feast in his father's castle, where the emperor was celebrating the wedding with his mother. Bevers wondered what the merriment was all about, and he took his club and went to his father's castle and spoke to the gate keeper: "I ask you to let me in, for I have some urgent business with the emperor."

The gate keeper responded angrily: "Get lost, you evil whore's son, you churlish and wicked person."

Bevers answered: "So help me God, indeed I am a whore's son, as you say and I understand, for you are right. But you lie, when you call me a churlish and wicked person, and you shall now find out whether it is as you say," and Bevers now raised his club like a grownup, and not like a child, and struck the gate keeper so hard on his head that his brains spilled out onto the ground.

After that he walked into the hall and up to the emperor and spoke boldly to him in the hearing of all: "Lord king," he said, "who gave you permission to embrace the woman who is sitting next to you? I do not want to deny that she is my mother. But because you did not request that I grant her in marriage nor asked for my permission,[1] you shall pay dearly for her love. I know for sure that you killed my father without cause, and therefore I ask you for God's sake that you return to me my estates and patrimony."

At this the emperor answered: "Be silent, you fool and idiot, you don't know what you are saying."

When Bevers heard this he got exceedingly angry and raised his club and struck three blows on the emperor's head, each time inflicting a great wound,

1. Bevers's statement that the emperor did not ask him to be allowed to marry his mother and that he did not give his permission for him to do so, reflects what happens in the Sagas of Icelanders, where marriages are agreed upon between a woman's father and the prospective groom. Here Bevers takes on the role of the father. See Jenny Jochens, *Women in Old Norse Society* (Ithaca and London, 1995), 44–45.

THE ROMANCE EPIC OF BEVERS • **163**

and he swore by the Holy Spirit that this should end with his death, since he wanted to deprive him of his patrimony.

When Bevers's mother saw this, she cried out in a loud voice and said that the boy should be seized. But the knights who had served his father ran up and recognized him and were greatly distressed that the boy was so poorly dressed, and they pretended to be seizing him, but they let him escape.

He now ran back to his foster-father. When Sabaoth saw him, he asked why he was running so fast. Bevers answered: "I have killed my stepfather, the emperor. I inflicted three wounds on him, which will never heal." When Lord Sabaoth heard what Bevers told him, he said: "My dear son, now you are quite guilty of not following my advice, and your mother will have me killed because of you." When Bevers heard this he cried greatly over his foster-father's anguish.

Lord Sabaoth now took the boy and put him in a secret chamber. The lady, the boy's mother, came and called on Lord Sabaoth and asked where the wicked boy was. "My lady," said Sabaoth, "you should not be asking me that, since you commanded me to kill him, and I did indeed kill him and hanged him by a mill. Afterwards I threw him into a lake." "God knows," said the lady, "you are lying. If you do not want to give my son back to me, I shall have you burned."

When Bevers heard her in his hiding place, how she threatened Sabaoth, his foster-father, he was displeased and ran out to his mother and said: "Lady," he said, "don't ask about my whereabouts. I am here and you must not accuse my lord and harm him on account of me. Let me pay for this myself."

With evil intent the lady then took ahold of her son and summoned two knights and ordered them to take Bevers, go out to sea with him, and sell him if someone wants to buy him – "otherwise drown him, so that he won't ever come back."

5. Bevers comes to Egypt.

They now seized the boy and sailed with him out to sea and there encountered a sailing galley full of Saracens. And the knights offered the boy for sale. When the Saracens saw how beautiful the boy was, they bought him for four times his weight in gold. When they were ready, they set out to sea and came to Egypt. Bevers never stopped crying over the death of his father.

The king of this country was named Erminrik. He was an old man with white hair and a long beard. His wife, who was named Marage, had died. He had a daughter who was both wise and beautiful. Her name was Josvena; she was young and no one in the world was more beautiful than she. Her father loved her above all else. The Saracens came to this king and brought him the boy. Even though he considered the boy an honorable gift, he asked from where he had come and

164 • THE ROMANCE EPIC OF BEVERS

what his name was. "Mahomet, my god, knows" he said, "I have never seen a more beautiful child. If you are willing to believe in Mahomet, you shall never be parted from me."

Bevers answered: "I am the son of an English earl named Gujon in a place called Hampton. My mother had him treacherously killed and then she married an emperor against my will. And I swear to Almighty God that if I live long enough to be able to bear weapons, I shall ruthlessly avenge this."

When the king heard this, he thought it troubling and spoke: "I swear by Mahomet, if you are willing to become a Saracen, you will become a valiant man. I have nothing better to offer you than my daughter, who has no equal. I will gladly give her to you in marriage, bestow knighthood on you, and give you my kingdom, if you are willing to worship our gods."

But Bevers responded: "What you propose is great folly, not for all the lands in the world would I ever forsake Jesus Christ, who was born by the power of the Holy Spirit of the Virgin Mary. But Mahomet, your god, can't do as much as can a mouse, for a mouse can move, but your god cannot do that, and everyone who believes in him perishes."

The king then said: "Bevers, you have a steadfast heart, and if you do not want to worship my god Mahomet, then you shall serve me at table, and when you have reached the age that you are able to bear weapons, I shall dub you a knight and you will be my squire and counsellor, and in battle you will carry my standard." Some time now passed.

6. Bevers slays a wild boar and kills seven men.

Bevers now lived with King Erminrik, and the king loved the boy very much. There were eleven knights at the royal court who were most displeased that Bevers was so intimate with the king, for they knew that Bevers had been purchased and subsequently given to the king. They hated him and spoke rudely to him. Now when he was sixteen years old, he was so advanced in valor and strength that no knight at the royal court dared joust or tilt with him, for he was exceedingly strong.

At that time there was a wild boar in the country which killed everything in its path, both large and small. And even though twenty fully armed knights confronted the animal, it took no more notice than if they had been ptarmigan, even though they were all hardy and dauntless.

Since Bevers often heard stories about this wild boar, he got up early one morning, took his sword and spear and mounted his horse. He wore neither plate armor nor a gambeson nor a hauberk and he had no other weapons than the aforementioned.

Josvena, the king's daughter, had risen early in the morning and stood in the castle's tower. As soon as she saw Bevers ride forth, she fell in love with him, and she spilled and shed many a tear on his account.

When Bevers came into the woods looking for the wild boar, he soon found the animal. When the boar saw him, it rushed at him and began to snort and grunt terribly, as though it intended to devour him, and it rushed at Bevers with gaping jaws. When Bevers saw this, he spurred his horse on and held his spear at the ready and thrust it with such energy into the boar's open jaws that the spear broke, but the spearhead struck the boar's heart and the boar died at once. Bevers then cut the boar's head off and set it on the spear's shaft.

The maiden Josvena closely watched what Bevers was doing and considered it most notable, and she said: "Mahomet, my god, see what a valiant man Bevers is, who was begotten in a good hour. May Mahomet grant me to become his beloved. Were I to be deprived of his love, I would cease to live." She often said this while weeping and sighing wholeheartedly, but Bevers did not know this.

When Bevers had mounted his good horse again and came out of the woods, eleven armed men rushed at him. They were his utter enemies and they shouted all at once and said that he ought not ride onwards. When Bevers heard them and wanted to grasp his sword, it was gone, for he had forgotten it after he had struck off the boar's head. The four men struck Bevers's shield all at once and their spears broke. Bevers quickly took the broken spear he had in his hand, however, and killed two with one blow and then one after the other, until seven were dead. And when the others saw their companions slain, they turned around and fled.

When the maiden saw their fighting, she was much heartened and asked Mahomet to grant her the affection of Bevers, the valiant.

Bevers now returned to the castle and brought the king the head of the wild boar. The king thanked him very much for his catch.

7. Bevers defeats Brandamon.

Some time later King Erminrik went into the castle to his daughter and saw down through a window that a large army of Saracens had arrived on the plain. The captain of this army was a king named Brandamon from Damascus. He had an army of 100,000 knights. King Brandamon now had a message sent to King Erminrik that he had sworn by Mahomet that he would either obtain his daughter in marriage or else he would lay waste his land so that he then would not have any more than what was needed, or even less, to set his two feet down.

When the king heard this, he became so angry that he nearly lost his mind, and he convened all his knights and special forces and gave them this news and

166 • THE ROMANCE EPIC OF BEVERS

asked what might be the best decision to take in this matter. But there was no one in the king's court who wanted to take on the command of his army, because they were all afraid and cowards. Josvena came into the hall now and went to her father. He informed her of the news he had received and also that his knights were terrible cowards. Josvena then said to her father: "I witnessed earlier today the great prowess that Bevers demonstrated. If you were willing to dub him a knight and give him your standard and appoint him captain of your army, then I expect that he will lack neither the temper nor the prowess to lead your army."

And King Erminrik immediately had Bevers summoned and said to him: "I shall dub you a knight, and you will bear my standard." "I shall gladly carry out your command," said Bevers, "whatever you want me to do."

Now appropriate greaves were put on his shins. Then he was outfitted with a hauberk that was so good that never was there a better shield, for no weapon could pierce it. Then the king attached golden spurs to his feet. Afterwards the king girded Bevers with a good sword; no better was ever made of steel or iron. It was named Myrklei, and with this sword Bevers subsequently acquired many a kingdom. The maiden Josvena gave him her good horse; never was there a better or a swifter horse. Bevers was now a knight and had weapons as he wished and the horse Arundele. The horse was of such a nature that no one could ride it unless one was a good knight and came from a noble family. Bevers now mounted the horse and let it run while everyone there watched. Everyone praised his valor and bravery. Bevers now blew his horn very loudly and everyone in the place immediately got armed. King Erminrik, the White-bearded, now came, and all his knights were commissioned under Bevers's leadership. Bevers rode out, carrying the king's standard. A lion was depicted on his shield, which symbolized his bravery.

King Brandamon, the Powerful, now approached with an army that was twenty times greater than Bevers's army. A large and evil Saracen carried the standard of King Brandamon. His name was Radifann, and he was as hairy as a bear or a wild boar. He carried a big spear to which the standard was affixed with four golden nails. When Bevers saw him, he spurred Arundele on and galloped toward him and attacked him with all his might. And the Saracen's shield served him not a whit, for Bevers washed the spear and standard in the Saracen's blood, and he fell dead to the ground. "You filthy whore's son," said Bevers, "it would have been better had you stayed at home than come here." Then Bevers called out loudly to his companions and asked them to advance boldly: "Ours is the first strike and we shall be victorious." When they heard what he said, they rejoiced and vigorously dashed forward and killed 400 of Brandamon's men. Bevers drew his sword Myrklei and struck on either side, so that no one survived. When his enemies saw this, they were as afraid of him as a little bird facing a hawk. They saw that their standard bearer had fallen and they rushed off and fled. Bevers's companions were now intrepid and valiant and they feared their enemies no more than wolves fear lambs.

When King Brandamon saw his men fleeing, he shouted at them and told them to proceed boldly forward and kill King Erminrik's men – "or else receive from me not a thing that is worth even one penny."

When Bevers heard what he said, he laughed at him and spoke: "Why have you come here? Did you think you would get the lady Josvena? You will never obtain her as your wife, but you will be hung instead on the gallows for your wiliness, and all of your men will die here."

Bevers now rode boldly forward and emptied many a saddle. And before midday all of King Brandamon's men had been killed, and the king himself fled. He had tied up twelve of King Erminrik's men, whom he wanted to take back with him, and he swore by Mahomet that he would have all of them flayed alive.

When Bevers saw King Brandamon riding off, he spurred his horse on and called out to King Brandamon with a loud voice: "You will wait for me whether you like it or not," and he brandished his sword Myrklei and dealt the king such a great blow that he fell instantly to the ground. Bevers stood over him and wanted to cut his throat.

And when King Brandamon realized that he had been defeated and that Bevers was holding a sword over his head, he got on his knees and said: "In exchange for your sharp blow, I surrender my sword and also myself, and additionally give you four hundred market towns and more than a thousand castles and fortresses, and I shall hold my entire kingdom in fief to you."

Bevers answered: "I shall save your life on condition that you become King Erminrik's vassal and hold your entire country in fief to him. Moreover, you must swear never to attack me."

When King Brandamon had promised this, Bevers had him get up and return home – which was rather imprudent.

Bevers now went to where his companions were tied up and released all of them. Then he rode to the castle and stepped before King Erminrik and told him that all the lands belonging to King Brandamon were now held by him in fief, together with their taxes and duties, "and the king himself is now your vassal."

King Erminrik now thanked Bevers exceedingly and asked his daughter Josvena to take him to his chamber and remove his armor – "and you yourself shall serve him food and drink in your room; he is well deserving of this."

"I shall gladly do so," she said. The maiden took him by the hand and led him to a room and removed his armor and brought him suitable garments.

168 • THE ROMANCE EPIC OF BEVERS

Afterwards they sat down to eat in a small well-furnished room. She served him attentively and respectfully, and she was both beautiful and polite. She cut the meat for him and poured his drink, while secretly hiding her anguish.

8. Concerning Bevers and Josvena.

When they had eaten and drunk, Josvena started to speak: "Fair lord and valiant knight! I am not able to conceal from you that on account of my love for you I have wept many a tear and had many a sleepless night. And for that reason, I ask you not to spurn my feelings for you. Otherwise I shall not live long, if your feelings for me are not similar to mine for you."

To this Bevers responded: "My dear lady," he said, "you should not dwell on this, since it is imprudent. I do not intend to betray my lord, King Erminrik. King Brandamon was here the other day and asked for your hand in marriage, but you refused him. I know of no gallant king who would not long for your love once he sees your beauty. I am a poor man, however, from a foreign country, and it is childish of you to want to throw your lot in life with someone like me."

The king's daughter answered: "I would rather have you with nothing but a tunic than some king with thirty kingdoms. Return my love as beseems a noble from a reputable family."

"I would not do that so recklessly," said Bevers, "for you do not believe in the God in whom I believe."

Now, when she heard this, she turned black as coal, and in her sorrow she fell down unconscious. When she recovered consciousness, she began to cry in her heartfelt anguish. "God knows," said Josvena to Bevers, "it is true that there is no nobleman who would not gladly marry me, if I agreed to do so. But you have refused me and have behaved like a rude peasant, and it would be better for you to herd cattle, guard horses, and run around barefooted like a ruffian than to be a knight at a court like the one my father holds. Go back to your country, you cruel man."

Bevers answered now: "Fair maiden," he said, "what you say, that I am a peasant and a cruel man, is not true, and you have reproached me without cause. This is how you reward me for the service I have rendered today to your father and you! I now want to return to my own country, and you shall never see me again. You gave me a horse: take it back, for I do not want to have anything of yours, considering your resentment and threats. But you will not get back the sword Myrklei, for I have paid enough for it."

When Josvena heard this, it nearly broke her heart. But Bevers left and found lodging with a burgess, and there he was able to rest up after his great physical exertions during the day. He lay down on a bed and was exceedingly angry about the maiden's words.

THE ROMANCE EPIC OF BEVERS • 169

When Bevers had left, Josvena stood up and thought about how she had wrongfully accused Bevers, and now she cried her eyes out and greatly regretted her offenses, and she called a devoted young man to her and said: "My dear," she said, "do me a favor and go to Lord Bevers, wherever he might be, and ask him to heed my request to come talk to me. And tell him that I want to make up for having offended him."

"My lady," he said, "I shall gladly do as you wish." And he now went looking for Bevers and found him in the middle of the city and spoke to him: "My lady Josvena has sent me to you with the message that she is asking you with all her heart to come speak with her one last time before you depart."

Bevers answered: "You can tell Josvena that you gained nothing from your errand other than that you conveyed her message, and that I have given you an outer garment." This was a garment of costly silk fashioned far beyond the sea.

The messenger thanked him profusely and went back to Josvena to tell her what had occurred.

When Josvena saw the young man, she asked him where he had gotten the costly silk. He said that Bevers had given it to him as thanks for his errand. "By Mahomet," said the maiden, "Bevers is both generous and chivalrous, and I know for sure that he was never a peasant or kinsman of one. Since he does not want to come to me, I shall instead go to him myself, whether he likes it or not."

She now went to the place the young man had indicated. When Bevers saw that she had come, he pretended to be sleeping and snored loudly, for he did not want to talk to her. Josvena went to the bed in which he was lying, and spoke to him: "Wake up, my dear" she said, "good friend and dear beloved. I would like to talk with you."

When Bevers saw her, he spoke: "Lady Josvena, let me rest, for I am very tired from today's exertions. You have rewarded me poorly, when you called me a ruffian and a wicked man."

When she heard this, she began to cry, and her bright tears moistened her face. When Bevers realized this, he thought her grief quite distressing.

Then she said to Lord Bevers: "Gracious knight, Lord Bevers," she said, "forgive me. I will gladly make up for anything I have done to offend you. I want to reject all idolatry and to believe in the true God, who was born of the pure maiden and virgin, and who was crucified."

Bevers answered: "I happily want that." And immediately he kissed her more than a hundred times. But what he did was a poor decision, which he would soon regret, because the two knights, whom he had freed from King Brandamon's shackles, were aware of what had happened, and went to King Erminrik and said:

"Lord King, you ought to be exceedingly angry at Bevers, since he has slept with your daughter, that wicked miscreant."

Those evil men lied, however, for Bevers had not done any more than kiss her, as was told earlier, because he did not want to engage in sexual intercourse with her before she was baptized.

9. The betrayal of Bevers.

When King Erminrik heard this, he shook his head and spoke: "Do you know whether this is true?"

One of them answered: "Mahomet knows that I am not lying."

"Good lords," said the king, "what advice do you give me concerning this? Ever since he first came here, I have loved him greatly, and I think it would be quite grievous to have him killed; indeed, I would soon die if I were to see him killed."

"Lord," one of them said, "we have good advice at hand: Have a letter with your seal quickly readied. Give this to Bevers and have him swear that he will not deliver the letter to any man other than King Brandamon. The letter should state that King Brandamon should put Bevers in a place where you will never see him again or hear any news of him, provided Brandamon wishes to do something to please you."

The letter was now prepared and Sir Bevers was called. The king then said to Bevers: "You are to be my emissary to King Brandamon in Damascus, and you are to swear that you will show this letter to none other than King Brandamon."

"Lord," said Bevers, "I shall gladly do as you bid; give me the letter and have my horse fetched and also my sharp sword."

"Sir Bevers," said the king, "a good palfrey would be better, since it would carry you more comfortably on this journey. And your sword Myrklei is too heavy. I shall give you another sword that is just as good."

Bevers now got the letter and took leave of the king. The maiden Josvena knew nothing about this. Bevers now rode his way; may God keep him.

He rode for some three days, over mountains and through valleys, and he encountered no one. But one day, as he was riding along, he ran into a pilgrim sitting under a tree and starting to eat. He had three loaves of good French bread and two casks of spiced wine. He was the son of Sabaoth, Bevers's foster-father, and had gone looking for him, ever since he was sold to the Saracens. The pilgrim said: "Welcome, fair lord, dismount for God's sake and eat with me."

Bevers gladly accepted this, dismounted, and sat down to eat. He was very hungry and ate quickly, but nonetheless with fine manners. The pilgrim willingly served him good food.

THE ROMANCE EPIC OF BEVERS · 171

When Bevers had eaten and drunk, he looked at the pilgrim and said to him: "Tell me the truth, friend, and don't fool me: From where do you come, and where were you born?"

"Sir," said the pilgrim, "I was born in a fine place, in Hampton. My father's name is Sabaoth and I am called Terri. When we parted, he asked me to look for a child who was by chance sold to Saracens. His name is Bevers; may God keep him. I have not found him anywhere, and I am therefore upset. If you know anything about his whereabouts, please tell me."

"You need not look any longer," said Bevers, "for I saw that the child for whom you are looking was hanged."

When the pilgrim heard that, he cried out loudly, greatly distressed, and spoke: "Lord God, who created me, if only my companion Bevers had not been killed like this!" And he fell unconscious. When he came to, he asked: "What is your name and on what errand are you? If you are carrying a letter, you would do well to show it to me."

"No," said Bevers, "I shall show it to no one but King Brandamon."

"By my troth," said the pilgrim, "this is not proper, for your letter might mean nothing else but your death."

Bevers answered: "I do not fear that, for my lord would rather lose ten market towns than me." Bevers did not want to give the pilgrim his name.

10. **Bevers kills a temple priest.**

Bevers and the pilgrim parted after this and kissed each other. He rode his way, laughing and singing, and did not stop until he reached Damascus. This was the most famous market town in the world, and everything one might desire could be had there. On top of the tower of the castle in which the king resided, there was an eagle cast of gold and in its claws it held a carbuncle that shone so brightly that there never was darkness, for it radiated like the sun.[2]

When Bevers entered the city, he rode boldly into the pagan temple, where he heard singing, as the Saracens worshipped their god, and there were more than a thousand priests. Bevers dismounted and went fearlessly into the temple and broke one priest's neck. When the others saw this, they fled as fast as they

2. The motif of a light-radiating carbuncle appears in one of the oldest *chansons de geste*, namely in the *Pèlerinage de Charlemagne*, which is translated in *Karlamagnus saga*, where it is entitled *Af Jorsalaferð* (Voyage to Jerusalem). Here Charlemagne is wined and dined in Constantinople by King Hugon, and subsequently he is taken to the dormitory which is lit day and night by a carbuncle. For the passage in *Jorsalaferð*, see *Karlamagnus saga ok kappa hans*, ed. C.R. Unger (Kristiania [Oslo], 1860), 473. See also Margaret Schlauch, *Romance in Iceland* (Princeton and New York, 1934), 157–58.

172 • THE ROMANCE EPIC OF BEVERS

could and told King Brandamon that a knight had come and had smashed their gods Mahomet and Tervagant, "and would have killed and disgraced us, had we not fled."

"Stop your babbling," he said; I think I know that it is the knight Bevers, my lord, who has come. Let him do whatever he wants and don't be so impudent as to criticize him."

11. Bevers is incarcerated.

On that same day King Brandamon held a great feast and he sat on the golden throne amid his knights. When King Brandamon saw Bevers enter the hall, he stood up to greet him and asked him to sit next to him.

Bevers spoke: "Quickly read this letter, else I shall behead you." King Brandamon got angry at Bevers and quickly took the letter and read it. When he realized what was in it, his heart laughed, and he reached for Bevers's right hand, so that he could not draw his sword, and he ordered his men to stand up and securely shackle him. "King Erminrik has commanded me to have him hanged, for he said that he had slept with his daughter." They shackled him thoroughly, and around his neck they placed fetters that weighed fifteen pounds.

Then the king spoke to Bevers: "I swear, had you not vanquished me with your sword, you would be hanged at once. But I shall have you first feel some pain: you will end your life in the deepest and worst dungeon, which is thirty steps down to the bottom, and you will never be able to satisfy your cravings or needs. Snakes and toads and other poisonous animals shall rip you apart. Such thick steel spikes are placed there so that your entire body will be maimed. And on no day will you have more food than a quarter of a barley loaf. But before that happens, you will first go to table and eat your fill for the sake of our gods whom we are honoring today."

When Bevers was sated they led him, hands and feet bound, to the dungeon, and threw him headfirst into the dungeon. But God helped him so that he was not injured. When he landed down there he encountered all kinds of poisonous creatures seeking to sting him. He managed to free his hands, however, and looked around and found a staff and with it he killed all the poisonous creatures. He now suffered excruciating pain, for his hunger was never satisfied by the bread. Two knights guarded the dungeon.

Bevers spoke to himself: "Lord God," he said, "help me for the sake of your holy name out of my torment. If I am freed, I swear by St Peter in Rome that I shall take away King Erminrik's crown and strike him myself so many times that he will never again deceive any man, for he has betrayed me dreadfully, even though I never deserved this."

THE ROMANCE EPIC OF BEVERS • 173

Bevers now lamented; he cried grievously and asked for God's mercy. Then one night an adder bit him on his forehead as he was sleeping. But when he woke up, he was able to get ahold of the poisonous creature and kill it.

12. Josvena seeks information about Bevers.

Now it is time to tell about King Erminrik and his daughter Josvena. She knew nothing about Bevers's betrayal. One day she went to her father and asked: "Where is Bevers whom you loved so much?"

"My dear daughter," he said, "he has gone back to England to kill his stepfather. And I do not think that he will ever come back."

When the maiden heard this, she could only speak softly to herself: "Alas, Bevers, how can I live if you are gone? How am I to endure my grief? My love for you will only bring my life to an end. Alas, what a cruel heart you have, to have left without letting me know this. But if you are, as I believe, a genteel knight, you will not forget my love.[3] For your sake I shall remain chaste and take care of your sword and your horse and never part with them until I hear news of you."

13. Josvena is married to Ivorius.

At that time a king named Ivorius of Munbrak arrived. He brought along twelve other kings. He had come to King Erminrik to ask for the hand of his daughter in marriage. Erminrik granted this readily.

When Josvena became aware of this, she made a belt for herself that was of such a nature that no man's desire might defile her, when she was wearing it. She put this belt on so that King Ivorius would not be able to assault her.[4]

Now one day King Ivorius got up and took leave of King Erminrik and returned to his kingdom with Josvena. She cried pitifully. She allowed no one, other than herself, to take care of the horse Arundele. And there was no one so

3. The romance epics were very much influenced by the courtly romances, from which they borrowed various motifs, chiefly that of courtly love. Josvena's grief calls to mind Blensinbil's lament in *Tristrams saga ok Ísöndar*, when Kanelangres, Tristram's father, is about to die: "How could I survive such a glorious, gallant man? I was his life and his comfort, and he was my beloved and my life. I was his delight, and he was my joy. How shall I live on after his death?" *Tristrams saga ok Ísöndar*, trans. Peter Jorgensen, in *Norse Romance*, vol. 1: *The Tristan Legend* (Cambridge, 1999), 47, 49.

4. The account of this belt is somewhat longer in *Boeve de Haumtone*: "She had learnt a little magic: she made a tight belt of silk. The belt was made in such a fashion that if a woman put it on underneath her clothes, there was not a man in the world who would have any desire to sleep with her, or approach the bed where she lay." See *Boeve de Haumtone* 1000–1005, in *Boeve de Haumtone and Gui de Warewic: Two Anglo-Norman Romances*, trans. Judith Weiss (Tempe, 2008), 43.

174 • THE ROMANCE EPIC OF BEVERS

bold as to approach the horse other than Josvena. She had a stable built, which was secured with two very strong iron chains. Whoever wanted to feed the horse had to come down from another house. King Ivorius very much wanted to ride the horse. But when he came to where the horse was standing, and wanted to take it, and the horse saw the stranger come in, it became frenzied and struck King Ivorius such a great blow with its forelegs that his head nearly broke. And the horse would have killed him, had not six knights helped him. They took him to his bedroom, laid him in his bed, and sent for a doctor.

14. Bevers is freed from the dungeon.

Something should now be told about Sir Bevers. When he had been in the dungeon for seven years, he began to lament one day and prayed for God's mercy, saying: "You, pure God, who created me and died on the cross and redeemed me with your blessed blood, I beg you with all my heart not to let me be tortured here any longer. Either let me die or else let me be freed soon."

The two men who guarded the dungeon heard this and spoke: "Today you are going to be hanged, you evil traitor." One of them let himself on a rope down into the dungeon and when he had come down, he struck Bevers with his fist so that he fell down, for he had become so skinny from lack of food that he could barely stand upright. Nonetheless, Bevers jumped up, grabbed his staff and struck him on the head and he fell down dead. Bevers then took his sword. The one who was on the upper floor called and asked why he was so slow bringing up Bevers, who was to die without delay.

Bevers answered: "I am so heavy that he cannot lift me; come down and help him."

The other guard lowered himself on the rope, and when he reached the dungeon, Bevers stabbed him with the sword.

Bevers then hauled himself up on the rope. When he came to the area where the guards had been, he took a sufficient number of weapons and garments. He also got a palfrey, saddled it, and mounted the horse. He rode out through the city gate. It was so early that the gate keeper was not yet dressed, nor were the city folks. Bevers then ran into the guards who had opened the city, and they asked who he was and where he was going. He answered: "I am one of King Brandamon's men and I am looking for Bevers who has escaped from the dungeon."

They told him to hurry and catch him, "and may Mahomet strengthen and attend you."

Bevers now rode through the night as fast as he could and in the morning he came to a crossroads. Because he had been in the dungeon for a long time, the roads were not familiar to him. And he took a road he shouldn't have. Around

THE ROMANCE EPIC OF BEVERS • 175

midday he saw before him a large city and realized that it was Damascus, which he had left only that morning. He then spoke: "Alas, God, what should I do now? Here I am burned out and injured and I cannot ride any farther. I need to rest here and sleep." Bevers now dismounted and laid his head on his shield and slept for a while. When he woke up he mounted his horse and rode in the direction leading away from the city. He was skinny and weak because he had not eaten anything for four days.

That morning King Brandamon rose early and called for his nephew, named Grandier, and spoke: "Call the two knights for me who are guarding the dungeon." He went and called, but no one answered. He lowered himself into the dungeon and found the guards dead, but Bevers gone. He went and told the king. The king got so angry that he grabbed a staff and charged at Mahomet, his god, and smashed the idol to pieces and spoke: "You wicked and fickle god. If you do not have Bevers return, so that he can be hanged today, you will never again get even the smallest bit of my wealth in your honor." After that he called for his army and told them to get armed and capture Bevers. And 300 men armed at once. The king was very quick and mounted his horse, as did Grandier. No horse was better or faster than the king's; he had paid four times its weight in gold for it.

King Brandamon now rode on his swift horse at the head of all his men. When he had ridden for a while, he gained on Bevers. And when he saw him, he shouted and bade the wicked traitor to wait for him and turn back, "for before evening comes you shall be hanged."

"Lord," said Bevers, "I dare not turn back, since I am much pressed by hunger and lack of sleep, and you might overcome me. Yet I shall nonetheless try to strike you."

When King Brandamon heard this, he became exceedingly angry and spurred his horse on and galloped at Bevers and delivered such a mighty blow that his shield split. Bevers now drew his sword and struck the king and sliced off a quarter of his helmet so that his brain fell out of his skull and onto the ground, and he fell dead off his horse.

Bevers then said: "You can thank me for having ordained you a bishop, and now you resemble other bishops with your tonsure."

At this moment Grandier rode up on his good horse, named Tronchevares, and he shouted at him and said that it was useless for Bevers to flee.

"Grandier," said Bevers, "I suggest that you turn back and return home with your uncle Brandamon, who has now been ordained a bishop, and I swear, if you come near me, I shall ordain you a deacon with my sword."

Bevers now took the spear that the king had held and rushed at Grandier with such great force that he bathed the standard in his blood. Grandier now fell

176 • THE ROMANCE EPIC OF BEVERS

dead off his horse. Bevers quickly took the horse with its golden bridle, mounted, and thought he was safe, now that he had taken hold of the horse. He rode off, but the king's men quickly pursued him.

When Bevers had ridden for a little while, he looked around. He had come to a large river and thought it an ill-fated spot to be, for the river was both deep and rapid, and the spear shaft was ripped out of his hand when he stuck it in the water. He hardly knew what to do. He fervently asked God to save him from the Saracens. He spurred on his horse, which ran far out into the water and swam with difficulty across the river, which was rapid, and the current bore them downstream. The horse swam all the more against the current and it foamed at the mouth. Thanks to merciful God, the horse managed to cross the river and Bevers was very happy. But then the horse shuddered, and at that Bevers fell off its back, yet he quickly got up again.

The Saracens now saw that Bevers had crossed the river and they were quite distraught and rode home with their dead king.

15. Bevers kills a giant and searches for Josvena.

Bevers now went his way and as he rode all alone, he talked to himself under his breath, saying: "God knows that I would willingly give all my armor and my good horse for just half a loaf of wheat bread, given how long I have now suffered hunger pangs."

He kept riding until he came to a castle built entirely of marble. He looked around and saw a beautiful tower, and at a window of the tower he saw a beautiful woman. Bevers rode to where he had seen her and spoke to her. "My fair and most gracious lady," he said, "for the sake of God in whom you believe, give me something to eat so that my hunger may finally be satisfied."

"Mahomet knows," she said, "you are speaking very foolishly, asking me for food, since you are a Christian. My husband is a big giant, both strong and fierce, and I shall now go to him and ask him to give you a meal with his iron club."

"I swear," said Bevers, "I am going to stay here and get enough food so that I am sated."

The lady then went to her husband and told him that a man had come and over her objections wanted food. The giant said that he would try to see what kind of a man he is before they part.

The giant now took his spear and sword and a large club and ran to where Bevers was and asked him whether he had stolen the good horse he was riding: "I think I recognize the horse that King Brandamon, my brother, owned."

Bevers said: "Yes, that is right. I killed him with my sword before we parted."

THE ROMANCE EPIC OF BEVERS · **177**

When the giant heard this, he intended to kill Bevers at once, and struck him with his iron club. But he missed Bevers and killed the horse instead. Bevers jumped up and brandished his sword and struck the giant's head, taking off a quarter of his fleshy tissue. The giant now flung his spear at Bevers and severely wounded him in the thigh, and he grabbed his sword and wanted to strike Bevers, but God helped him, and he did not succeed. At this the giant fell. Bevers was happy at this; he jumped on his chest and cut off his arms and his legs as well as his hideous head.

After this victory, Bevers went into the castle and asked the lady to give him food. And she did so, and neither drink nor food was lacking, and now he felt his strength return. When he had eaten enough, he had his wounds bound. Then he asked the lady to get him a horse, and she did so.

He mounted and rode on his way until he arrived in Jerusalem, where he met the patriarch and told him the story of his life, what had happened to him at the beginning when his father was killed, and up to what had now happened. When the patriarch heard this, he thought it distressing, and he gave Bevers a mule along with thirty-four gold coins, and Bevers took leave of the patriarch, but he did not want to go home, but rather find out where Josvena was, and he now went to Egypt. But he could not find her there.

One day, as he was riding along, he met a man whom he knew quite well, for they had both been with King Erminrik. He asked the man how Josvena was, and the knight responded: "A mighty king has captured her. He is Ivorius of Munbrak, and I can easily tell you how to get there. You should go all the way to Iturea and on to Carthage and to the city called Orphanies. After that you come quite quickly to Munbrak." Bevers thanked him and rode very fast to Munbrak.

That day King Ivorius had gone hunting with all his knights. Josvena was at home with a few squires. Bevers was happy now and he went to the door of the hall where she was, and he listened for a while and did not want to enter too soon. He heard Josvena sobbing grievously and in great distress, while she said: "Alas, Lord Bevers, how greatly I have loved you! My love for you will be my death. I have lost you, and therefore I do not care to live any longer."

When Bevers heard this, he realized her great sorrow, and he entered the hall, dressed like a pilgrim, and asked Josvena to give him something to eat. "Welcome, pilgrim," she said, "you shall not lack food." And she herself got up and gave him food and graciously served him.

When he had eaten his fill, she spoke to him in tears and asked: "Pilgrim, where were you born? So help you God, tell me the truth."

"Lady," Bevers said, "I was born in England."

When Josvena heard this, her heart warmed, and she asked: "Do you know a person named Bevers, from Hampton?"

178 • THE ROMANCE EPIC OF BEVERS

"Yes," he said, "quite well, because his father is related to me. And not yet twelve months have passed since I saw him kill a crowned king and a giant. Now he is back in his kingdom and he has avenged his father, and gotten his kingdom back, and there he has married well and honorably. Never was a more beautiful woman born than his wife.

Josvena was now very upset, when she heard that Bevers was married, and she fell unconscious. When she recovered, she cried out and said: "In a cruel moment was I born, and I shall be yearning for Bevers in great sorrow." Now she looked at him and spoke: "So help me God, if I did not know that Bevers is back in England, I would say that you are that very Bevers for whom I have long yearned. But because of the scar on your forehead, I do not recognize you."

"No," said Bevers, "I am not Bevers, and you are not perceiving this correctly." But Bevers now said to Josvena: "I have often heard a horse mentioned that you are stabling. If you have that horse, I would like to take a look at it." "Good lord," she said, "that can't be, for ever since I lost Bevers, the valiant knight, no man dares to approach it."

One of her squires now came in, whose name was Bonifrey. She asked him: "Whom do you think the pilgrim sitting there resembles?"

"Lady," said Bonifrey, "I think he is Bevers of Hampton."

When the horse Arundele heard Sir Bevers mentioned, it broke out of its iron tethers, ran into the yard, and neighed. Then it rolled around on the ground.

"God knows," said Bevers, "I am going to try to see whether I can mount the horse."

When the horse saw Bevers, its lord, it stood still and did not move until Bevers had mounted. He then let it run quickly and the horse carried Bevers to Josvena, where it frolicked before her.

When she saw this, she spoke: "Now I know that you are the one whom I have long desired. For God's sake, dismount. You are going to keep your horse and get back the good sword Myrklei, which I have long looked after for you."

"Lady," said Bevers, "fetch me my sword. I now want to go home to England."

But she answered: "You are not going to go there, unless you take me along."

"Lady," he said, "you shouldn't be saying that. You are a mighty queen, but I am an unknown man who should hate you rather than love you, because your father viciously betrayed me, when he held me so long imprisoned in a dungeon. And I want to tell you another thing: I made my confession to the Patriarch, who directed me that I should never marry a woman, unless she is a virgin. If you are a virgin, it would be a great miracle, since you have been together with King Ivorius for seven years."

Josvena now answered: "The God in whom Christians believe knows that I was not aware of how my father betrayed you. And after King Ivorius and I were married, he was never able to touch my body in sinful acts. And I ask you to take me along to England. When you have me christened, and it is proven that I am not a virgin as I am telling you now, then send me back, penniless, with nothing but my nightgown on my back."

"I shall gladly do so," said Bevers. And he immediately kissed her with great happiness.

16. Bonifrey's advice.

King Ivorius now returned from the hunt with the twelve kings subject to him. He had bagged a good hundred lions and leopards, and so many wild boars and bears that they could hardly be counted.

When Josvena saw this, she was troubled and called Bonifrey, her secret squire, to herself, and spoke: "Give me some good advice. King Ivorius has now returned and we won't be able to get away."

"My lady," said Bonifrey, "don't cry. I'm going to give you good advice: King Ivorius has sent one of his friends and his dearest brother to a place or castle called Abilant. The king there is named Bibilant, and he is under siege and shut in with his entire army. When King Ivorius returns to court, Bevers should come forward and tell the king this. I know for sure that King Ivorius will be very unhappy, and have his people get armed, and he will go to help his brother. We shall be here with but few people and thus be able to get away."

"By my troth," said Bevers, "this is good advice."

17. Bevers escapes with Josvena.

After this, King Ivorius returned with his booty and showed it to Josvena. The king saw Bevers standing there and asked who he was and from where he had come.

"Lord," said Bevers, "I have been in many lands, both Saracen and Christian, other than the castle of Abilant, where I could not get in, because Bibilant, your brother, was locked in there with all his people. The king of Vamera has done this."

When King Ivorius heard this, he spoke: "This is distressing news, should my brother be hanged there or mutilated." He told all his men to arm as quickly as possible, "and let us go and help my brother."

King Ivorius now made his way with all his men to the castle of Abilant, but he left a king named Garsich behind and 1,000 knights to protect the kingdom and Queen Josvena.

180 • THE ROMANCE EPIC OF BEVERS

When King Ivorius had left, and Queen Josvena and King Garsich were left at home, Josvena was very sorrowful. Bonifrey, her squire, gave her confidence "that I shall get you away from here. I am going to go into your garden and collect a certain herb, and such a great amount that a horse could not carry more, and I shall mash the herbs and extract all their juices. Afterwards I shall have a wine blended for King Garsich and give lots of it to all his men, so that none of them will know what to do. And everyone will fall asleep, wherever he is. And we, together with Bevers, shall get ready as quickly as possible. We shall have come a long way on our journey, before King Garsich becomes aware of this."

Now Bonifrey did what he had said: he took the herbs and made the drink and gave it to King Garsich and his men to drink, and they ended up lying on top of one another, as they were sleeping. Bevers now put on his armor, and Josvena prepared for their journey. When they were ready, they left with twenty horses loaded with gold and silver and all kinds of precious objects.

King Garsich awoke the next day and now became aware that Josvena was gone, and he realized that he had slept too long. He owned a ring with a stone, the nature of which was that if one looked at the stone one could see whatever one wanted.[5] When he now looked at the stone, he saw that they had speedily ridden away, and saw that the same pilgrim who had been there had taken Josvena away, and he considered this a great disgrace. He saw that all his knights were sleeping, and he went and awakened them, and he ordered them to get armed and to pursue them. "And if King Ivorius learns of this, we shall suffer severe consequences."

When the knights heard this, they got armed, and 1,000 knights pursued Josvena.

They rode so rapidly that they now spotted Bevers. "By my troth," said Bevers, "I shall now turn back and smite King Garsich with my sword."

But Bonifrey replied: "I have a better suggestion for you. I know of a rocky precipice not far from here, and there is a path on which we can ride. If we can get there, we need not be afraid, for no person alive can find us there."

When Bevers heard this, he thought it the best plan. Bonifrey showed him the way, and they came upon a cave, without King Garsich and his men becoming aware of this. The Saracens looked everywhere for them, but could not find them, nor anyone who could tell them their whereabouts. And they now returned as things stood, distressed, as was fitting.

5. This ring with its magic stone is a variant of a ring found in Chrétien de Troyes's Arthurian romance *Yvain*, where the protagonist is given a ring which, if worn with the stone facing the palm, renders him invisible. See Chrétien de Troyes, *The Knight with the Lion*, in *The Complete Romances of Chrétien de Troyes*, trans. David Staines (Bloomington, 1990), 269.

THE ROMANCE EPIC OF BEVERS · 181

While Bevers and Bonifrey were in the cave, they kept careful watch for fear of the Saracens. Then Josvena spoke to Bevers, saying: "My beloved, I am so hungry that I can hardly speak, and I cannot do without food any longer."

"Lady," said Bevers, "I think that is awful, and I shall try at once to hunt down a deer in the woods. Bonifrey will protect you while I am gone." Bevers now rode off quickly, but Bonifrey and Josvena stayed behind.

When they had not been waiting long, they saw two lions approaching. They were quite fierce and leaped at them. When Bonifrey saw that, he seized his weapons and mounted his horse and struck one of the lions with all his might, but the lion's skin was so tough that he could not pierce it. The fierce animals now attacked Bonifrey; one of them tore him apart and the other his horse, and they did not stop until he was completely ripped apart, as was his horse. Thus he unfortunately lost his life in this way.

When Josvena saw this, she began to cry and weep sorrowfully out of fear. The animals now leaped at her and tore off her clothes and dragged her onto a rock. She now realized her terrible situation.

At this moment Bevers came riding, having bagged a roe. He saw Bonifrey's arms lying in one spot and his legs in another. He called out to Josvena, and when he did not see her, he could not go on and he fell unconscious. When Arundele, his horse, saw this, it gently nudged him with its foot, as though to wake him, and at last Bevers regained consciousness. Bevers now resolutely took heart, and he mounted his horse and spurred it on. He looked up at the rock and saw that Josvena was being guarded by two lions.

When Josvena saw him, she called out: "Lord Bevers, Lord Bevers," she said, "come here and help me, for I am now in a wretched situation."

When the lions saw Bevers, they leaped up. Bevers dismounted and did not want them to harm his horse. He took his shield now and his sword in the other hand and walked toward the animals. Both now leaped at Bevers simultaneously. One of them reared on both legs and broke Bevers's shield in half. But with great energy he struck his sword down on the head of the lion, yet it was so hard that the sword could not split it. The lion now leaped so savagely and fiercely with gaping jaws at Bevers as though to devour him. At this moment Bevers struck down onto the animal's neck and the point of his sword reached the heart. Bevers pulled out his sword and the animal died at once. Now when the other lion saw its companion slain, it sprang at Bevers and ripped his hauberk, as though it were a threadbare tunic. And the lion raised its forefeet and struck at him, but Bevers defended himself so bravely that he received not a single wound. Bevers now became angry that this animal should so long stand in his way, and he struck the lion and cut off both of its front feet, and the animal fell to the ground. And

182 • THE ROMANCE EPIC OF BEVERS

that is how Bevers was able to kill it. Then he went to Josvena and gave her something to eat from what he had bagged. After this they rode on their way.

18. Bevers encounters Eskopart.

When they had now been riding for a long time, Bevers saw a very large giant ahead on the stump of a tree. He was a goodly fifteen feet tall. In his hand he was holding a big club that was so heavy that a group of ten peasants would not be able to carry it. At his side he had a heavy, sharp sword. The space between his eyes was three feet; his skin was black as coal; his nose was ugly and on its tip were two knobs. He had large, long legs; his feet were ugly in shape. He could run faster than a bird could fly. His voice sounded as though ten dogs were barking. His hair was as long as a horse's tail. His eyes were large and black like the bottom of a kettle. He had teeth like those of a wild boar. The mouth was very wide, and he was altogether a hideous creature.[6] King Ivorius had sent the giant out to look for Josvena and to bring her back.

When this giant saw Sir Bevers, he shouted at him and spoke: "You evil traitor, you are going to hand over the lady whom you have with you."

When Bevers saw that he was so huge and hideous, he laughed at him and asked: "Where were you born and what is your name?"

The giant answered: "My name is Eskopart, and I am a strong and very valiant man."

Bevers said: "You are a hideous creature, and is everyone in your country as tall as you?"

He answered: "Mahomet knows, people there called me a dwarf, and I was ashamed to stay there and I fled, because there I was considered little, and ever since I have served King Ivorius. And on the spot I shall break your head with my club, because you have abducted my Lord's queen."

Bevers said: "It won't be long before you shall pay for your boasting." He now spurred his horse on and struck Eskopart's chest, but the spear shaft broke, while Eskopart stood still and was not wounded. He then cast his thick iron staff at Bevers, but it was aimed too low and did not strike Bevers, but instead hit a tree, and it split. Then Eskopart drew his sword and wanted to strike Bevers, but his horse Arundele saw that and reared and with both legs struck the giant's chest so that he fell down. When Bevers saw this, he jumped off his horse and wanted to behead him.

But then Josvena spoke: "I advise you, Bevers," she said, "that you spare his life and make him subservient to you and have him baptized."

6. The portrayal of this giant was presumably inspired by Chrétien de Troyes's *Yvain*, where the Arthurian knight Calogrenant encounters a similar giant. See Chrétien de Troyes, *The Knight with the Lion*, trans. Staines, 260.

THE ROMANCE EPIC OF BEVERS · 183

Bevers said: "No, he shall die instead."

And when Eskopart heard this, he shouted so loudly that the woods echoed: "Lord Bevers," he said, "do not kill me, for I shall gladly become a Christian and serve you."

Josvena said that one might well trust him. Then Bevers let him stand up, and Eskopart gave his word of honor that he would serve him faithfully.

After this Bevers mounted his horse, as did Josvena, while Eskopart took his club and followed them and became their servant.

They now rode until they came north to the sea. There they saw a ship loaded with Saracens who intended to fight against Christians.

Eskopart asked them to give him their ship, but they refused to do so. He jumped on the ship and with his club he killed everyone on the ship. Many jumped into the water and drowned. And when the ship was empty, Eskopart carried Bevers and his beloved as well as their horses and all their possessions onto the ship.

19. Bevers comes to Cologne.

Now we must tell about King Ivorius. He had learned how Bevers and Josvena had sailed away. He called to his kinsman, whose name was Amonstrei.

"You shall go," he said, "and bring back Bevers and Josvena as well as the evil traitor Eskopart."

"I shall gladly do so," he said. Amonstrei now went to the sea and got a ship for himself and sailed after them, and he found them in the middle of the sea. When they met, Amonstrei shouted, saying: "I swear by my head that you, Eskopart, shall pay dearly for the treason you have committed against my lord, King Ivorius."

When Eskopart heard Amonstrei's threat, he became very angry and spoke: "Go back," he said, "you evil brute, your threat is not worth anything to me, and if you come near me, you shall pay for this."

Amonstrei now became very frightened and did not want to wait for Eskopart, and they parted as things stood.

They now continued on their way across the sea and came to Christian territory and landed in the city called Cologne. An archbishop had jurisdiction in the city. He had risen early in the morning and gone to the shore to amuse himself where the ship landed. The archbishop was Bevers's uncle, but he did not know that. The archbishop went to where Bevers had landed, and when Bevers was no longer occupied, he approached the archbishop and they greeted each other. The archbishop asked: "From where did you come, knight, or where were you born? You are handsome and well mannered."

184 • THE ROMANCE EPIC OF BEVERS

"My lord," he said, "I was born in England; I am the son of Earl Gujon who was treacherously killed."

When the archbishop learned what he told him, he was overjoyed and hastened to him and kissed him and said: "My good nephew, you are welcome. But who is that maiden with you, so fair and beautiful that I have never seen another maiden equally fair?"

"Lord," said Bevers, "she has loved me and I have loved her, and on account of my love of her I spent seven years in a dungeon. She wants to become a Christian now and to be baptized."

"God be praised," said the bishop.

At this moment Eskopart came running. When the archbishop saw him, he blessed himself more than twenty times and asked Bevers who that monster might be. "Lord," said Bevers, "he is my servant and I would like you to baptize him."

The bishop spoke: "Sabaoth, your foster-father, is very angry and sad because Terri, his son, told him that you had been hanged. Sabaoth has built himself a fortress on a high cliff. It is so stoutly constructed that no one can conquer it. My advice is that you go to him, on account of your great enmity with the emperor. I shall also provide you with a force of 500 well-armed men."

Bevers thanked him profusely.

The archbishop now led him to his chamber, and he was very happy that he had come. Afterwards they went to church, and Josvena was baptized. Then Eskopart was led forward, but a large tub had to be readied for him, because the baptismal font was too small. And Eskopart had to jump into it himself, because he was so heavy that the city's entire population could not lift him. Afterwards they all went to dinner.[7]

Afterwards Bevers prepared to sail to England, but he left Josvena in Cologne, together with Eskopart. He rode off with the 500 men whom the archbishop had provided. Josvena remained behind, however, sad and sorrowful.

Bevers and his men now sailed over the sea and arrived in Hampton, England. The emperor ruled there and he went to meet Bevers to ask who he was and what his name was.

---

7. In *Boeve de Haumtone* the account of Eskopart's baptism is longer and more comical. Twenty men are not able to lift him and Eskopart jumps in with his feet together, but the water is cold and he gets chilled. Eskopart begins to yell and upbraid the bishop: "'What is this?' he said. 'Base, wicked shepherd, do you want to drown me in this water? Let me go; I've had enough of being a Christian.'" And he jumps out, naked, and everyone who sees him, according to the narrator, thinks him a hungry devil (*Boeve de Haumtone* 1969–77, trans. Weiss, 62).

He answered: "I am Geirard of France from the castle called Digon."

"Sir Geirard" said the emperor, "I would like to tell you that there is an evil old fellow who lives in a strong castle by the sea. His name is Sabaoth and I am not able to overcome him, yet he has done great damage to me and harmed my knights."

"Lord," said Bevers, "if you give all my men weapons and armor, I shall attempt to seize him and deliver him to you in shackles."

The emperor agreed to this and had weapons and fine armor provided. They then left and did not let up until they arrived at the castle. When Sabaoth saw Bevers, he asked him for his name, for he did not recognize him.

"Lord," said Bevers, "I was born in England in the good city of Hampton."

When Sabaoth heard this, he did not need to ask any longer, but went to him and kissed him lovingly, and joyously led him into the castle.

20. Josvena kills Earl Miles.

Now we must tell of the fair Lady Josvena, the faithful maiden. She was in Cologne, together with Eskopart. In this country there was an earl who had seen Josvena one day and his heart had immediately become inflamed with great love for her. He repeatedly considered how he might win her love. He often went to see her, but the more he cajoled her, the more she resisted him. When he saw that she could not be seduced with gallant words, he swore by his head that he would take her by force and against her will, for she was not that properly sheltered. The name of this earl was Miles. Josvena said to him: "Miles, let me be, and don't do me any harm. If Eskopart finds out about this, he will avenge me on you."

When the earl heard this, he began to consider how he might deceive Eskopart, and he said: "Brother Eskopart, Lord Bevers sent you his greetings and he asked you to come to him, since he needs you. He is in the castle that you can see across the sea, and he is awaiting you there."

Eskopart believed this and said to the earl: "I very much ask you to take me there."

"Gladly," said Miles, "let us go abroad without delay." They took a ship and sailed to the castle. When they arrived there, Miles asked him to go into the castle, and then he locked the gate tightly behind him.

Eskopart looked everywhere in the castle, but found no one there. When he realized that he had been betrayed, he called out loud to the earl and said: "For God's sake, let me out of here."

"You should know, Eskopart," said Miles, "that I am now going to sail home and marry Josvena."

186 • THE ROMANCE EPIC OF BEVERS

When Eskopart heard this, he became exceedingly angry, and began to tear down the stone wall with his nails. He was so strong that he was able to break the stone wall all the way down to the sea. Then he dived into the sea and began swimming with all his might. When he had swum for a while, he saw a merchant ship and called out to those aboard, saying: "Let me up onto your ship."

Now when the merchants saw such a huge and hideous creature swimming so powerfully in the sea, they thought that it was the devil himself, and full of fear they all jumped overboard. Eskopart seized the ship and with great strength rowed to land.

On that very day a messenger arrived in Hampton and told Bevers that Josvena had been married against her will to an earl. When Bevers heard this, he took his horse and weapons and rode all alone to Cologne.

Now it is time to tell that Earl Miles married Josvena, overpowering her and against her will. In the evening, when they were to go to bed, he had the door locked. He quickly undressed and wanted to deprive her of her virginity. But Josvena began to worry and to think about how she might avoid this disgrace and get rid of him. She took her good silken girdle and made a noose with it. And when he was about to go to bed, she cast the noose around his neck. The bed in which they were to sleep was very high, however, and Earl Miles jerked when he felt the noose and slipped down on the other side of the bed, but Josvena yanked the girdle hard toward herself, so that his feet did not reach the ground and she strangled him to death.

In the morning when it had become light, the knights came to the loft and called out to the earl, saying it was time to get dressed. Josvena said that he was dead, "and I killed him." When they heard this, they broke into the loft and took Josvena and shackled her. Then they made a huge pyre and intended to burn her. They led her there in disgrace, without showing any mercy.

Josvena now cried out loudly and spoke: "Woe, Lord Bevers, you have lost your beloved in a heinous way. I gave you all my love, but now you have forgotten me, and I shall now be killed, because I did not want to betray you." After this, Josvena asked for a priest, and one was fetched, and she spoke with him for a long time.

Bevers now came riding along and met a courtier and asked him the reason for the large pyre.

"Lord," he said, "there is much grief. A maiden is to be burned there because she strangled an earl who intended to rape her."

"That is not going to happen, God willing," said Bevers, and he spurred his horse on and raced to the fire.

Eskopart now came from another direction; he met a man and asked why such a large fire had been lit. When the man saw him, he fled and cried loudly:

THE ROMANCE EPIC OF BEVERS • 187

"*Benedicite*," and made the sign of the cross on himself. But Eskopart went after him and grabbed his hood and asked him to stop and answer his question. The man cried out and asked for mercy and said he would gladly tell him what he wanted to know: "A maiden is to be burned for having strangled an earl to death who wanted to rape her."

"I swear by my head," said Eskopart, "that will not happen, if I can help it, and if my club is any good," and he now ran to Bevers without delay and the two arrived simultaneously at the pyre. Bevers drew his sword Myrklei and many a head fell to the ground. And Eskopart straight away killed ten or twelve men with his club. When they had killed their enemies as they wanted, Bevers turned to Josvena, quickly freed her and kissed her. Bevers now asked the bishop to obtain a palfrey for him, and he did that willingly. Bevers had Josvena mount the good horse, and they went their way until they came to the castle where Sabaoth was. He received them with great joy. Sabaoth had the castle buttressed now, so that no one could get in without his consent. He was now safe and no longer afraid.

21. Bevers avenges his father on the emperor.
Bevers now sent one of this knights, his kinsman by name of Kuripus, to the emperor to tell him that he would shortly be hanged, "for now I have the support of my kinsmen and friends." He went to the emperor and spoke: "You evil traitor, may God condemn you for the evil you have done. The knight who appeared before you the other day was not named Geirard, but rather Bevers: may God support him, but chasten you. He sends word with me that you shall be hanged."

When the emperor heard this he nearly went out of his mind and grabbed a sharp-bladed knife and threw it at the messenger, wanting to strike him in the chest. But he missed, and instead struck his own brother, who fell dead to the ground. And Kuripus mounted his horse and spoke: "You are a great fool and out of your mind, since you killed your kinsman instead of me." And he now rode off. The emperor was left behind and was ill pleased with the outcome of the matter. The messenger returned to Bevers and told him what had happened.

Now there is this to tell about the emperor: He was so upset at what happened that he sent for his friends in Germany and asked them to come to him. He also sent a message to the king in Scotland and asked him for help in his great need. Knights from both Scotland and Germany arrived, and the emperor now had a large army. The emperor had everyone get armed. His army was divided into two companies, each of the kings with his own company. The emperor intended to attack Sabaoth the Old. They had such a large army that 1,000

188 • THE ROMANCE EPIC OF BEVERS

knights were pitted against 100 of Bevers and Sabaoth's men.[8] They divided their army into three companies: one led by Bevers, the other by Sabaoth, and the third by Eskopart.

Sabaoth led with his company; he had 10,000 men. When the emperor saw this, he shouted to his men and bade them make sure that Sabaoth would not get away. The king of Scotland mounted his horse from Orphanie, and holding a spear in this hand, he charged at Sabaoth, who saw this and charged toward him. And it happened, as the saying goes: "Tough are an old man's sinews." As soon as they met, Sabaoth struck his shield, which was of little use, and he bathed his spear in his heart's blood and hurled the Scottish king dead to the ground. Sabaoth spoke to him: "No thanks to you for failing your companions with the first strike." He now drew his sword out and no one could withstand his strikes; the army was riven and right afterwards the first battle-array. When the emperor saw this, he was most irate; he mounted his horse, as did all his knights, and they charged at Sabaoth.

When Lord Bevers saw this, he had the trumpets announce the attack by his company. He himself mounted his horse Arundele. His knights were well armed, bold, and dauntless. Bevers spurred his horse on while tightly holding his shield in front of him, and he charged. With his first stroke he killed the chieftain named Ivore, and with the next he killed the man named Obbi of Moruel. And his companions did not spare their enemies.

Shortly after this, Bevers saw the emperor, his stepfather, for whom he bore little love. "God knows," said Bevers, "you vile traitor, if I can get hold of you, you will quickly lose your head."

When the emperor heard this, he said: "You need not threaten me. If you wish to fight with me, then quickly meet me on the level plain near here, where we can engage in a duel."

When Bevers heard this, he was never more overjoyed.

The armies now separated into two, and the length of a field was between them. Bevers took his spear and clasped it tightly with all his might. Then they rushed at each other with great force. Bevers struck the emperor so hard that he fell off his horse, and he came down so hard on the ground that his shield split and his sword broke. The emperor nimbly jumped up, because he was exceedingly angry and afraid of being killed. He found a large stone on the ground. The emperor was very strong and hurled the stone at Bevers, at his shield, so that it split. Bevers now drew his sword Myrklei and hewed at the emperor. When his

8. The size of the opposing armies makes no sense, to judge by what follows. For Sabaoth now has a company of 10,000 men. The reading in *Boeve* does not clarify the matter. See *Boeve de Haumtone*, trans. Weiss, 67–68.

men saw that he was going to be overcome, if he did not get any help, they rushed to help the emperor and got him onto his horse.

The two armies reunited and the battle began anew. Now Eskopart arrived with the third company. In his hand he held the iron staff, and whoever crossed its path, found death. With every strike he killed ten or twelve men. Bevers called out to him and said: "My dear friend Eskopart, do you see the emperor sitting on a white horse? I ask you to seize him and bring him to me."

Eskopart responded. "I shall gladly do that." Eskopart now slew everyone he came across with his staff. He reached the emperor and seized him and brought him to Sabaoth's castle, shackled him, and thus left him lying there. After this he returned to the battle. When the German knights of the emperor saw that they were not able to help their lord, they surrendered to Bevers.

At the conclusion of the battle they went back to the castle, where the emperor had been left. When he saw that Bevers had come, he spoke: "Lord Bevers, I know that I may not ask for clemency. I willingly forgive you my death, if you want to end my life with one stroke."

Bevers answered: "So help me God, you will now learn how you showed clemency to my father, when he begged you for mercy, and you so cruelly betrayed him." Bevers had a large pit dug now, and had it filled with boiling lead, and he had the emperor cast into it. Thus he left this life.

At this time a messenger arrived before the emperor's wife and gave her the news. When she heard this, she picked up a knife and threw it at the messenger, and the tip of the knife struck his heart, and that was his death. After this she went to the tower of her castle and decided to throw herself down, and that was the end of her life.

22. The wedding of Bevers and Josvena.

After this Bevers rode home to his own city and castle and took control of the entire kingdom that the emperor previously had held, but which was his own patrimony. He gave gifts to all those who had supported him, each in accordance with his station. Bevers had now splendidly overcome his enemies. After this he sent for Josvena and she was escorted there. Then he invited the archbishop of Cologne and all the lords of his kingdom to his wedding. And when the entire multitude had arrived, the archbishop married Bevers and Josvena, and there was a most splendid feast with all kinds of entertainment.

As Bevers had not been home long in Hampton, the king of England invited him to come to a meeting with him. Bevers immediately left with many knights. And the king rode out to meet him and led him with great honor into the city, and arranged a splendid feast for him.

190 • THE ROMANCE EPIC OF BEVERS

On the second day of the feast the king convened all his best men, and he spoke to Lord Bevers: "You know that your father was chief justice over all of England and we wish you to be the same. Furthermore, I give you all the money that the kingdom of England took from your possessions, from the time your father was killed to the time when you recovered your kingdom." Moreover, he gave him a rod made of pure gold.[9]

Bevers thanked the king and said he would gladly carry out his orders. Bevers was now lord, after the king, over all England. In one tournament that the king had arranged, Bevers won two hundred marks of pure gold with his horse, because it was faster and more agile than any other horse in the country. And at the spot where Bevers won this money, he had a castle erected, which he named Arundele after his horse.

23. Arundele kills the king's son.

The king of England had a handsome and accomplished son. He knew that Bevers owned a horse which was the best in the world, and he asked Bevers to give him the horse or else sell it to him. When Bevers did not want to do so, he went, along with forty knights, to steal the horse while Bevers was at dinner. They cut off the horse's iron chains, but when the horse saw that unknown men were grasping it, the horse reared and with its forefeet struck the king's son, who was standing next to it, on the forehead so that his entire skull broke into small pieces.

The king was told that Lord Bevers's horse had killed his son. He became so angry that he nearly lost his mind on account of his sorrow and he shouted to his knights to seize Bevers and hang him. Bevers was now seized and cruelly led off, because he knew nothing to fear.

His kinsman, the earl of Gloucester, saw this, as did Carmen of Britta and Clare of Leicester, and they got hold of Bevers and spoke to the king: "Lord," they said, "your judgment of Bevers is wrong, for he is innocent, and we want him to be freed on condition that he give you his horse." Bevers said that there was no chance that he would give up his horse. The king became so angry that nothing else was to be done but to banish Bevers. And his kingdom was to be entrusted to Sabaoth, his foster-father.

Bevers's authority changed swiftly now: in the morning he had been administrator of all England, but now he was stripped of all his possessions.

Then he mounted his horse and spoke to the king: "I ask you in the name of God that you and Sabaoth, my friend, remain good friends. But if you harm him

9. In her translation of *Boeve de Haumtone*, Weiss suggests that this rod (*verge*) may be "a staff of authority, but it is unclear of what sort – perhaps an entitlement to carry a royal staff in front of the king in procession." See *Boeve de Haumtone*, trans. Weiss, 71 n218.

THE ROMANCE EPIC OF BEVERS · 191

and he cannot freely hold on to the land which he received from me, then, God knows, I shall come to his aid, even if I were over four seas away. And you should not have to fear me, unless you are absolutely guilty."

Bevers now took leave of the king and did not stop until he came to Hampton and there met Josvena. He convened all his knights and told them what had happened, and he asked them to promise to be loyal to Lord Sabaoth. They were sad at this. He said that Josvena would accompany him, and also Terri, Lord Sabaoth's son. Eskopart was to stay behind to support Lord Sabaoth. In exchange for his service he gave him a country called Larthe, along with two hundred knights. Eskopart did not thank him, but left very angry, because he would have preferred to go with Bevers rather than stay behind.

The next day Eskopart immediately set out on his journey and came to the sea, where he found a ship for himself. He did not stop until he arrived in Munbrak and saw King Ivorius who had sent him out to look for Josvena. When Ivorius saw Eskopart, he asked where he had been so long.

Eskopart said: "I went in search of Josvena, your wife, as you asked me. And it has now been a year since she left with the pilgrim whom you had lodged here. I found him in England, where he had a great kingdom, cities and castles. But all of this has been taken away from him and he has been banished, because his horse killed the son of the king of England. And if you want me to get them and bring them to you – all the roads are known to me – then give me men to support me."

The king was now really happy and gave him everything he asked for. Then he went on his way to look for Lord Bevers and Josvena.

24. Josvena is abducted by the traitor Eskopart.
Now one should tell about Lord Bevers who made preparations for the journey and brought along much gold and silver. There was much sorrow and grief when he parted from Lord Sabaoth and his knights. Bevers, Josvena, and Terri put out to sea, and when they came to land, they mounted their horses.

One day, as they were riding along in some forest, Josvena went into labor and could not ride farther, and she spoke to Bevers: "My lord," she said, "I cannot ride any longer because I have become quite infirm. Help me down from the horse and make an arbor for me from the thick shrubs growing here."

When Bevers heard this, he was distressed that she should be ill at this time. They gently took her down from the horse and erected an arbor as best they could. Now she went so quickly and painfully into labor that she cried out. When Lord Bevers heard that, he went to her and spoke: "My dearest, I would like to be with you and serve you in your time of need and help you as best I can."

192 • THE ROMANCE EPIC OF BEVERS

She said: "Gentle lord, that cannot be, and it is not becoming for you. You should rather leave, so that you will not hear how wretched I feel. God's grace will be with me, and Mary, the most merciful mother of God."

Bevers now went away, and she was left alone, and in good time she gave birth to two sons.

At this moment unmerciful and damnable Saracens came along. Their leader was the evil traitor Eskopart. They took her away in such straits, and because of her infirmity she was not able to cry out to Bevers for help. The Saracens thus left with her, and she now thought herself to be in dire straits.

When Bevers and Terri thought they had been away long enough, they came to the spot where Josvena had lain, and they saw that she was gone. They heard babies crying and found them in the leaves. Lord Bevers then cried out that Josvena was gone, saying: "Where are you, my dearest love? I loved you more than any woman alive." And when he did not hear her, he thought this absolutely horrendous. Lord Bevers cut the sleeves from his mantle and swaddled the boys in them, and he and Terri took one each. They mounted their horses and looked for Josvena all over the woods, but did not find her anywhere.

Thus they returned to Greece.

25. Eskopart is killed by Sabaoth.

Now there is this to be told of Lord Sabaoth: One night, as he was sleeping in his bed, he dreamed that a fierce lion approached Bevers and wanted to tear him to pieces and took his good horse from under him. And again he dreamed that he was ordered to go on a pilgrimage to St Gilles[10] in France and there ask God for forgiveness. When he woke up, he donned a pilgrim's garb and quickly sailed over the sea, together with nine companions. They did not let up until they came to the city of Orleans in France. From there they went to St Gilles, as they had promised, to his church and asked God for forgiveness, and gave their offering to St Gilles in good faith.

After they left the church they wanted to find lodging. And now he met Josvena, recognized her, and thought it strange that she was alone, yet he was very happy to see her, and asked where Lord Bevers was. But she told him that she did not know, and she told him the whole story of their parting, and that Eskopart intended to bring her to King Ivorius.

---

10. The reading in *Bevers saga* is: "fara j Franz pilagrims ferd til hins helga Juliens" (go on pilgrimage to St Julien; *Bevers saga*, in *Fornsögur Suðrlanda*, ed. Gustaf Cederschiöld [Lund, 1884], 247.35–36). This appears to be a scribal error. In *Boeve de Haumtone* Sabaoth is ordered to go on pilgrimage to "Sen Gil" (v. 2736), and Weiss writes that this is "probably St Gilles-du-Gard, near Nimes: many pilgrims flocked to the saint's shrine in the reliquary abbey there" (*Boeve de Haumtone*, trans. Weiss, 76 n239).

THE ROMANCE EPIC OF BEVERS • 193

At this moment Eskopart came toward them, and when Sabaoth saw him, he rushed at him and struck such a strong blow under his ear with his staff, that Eskopart fell down dead. The city folk now came to their help and killed all the Saracens, with none getting away.

Lord Sabaoth now took charge of Josvena, and they traveled everywhere looking for Bevers and Terri, and they came to a place called Abbaport. Lord Sabaoth became very ill there, but Lady Josvena took care of him and served him, and she was never separated from him while he lay ill.

26. Concerning Bevers and Terri.

We are now going to turn back and tell something about Bevers and Terri. When they had been searching for Josvena but had not found her, they worried greatly whether she was alive. As they were riding out of the woods, they met a forester, and Bevers spoke to him: "What is it that you do here?"

He said: "I take care of the woods. From what country are you? The two of you look weary and exhausted to me."

"God knows," said Bevers, "that is true. I was married to the most beautiful woman a man could ever love, and she gave birth to my two sons here in the woods. But then she was abducted and I do not know where she is."

The forester thought this most distressing and said: "Give me one of your sons and I shall love him and have him christened. Leave him with me until you come back or send for him."

Bevers thanked him very much, and he took one of the boys, and Bevers told him that his name was to be Gujon. At this they parted and each went his way. Lord Bevers gave the other child to a fisherman, together with twenty English marks for fostering the child, which was to be baptized and named Miles.

They now rode their way and came to a city called Civile. They took lodging in the city with a resident. Around the same time an earl had been besieging this very city with 60,000 men. They had burned and laid waste the land around the city, and now they would have captured the city, had there not come help, as you shall now hear.

When Bevers and Terri heard this story, they rose early in the morning, got armed and rode at once out of the city. Lord Bevers sat on his good horse Arundele and galloped toward the standard-bearer and hurled him dead to the ground, and thereafter one after another as his spear struck. Terri too did not forget his duty and spurred his horse on and charged at a strong knight with such great force that he fell dead to the ground. Terri immediately took his horse and handed it to their host. The citizens quickly came to their help, and a tremendous battle ensued. Bevers and Terri boldly went on the attack and killed so many men that the ground was full of their corpses. In this battle Lord Bevers was able to capture two earls,

194 • THE ROMANCE EPIC OF BEVERS

but he did not know where they were born. When he turned back, he killed the earl who was captain of the army, and after his death everyone fled who was still alive.

Ruling the city of Civile was a distinguished Lady. The entire realm that the earl had been besieging belonged to her. One day this Lady had gone up into the highest tower and had seen how an unknown knight had killed her enemies. She was inflamed with love for him and asked God to have her become his beloved.

Once the earl had been killed, the citizens pursued the fleeing army and killed many of them. After their victory they came back and praised the prowess of this one knight. Bevers and Terri and their companions returned together with their host. Lord Bevers sent the three earls he had captured in battle to the Lady of the castle. She praised his prowess greatly and sent men to Lord Bevers, asking him to come to her. But the messengers did not succeed in their mission, and returned to her, saying that the knight did not want to come, as she had asked. She now put on her mantle and visited Lord Bevers. When he saw her coming, he stood up and they greeted each other courteously.

She then spoke to him: "May God keep you, courteous knight! I sent you an invitation with my knights, but you did not want to visit me."

"Fair and gracious Lady," said Bevers, "you should not think that is the case; I would gladly have come," said Bevers, "but I was angry this morning and perturbed, because my beautiful and faithful wife was abducted in the woods. Her name is Josvena and never was a more beautiful woman born. Yet God be praised, she left me two sons."

When the Lady heard this, she thought this was sad, but said: "Then you are going to take me to wife now, and I shall entrust my entire kingdom into your hands."

When Lord Bevers heard this, he said: "God knows, never for your entire kingdom would I take you to wife."

This is how they talked, and both were angry, and the Lady threatened to have his head cut off.

When Bevers saw how angry she was, he spoke again: "I shall certainly take you to wife, if I do not get Josvena back within seven years."

Then the Lady responded: "That is well put, but I shall give you a period of four years,[11] and should she come in that time, then you shall give me Terri, your companion, in marriage, but you shall nevertheless stay here and defend my kingdom."

11. In her translation of *Boeve de Haumtone* 2887, Weiss writes "four [months]" on the basis of Stimming's emendation, where the word is lacking in the manuscript (*Boeve de Haumtone* 2887, in *Der anglonormannische Boeve de Haumtone*, ed. Albert Stimming [Halle, 1899], 160; see *Boeve de Haumtone*, trans. Weiss, 78 n248). Four months does not make narrative sense, since the bargaining so far has been in years. Thus the Icelandic text, which is based on a no longer extant French manuscript, and confirms that the original reading had been "years."

THE ROMANCE EPIC OF BEVERS • 195

Bevers agreed to this and he now oversaw everything for her, and all her knights now became his men. And there was a most splendid celebration.[12] On that day the earls whom Bevers had captured in battle, were spared their lives, and they swore fealty to him and became his men.

27. Bevers defeats two earls.

Two earls, with their entire armed forces, attacked the city of Civile. They envied the fact that the Lady had acquired a captain for her forces. One earl was named Vallant, and the other Doctrier. They had 10,000 men and laid waste and burned everything in their path; they killed men and unmercifully committed all kinds of misdeeds.

Lord Bevers rose early one morning and heard loud trumpets, but did not know the reason for this. He went onto the highest tower of the castle and now saw that an overwhelming army had come. He left the tower, had all his knights arm, and rode out of the city with his men, with Terri and his knights. Bevers rushed forward at the helm of the army, in order to lead the first charge, as he was wont. He charged at a chieftain, named Ysier, and cast him dead onto the ground. Terri, his companion, did not want to forego helping Lord Bevers and charged at a Saracen named Saladin, and with his spear hurled him forcefully to the ground, dead. A hard battle ensued and a great number of men fell on either side. Lord Bevers rode boldly forward holding his sharp sword Myrklei, and everyone who was struck was condemned to death. Terri was not to be reproached, for no one who met him could boast of victory.

Bevers now saw the earl of Vasteva, who was the leader of this battle. They charged at each other with such great boldness that each broke his spear shaft on the other's shield, and the earl received such a great blow from Lord Bevers that he was thrown from his horse, and not to his pleasure. Lord Bevers now drew his sword Myrklei and wanted to behead him. When the earl saw this, he feared dying and surrendered to Bevers, who gave him quarter.

Lord Bevers now went looking for Earl Doctrier. He found him in the midst of the army, and wounded him so severely that there was no cure for him.

When those who were left saw their leaders overcome, they fled as fast as they could. Thus ended the battle: most enemies either fled or were felled by the

12. Here *Boeve de Haumtone* provides the most telling evidence that this Anglo-Norman version is not the source of *Bevers saga*, for that text here reads: "Next morning, the counts rose and crossed the bridge to church. Then Boeve married the lady." Weiss comments on verse 2895: "Such a marriage could be annulled, under certain conditions, if the partners initially promised marriage 'in the future tense'" (*Boeve de Haumtone*, trans. Weiss, 79 n250).

196 • THE ROMANCE EPIC OF BEVERS

earls, and this victory was now much praised. Lord Bevers rode into the castle with great pomp, and the Lady[13] went to meet him and thanked him very much for this victory.

After this, Lord Bevers was in the city of Civile for a long time, but he continually lamented the loss of his wife Josvena. Now it was close to the four years that the Lady had agreed on with him, and one day she talked to Lord Bevers, saying: "Lord," she said, "now it is close to the extension I gave you for our marriage to take place, and you still have not heard anything about your wife Josvena."

Lord Bevers responded: "My gracious Lady, I cannot dispute this, but now I ask for your permission of a delay of another two years, and then do as you will if by then I have not heard anything about Josvena."

The Lady said: "It befits me to grant your wish and request on account of the great magnanimity you have shown me. You asked for an extension of two years, but I shall gladly give you three years, which will then come to the seven years that you asked of me initially."

Lord Bevers thanked her very much for her support and kindness and said that he could not himself have asked for anything better. In the course of these seven years Lord Bevers enhanced her kingdom in every way and killed her enemies wherever he encountered them.

28. Lady Josvena and Sabaoth encounter Bevers.

There now is to be told about Lord Sabaoth and Lady Josvena that he recovered from his illness, during which time Lady Josvena had diligently ministered to him. One day he spoke to her and said: "Now we must again go look for Lord Bevers, your husband, and Terri, my son."

She said that she would gladly do so.

They wandered far and wide but learned no news of them.

One evening they came to a place where they were told that Bevers and Terri had earlier passed through. And that evening they came to the city of Civile and found lodging there. They made inquiry concerning Lord Bevers and Terri, and were told that the knight had been there for seven years, and leading the army he had engaged in many a battle, but now his wedding and that of the Lady was soon to take place. When they heard this they were happy that Bevers and the Lady had as yet not had sexual relations and were above reproach.

13. The Icelandic text here reads "hans unnasta" (his beloved), which cannot be right, since the reference is to the Lady of Civile. The translator misread the syntax of the corresponding Anglo-Norman verse 2953: "Mult eyme Boun la pucele gentiz," which Weiss translates: "The noble maiden loved Boeve very much" (*Boeve de Haumtone*, trans. Weiss, 80).

THE ROMANCE EPIC OF BEVERS · **197**

Lord Sabaoth now hurried to the hall where he had been told he would find Lord Bevers. He saw them now and greeted them. They prayed God to keep him and asked from where he had come. He said that he was a pilgrim from a foreign country.

Lord Bevers said to Terri: "I have never seen a man looking more like Sabaoth, your father; grant him anything he needs."

Terri now stood up and spoke to Lord Sabaoth: "You, old fellow, come here. You resemble my father, and I am therefore going to give you enough to eat."

"Thanks be to God," said Sabaoth, "for some time now people have said that you are my son."

Terri now looked at him and realized that indeed it was his father, and he kissed him and asked him to forgive him for having spoken so rashly to him. Then they went to Lord Bevers, and Terri told him that his father had come. When Bevers learned this, he rejoiced and was happy and embraced Lord Sabaoth, and he asked him if he knew anything about Josvena. And Sabaoth told him everything that had happened to them and that Josvena was in the city, lodging there with a resident.

When Lord Bevers heard this he was happier than can be imagined, and they went to where Josvena was lodged. When Bevers and Josvena met, it was such a great joyful reunion that they could hardly hold back their tears. They now led Josvena to the hall where the Lady was sitting and where they were wont to be.

When the Lady saw how beautiful she was, she asked Lord Bevers whether she was the wife for whom he had longed, and he said that this was the case. "Thanks be to God," she said, "the two of you shall enjoy each other," she said, "but you must give Terri to me as husband."

He gladly agreed to this. The Lady went to Josvena and welcomed her with great friendliness and graciousness.

Lord Bevers now had his sons sent for and they both came, and Bevers as well as Josvena were glad, and thanked their foster-fathers well, giving them a generous sum of money.

A beautiful feast was now arranged, and Terri married the Lady of Civile, and this wedding was celebrated with all the pomp and entertainment that people might wish. Terri now became Lord over the entire kingdom and all the possessions held by the Lady. All the men in the country, dukes and earls, became his subjects and swore fealty to him.

29. Reconciliation of Bevers and King Erminrik.

Lord Bevers now heard the news that King Ivorius was harrying with all his forces. He met up with King Erminrik, Josvena's father, and blamed him that he had lost

198 • THE ROMANCE EPIC OF BEVERS

her. Lord Bevers now asked Terri for advice and said: "I want to go meet with King Erminrik, my father-in-law, and help him, for I believe that it was not his fault that I was cast into the dungeon by King Brandamon. Rather I think it was because of his evil counsellors, whom he trusted too much, and God willing, I shall avenge myself on them."

Lord Terri answered: "I shall accompany you with all my forces."

Bevers had been in the castle of Civile such a long time that he had a daughter with Lady Josvena, and her name was Beatrix. Terri had a son, who was named Bevers, and Lord Bevers was his godfather, while Terri became the godfather of Beatrix.

After this they prepared for their journey: Bevers and Terri, Sabaoth and Josvena, and their children. In all they were accompanied by 15,000 knights. They started on their journey and did not let up until they came to Abbaport, the city that King Erminrik ruled. Bevers now sent a messenger to the king and bade him tell of their arrival. And the king stood in the towers of his castle and saw Bevers arrive with his entire army. The king had all his chieftains and counsellors convened and asked them for advice as to what he should do, "for our deadly enemy, Lord Bevers, is here and he will kill us and conquer our kingdom."

At this moment the messenger of Lord Bevers arrived and stepped before the king, saying: "You need not fear Lord Bevers, for he has arrived with 15,000 men in order to assist you against your enemies."

When the king and his knights heard this, they gave thanks to Mahomet, their god. And when King Erminrik saw Bevers coming and dismount, he went to meet him and fell on his knee before him and said: "I ask for your forgiveness for the sake of God who is in heaven, for I have greatly transgressed against you, and I gladly want to make up for what I have done."

Bevers now walked toward him, raised him up, and spoke: "I shall gladly forgive you for this, provided you bring me the traitors who condemned me to death."

"I shall gladly do so," said the king. He then had the two knights seized and handed them to Lord Bevers, who had them flayed alive. One of them was named Gistilin, and the other Fures.

Afterwards they went with their entire retinue into the hall, and King Erminrik was much delighted at his daughter and her children with Bevers. Now there was great joy and a most splendid feast.

30. King Ivorius is vanquished.

Now we must first report about King Ivorius: He conscripted an army in his entire kingdom. He had a spy among King Erminrik's troops who told him everything that went on there. A multitude of men gathered, so that King Ivorius had an army of no fewer than 34,000 men. Fifteen kings also came along, and with this army he went to Abbaport, where King Erminrik was residing. They set up their camp on a level plain outside the city, and there was a great din from the clattering of weapons.

Lord Bevers now had his men arm, and he rode out of the city at the head of 30,000 well-armed men. And when they met, Bevers charged at a Saracen and cast him dead to the ground. Lord Sabaoth now rode forward and struck another Saracen to death in the same way. And all of their men advanced so bravely, that no one withstood them. The battle now began in earnest and with great din, and the Saracens fell in such numbers that they were stacked one upon another. King Ivorius finally fled back to Munbrak, with 15,000 of his men dead.

When he returned home, he summoned an earl named Fabur and spoke: "I am exceedingly angry that I have lost so many men. What advice can you give me? King Erminrik now wants me to become a Christian. Josvena has become a Christian and I shall never get her back."

Fabur replied: "I can give you good advice. You should summon everyone in Saracendom and in Babylon and ask all the rulers to come here with their entire armed forces and help you in your need."

King Ivorius realized that this was the best advice, and he now sent messengers throughout all of Saracendom and summoned all the kings subject to him, together with their forces. They quickly got ready, when they received their lord's summons, gathering as great a force as they could, and they did not stop until they arrived before King Ivorius in Munbrak. Altogether fifteen kings had gathered, and each brought along 15,000 well-armed men. When they arrived in Munbrak, King Ivorius was mighty glad, and they now considered themselves secure.

King Erminrik had sent his spies to Munbrak and he learned now how large their army was. When King Erminrik and Bevers became aware of this, they sent word to Civile that Terri should come to support them. He immediately set out with 15,000 men for Abbaport, and Lord Bevers was exceedingly happy, as was Lord Sabaoth, his father. Terri brought his son Bevers along with him.

Bevers now told Terri how large an army King Ivorius had. After Terri had been there for one night, they did not want to stay any longer in the city, and they armed their large force and rode vigorously to Munbrak both day and night, until they arrived in Munbrak. But they stopped in a forest to rest up for a while, because they were exhausted. 10,000 of their armed men teamed up to ride ahead in order to kill the watchmen and the spies they came upon in the army of King Ivorius outside the city.

200 · THE ROMANCE EPIC OF BEVERS

When King Ivorius became aware of their arrival, he had 60,000 men get armed and had them ride out to attack Bevers and Terri. At the head of the Saracen army rode a knight who charged ahead as though from hell. His name was Fauker, and he was lord over all of Araby, and he called out in a loud voice to Bevers and Terri, saying: "None of you evil traitors will escape."

When Terri heard this, he spurred his horse on and charged at the Saracen king and struck him with his spear, but neither arrogance nor pride nor his good armor availed him now, and he was hurled dead off his horse.

The Saracens now came in full force, and Bevers confronted them with 30,000 knights. The battle commenced and there was a great loss of lives on both sides, indeed so great that it was difficult to advance through the Saracen corpses. Lord Bevers rode swiftly forward. Terri and Sabaoth acquitted themselves well in this battle, and anyone in their way was doomed to death.

King Ivorius now advanced with his entire force, galloping at the forefront of his men. When Lord Bevers saw him, his only thought was bent on him and he spurred his horse on and galloped at the head of his men. He charged at the king with such great force, that the horse's saddle girth and the front saddle bow broke, and the king fell ignominiously off his horse. Bevers now drew his sword Myrklei and struck the king so hard on his helmet that he would have lost his life, had he not surrendered himself and his kingdom into the hands of Bevers. He also gave up his sword, and thus he kept his life. Bevers readily received his sword, and he now sent King Ivorius to King Erminrik and Josvena. At this moment the Christians let out a great battle cry, but the Saracens fled, and the Christians pursued those fleeing for about four miles, killing most of them.

When Lord Bevers returned, he rode to the hall, where King Ivorius was. He jumped up in greeting and spoke: "My Lord Bevers, my life is in your hands. Do with me as you will, but I would like to ask for my life in exchange for gold."

Bevers said: "You are to have 20,000 marks of pure gold sent to me and you are to stay here until this arrives."

King Ivorius gladly agreed to this and he sent at once to Munbrak for the money. The shepherd Fabur himself came with this money and handed it to his lord. This was now delivered to Lord Bevers, and he gave Ivorius leave to go back to his kingdom. They parted for the time being.

31. The death of King Erminrik.

Not much later King Erminrik fell ill. When he realized that his illness grew worse, he called Bevers and his two sons to him and said: "I have ruled this kingdom for a long time, and I see that God now wants to call me from this world. Therefore I want to take care of my kingdom now, two-thirds of which I want to give to

Gujon, my daughter's son, as well as bestow on him the title of king, and one-third to Miles, together with the title of duke."

The next morning they were dubbed knights, as well as Bevers's son Lord Terri and many other citizens. After this the title of king was bestowed on Lord Gujon, and on Miles, his brother, the title of duke. Not much later King Erminrik died and he was buried with every honor. Three days later, Gujon spoke to Miles, his brother: "It is now proper that we and the others who were dubbed knights, participate in a tournament and compete in chivalric tests."

They did so, got armed and rode out. And each jousted with another, and no one could lift either Gujon or Miles out of his saddle, but the brothers succeeded in doing so to anyone they came across. Bevers, Terri's son, was the best knight, and now the brothers Gujon and Miles jousted and neither could lift the other out of the saddle. Then Bevers called that they should ride home, and he thanked them for the tournament and said that they would turn out to be good knights.

At this time Lord Sabaoth took leave and went home to England. He had been gone for seven years. Lord Bevers sent to Lady Herinborg, his wife, a mantle shot through with gold, of which there was no better, and a golden goblet as well as many other precious objects. Sabaoth did not let up until he came home to England, to his wife and to his son Robert. There was a joyous reunion, and he now stayed home for a time.

32. Arundele is stolen.

Now it is time to tell about King Ivorius. He was thinking about how he might avenge himself on Lord Bevers. With him there was a thief named Jupiter. There was no wall so high or so smooth that he could not climb it. His nails were as strong as eagles' claws. The king called this thief to him and spoke: "You shall go to Abbaport and there steal Bevers's horse Arundele. If you bring the horse to me, I shall give you as much gold as you want and additionally a mighty castle."

"By Mahomet," the thief said, "you shall get that horse." He now rode off until he came to Abbaport. And when he came to the castle where the horse was, he opened the locked door, for which he did not need a key, and by means of witchcraft he managed to seize the horse, mount it, and ride off until he reached Munbrak and brought the horse to the king. He was happy and said that he had now gotten the horse that was the best in the world. When Lord Bevers was told that his horse was gone, he became exceedingly angry, but he could do nothing other than accept this fact.

At this time Lord Sabaoth at home in England dreamed that he thought Lord Bevers had broken his thigh-bone. He told his wife about the dream. She spoke: "That means one of three things: that he has lost his wife; or else his son; or else

202 • THE ROMANCE EPIC OF BEVERS

his good horse Arundele, and this last is the least loss. My advice is that you go to him as quickly as possible to aid him with your counsel."

He said that he would do so.

He now readied for the trip. He took a palm branch as well as his iron staff, took leave from his wife, and then went abroad and came to the harbor in Jerusalem, where he got a ship, and did not stop until he met Bevers in Abbaport. He was happy to see him and said that King Ivorius had his horse stolen. Sabaoth replied: "Alas, God," he said, "this will be a difficult task for me. But before I manage to find this horse, I shall have many a wretched night."

After that he got ready for his journey and left, and he came to Munbrak. King Ivorius had now had custody of the horse for seven years, and the horse had sired a foal so similar to Arundele that in every way it looked just like its sire. The king loved this horse very much, for it was younger and the best and fleetest of all horses. At this time King Ivorius had summoned all the kings subject to him, together with their forces and also those Saracens who as mercenaries wanted to engage in battle against Bevers. Ivorius had great confidence in his good horses, which he had stolen from Bevers.

33. Lord Sabaoth obtains Arundele.

It happened one time that Lord Sabaoth saw that the thief rode the horse to water. He approached him and spoke: "Good fellow, let me look at this beautiful horse."

The thief turned the horse's chest toward him and let him look at it, but he did not know with whom he was talking. Lord Sabaoth also asked to see the horse's haunches, and he praised the horse greatly. The thief turned the horse around, and Lord Sabaoth now jumped on the horse and thrust his iron pike so hard through the thief's shoulders that it came out through his chest, and he fell down dead. But Sabaoth rode off as fast as he could.

The fellows who had ridden the other horses to water saw this and galloped after him, wanting to find out who it was who had done this. Sabaoth, however, did not want to wait for them and drew speedily ahead of them. When they saw that they could not reach him, they went to tell the king that his good horse was gone and the thief had been killed. When he heard this, he became so angry that he nearly lost his mind, and he ordered his men to get armed and ride after Sabaoth. They did so and galloped as fast as they could.

The king called Fabur and gave him the news. When he heard this, he said: "By Mahomet, I shall quickly bring the horse back to you." He now took his weapons, mounted Arundele's foal, and rode with great speed after Sabaoth.

THE ROMANCE EPIC OF BEVERS • 203

Sabaoth had ridden through the night with great speed and kept hearing his enemies in pursuit, who were a great threat to him. And when day came and the sun rose, Lord Sabaoth looked back and saw that an overwhelming army was in pursuit. In the lead was the person who was riding a horse that looked just like Arundele. This horse was even faster and was able to gain quickly on Lord Sabaoth.

Josvena had risen early this morning, and she stood in the highest tower of the castle and saw that a huge force of unknown men came riding and at the head of the army galloped two men, one behind the other. Their horses were so similar that she could not distinguish one from the other, but she thought she knew that one of them was Arundele, a horse she very much used to love. But she did not know where the other man came from who was riding the other horse, which looked so much like Arundele. Then she descended into the castle and told Lord Bevers that a man was riding a horse looking very much like Arundele and behind him came a large army. When he heard this, he ordered his knights to get armed and help him, "for that must be my good friend Sabaoth, and he must be bringing back my horse Arundele." The knights did as Bevers had ordered and rode out of the city.

When Lord Sabaoth saw that he could no longer escape the man pursuing him, he turned around and faced him with his sturdy pilgrim's staff in his hand. Fabur rode toward him and held his spear ready to use with great force and wanted to stab Lord Sabaoth, but God's mercy prevailed and he did not reach him. And as Fabur galloped toward him, Lord Sabaoth struck him with his iron pike and delivered such a great blow on the Saracen's helmet that his neck broke and he fell dead to the ground. Lord Sabaoth took his horse and mounted it, and let Arundele run loose, because by then the horse was old and tired more quickly.

Sabaoth now rode as fast as he could, because the large Saracen army was bearing down on him. But now he met Bevers's men who were going to help him. He asked them to ride vigorously at the Saracens, and they did so, and a huge battle commenced. At this moment such a large number of Saracens came attacking the Christians that they could not repel them and had to retreat; yet they defended themselves manfully. And while the battle was raging, Lord Sabaoth met Bevers and gave him his horse Arundele. Bevers was grateful and did not fear for himself anymore, and Lord Sabaoth rode the foal. The two horses were so much alike that no one could tell the two apart.

Sabaoth asked Bevers to help his men now and said that an overwhelming host of Saracens had arrived. Bevers had the trumpets blown for his knights to assemble. King Gujon and Duke Miles were together amidst the army. They rode to the aid of their men, and now the battle commenced. The brothers advanced

204 • THE ROMANCE EPIC OF BEVERS

with great force, and anyone confronting them was certain of death. Now such a
large force of Saracens came anew that the Christians could barely resist them. At
this moment Lord Bevers and Sabaoth arrived with a large group of bold knights.
When they pressed forward against the Saracen army, they charged with such
great boldness at them, that it was like a lion charging into a flock of sheep: that
is how the Saracens flinched before their weapons. There was a hard attack at
their arrival; many a man fell on either side, yet more among the Saracens. There
was a hard assault now by Bevers and Sabaoth, King Gujon and Duke Miles, with
no one withstanding them, and the Saracens, thankless, were forced to flee. The
Christians pursued them some eleven miles and killed a large number of the
accursed folk. After this victory, the Christians returned home.

When King Ivorius became aware of the catastrophes suffered by his men
and that Fabur had been killed and he had lost his best horses, he considered various means of avenging this disgrace, and he issued a decree throughout his entire
kingdom, mustering every man who could bear weapons. He also summoned
Soldan of Babylon to come to his aid. King Soldan was ruler over all of Saracendom. When Soldan learned this, he assembled an army from the entire kingdom
and appointed as captain his son Ammiral. He then sent this large army to King
Ivorius. When they arrived, he was most pleased.

At this time Bevers had a spy at the court of King Ivorius. When he learned
of Ivorius's call to arms, he went to meet Bevers and gave him the news. When
Bevers heard this, he issued a decree throughout his kingdom, calling up his entire
army, as many men as there were in the kingdom. He also sent word to Duke
Terri, his good friend, and asked him to come in his great hour of need. When
Lord Terri learned this, he rode as fast as possible with his entire army to meet
Bevers in Abbaport. Bevers was happy at his arrival and told him all about King
Ivorius's doings.

34. Gujon, Bevers's son, kills King Ivorius.

Not much later, trumpets summoned the entire army out of Abbaport, and
they did not stop riding until they arrived in the kingdom of King Ivorius. They
set up their camp on the plain outside the city of Munbrak. When King Ivorius learned this, he ordered his forces armed. Ammiral, chief of the Saracens,
who was mentioned earlier, had an innumerable army. They now had trumpets summon the troops of Munbrak who drew up in battle array. The city was
left in the hands of 20,000 Saracens. When Ammiral came onto the plain and
saw such a large army of Saracens and Christians assembled, he thought it
momentous that so many knights and noblemen should spill their blood on
account of two men. He had the circumstances and nature of the case looked

at carefully, and who had a greater claim, and realized that it was best for King Ivorius and Bevers to engage in single combat, and whoever was victor was to obtain both kingdoms. When King Ivorius heard this, he willingly agreed. He rode at once with great speed into Bevers's army and said as follows to him: "I challenge you to single combat and the victor shall obtain the other's kingdom, and each shall swear to this."

Bevers gladly agreed to this, and they raised their hands and swore that what they had said should stand. Then they immediately got armed.

There was a field on which they were to fight. When they had armed, they rode onto the field. Lord Bevers called upon Almighty God to help him, whereas King Ivorius called upon Mahomet. He was a fierce man and a great champion. Both spurred their horses on and rushed at each other boldly and with great keenness. Each struck the other's shield so forcefully that the shields split and their spears broke. Their hauberks, however, were trusty and were not scathed in this assault, and neither fell off his horse in this assault. Lord Bevers now drew his sword Myrklei and struck the helmet of King Ivorius, so that both the leaves and gems fell off and the handle of his shield broke, as did the front of the horse's saddlebow, so that the horse's head was struck off and it fell down dead. King Ivorius jumped up adroitly, however, and struck down on Bevers's helmet with full force so that all the leaves and gems flew off. That strike would have wounded Bevers, if the sword had not veered as it struck. They now had a brutal clash.

When King Gujon and Duke Miles saw their father in such straits – it happened now as the saying goes: "quick are children's minds" – they thought that he would not survive the strong strikes of King Ivorius. King Gujon rushed forward with much clamor and struck King Ivorius with such great force that none of his armor protected him and he fell dead to the ground.

Bevers was much displeased at this and reproached his son greatly and said to him: "Why did you want to humiliate me in this way? You saw that I was neither defeated nor overcome."

King Gujon said: "I thought I was doing a good thing, for I thought it was evil that this Saracen should strike you so hard. And if I have done wrong, I beg you to forgive me."

At this moment the two armies, the Saracens and Christians, gathered and a mighty battle ensued. One could hear there a great clash of weapons. King Gujon rode straight into the Saracen army and many men fell on either side. The king of Damascus, the son of King Brandamon, who was named earlier, took part in this battle, and proved to be a fierce warrior. The Franks acquitted themselves well and struck hard, killing their enemies right and left. Lord Bevers rode boldly

206 • THE ROMANCE EPIC OF BEVERS

forward and in a short time he had killed 100 Saracens. The Franks drove the Saracens toward the water[14] and there killed a great number of this accursed folk.

And now they had come to the city of Munbrak. When the Saracens saw that they could not hold out against the Christians, one nobleman, the leader of the Saracens said: "I shall gladly believe in the true God and renounce Mahomet and accompany you and advise you as to how you might conquer the city, for there are 20,000 valiant knights drawn up there, who are prepared for battle. You should get armed with the Saracens' weapons so that they will think you are their colleagues, and they will open up the gate for you. I shall go in first, in front of you."

Twelve kings subject to King Ivorius were there and they saw that the best alternative was to denounce their gods and to believe in the true God. The Christians thought this was a good decision and they armed themselves, taking the weapons of the Saracens. The name of this chieftain was Leomacior. He took the standard of the Christians and rode as the first person into the city. Those who were in the city thought they were their own men and opened the city gate. King Gujon rode in with 20,000 knights and killed everyone confronting him. The Saracens became so frightened at this that the most daring among them now was faint-hearted.

Lord Bevers also came riding into the city with his entire army. King Gujon rode to meet him, greeted him, and said: "I want to give this city to you, father, which I have won with my sword, and killed all those who did not want to believe in God."

Bevers thanked him for this gift and said that he would gladly accept it. After this, Bevers had the bishop and priests sent for and had everyone in the city of Munbrak christened, as well as the entire country.

35. Bevers christens everyone in Munbrak.

The king of Damascus went to Bevers and to King Gujon and said: "I now want to be a Christian and believe in the true God, and to renounce Mahomet and all idols, provided that I see that your God is mightier."

When they heard this, they rejoiced. And King Gujon had Tervagant, their god, brought forward, and this was done. The Saracens had decorated the idol magnificently with all kinds of gems. The idol was placed on four pillars, and when King Gujon saw it, he said to the idol: "Were you ever powerful? Where is the might now that you demonstrate? Let me see this as well as the others assembled here. Show us your might and power, if you have some."

---

14. Here *Boeve de Haumtone* reads: "Now, armed and on excellent horses, they crossed the ford and reached the other side" (*Boeve de Haumtone* 3583, trans. Weiss, 90). In note 287, Weiss comments: "There is a possible reference to a combat on an island (a *holmgang*) here."

King Gujon had a large club and he struck the idol so that it shattered into little pieces. And a bishop threw holy water onto it, and a fiend in the likeness of a dog jumped out, howling terribly, and spoke thus: "Wretched is anyone who believes in me, and whoever places his trust in me is lost."

Those who were present threw anything at hand at the fiend and asked God that the fiend not harm anyone there.

When Lord Bevers saw this, he spoke: "Now, you wretched men can see in whom you have believed."

The king of Damascus said: "Our beliefs were in error and very dangerous, and anyone who still believes should be condemned."

When the Saracens heard this, they cried out in a loud voice, wanting to be christened. Then all those who had come there were christened. And for three weeks nothing else occurred except the christening of the Saracens.

Lord Bevers then sent word to the pope and asked him to come with as many clerics as possible, and he asked that the pope himself crown Bevers. When his message reached the pope, he sailed over the sea in fine company and with a great number of clerics. When he arrived in Munbrak, King Bevers rode to meet him, along with all his preeminent men and welcomed him with the utmost cordiality. And on the feast of Pentecost the pope crowned Lord Bevers and Lady Josvena. The festivities lasted for a month, after which the pope departed with fine gifts, now that Bevers's entire kingdom had been Christianized, and they parted in great friendship.

Not long thereafter a messenger arrived, telling Lord Bevers that Lady Herinborg and her son Robert had sent to him and Sabaoth the news that the entire kingdom in England that Lord Bevers had given Lord Sabaoth had been seized by the king of England from his son Robert, who now had no more than the castle that Lord Sabaoth had built by the sea.

When King Bevers heard this news, he convened all his knights and barons and told them that he intended to go to England and take vengeance on the king in England for having dishonored Sabaoth, his foster-father. Lord Gujon, the king, and Duke Miles as well as Sabaoth the Old, and Terri, his son, accompanied King Bevers. Additionally, there were 20,000 knights and other folk. Lady Josvena stayed behind, sad and unhappy, and feared that she would never see Bevers again.

36. Bevers regains his possessions in England.

When Bevers was ready, he put out to sea with his entire army. They had a fair wind and did not stop until they arrived at Hampton in England. And the city surrendered to him at once, because no one dared to refuse to give it to him.

208 • THE ROMANCE EPIC OF BEVERS

When Lady Herinborg and Robert learned this, they went to King Bevers and complained about their troubles, and said that the reason he had needed to come was in order to avenge them.

When the king of England learned that Bevers had come with an overwhelming force and had been crowned king, he sent word to all his best men that they were to meet him in London. He told them that Bevers had arrived, together with his two sons, and that he had been crowned king. Additionally, a multitude of men had come along. He said that they were great warriors, and if he were young and healthy, he would fight them, "but I am now sick and old, and therefore we must not engage them in war. My conduct toward him has been appalling, and I want to ask him for clemency. You know that I have a daughter; I want to give her in marriage to Miles, along with my kingdom, if that meets with your approval."

All answered and agreed that this was a good plan. He sent an archbishop and additionally two earls to King Bevers with the message that they were all very much obliged to him. When they met Bevers and showed him the king's letter, and King Bevers realized the nature of their business, he welcomed them in a most friendly manner and willingly listened to what they had to say, and they enjoyed a good reception there.

Afterwards King Bevers invited them to ride along to London. He had with him his two sons as well as 3,000 knights. When he arrived in London, he went to the chamber in which the king lay. He got up to greet him and said: "Welcome, Bevers," and he kissed him, "and with this kiss I give to Miles, your son, my daughter in marriage and my entire kingdom."

Bevers sat down now beside him and they chatted with one another. The king of England then told Bevers that he was seriously ill and that he realized he would not live much longer, "and therefore I shall have my daughter married to your son today."

And that is what was done: the two were married in the morning, and there was a great celebration. After this had lasted for three days, the king died, and his burial was praiseworthy. Then the celebration continued anew. Miles became king and was crowned, and King Gujon, his brother, attended his brother at this celebration. Bevers had been crowned king, as had his two sons, and he had overcome all his enemies. The feasting went on for fifteen days, and then everyone went back home.

Bevers went back to Hampton and had his ship prepared and he took leave of his friends and asked Lord Sabaoth to help his son Miles as his advisor. He swore that he would never fail to do so. There now was much sorrow at their parting.

37. The death of Josvena and Lord Bevers.

Lord Bevers now boarded a ship and sailed to Flanders, where he got horses and rode to Rome, and there he got another ship, and came to Jerusalem, from where he had a fair wind, and he did not stop until he arrived home in Munbrak. Everyone welcomed him. He went to the room where Josvena was, and he saw that she was lying there, sick. When she saw Lord Bevers, she said: "I am very ill and I believe that I shall not be enduring this illness long."

When Bevers heard this, he was so sad that he nearly lost his mind, and he spoke: "If I were to see you dead, I would not want to live any longer. And God be praised that he has given us three children to manage all of our possessions."

He then had the archbishop called and he had the necessary service provided for Josvena. Bevers was now so grief-stricken that he nearly died of grief.

While the archbishop heard Josvena's confession, Bevers went to look after his good horse Arundele, which Lady Josvena had given him. When he got there, the horse lay there, dead. It seemed that this was more than he could bear, and he left deep in sorrow. He met his son King Gujon and told him that his horse Arundele was dead. At this King Gujon was very sad and he went to his mother, wanting to comfort her, and spoke: "My dearest mother," he said, "look after my father. I have never seen a more sorrowful man."

Lord Bevers then came, and he saw Josvena passing away, and he spoke: "Alas, God in heavenly glory, how great is the sorrow that has overcome me, now that I see my wife lying here nearly dead, whom I have loved above all else in the world. How can I live any longer? Now I ask you, glorious Jesus Christ, who knows and governs everything, let us both leave this world together."

When Bevers had finished his prayer, he was immediately stricken with a deadly illness and he lay down in the bed next to Josvena. He had Bishop Mauricius called to hear his confession and then he received Holy Communion, and commended himself into the hands of God. When he had arranged everything as he wanted for his kingdom after his death, and he had made a last will and testament for both himself and Josvena, the couple commended all their friends into God's hands. They embraced each other, as was fitting, and gave up their ghost. God's angels carried their souls up to the heavenly realm.

Both near and far mourned their death. King Gujon did not want to have them buried in the ground, like other people. He had a marble sarcophagus built instead and their bodies were placed in it and were taken to the church of St Laurence, where they were set down with great honor, amidst the sorrow of their friends.

Afterward King Gujon had himself crowned king of Munbrak and over the entire land his father had held.

Here there now ends the saga of Bevers and his wife Josvena.

The Romance Epic of Baering

1. Heinrek the Fraudster appropriates the duchy of Holstein.[1]
There are three rivers named Elf: one is called Gotha in Sweden; the second is the river Raum in Norway; and the third is the river Elbe in Saxony.[2] Along the Elbe is a little market town or castle called Eutin.[3] Duke Baering ruled this town. His sister was Lady Gertrud, who was married to Walter of Holstein. At the time when Walter died, Heinrek the Fraudster, who was Baering's knight, came with a Frisian army and killed his lord Baering and unjustly seized the duchy. All the dukes' courtiers fled to various places, because the evil Heinrek deprived them of the honors which the duke had bestowed on them. Through great warfare he subjected the land by force to his rule and had himself declared king of Holstein and Saxony and their entire population. He resided in the city called Bard, not far from the Elbe, and now rode to a wedding he wanted to celebrate with Lady Gertrud.

As soon as she heard this, she said to him: "Your intentions are evil, you accursed dog. You know that you have pillaged my husband's land and killed my brother. And now you want to have me, a pregnant woman, as your wife. I am in my ninth month and by rights am to give birth. Stop what you have in mind and let me have my own say."

He answered: "I shall wait until you have given birth, and then you will become my wife."

Soon thereafter Lady Gertrud gave birth to a son and she was very happy at the beautiful child. She expected the child to be his father's heir and to avenge the murder of his mother's brother.

Heinrek now learned that Lady Gertrud had given birth to a baby boy, and he spoke to his counsellors: "I fear," he said, "that once the boy has grown up he

---

1. Here, and subsequently, many chapters lack titles or they are partly illegible in the manuscript, and I have supplied them.

2. In the manuscript the rivers are named *Gautelfr*, *Romelfr*, and *Saxelfr*. The second syllable in each case, -*elfr*, means river in Icelandic.

3. In the manuscript this is *Ertinborg*, literally "Ertincity," which is a corrupt form of Eutin in Holstein.

THE ROMANCE EPIC OF BAERING · **211**

will inherit Holstein. It would be prudent to kill the child before it grows strong enough to want to avenge my killing of his uncle."

His counsellors agreed with him that it would be much safer to kill the child so that his kingdom would not be encroached upon.

2. The search for Gertrud and the baby.
When Heinrek came into the room where Gertrud tended to be, he found neither her nor the baby. The evil king then had them searched for everywhere, and every spot in the kingdom was ransacked. He was now quite vile and had the men killed who were supposed to find them. For a long time no one heard a kind word from him.

3. The dream of Heinrek the Terrible.
One night, as Heinrek was asleep, the hall in which he was sleeping began to shake. His knights thought they were going to die of fright. Heinrek bellowed like an ox and thrashed about with both hands and legs in his bed, and this went on until midnight, and after this until daybreak he lay there as though dead. But at the hour of prime[4] he sat up in bed, pale as a corpse, but did not feel ill. He now asked his counsellors to interpret his terrible dream.

"I dreamed," he said, "that I was standing on the banks of the Elbe, together with my entire army. It seemed to me that a lion was swimming against the current in the river and it had come to the city of Eutin. A big dragon came, flying downstream, who approached the lion and attacked the animal, biting it for a long time. Thereupon it seemed to me that the dragon flew off and the lion pursued it and with flaming teeth it ripped the dragon to pieces. And the river was filled with blood. Thereupon the lion ran with gaping jaws toward me and all of us on land. It seemed to me that you ran away and the lion tore me alive into pieces. That is the reason why I cried out so terribly in my sleep and found this dream so horrific." No one dared to advise him, but most expected that his injustice would be avenged.

4. Concerning Lady Gertrud.
It is time to tell about Lady Gertrud and her wanderings. While King Heinrek's entire court was searching for them, Lady Gertrud got into a dinghy and floated down the Elbe, which took her downstream all the way to the sea. By the sea there were some fishermen, and they heard the baby's cries even before they saw the dinghy and thought there was a troll. But when they saw the dinghy, they rowed toward it and saw a woman lying in the dinghy with a baby in her arms. They took

4. The canonical hour of prime is at 6 a.m.

212 • THE ROMANCE EPIC OF BAERING

hold of her and wanted to lift her out in her silken mantle, nearly half dead, afflicted by both illness and lack of food. When they turned her over, the baby began to cry.

And it was as though she awakened from sleep, and she said: "Good men," she said, "kill me before I end up in King Heinrek's clutches. And do not harm my child, for there is no one left alive after Duke Baering, my brother, and Walter, my husband, who was the earl of Holstein."

They were touched at her sorrowful and despairing words.

One of the fishermen spoke: "I am happy to have found you and the baby. I was Duke Baering's knight, and the evil Heinrek deprived me of my knighthood when he killed my lord Baering. Since then I have been a fisherman, because I did not want to serve the evil betrayer of my lord, and my residence has been mostly in England, in the market town of London. I can take you there, far from Heinrek and his control. There you will meet King Richard who will have authority over all of us. He has heard of all of Heinrek's evil actions. Now I shall no longer have to be a fisherman, since God has enriched me by meeting you. Blessed be the West winds that guided me here, since it is a lucky meeting for all of us."

Lady Gertrud was happy now to have met the man willing to help her in the great adversity she was experiencing, and she asked him for his name.

He said: "My name is Adalbrecht. I was Duke Baering's treasurer. I escaped and was wounded twice."

"I know you," said Lady Gertrud. "You accompanied me to meet my Lord when I was married to him. He gave you a splendid garment and sent you back to my brother."

When they were talking about their happy lives and that Heinrek had destroyed them, everyone thought it sad to hear how a wealthy and high-born woman should now be so wretched. They now gave her the best food they had, serving her gently, and she accepted this graciously. She asked God to give them a fair wind to England, so that Heinrek would no longer have power over them. God granted her prayer with an eastern wind, and they sailed with a fair wind for four days, after which time they saw England and came to the river Thames in London. When they arrived, they received lodging in the king's palace.

5. Concerning Lady Gertrud.

When they had been there for two nights, Lady Gertrud spoke to Adalbrecht, and asked him to meet with the king and ask him for some useful advice. He approached the king and told him the nature of his errand. The king asked that Lady Gertrud and all those with her meet with him. She went to him, as he had asked.

When he saw Lady Gertrud, he kissed her and said: "Welcome, Lady Gertrud, and your son, my kinsman, and your entire company. God grant that I

THE ROMANCE EPIC OF BAERING · 213

might be able to support your son in attaining his patrimony and avenging his kinsmen. Moreover, when the boy has grown up, he shall be welcome here and enjoy my royal respect. And Adalbrecht shall become my knight and enjoy the same respect from me as do my other knights. And he shall protect you on my authority. He shall enjoy your trust, inasmuch as he did not betray his lord. The fishermen who came here with you will be your servants. Food and garments you will receive from me. But now I am curious to learn how you managed to escape from Heinrek."

Lady Gertrud spoke: "I escaped the second night after having given birth to the baby. The men and their wives who were in the same house as I were all asleep. I took the baby in my arms and left without anyone knowing this. After I had gone out of the gate, I went to the river that flows from Braunschweig into the Elbe. It was very dark and I did not know the area. And I walked with wobbling steps, because the pains of childbirth and my weakness affected me, and I fainted together with the child. At daybreak I regained consciousness, but the child had fallen two feet away from me and an eagle had its talons on it intending to fly off with it. But I hastened there so that it could not take the baby. But then I heard many men talking, saying that they should look carefully for me. And I jumped down from the Elbe's banks and fell into the reeds, and I was covered with reeds and sand, and the Elbe was so close and it flowed all around me. In the meantime, the baby suckled. Heinrek and his men were looking for me on the Elbe, and the boat he was in was at my head, drifting alongside me. I would have been killed, if the keel had dragged me along the edge of the boat. Nonetheless, three of my ribs broke on one side, but I thought it worth enduring, to keep the baby quiet, which Heinrek would have wanted to kill. God, however, did not want that and was merciful to us and sent us here, for if Heinrek had killed the baby, I would no longer have wanted to live. But the baby was silent and was not frightened by either the noise or din caused by those searching for us. When evening fell, Heinrek told 200 men to guard the Elbe and threatened them with their lives if they did not search every ship they saw. They did this the entire day until it was dark. Then they headed in their boats for land, set up tents, and started to eat. A dinghy was at my feet where I lay in the reeds. I stood up and we lay down in the dinghy and pushed it from shore. Then such a great storm arose that the dinghy was transported a little faster than Heinrek's ships, and it seemed to be around midnight that Heinrek shouted to his men and told them to sail to Frisia, for he had been told that I might have gone there. And I was very much afraid that he would see me, but the night's darkness prevented him from seeing me. And then I no longer heard him. I was driven out to sea where there were such heavy swells and waves that I fell unconscious. I do not know what happened after this, until Adalbrecht and his squires came to my help. The baby has not been christened and by now it is three months old. It would be the greatest honor for me if you were to stand as the baby's godfather when the baby is christened. And this would make up for the need and misery I have suffered with him."

6. The baby Baering is christened.

Everyone who heard Lady Gertrud's words was sad. The king declared himself ready to be the baby's godparent, together with his queen, Lady Margaret. A deacon named William, from the monastery of St Paul, baptized the baby, and it was called Baering after his mother's brother. The mother rejoiced at her beautiful baby. The king proceeded to table, and the queen sat on one side of him and the deacon William on the other, while Lady Gertrud sat next to the queen. All kinds of dishes were brought to the table and splendid drinks were generously offered to everyone at the table. After finger bowls had been brought, the king asked for silence and spoke: "Most people must be familiar with the fact that Lady Gertrud has suffered a great loss in the death of her husband and my kinsman Walter, and that the evil fraudster Heinrek betrayed and killed Duke Baering, her brother. She has come here into our realm seeking protection for her son. If young Baering resembles the men who are his kinsmen, then those who behaved dishonorably toward him will be rewarded in kind. I now ask you, my queen, and my entire court, both learned and unlearned persons in my entire kingdom, that you express honor and fine respect to Lady Gertrud and her son, young Baering. Those who do so shall have our thanks and gratitude; but those who are opposed and disobey will reap harsh consequences." The king received much praise from the people for his words, but most of all from Lady Gertrud. And she was now well respected by the entire royal court, as a result of the king's words.

7. Baering's education.

When Baering was eight years old, his instruction started with books, and he was schooled for twelve years, during which time he studied and learned the seven liberal arts. He surpassed others in learning, intelligence, and eloquence. Indeed, he was superior in knowledge, physique, and strength over other men. He was modest by nature and generous to the poor.

When he turned twenty-three, he asked King Richard, his kinsman, to dub him a knight. "I shall gladly do so," said the king, "because you are a most accomplished person. And I shall give you squires and a ship to sail to Holstein to attempt to regain your patrimony and to avenge your mother's brother, and also as much help as I can put at your disposal." Baering now thanked the king for his promises and he asked Adalbrecht to buy weapons for him, and he did so.

THE ROMANCE EPIC OF BAERING · 215

Christmas had now come. Many lords had arrived at the court of King Richard. Many earls had also come to London, as well as the king of Scotland, and many mighty men and those who held land in fief to King Richard. They all wanted to celebrate Christmas with him.

On the first day of Christmas, when the large group had come to table in the palace, the king of Scotland asked for his son to be advanced in rank by King Richard and said that no one equaled him in vigor and courage. And King Richard announced to the assembled court that he intended to dub John, the son of the Scottish king, a knight, and at the same time young Baering, his kinsman, as well as 300 other young men. King Richard now bade the bishops and earls to observe who among the knights proved superior at jousting and who accomplished and performed best and was able to lift the most men from their saddles. Everyone there praised the king for his benevolence in wanting to advance his vassals in rank. The queen herself asked to observe this tournament.

8. Baering and other young men are dubbed knights.
At daybreak on the second day of Christmas the king went to the cathedral of St Paul to attend the chanting of hours and Mass, as did all the young men who were to be put to the test that day. After the celebration of Mass the king first dubbed Baering, his kinsman, a knight and presented him with splendid weapons and sumptuous garments, including a silken jacket. In the same manner he dubbed John, son of the Scottish king, a knight, as well as 300 knights whom he presented with horses and weapons. They left the church and mounted their horses. The king and the queen and the entire court went to observe the jousting. Of all those on their horses, Baering was taller by a head.

John, the son of the Scottish king, then said to Baering: "The one who dismounts the other shall take the spurs off his feet and turn his horse around for the queen to see, and also Elena, her daughter."

Baering answered: "You want to demonstrate your prowess now, and you shall decide this."

9. Baering is victorious at jousting.
Now they rode at each other and when they met, people heard and saw them striking at one another with their spears, and this went on for a long time. Baering then said to John: "Take back your words, for I could have lifted you out of the saddle a long time ago if I had wanted to do so. But I don't want you to veer before my horse for her to see, since you are wooing her."

"No," said John, "we are going to continue jousting."

216 · THE ROMANCE EPIC OF BAERING

At this Baering directed his spear at John, the Scottish king's son, and lifted him out of the saddle, throwing him to the ground. And afterwards he lifted one knight after the other out of the saddle and defeated everyone. Baering now earned praise and great renown through his jousting. John asked him for restraint, so that he would not be disgraced in front of his beloved, and Baering agreed to this.

The king and his entire court now went to table in the palace. The Scottish king thought that he had boasted too much about his son and now believed that the wooing might not be supported. But King Richard cheered him up, as did all his guests, and he said that there was no blame or disgrace in having been overcome by Baering. King Richard celebrated Christmas with much pomp and good cheer. At its conclusion the kings, earls, and the mighty men who were the king's vassals went home to their families.

10. **Baering is shipwrecked.**

Afterwards King Richard had one hundred big ships built that measured a hundred fathoms, and gave them to Baering, his kinsman. On board the ships were two earls and a large army. Baering was now chief of this army and he intended to regain his patrimony and avenge his mother's brother with King Richard's army. They were now ready to sail from the harbor of Yarmouth. They had a fair wind filling the sails, and they began sailing into the sea with their large army. Then an eastern wind arose, bringing much rain, and they had to take the sails in and drift with the wind. Then the wind turned to the south and thereafter to the north of the land. The storm was such that they could not drift before the storm and they were borne onwards. But the rigging did not fare well when the northwest wind came: the shrouds broke; the braces of the sails gave way; and the sea washed over them, and no one on board expected to live. When the storm was at its fiercest Baering's ship was thrown onto the seashore and it broke to pieces. Of the men on board no one came away alive except Baering. He lay in an inlet for three days and some fishermen found him on the flooded bank and thought he was dead. They wanted to strip him of his tunic, but then Baering regained consciousness and spoke:

"Where am I," he said, "and where are my squires and the good sailors and the mighty army that King Richard had given me to take vengeance on my enemies for my great disgrace? And you, merciless and cruel storm, have taken from me all my good luck with the raging swells. And you strangers want to strip me like robbers? Give back my garments and leave as you came!"

At Baering's words, they came and gave him back his garments, and asked who he was. He answered: "That is none of your business. You can see that I have been shipwrecked. But what is the name of the country in which I find myself?"

The fishermen answered: "You have come to the country called Flanders. Earl Ferant is the ruler here and he is a vassal of the king of France. You can see his capital, which is called Bononia,[5] and we promise to take you there. You must be of good family, and we shall also receive a good reward for our effort, since God safeguarded your life."

Baering answered: "Thank you for your fine offer, which I gladly accept."

Now they brought him to a good merchant, who gave the fishermen English marks, and they went their way. When he had been half a month with the merchant, Baering spoke to him.

11. Baering participates in a joust.

"I have now dwelled with you most generously, but you have not received anything for your hospitality. I have recovered from my injuries at sea, and I would like you to receive my garments. I have three English marks and I would like you to buy for me fine white garments and along with them appropriate white weapons as befit a knight. Every day I see the earl's men challenge each other's prowess, and I wish to participate in their jousts, since what I see there is what I was born to."

The merchant answered: "I think it likely that you are a good knight, for you are a tall man and most handsome. And I shall obtain both for you, but I do not want your garments in exchange."

"It is not customary in our family," said Baering, "to give something and then take it back."

The merchant answered: "I shall repay your goodness and give you my horse which the earl offered for ten English marks."

"God reward you!" said Bearing, "Now you have dubbed me a knight, and I shall reward you well for that."

The merchant now brought him the weapons and garments, and Baering received them with thanks. He got armed and mounted the horse which the merchant had given him, and he rode to the place where men demonstrated their prowess.

When Robert, the earl's son, saw him, he spoke to his squires: "I've seen an unknown knight come here, and I am curious about our joust. The one who is our best knight shall joust with him and find out what he is capable of."

And the earl's man at once spurred on his horse and galloped toward Baering, but the latter thrust his spear at him and cast him far from his saddle and to the ground. Robert, the earl's son saw this and spoke to his squires:

---

5. Bononia is today's Boulogne-sur-Mer on the French coast of the English Channel.

218 • THE ROMANCE EPIC OF BAERING

"Repay him," he said, "for he has lifted our companion out of the saddle."

Baering, however, rode back to the knight against whom he had contended and spoke: "I don't want you to behave despicably toward me, at my having thrown you out of the saddle, since you are unaccustomed to chivalry. Let us meet here tomorrow morning. And if I am better than you, then I shall teach you."

The earl's son Robert answered: "I would like that, and come back with us, but tell us who you are and what your name is."

"I shall not tell anyone my name," he said. "Christ knows me, but my christening name will be hidden for now. Let us go home now, and in the morning meet here where we have been speaking."

12. Baering bets his life in the joust.

The first to come in the morning was Robert, the earl's son, together with all his father's best knights. One of them was Kleokan, who had never yet been lifted out of the saddle. He spoke to Robert, the earl's son, in this fashion:

"The knight should now be coming who lifted you out of the saddle yesterday. I bet 100 silver marks that he won't lift me out of my saddle."

He had barely spoken, when Baering arrived and spoke: "I heard what you said and that you bet 100 marks; I shall bet my life, however, for I have no money."

They shook hands and pledged this, which Robert, the earl's son, and other knights witnessed. They attacked each other now and each broke five spear shafts against one another. Baering spurred on his horse and galloped at Kleokan, grabbing him by the neck and lifting him out of the saddle, and he galloped with him around the whole field and then flung him to the ground and spoke:

"You shall give me 100 marks, as the earl's son Robert and other knights can attest."

They said that he was right. "And you deserve this, for there is scarcely another man as strong as you."

And then Kleokan got up and paid Baering the money, as agreed. The earl, however, and Robert honored Baering in word and deed, and said that it was clear that no one equaled him in chivalry. And the earl's son did not part from Baering's side either at meals or in their chambers.

13. Easter celebration in Paris and arrival of Emperor Emanuel of Greece.

During the day, as the earl sat at table, a handsome knight came riding who approached him. He came with a greeting from King Pippin of France, with an invitation to visit him in Paris together with all his best knights. He wanted to celebrate Easter in the city of Paris, and on Easter Monday he wanted to stage chivalric jousting. After this the earl set out with 800 men, pages excepted. The earl arrived in Paris on Easter Eve, where the king was presiding, and his men, who knew the earl, accompanied him to the king, who welcomed him and those attending him.

On Easter Sunday King Pippin went to the church of St Mary, accompanied by all the best knights, as well as Earl Ferant and his men. The archbishop of Sanz celebrated Mass, assisted by eight suffragan bishops. At the conclusion of Mass, the king went to the hall, accompanied by the archbishop and the suffragan bishops, as well as Earl Ferant of Bononia, Earl Stefan of Byrgum, the duke of Normandy, Count Lafranz of Brittany, and all the other noblemen who were King Pippin's vassals. All had now come to table with the king. The table seating was thus: the archbishop sat on the king's right, and Earl Ferant on Queen Dionisia's left, and also the suffragan bishops. The throne-table was round and no one was assigned there except for two earls and the bishops.[6] This throne-table was in the middle of the hall, scintillating with fire-red gold. In all 500 persons were present, with no one of lower rank than knight. There were all kinds of food and drinks, wine and mead and royal delicacies.

As the king was sitting, he looked around the hall and noticed Baering. He looked at him for a long time and then spoke to Earl Ferant: "I have never seen a more handsome man than the one sitting next to Robert, your son. Where has he come from?"

The earl answered: "He is Robert's companion and a good knight. But his family is not known to me, and he does not want to reveal his name to anyone. We call him the Fair Knight."

The king said: "That name befits him, for I have never seen a fairer man who also is so valiant. And tomorrow he will be able to demonstrate his valor."

As the king was speaking about his beauty, the queen sat there despondent, as she looked at him.[7] The earls and knights and everyone else in the hall praised his beauty.

On the morning of Easter Monday the king had the trumpets blown for everyone to assemble for the tournament in Paris. When the king came onto the field with his army, a nobleman approached him and spoke to him:

6. The word I translate as "throne-table" is *hásæti* in Icelandic; it is the high-seat reserved for the head of household in the Icelandic sagas. Here it is round, and to judge by the above information, eleven persons are seated here. This suggests that it was inspired by King Arthur's Round Table, which was known in Iceland from the thirteenth-century translations of Chrétien de Troyes's Arthurian romances and which is described at length in the fifteenth-century *Skikkju rímur* (Mantle Rhymes). See Marianne Kalinke, "*Skikkjurímur*: We shall find ourselves better women," *Journal of English and Germanic Philology* 120 (2021): 1–17.

7. The queen's despondence is puzzling, but possibly presages the subsequent reactions of women to the young man known only as the Fair Knight.

220 • THE ROMANCE EPIC OF BAERING

"Greetings to you, lord king, and to your entire army. Emanuel, the emperor of Greece, has come here in peace and with amity, and he seeks your permission to test the valor of his men and yours. He also wants to ask honorably for the hand of your daughter Wilfrida in marriage. He has been told that there is no one who is her equal in beauty in the world. That is the reason for his coming here, and not war."

King Pippin welcomed Emperor Emanuel and invited him and his men at his expense. After this the jousting took place and each man charged at the other, and their assaults were so rough that the horses barely managed to dodge the broken spear shafts, and many hundreds of men were lifted out of the saddle. The Greeks were daring toward the Franks, and Arius, the nephew of Emperor Emanuel, threw many a good knight off his horse, for he was both agile and strong and did not fear the dexterity of any Frank. The sons of earls and dukes did not dare challenge the Greeks. Robert, the earl's son, and Philip, the son of Earl Stefnir, both charged at the same time at Arius, but he turned toward them and threw both of them off their horses.

14. A joust.

Baering now rode onto the jousting plain and was surprised when he saw that a foreign army had come to compete at jousting with the Franks, and he asked where Robert, his companion was. He was told that he had been thrown off his horse and that the nephew of Emperor Emanuel had beaten all the Franks. As soon as Baering heard this, he turned his horse toward Arius, whose spear shaft he seized and broke with his hands, and then he grabbed his neck with his left hand and lifted him out of the saddle and threw him a length of six feet onto the field, and three of his ribs broke. After this the Greeks stopped jousting, for no one dared to joust with Baering. As a result of this joust Baering was declared victor and earned great honor. Baering was now the most renowned of all the knights.

Afterwards they returned to Paris and ceremoniously accompanied the emperor to the king's hall. King Pippin was there, as were Queen Dionisia and Wilfrida, their daughter, who were sitting at the throne-table. The emperor and his people were welcomed enthusiastically and joyfully.

The archbishop began his speech as follows: "Emanuel, the emperor of Greece, is welcome here, as are his earls and knights. They have come out of affection and friendship for Pippin, the powerful king, and the queen and their daughter Wilfrida, whom the emperor would like to have as his queen, provided her father consents. She is the most beautiful and gracious maiden in the world. She has not appeared before among such a large numbers of persons, until the emperor arrived here. It is my advice, Lord, that you give your daughter to the emperor in marriage."

The king answered: "I shall gladly do so," he said, "if she agrees to that." Then the king asked Lady Wilfrida if she agreed to what her father and mother approve.[8]

"Yes", she said, "that is agreeable to me."

After the tables were removed, the emperor betrothed himself to Wilfrida, the king's daughter, and bestowed on her half of Greece, and this was witnessed by everyone in the king's hall, that is, ninety persons. One could now hear all kinds of entertainment with stringed instruments, with harps, rebecs, fiddles, and psalteries. And there was much feasting and merriment in all of Paris on account of the emperor. During this merriment Baering, who was known as the Fair Knight, walked into the hall. The king invited him to sit at the throne-table, next to him.

"No," he said, "I am neither a king nor a cleric. I shall sit among the knights."

The king answered: "You are quite worthy to bear the name of king, considering your beauty and your valor." The king's daughter kept looking at Baering, because she had never seen an equally fair man, and she very much regretted her betrothal to the emperor and her consent, which she very much wanted to annul. Her intense love for Baering overwhelmed her, and she was tortured by this both night and day.

15. Concerning the love of the king's daughter.

She now began to love Baering with all her heart, and this was not hidden on her face, as anyone in the hall could see, for she sometimes was red as blood, and sometimes pale as bast. And it happened in keeping with the old maxim: "if a woman loves a man, her eyes won't hide it."[9]

After that the tables were removed and the emperor went to his quarters, and the king and queen and their daughter to theirs.

Baering took the money he had won at jousting; it was no less than 500 English marks, and with all this money he bought weapons and garments and gave

8. By the end of the twelfth century a marriage was established in Iceland "as soon as a man had betrothed a woman 'with her own yes-word' (með jákvæði hennar sjálfrar) in the presence of witnesses." This is reflected in the question Pippin asks his daughter. See Jenny Jochens, *Women in Old Norse Society* (Ithaca and London, 1995), 44–45.

9. The source of the saying is *Gunnlaugs saga ormstungu*, which states: "Eigi leyna augu ef ann kona manni" (if a woman loves a man, her eyes won't hide it). See "Gunnlaugs saga Ormstungu," in *Borgfirðinga sögur*, ed. Sigurður Nordal and Guðni Jónsson (Reykjavík, 1938), 89, and *The Saga of Gunnlaug Serpent-Tongue*, trans. Katrina C. Attwood, in *Sagas of Warrior-Poets*, ed. Diana Whaley (London, 2002), 137.

222 • THE ROMANCE EPIC OF BAERING

them to those on whose account he had won the money. For this reason he gained the friendship of the emperor so much that he offered him the best earldom in Greece.

Baering responded: "I would like to accompany you, lord, and observe your customs and be paid by you as a mercenary, if you think my service is deserving; but I do not want to receive an earldom."

16. Concerning Wilfrida's wish to enter a cloister.

Now on the fourth day the emperor was ready to go home to Greece and he wanted to take his betrothed along. But she said that she had dreamed that she should observe chastity and abstain from carnal intercourse. Her father and mother asked her to accompany the emperor, however, but it was no use, and everyone considered this a serious matter, but for the emperor it was most distressing. When everyone was outside the city gate and they were ready to depart, Lady Wilfrida, the beautiful maiden, came and kissed the emperor and her father and all the noblemen.

"Stay well," she said, "I am dedicating myself to God and entering a holy cloister, for I want to abstain from all of life's pleasures."

When she had kissed the great noblemen, she turned to Baering, kissed him amiably, and said to him in a low voice: "I give myself to God, but I commend my love into your hands, and in return I want to have your love forever."

Baering did not want to respond, since it was neither the time nor the place for this. Many there suspected that her feelings were more for Baering than the emperor. After this the kings departed, and Baering traveled with the emperor to Greece. Lady Wilfrida entered a cloister, but did not want to don a nun's habit.

As soon as the emperor returned to Greece, many wounded men came to him, and they said some men had died in Constantinople, which we call Miklagarðr,[10] which was conquered by black men and the heathens they call Saracens. "They have an army of no less than 230,000 men and 10,000 ships. They have a chieftain named Livorius, and in all of Greater Saracendom there is none equally evil. His face is black like the bottom of a kettle, and his nose is crooked and two hooks are at its tip. He is eight ells tall and resembles more a devil than a man."[11]

At this the emperor became sad and with trumpets he called his men to arms. As soon as the black men saw this, they armed and rode against Emperor Emanuel's forces. But before they met, Livorius spoke to Emperor Emanuel:

10. *Miklagarðr* literally means "big stronghold." The use of the Old Icelandic name for Constantinople is another indication that *Baerings saga* was composed by an Icelander.

11. The figure of Livorius and his portrayal was clearly inspired by the giant Eskopart in *Bevers saga* § 18. On black Saracens, see Geraldine Heng, *The Invention of Race in the European Middle Ages* (Cambridge, 2018), 186–91.

"Your land and life are mine. Submit to me and be my man. I have conquered half of Greater Saracendom with my sword, and a battle against you seems an easy one. My two brothers, Vincent and Ambolicus, have been victorious in 1,000 duels, in addition to all the battles. Now choose one or the other: submit to me or do battle with us.

17. The battle.

The emperor did not respond, but had his trumpets blown, and now a hard battle ensued. At the beginning of the battle, Arius, the emperor's nephew fell, and also many other good knights. The emperor considered fleeing, but at this moment Baering came forward and with mighty force he struck down Ambolicus, the brother of Livorius, and ten of his earls. At this, the emperor and his army, which earlier had wanted to retreat, now advanced. When Vincencius saw that his brother Ambolicus had fallen, he rode toward Baering and spoke as follows:

"You have greatly humiliated and offended King Livorius when with a single blow you struck down his brother and sliced through ten of his earls as though they were angelica.[12] What is the source of your strength without the aid of our gods? I am now going to avenge my brother and my squires, the two earls, if you dare join battle with me."

Baering answered: "Attack bravely and valiantly. May one's heart break if he fears you, a single man."

Vincentius now thrust his spear at Baering's shield, but Baering moved adroitly and broke the spear shaft, chopping off his right hand. Then Vicencius turned to flee, but Baering struck his back and split his hauberk and chain mail and even Vincencius himself and his horse.

After this King Livorius fled into the castle in Constantinople and locked the gates of the city. The emperor, however, had his army set up tents all around the city, and he praised Christ for having granted victory to him.

He spoke to Baering: "Praised be the father who begot you and the mother who gave birth to the son that you are.[13] You avenged my nephew Arius, and killed two brothers of King Livorius, most valiant men, and ten other earls. On this day you gave me victory through God's mercy and your own prowess, and my empire, Greece, has been saved. Now tell me, you exceptional knight, your name."

12. Comparing Baering's killing of the earls to slicing through angelica is surely an Icelandic touch, since the plant grows all over Iceland.

13. The emperor's statement to Baering has biblical resonance, such as in Proverbs 23:25, "Let your father and mother be glad, let her who bore you rejoice," or Luke 11:27, "Blessed is the womb that bore you, and the breasts that you sucked."

224 • THE ROMANCE EPIC OF BAERING

Baering answered: "I dreamed that others will very soon reveal my name and background, family and circumstances. And I want to serve you. And it is true that I did not harm men before today – though they ought not be called men, but rather dogs. Those men have attacked Christendom, and we ought to repay them for their great injuries. And that is, as God wills."

When Baering had said this, a knight came running out of the city and told the emperor frightful news, as follows: "The accursed Livorius has told his idols about the loss of his brothers and innumerable knights, and he is blasphemously offering sacrifice to them and with devilish ruses in order to overcome you. To judge by his countenance, a swift death awaits Christians and Saracens who are in the city. His idols have given him frightful strength and the appearance of an unclean spirit, and anyone who sees him loses his mind; many Christians have died because of this. Early tomorrow morning he intends to wage battle. And you, Lord, if truth be told, must take action against this fiend."

At this news Baering went to talk to the emperor, and he now advised the emperor's entire army to follow him in battle array. And Baering told the emperor that trusting in God he would engage Livorius in a duel.

At daybreak the next morning many Saracens left their ships for the city. Livorius himself left the castle with such fiendish power that every Christian he looked at died instantly. Baering suggested that the emperor should engage those from the ship in battle until God granted their duel.

18. The death of King Livorius.

Baering now mounted his well-armed horse, made the sign of the cross, and charged through the ranks of 20,000 men. Livorius stared at him with flaming eyes and addressed him with harsh words in this manner: "*Ho, ho, niho, lot, makot, tolot.* Holy god, where now is your might and main? The bane of my brothers and earls singlehandedly assails our mighty army, not fearing your power, which filled me with his spirit, so that all my enemies fear me, except for this one person. Tell me, are you a king or a king's son, and what god has given you power? I have never seen an equally dauntless man. What is your name and from where do you come? Or don't you understand my language? If you understand me, then answer me. And you can reveal your innermost thoughts. I forbid all my men to attack you, for I alone shall kill you."

Livorius said this and then struck Baering's shield with his fine sword, splitting it. Baering made the sign of the cross, however, and with his spear struck into Livorius's shield, as though it were a wooden log, and through Baering's great strength Livorius's shield fell out of his hands and onto the ground. Baering then drew his sword and struck Livorius's helmet, but he returned the blow

THE ROMANCE EPIC OF BAERING • 225

and split Baering's helmet, and the sword knocked off his mail cap and came down on the armed horse in such a fashion that its head flew off. Baering was immediately on his feet and when the Saracen king wanted to run at him, Baering grabbed Livorius's waist and got ahold of the sword he held in his hand, and now both held onto it. Livorius's horse, however, was startled and Livorius fell to the ground and both men now grappled for the sword. Through God's mercy Baering was on top, managing to get the sword, and he struck Livorius and cleaved his waist. Then the loathsome fiend emerged out of Livorius and spoke: "Flee from me, Saracens."

It is not safe to overcome God's friends, and the power of idols is meager. There was not one Saracen who dared assault Baering once Livorius had fallen, and they all fled to the city. The emperor was there with his army and killed all the Saracens. Once Livorius had fallen, the emperor's army was able to fight and also to defend itself, and both the naval force and the Saracen army were defeated because of Bearing's command and prowess, and with the assistance of Our Lord, Jesus Christ. And because of Livorius's struggle with him, Baering lay long unconscious. The emperor raised him up and sprinkled cold water on his face and spoke:

"God preserve your life. I shall give you half of Greece and Vindemia, my sister, a most beautiful maiden, in marriage."

Baering then regained consciousness and spoke: 'Let us check out the slain to see whether Livorius is dead."

The emperor said: "He is lying here, rather fiendishly, among us. May God reward you. I shall give you half of Greece and my sister Vindemia in marriage, and additionally any rank you choose. But tell me your name."

Baering answered the emperor and said: "God be thanks for your good offer," and he went to the city gate, where the emperor's army was. They all praised him for his prowess. And after the field had been ransacked, the emperor went into his city and ordered a great feast to be prepared, and he led Baering and Vindemia, his sister, into the chambers. His armor was then removed and his bare skin showed. In many spots he was bruised and bloody, because the evil heathen king had punched him, but in between his skin was as white as snow. Vindemia gave garments of rich material and silk to him, and she said to her brother:

"His valor and chivalry and his snow-white skin will cause many a woman much anguish." Baering only laughed at this. The emperor now went to table, and Baering sat on his right hand and Vindemia on his left, as did the dukes and earls. One could see there much refined pomp at the emperor's feast. News of the victory and honor that the Fair Knight had won for the emperor was heard all over France, and no less in Greece.

226 • THE ROMANCE EPIC OF BAERING

19. Baering's beauty seduces women.

Now we must tell a bit about King Richard and Baering's mother, Lady Gertrud. The fishermen who had found Baering said that he was alive and that they had taken him to Bononia. They knew for sure that the person called the Fair Knight was Baering, and that he alone had survived in the great storm. They sent a letter to the king of France and the earl of Bononia to inform them of Heinrek's treachery and how Baering had escaped.

Now that they had learned this, they sent the earl's son Robert to Greece, along with many good knights, to find out whether Baering wanted to regain his patrimony and to avenge his mother's brother with the same courage he demonstrated when he rescued the emperor's life and country. As soon as Wilfrida, the king's daughter, learned this, she sent a letter to Baering, while the king dispatched two letters, one to Baering and the other to the emperor, concerning his betrothed. Months did not pass before Robert, the earl's son, met the emperor and Baering and delivered the letters from the king of France and his daughter. Through these letters the emperor learned of Baering's family and his prominence, and he honored him all the more in every way, when he learned what kind of a man he was. There now was a joyful reunion of Baering and Robert, his companion. And they went straight to the chambers of Vindemia, the emperor's sister, where they talked and played chess with her. She often inquired about the emperor's betrothed, why she had not wanted to accompany the emperor. But Robert, the earl's son, said that she would soon come.

One day when Baering had gone to dinner, Vindemia found the letter from the king's daughter Wilfrida, and this is what she had written:

"To the dearest Baering, the young and fair knight, son of Walter of Holstein, Wilfrida, daughter of King Pippin of France, sends God's greeting and her faithful love. You know that I have rejected my betrothed, the emperor of Constantinople, on account of my love for you, and have said that I want to observe chastity. Yet that was not my intention, as I told you when we parted, for I love you with all my heart. Now if you wish to receive lands and riches from my father, come to meet me. I shall firmly support our marriage, and you will be properly honored by my father and my relatives as well as the entire populace. Farewell."

Emperor Emanuel saw the letter sent by the king of France and he offered to give his sister Vindemia to Baering in marriage, along with half of Greece.

Baering answered: "I thank God for your good offer, Lord, but I long very much to go home and I have very much in mind to regain my patrimony. I shall never forget your sister, however, who is both wise and beautiful and who is prudent in her constancy. But I do not want to be engaged to her until I return. And I firmly intend never to be unfaithful to her."

THE ROMANCE EPIC OF BAERING · 227

Vindemia said: "I shall not offer myself to any man, and in keeping with my brother's advice I shall remain faithful to you, and I give you my word of honor, if you want to marry me."

"You have spoken well, maiden," said Baering. They now shook hands and accepted joint responsibility in keeping with the advice of the emperor, and Robert, the earl's son, and many other noblemen.

Vindemia then showed Baering the letter from Wilfrida, the emperor's betrothed, which she had found when he had left. Vindemia was now aware that Wilfrida loves Baering, and she asked him how he wanted to deal with this.

Baering responded as follows: "Although she is beautiful, she is not steadfast. And I could never love her, since she is a fickle woman. Convey my advice now to your brother that he ought not love her."

After their conversation Baering took leave of the emperor. The emperor offered him a large army, but Baering wanted to have no more than one ship. At Baering's departure many became sad, and Vindemia cried and bade him fare peacefully with God.

On the tenth day they came to the harbor of Venice. Baering disembarked and took along the weapon that had belonged to Livorius, as well as his horse. In battle the horse was stronger than a lion, more savage than a tiger, and faster than a bird in flight, but occasionally gentle as a lamb. Baering had two men as squires, and he told all the others to sail back to Greece. Robert, the earl's son, brought the emperor's letters to the king of the Franks and had much jewelry for the king and his daughter, which the emperor had sent. Baering, however, went through Normandy until he arrived in Bononia.

When he rode to the city, three armed knights rode toward him and said that he was not permitted to ride into the city until he had duelled with a knight named Samuel.

"He is a good knight and the hardiest of those whom Lucius, the Roman emperor has brought along. Any knight who does not want to duel with him has to give him 100 marks of pure silver and then go his way in peace."

But Baering did not respond, and struck one with the sword that Livorius had owned, and he cut him in two, right through the middle; and thereupon the other man, and then the third. The fourth managed to escape and told the earl of their deaths. He immediately got armed and found Baering where he had taken lodging, and he said: "Get armed, knight, you killed the emperor's knights and did not want to adhere to his rules."

"I am first going to eat," said Baering, "and then you can meet me outside the city, but do not let any more men fight with me."

228 • THE ROMANCE EPIC OF BAERING

As soon as Baering had eaten, he got armed and also his horse, which he mounted. His two squires, Osus and Nisus, accompanied him. Vindemia had chosen them from the emperor's entire court as the most trustworthy men. When Baering came to the outskirts of the city, the knight followed him, as did all the people in the city, both men and women, to watch his victory. The earl's wife was standing on the ramparts and asked Baering to flee. The earl was happy at her words, thinking that he himself would be victorious, and spurring his horse on, he rode fast at Baering. Baering turned his horse toward him and struck his spear into his shield and through it, and into the hauberk, and his spear was washed in the blood of his heart. Baering cast him, dead, to the ground. His wife wailed when she saw her husband's blood, and she asked the men in the city to avenge him. But that did not happen, since Baering had conquered many lands for the emperor by duelling, and if he were killed, there would be no one to avenge him. For this reason Baering rode peaceably into the city.

In the morning the earl's body was taken to be buried, and the city's entire population accompanied the body. Baering was standing nearby, and the beautiful woman who was married to the earl saw him, and asked who that handsome man was. She was told that he was the one who had killed her husband. When she saw his bare face, she was smitten by him more than was appropriate, and she mourned her husband's death but little. She sent word to Baering that he was to marry her, according to the laws of the land. She greatly praised his chivalry, and offered him much wealth, gold and jewels, possessions and property. Baering did not respond to this, and instead wondered how his beauty might be lessened, for every woman who saw him could not help but experience an ardent attraction. And this often resulted in difficulties for him, although his attractiveness did not come from indulgence or boasting or flattery, while mocking was not in his nature. And he did not want to be involved in killing, should there be no necessity. He had a strong desire to pray and to give alms for the sake of God.

One night an angel sent by God appeared to him in his sleep and spoke to him: "God has bestowed great beauty on you and he does not want you to hide this gift or your beauty. Your beauty will be a source of pain for you, because the daughter of Lucius, the Roman king, whose name is Lucinia, will tempt you very much, and many others will do so as well, for they will want to have their will with you. You must not trust any of the women, except Vindemia, who is a most gracious maiden, and you are to marry her, but not any of those who are led astray by your beauty and want to satisfy their lust, instead of observing chastity."

Baering then woke up and recalled the beauty of the angel and how he had appeared to him, and he went into the church and prayed that God mercifully

THE ROMANCE EPIC OF BAERING • 229

bestow on him the beauty that the angel bid him to welcome. And he did not dare veil his face or conceal God's gift any longer.

As Baering was going to his lodgings, he saw a large group of knights coming into the city, who ordered the streets cleared and bells rung at the arrival of Lucius, the Roman Emperor, and this was done. Bishop Astacius and all the city's clerics went to greet him and led him respectfully to the church, and also the emperor's daughter Lucinia. Afterwards they went to their private quarters.

A powerful noble named Tholomeus went to Baering's chamber. He looked at Baering for a long time and then said: "Are you the Fair Knight who killed Samuel, the city's earl, and our companions? We intend to avenge this, if the emperor permits it. Know that he will reproach you."

Baering said: "Let us go to the emperor. I shall not deny that I acted only in self-defense. Be assured that it will happen to others who want to harm me."

They now went to the emperor who was sitting at the throne-table, with Lucinia, his daughter, next to him. Baering went to the emperor and bowed before him and spoke:

"God keep you, Lord! Your power and might are wide-ranging. I have heard that you are just. I trust that you do not misjudge me on account of the avarice of the earl who was your vassal. God passed judgment on us as he willed. He was killed by me as a result of his arrogance. If you want to break the law in respect to me and avenge him, then have your men engage in battle with me, and let God decide who should be the victor." This is how Baering ended his speech.

All those who were in the hall paused, since they had never seen the man before, and they stared at him and said to one another: "Look at this handsome man, such a noble-looking and eloquent individual! See this exquisitely formed person. Look at how Lucinia's color changes, as she stares at this handsome man."

There was such a din in the hall on account of Baering's beauty that the emperor could barely be heard; nonetheless he began to speak and said: "You are a handsome man and likely to be a good knight. Let none of my men be so bold as to break the law in respect to you. I shall raise you in rank, if you become my man."

Baering said: "God be thanked, Lord! I wish to enter your service."

The emperor's daughter Lucinia experienced much heartache on account of Baering's beauty, but she bore this anguish secretly in her breast.

In the morning news reached the emperor that the sons of Heinrek[14] were sequestered in the city of Bern. A huge army had come into the country intend-

14. The text has "menn hans" (his men), but this can't be right, since it seems to refer to the emperor. I changed this to "the sons of Heinrek" in keeping with the next sentence.

230 • THE ROMANCE EPIC OF BAERING

ing to conquer it in war. The following chieftains were there: Geirard and Herman, the sons of Heinrek, who killed Baering of Braunschweig and seized Holstein from Lady Gertrud. When the emperor heard this, he left the city with his entire army and did not let up until he reached Bern.

20. Baering battles with the fraudster Heinrek's sons.

The sons of Heinrek, Hermann and Geirard, killed 400 men of the emperor's army and one nobleman named Tholomeus. The emperor was greatly stricken with grief that the men in his army had been slain. He continued to battle with them, yet without attaining vengeance. Baering had come with his squires, Osus and Nisus, and he went to the tent of Heinrek's sons and spoke to them: "You wretched sons of a villain, get armed. I want to engage in battle with the two of you, for I would rather die in battle than that my mother's brother, whom your father killed, remains unavenged any longer." They considered him impudent, yet got armed at once and mounted their horses. They attacked with their spears but the shafts broke. The brothers, who were accompanied by four knights, drew their swords and attacked Baering, but with his sword he struck down on Hermann's helmet and the sword went all the way into his chest, and he was hurled dead to the ground. Geirard, his brother, wanted to flee, as did the four knights. And Baering pursued them and killed all four, but he seized Geirard and tied his hands behind his back and had him lie on the ground, and the brothers' entire army was so scattered that Baering could kill anyone he wanted. His squires, Osus and Nisus, followed him so well that they had killed a great number before the emperor arrived with his army. Now that he had come, many were slain and the ground was littered with the bodies of the men in the brothers' army. Those who were still alive, fled. The emperor's knights divided the booty among themselves. The emperor took hold of Baering's stirrups and bade him dismount and go to his tent. Matters stood now as before: Baering was a valiant victor, and he was very much praised by the emperor's court. He sat next to the emperor, on his right, and his daughter Lucinia on his left. And Baering was ever most renowned and valiant.

21. Emperor Lucius interviews Geirard, Heinrek's son.

Baering now had Geirard tied up and brought before the emperor, and he said to him: "You son of a villain, are there more of you brothers? And how far to the south does the realm of your father, that fraudster, extend? And why did you dare to harry the lands of the emperor, who is the superior of all kings? You and your father wanted to treat everyone as you did me, and you have long set yourself above my station, but now God permits my revenge."

The emperor now realized from his words who he was, and spoke: "You are welcome before God and me. God has chosen you as defender of the good, but nemesis of the wicked. You have now won a victory for me and also for yourself, and I would like to reward you substantially for this, so that you can avenge your family. Choose the best duchy in my empire for yourself. I want you to be my principal in all my plans, and everyone in my court is to obey you."

Baering thanked the emperor for his good proposition yet asked the emperor to interrogate Geirard concerning the circumstances of his father Heinrek. The emperor and Baering now interviewed Geirard, and his fetters were removed. Then he spoke: "I did not think, when Hermann and I left home – and we had 3,000 knights in our army abroad – that I would have such misfortune: the death of my brother, and the slaying of our entire army, and myself bound like a thief. We, father and sons, should remember the saying: 'old sins bring on new shame.' Everyone told me that you, Baering, and the entire army given to you by King Richard in support had drowned. And now you have opposed us with great resolve and prowess when we did not expect it. To be sure, my father was the source of great harm to you, and most everyone knew that you were wronged by us. But the realm of my father is now extensive, and since he killed Duke Baering he has killed seven other dukes and seized everything they owned. Furthermore, since then he has conquered many lands and even one territory belonging to the lord Emperor."

22. Concerning Heinrek's wife, a giantess who practices witchcraft.

"Now although I have been captured there lives yet another brother, a most valiant and superlative knight. But he is a malicious man and resembles his mother in this respect. She was a giantess and lived under a waterfall of the Elbe river. Through sorcery she became intimate with my father and became his queen, and he loved her beyond all measure. She practiced witchcraft while she lived, and her son far more. Now and then he takes on the form of a dragon, which in battle spews poison at its enemies, who cannot endure this and flee.[15] Through his brute force many lands have become tributary states of my father. And father and son must be with their army in the city called Bozen in Trentino,[16] although they may not yet have learned of this. Now I have told you this and I ask for your

15. This brother, the son of a giantess, is a so-called shapeshifter, as will subsequently be seen. On Icelandic shapeshifters, see Margaret Schlauch, *Romance in Iceland* (Princeton and New York, 1934), 119–48.

16. The place names are guesswork on my part. The manuscript has *Bót* in *Trentodolum* (Trentino valley), which suggests Bozen (also Bolzano) in the Trentino region of northern Italy.

232 • THE ROMANCE EPIC OF BAERING

mercy for my misdeeds. It was not my plan to harry your land, but rather that was my father's and brother's plan, and I cannot tell you whether he is christened or not. He has never come to church and he never allows anyone to speak of God. All the evil deeds are his work and that of his counsellors. It was his plan for us to harry the emperor's realm."

Geirard now concluded his speech, and the emperor and Baering gave him quarter, and he swore fidelity to them and went his way. After this the emperor sent spies into the Trentino valley to find out what Heinrek was up to. In the meantime there was much merriment at the emperor's court, for he held a great feast, and all the citizens were well entertained at this feast.

23. The king's daughter attempts to seduce Baering.
One day, when the emperor was out riding for pleasure, Lucinia, the king's daughter, went into Baering's chambers and spoke to him in a low voice:

"God keep you, my most beloved friend. We two are together in this room now and I must tell you and reveal to you the heartache and anguish I suffer on your account. Ever since I saw you for the first time, my mind has dwelled on your beauty day and night, and I have not been able to eat or experience any joy. You know that I am the sole child of the emperor, a virgin, and I am my father's sole heir. You can now choose to marry me and inherit my father's empire. But to tell you the truth, I think it even better if you first make love to me in secret. That would end my heartache and torment and, to tell the truth, quickly bring me pleasure and joy, until the time when my father consents to what I want. He has pledged that I may choose to marry whom I want. Now if you are willing to comply with my wishes, it does not matter how you proceed. But if you reject my request and do not agree, I shall see to it that you lose both your life and your reputation."

To this Baering replied: "Good maiden," he said, "your words are strange, and I do not understand anything other than that you are seducing me. But I shall never give in to that temptation, since it would be dishonorable of me to bring disgrace on your father. It happens that I must first demonstrate my prowess before I feel love for a woman. Moreover, I am not saying this because I do not know that you are a proper match for me, since you are of higher birth than I am. It might seem childish for you to ask your father to let you have sexual relations with me, considering he is of such noble birth."

The maiden became angry and ran out of the room. She had people support their love and that Bæring should lust for her, and it was no use. For that reason she schemed how to deal with him, and devised a rather evil plan.

Early one morning, when the emperor had left his chambers to go to church, one of the emperor's squires hurriedly came to Baering and asked him to come to a meeting with the emperor. Baering was unaware of any treachery, and he went with him, but instead he found Lucinia, the emperor's daughter, alone in the room. He wanted to walk out, but the doors were locked, and he could not get out. Lucinia did not shy away from her evil act: she sprang at Baering, ripped his clothes off, and cried out loud so that all in the vicinity could hear her. People ran to the door and broke in, followed by the emperor who saw that his daughter had grabbed Baering's hair, and she said that he wanted to rape her. The emperor was quite furious and told them to shackle Baering. Many people wailed and most of all those who were closest to him. But the odds against him were great. Many a one said that it was a great shame to lose a man who was so fair and valiant. But this did not stop the emperor's anger; he had Baering dragged to the river Aare, which flows through the city of Bern, and Baering was cast into the deepest waterfall in the river. Everyone thought that it would be the end of his life. Everyone who was there, wept for him, and said what was true, namely that the lust of the king's daughter, not Baering, was to blame for this.

Baering's squires, Osus and Nisus, got away with his horse and weapons, and headed from the north to the town of Trento, and took lodging in a house outside the city. The third night after he had been thrown into the waterfall, Baering got safe and sound out of the waterfall and came to the room where his squires were and greeted them. They were afraid and thought that he might be a troll, yet also thought that it might be Baering, were his death not a fact. Thus they were afraid and wanted to run away.

24. Battle with the fraudster Heinrek.
Baering spoke to them: "Do not be afraid, good friends, for God has wrought miracles for me, a sinner. The emperor's daughter was not violated by me and I was innocent when I was thrown into the waterfall. But God's angel bore me out of the waterfall, and I seemed to be sitting on the angel's wings. The angel flew with me like a ship under sail, and brought me onto dry land. God willed for us to meet here hale and hearty, and with his guidance we shall be able to dispel our sorrows."

They were happy to hear what Baering said, and they praised God. Then they went into the Trentino valley, but with heads covered, because Baering did not want anyone to hear about him before he had accomplished a heroic deed.

When they came to the city of Bozen, Heinrek, the fraudster king, was there with 40,000 knights, and the fells were teeming with them both in and outside the city. When Baering saw this he turned to go up the mountain above the city. On this mountain was a smooth rock surrounded by willows in leaf, and they stayed there for the night. In the morning Nisus went into the city to

234 • THE ROMANCE EPIC OF BAERING

buy provisions for them, and he found good bargains, since Heinrek was out-side the city with his army, and everyone feared his attacks, which proved to come true. Nisus had hardly come back to Lord Baering, when they saw the battle array on the heath and heard the loud trumpet call, and a great battle began. Baering and his squires got armed and rode down the mountain. They asked with whom he wanted to fight, "since both of these two noblemen have greatly dishonored you, yet one of them was the source of much disgrace and humiliation."

Baering answered: "Old injuries should be avenged first." From this they knew that he wanted to kill Heinrek, and help the emperor this time.

Heinrek had two dozen knights who came from Russia and were taller and stronger men than there had existed earlier. They had killed many of the emperor's nobles. Their swords were tempered with poison and they themselves were full of poison. The emperor could not hold out against them, for they had surrounded him, and he did not think he would be able to escape. At this moment Baering charged at them on his horse and struck one fighter, named Seness, with his sword on his left shoulder, cleaving all the way through him and down through the horse. This stroke caused such a great din and crash that everyone was frightened. The emperor and his army were emboldened and killed a great number of Heinrek's soldiers and thus avenged their men well. Now Baering encountered the fraudster Heinrek with many knights, and Osus and Nisus were wounded, but Baering avenged them so well that Heinrek fled into the city of Bozen. Baering was too slow in pursuing him, however, and Heinrek got into the city before Baering could catch him. All the city gates were locked, and in attempting to reach him Baering struck the gate hinges and said: "Too fast have you escaped me, you villain." The city was now locked, and Hein-rek's forces that got away were inside the city. The emperor's knights divided the booty among themselves, but Baering rode up the mountain and bound the wounds of his squires so they would heal. And the three of them were now of good cheer and merry.

25. The talk of the city's inhabitants.
Now there was much talk by Heinrek's men about the emperor's victory, won-dering who the valiant man was who could slash so mightily. Some said that it was a troll who had come down from the mountain. Others said that it was a giant, along with his two sons.

But Geirard, Heinrek's son, answered: "That must have been young Baering, for he had the sword which killed Hermann, my brother, and our army. Never have I seen a man who resembles him more in both stature and prowess."

THE ROMANCE EPIC OF BAERING • 235

But his father asked him not to say this, "since the emperor threw him into the waterfall on account of his daughter. And we need not fear him."

Thus they concluded their discussion.

26. Heinrek attacks the emperor during the night, but he is saved by Baering.
The emperor spoke to his knights as follows: "Who could it have been who gave me victory today? Twelve of Heinrek's men had surrounded me and also other knights, and they would have killed me if that valiant knight had not come to my assistance."

"Yes," said all his men, "blessed be the knight who wielded the sword. He is tall and strong and greatly resembles Baering."

"No," said the emperor, "what is worse is that I lost him, for he was unsurpassed as a man, but he is not this more unaggressive man, and I would like to know who he is and also his two squires."

One earl from Florence said that he recognized Baering for sure and he asked the emperor and his daughter to confess to their ugly deed of falsely accusing him. As they were talking, Heinrek sent hostages, so that a reconciliation might take place. And the emperor in turn sent hostages to Heinrek. They discussed the terms of the settlement, which were as follows: Heinrek, the fraudster king, was to obtain the emperor's daughter in marriage, together with all of the Trentino valley, in addition to all the emperor's other land that he had conquered, and both swore oaths of fidelity. This allegiance, however, was poorly upheld, for Heinrek was deceitful and intended to betray the emperor, and this betrayal now occurred.

One night Heinrek and his entire force got armed, and without anyone being aware of this they rode toward the emperor's tent and killed a large number of people before the king and his men were yet awake. Those who woke up now wanted to flee. Baering got to hear the noise and he rode immediately toward the battle and saw that the emperor was fleeing as well as more than half his army. One warrior, named Otenek, a great chieftain in Russia and a sworn confederate of Heinrek, who often claimed victory in single combat, was accompanied by 400 knights, and they brutally attacked the emperor. Otenek would have killed him, had not the emperor's hauberk prevented this. Baering now charged at Otenek, who thrust at Baering's shield, but in turn Baering thrust his spear, which was more than three ells long and two spans broad, and was made of holly, into the armed chest of Otenek's horse and its shoulders, continuing through Otenek's shield and his body armor, and the horse fell dead to the ground as did Otenek, while Baering's spear bored more than three ells down into the ground, and the shaft split in two. Baering now took his sword and struck everyone before him and

236 • THE ROMANCE EPIC OF BAERING

also many who tried to flee. His squires also turned out to be good warriors, and the three slew many knights who fell before them in a heap. When the emperor saw this, he turned around with his army, because he saw that he had assistance, and charged hard at Heinrek, and a great number fell in a fierce battle. Heinrek now fled, calling out: "Let us flee. A giant and his two sons have come down from the mountain." But Geirard responded: "This giant is young Baering and he is fittingly avenging himself on you for your wicked deeds."

27. The emperor suspects his daughter of having falsely accused Baering.

Heinrek fled now and had no more than 240 men, and all of them were wounded. He went back north to the Trentino valley and the city called Anguriss. The emperor was in Bozen, however, and thanked God for the splendid victory. He asked whether anyone knew the fine man who fought so boldly on his behalf and delivered his empire and himself from mortal danger. Everyone said that it was young Baering. After their reply, the emperor and his daughter rode out of the city, together with 400 men, in order to find Baering. The emperor asked his daughter whether he was truly guilty of the offense charged against him. She did not reply, but only wept. The emperor suspected that she was malicious and deceitful, and that because of her charges he would experience difficulties in being reconciled with Baering. When it had become most difficult for the emperor to discuss the matter, Baering rode down the mountain and headed north of the city, since he did not want to encounter either the emperor or his daughter. The emperor sent his men looking for him, wanting to speak with him, but did not find him. And now the emperor's fear increased. He went back to the city of Bozen and searched the slain and found Otenek, whose horse had fallen on top of him with its legs up in the air. The spear had pierced both, the horse and Otenek, yet both wore body armor, and the spear was stuck some three ells into the ground. This thrust surprised everyone and they praised the strength of the one who had thrust the spear.

All who saw this said: "That is Baering's thrust." Others said: "Look at Baering's sword stroke. God preserve his hands. He is a valiant man. By God's mercy he was saved from the waterfall in order to be able to destroy God's great adversary and his own. It is most distressing to lose such a comrade. May his hands be blessed. But woe to the emperor's daughter, whose lust brought this about." They ended their wishing Baering to fare well, and they praised God for manifesting his mercy to Baering.

28. Baering arrives in Holstein and prepares to wage war against Heinrek.

It is time to tell about Baering and his squires. They were pursuing Heinrek and found quarters for the night. When they came to the city of Anguriss Heinrek

THE ROMANCE EPIC OF BAERING · 237

had already left. He had collected an army and headed north to the town of Vicilior with 2,000 knights. The earl of Sarnak joined Heinrek with 1,000 knights. Heinrek summoned all who were rendering tribute to him, and when all had come, there were 3,000 knights in addition to the infantry. Heinrek often told his men that the emperor had a giant who had killed his entire army.

One day Heinrek organized a tournament and there was a lot of jousting on a field outside the city. And Baering saw this and said to his squires: "Look at the jousting, or better, battle. A large army has assembled here."

"Yes," they said, "the fraudster Heinrek has assembled his army. We shall gladly accompany you if you want to attack them, and we shall gladly die for your sake."

Baering answered: "That is well spoken, fellows, let's test ourselves against them now." They now rushed at them with great bravery and good luck, and the army became frightened and fearful. Baering and his squires ran into the city and killed seven knights in Heinrek's army and that of the earl of Sarnak. After that they rode on their way, some ten miles north from the city on that day.

On the fifth day they arrived in a city called Mylnar, and came to the wealthy wife of an earl in the city. She provided full lodging for them, but asked Baering to sleep with her in one bed, and he agreed. She had a beautiful daughter who asked Baering the same thing, and he agreed. When they had eaten, a bed was prepared for them in the loft. The three men were to sleep in one bed, but mother and daughter each in her own bed.

When it got dark Baering said to his squires: "You should enjoy yourselves tonight with the mother and her daughter." And they did so: Osus lay next to the wife of the earl, and Nisus lay next to the daughter. They lay there and amused themselves for the night, while the mother and daughter each thought it was Baering. In the morning, before daybreak, Osus and Nisus returned to their own bed.

When they got up and were ready to leave, the earl's wife spoke to Baering privately, and said to him: "You handsome man shall be mine, since I am now without my lord. Otenek was the name of my husband, a powerful nobleman and a sworn confederate of King Heinrek. You shall be honored and possess wealth, if you accept me as your wife; but if not, then I shall arrange for you to be repaid for the shame you brought on me during the night."

Baering answered: "Good woman, you have not been shamed by me, and I want to both live and die with you."[17]

17. The first part of Baering's response is true, but the second is a lie. This is the only time in the entire saga that he prevaricates.

238 • THE ROMANCE EPIC OF BAERING

She thanked him and gave him 100 silver marks, and asked him to go to King Heinrek to tell him about this matter, since the king was responsible for arranging her marriage.[18]

Baering, however, traveled north to the river Elbe, and crossed it, and he was now in his father's land, Holstein. He met many knights there, but did not want to harm them, because they had been forced by Heinrek to serve him. They would rather have had Baering as their lord. Baering went to a castle named Mylnar, and there he lodged well with a merchant. It was summer time and the great feast of Saint John's Eve,[19] and everyone left the castle for the vigil in the city of Lübeck. Baering went there as well. People had come to the city from many lands, from Denmark, Frisia, England, and Vlieland.[20] People from all lands had come there, and they all thronged there to look at the handsome man, Baering. They asked each other from where that man and noble lord had come. All missed the vigil and could do nothing but gaze at Baering's beauty and comeliness. They thought of no other pleasure but to look at him. The eyes of both women and maidens experienced such great pleasure that each thought herself blessed to see such beauty, and wanted to be married to him.

On the Feast of St John, the bishop invited Baering to sit at his table for the fine banquet, and Baering sat to the bishop's right. The bishop now asked him about his background.

Baering said: "I am a knight, and because of a number of troubles I have served various rulers."

The bishop asked: "What are your troubles?"

Baering answered: "The death of relatives and the theft of lands."

"Yes," said the bishop, "many know of the crimes of Heinrek, who is now called our king. He has annihilated all the best men of this country. Day after day we thought that Baering, who defended Greece, would come. He was well regarded everywhere, but people say that Lucius had him drowned in a waterfall on account of his daughter. Yet some say that he is alive and has killed a great part of Heinrek's army."

18. This final scene is poorly motivated. While Baering implies that he has not engaged the widow sexually, his statement that he wants to live and die with her is a lie. This is uncharacteristic of the highly moral person depicted throughout the saga. The author seems to have fallen asleep. For a discussion of Baering's relationship to women, see Marianne Kalinke, *Stories Set Forth with Fair Words: The Evolution of Medieval Romance in Iceland* (Cardiff, 2017), 116–20.

19. The evening before the feast of St John Baptist, that is, June 24.

20. The manuscript writes "Vinland," but this is surely a mistake, for *Vínland* (Wineland) was the name given to an area of coastal North America explored by the Norse in the Middle Ages. I have corrected this to "Vlieland," a West Frisian island.

THE ROMANCE EPIC OF BAERING · 239

"Yes," said Baering, "that may be the case. Would he have the support of brave men, if he were to come here?"

"Yes," said the bishop, "I would grant him 1,000 men."

Baering said: "Thanks be to God, Lord, you are speaking with young Baering."

The bishop answered: "This is a great gift for all of us countrymen. I now recognize you because of your father, but you are both taller and more handsome. May God assist you in destroying God's adversary in your grief. I shall gladly grant you the support of holy church."

Word now got around the city that the fair man who had arrived was young Baering, son of Walter of Holstein. Farmers and city men and knights came to him now and became his retainers, so that he now had 3,000 well-armed men bearing a variety of weapons. He raised his standard and set up the battle array. He elevated the status of Osus and Nisus to duke, and those who had previously been his squires were now lords. Baering put two other dukes in charge of his army, Benedict of Stettin and Baldwin, the nephew of Bishop Peter. Baering left Lübeck now and searched throughout Holstein, and the entire populace submitted to him, including their property and possessions. From there Baering headed south across the Elbe and set up camp near the city of Eutin.

King Heinrek was in Bardwick with 40,000 knights and received news that Baering had assembled an army not far away. He was most unhappy because Baering had killed Herman, his son, and many of his most valiant knights. There was a giant from Frisia with Heinrek.

He said: "Cheer up, lord. This very day I shall bring you the head of the Fair Knight on the pike of my spear. I fear neither trolls nor men in battle. I can lift 144 pounds and my horse can carry four loads of cargo. I know of no one who is my equal, except for Skadevald,[21] your son. Cheer up, lord," said the giant, "and be merry. Let's leave the city now. I know that Baering won't escape. He does not have troops, whereas we have a large army." And this was done.

29. Baering's victory.

Heinrek had now come outside the city with his armed militia, and Baering confronted him with his army in battle array. The sound of trumpets and cornets could be heard, but it was actually the shrill and loud shouting of the huge giant.

He spoke to Baering and his men: "You wretched and poor beggars, get lost!"

Baering spurred his horse on, however, and did not answer, and the horse galloped forward as fast as a hungry hawk flies toward its prey. And Baering drew

21. The name means "wielder of harm."

his sword and struck down so hard on the giant that both his head and trunk flew off. In this assault Baering and his knights attacked so fiercely that Heinrek and his knights fled, since Baering and his men killed many thousands of Heinrek's army. Heinrek now fled into the city with an army numbering no more than 500 knights. But the victorious knights divided the money and weapons and good horses among themselves, and afterwards said to Baering: "We owe thanks and praise to God and to you, Lord, that we, few knights that we are, won such a great victory over many thousands of men. It is through God's mercy that this victory has been achieved on account of your prowess, and your great assault of the giant goaded everyone on to attack.

30. The Holmgang.
"We should always praise God and his saints," said Baering, "and I want to thank you for the great support you have granted me today. But now we shall divide our troops: Baldwin, the bishop's nephew, and Benedict shall go to Hildesheim with ninety knights; Osus and Nisus to Bremen with ninety knights; and I shall go to Braunschweig. I expect that these cities will not offer us any resistance." Now let everyone go to their respective places and overcome these cities without a battle."

In the meantime Skadevald, Heinrek's son, came to Bardwick. He greatly rebuked his father for not having sent word earlier, and he said that Baering would be killed if he attacked him. Heinrek responded, however, that he would not be overcome except through duplicity and sorcery.

"Yes," said Skadevald, "I shall challenge him to a duel, and there is no chance that he can withstand my witchcraft, sorcery, and prowess. I maintain that there is no one more valiant than I and no one more adept at sorcery. You know very well, father, that I have conquered many lands for you, both because of my prowess and my knowledge of witchcraft, which my mother taught me."

An innumerable army accompanied Skadevald. Father and son did not want to lose any more of their men. They said that Skadevald was going to engage in a duel with Baering to determine whose life will be lost. Whoever is victor shall receive the lands and the kingdom. When Baering arrived with his army, he realized that Skadevald wanted to engage him in a duel, and Baering agreed to this.

31. The Duel with Skadevald, the Shapeshifter.
The day of the duel now arrived, and Baering had the Mass of the Holy Spirit, and of the holy queen, Saint Mary, and of the holy angels celebrated. Bishop Peter was the celebrant, and Baering commended himself to God, and then got armed. The bishop asked him to beware the witchcraft of Skadevald. Baering answered: "I trust so greatly in God's mercy that I am not afraid of any witchcraft."

THE ROMANCE EPIC OF BAERING · 241

Baering now stepped into a boat and rowed out to the isle. Skadevald rowed down the river, with envenomed witchcraft, and accompanied by the fiend. Baering blessed himself before stepping on the island, and at once the island disappeared.

Baering then spoke to Skadevald: "Woe to you, villain's son," he said, "heart and strength are demanded for a duel, not witchcraft. Let's tie our boats together and fight on them; that way we shall be far from land."

"Yes," said Skadevald, "wait for me, we'll both be in the same boat," and he jumped up and onto Baering's boat by the prow. Baering attacked him from the middle of the boat, and they struck at each other for a long time until their shields were split. Their boat drifted downstream in the river. Those who were on land watched all their fighting. When their shields split, their hauberks were slashed, as they struck hard.

Skadevald then spoke: "Let us rest for a while."

"No," said Baering, "rest in hell instead, for I shall send you there to rest."

With both hands Baering now struck with his sword at Skadevald, but he avoided the blow adroitly, and transformed himself into such a terrible dragon that no one on land dared look at it. Everyone thought that Baering would die, for a red flame rushed out of its jaws which spewed poison at Baering. But he protected himself with the planks on the boat. But his greatest help, with the mercy of God, was the leather jerkin which Vindemia had made for him. It was lined both outside and inside with red silk, between which there was the soft skin of an animal called Asalabia.[22] Poison cannot penetrate it nor water nor other kinds of moisture. The poison was so strong that the planks broke apart like rotten bark. Baering was now no longer striking at the dragon, for at this moment it turned back into the likeness of a man and spoke: "You are mighty," he said, "no one was able to tolerate this before you. By now I am rested while you are exhausted. Give up your kingdom and lands now, else you shall die."

"This is for God to determine," said Baering, "not you or your witchcraft." At this moment Baering struck down on Skadevald's helmet and cleaved his right ear and also his right shoulder, and Skadevald fell on the planks with his sword at his feet. Skadevald now asked for mercy long enough for him to throw his ear into the water.[23]

22. There are only two attestations in Icelandic of an animal named *Asalabia*, in *Bærings saga* and also in *Viktors saga ok Blávus*, an indigenous *riddarasaga* like *Bærings saga*; there the animal has the quality that it cannot be poisoned. See Sophie Charlotte Maria Fendel, *Tierische Wege gen Norden: Zur Physiologus- und Bestiarienrezeption in Nordeuropa* (Munich, 2023), 297–99.

23. Throwing his ear into the water seems rather strange, but perhaps this is meant to summon Skadevald's two poison-spewing serpents. On shapeshifting, see Schlauch, *Romance in Iceland*, 119–48.

242 • THE ROMANCE EPIC OF BAERING

"Now what are you thinking," said Baering. Then Skadevald turned into an ox and bellowed incomprehensible words. At its bellowing two long and fat serpents came swimming; they were long and thick like wooden logs and slid over the sides of the boat, spewing poison at Baering. With his sword Baering struck the neck of the serpent from the starboard side of the boat, and the head fell into the boat, while the tail landed in the water. Skadevald turned back into a human being, however, seized his sword with his left hand, and struck, as though he had not been wounded, through Baering's double coat of mail and the jerkin, and to the very bone.

Baering spoke: "You are the first man to wound me, and you shall pay dearly for that." And Baering now struck Skadevald's left thigh, which was cut off together with the double coat of mail, and Skadevald plunged overboard and onto the serpent. And it stuck out an ugly two-pronged tongue as though intending to defend Skadevald. But Baering was not afraid of the serpent and cut off the tongue and the lower jaw. At that the serpent curved its tail and struck the prow, so that it broke. At this Baering seized Skadevald's sword and pierced his hauberk and also struck it into the back of the serpent and its heart. Baering held onto the haft of the sword, while the serpent ran with Baering and the boat up onto dry land, and at this point both monsters burst, while the river turned red from the blood of the fiends.[24]

Baering now returned to his men and they sang a hymn of praise to God. Afterwards they mounted their horses and dissolved the truce. Heinrek was quite shrewd when he saw that Baering had killed his son and had won a great victory over so many huge monsters and he wanted to flee now. But Baering pursued him with his army, and captured him, and killed almost his entire army. He was beaten, buffeted, and flogged, and cast into the dungeon, together with Geirard, his son.

Baering went with his army to Braunschweig. There the archbishop and other bishops greeted him and led him with respect and honor into the church. With the counsel of all those present Baering was chosen king over all of Saxony, Westphalia, Holstein, Hildesheim, and Frisia. The land down to the sea and up to the mountains in France and in Lombardy, and east to Kiev and north to Denmark was now Baering's empire. And there was no one so powerful who begrudged him this on account of his father and his lineage, as well as his prowess and bravery, and he enjoyed the good will of all his liegemen.

His deeds of prowess were the subject of much talk in France and England, in Greece as well as Rome. Emperor Lucius was most unhappy that he had Baer-

24. Baering's duel with the shapeshifting Skadevald returns the narrative to § 3 and Heinrek's premonitory dream, in which he bellows like an ox; a lion rips a dragon and Heinrek to pieces, and the river is filled with blood.

THE ROMANCE EPIC OF BAERING · **243**

ing, who was innocent, thrown into the waterfall. And he now wanted to set matters aright and wanted to give Baering his daughter in marriage and also half his empire. Baering, however, did not accept this offer, and instead went to meet the emperor with 8,000 knights and surrounded him in the city of Florence. Not a single person dared to leave the town and come outside, because everyone knew of Baering's prowess and capabilities.

Bishop Peter, and Baldwin, his nephew, and Bendict the mighty were with Baering. Their plan was for Osus and Nisus to go to Greece, taking along ninety knights, with the message that the Greek emperor give his sister Vindemia in marriage to Baering in keeping with their agreement before they parted. They boarded a ship in Venice and sailed in great state on their mission.

This company now sailed to Greece. The emperor wondered from where the handsome group had come. But Vindemia recognized Osus and Nisus and welcomed them. They delivered Baering's greetings and showed the emperor his letter. He now understood the nature of their mission, and learned that Osus and Nisus were now dukes, and also heard about Baering's family. Each of them was now to be addressed as Lord, when previously they had been Baering's squires. The emperor spoke: "God keep you, young Baering, for having raised the honor and reputation of your squires. It is good to serve those who are upright." And their conversation ended for the time being.

32. Baering meets with the emperor and the French and English kings.
The emperor and his sister gathered gold and jewelry together and all kinds of precious objects, and Vindemia was now readied with every honor and started out on her journey. May she fare well.

Now we shall hear what Emperor Lucius and his daughter Lucinia did. He left the city with her, and they surrendered to Baering's authority and also their entire realm. Baering was now the Empire's ruler. King Pippin and King Richard learned this and traveled together with Lady Gertrud, Baering's mother, to visit Baering. They met him in Venice and there was a joyful reunion. Never before had a city been occupied with as many nobles and powerful men as there were in Venice. And Baering was always the fairest of them all.

On the feast of the Assumption of Mary,[25] Baering met with Emperor Lucius, King Pippin of France, King Richard of England, and the bishops there assembled. They agreed that Baering had comported himself well in face of the sexual desire of two kings' daughters, Lucinia and Wilfrida; the latter had rejected her betrothed, the emperor of Constantinople, while the former lost her father's empire. They were unable to refrain from love's passion, but Baering firmly resis-

25. August 15.

244 • THE ROMANCE EPIC OF BAERING

ted sexual desire and did not dishonor them; instead he preserved his chastity and did not let himself be governed by lust. And all agreed that Baering was innocent and guileless in respect to the women and their guardians.

Baering now spoke: "God knows, as you also do, as well as other valiant men what my conduct has been in respect to women and their disgrace. Since you have placed the matter in my hands, I shall give you good advice, if you choose to accept it. Since I love and am kindly disposed to the sister of the Greek emperor, who has agreed that I join her in holy matrimony, my advice is as follows: Since your queen has died, King Richard, I would like you to marry Lucinia, the emperor's daughter, and I shall give her all of Lombardy in the empire, because of our kinship and your kind actions toward me and my mother. And the Greek emperor should marry his betrothed Wilfrida. I give this advice for the sake of our honor, and am unable to give you any advice that is more fitting."

33. Baering's wedding.

All now thanked him for his advice and followed it. A short time later Lucius, the Roman emperor, fell ill and died. His burial took place most honorably. In his place young Baering was chosen as emperor on the advice of the sovereigns present there. On coronation day he presented his mother with Saxony. Lady Gertrude had Heinrek released from the dungeon as well as his son Geirard. Heinrek now remembered his terrible dream, and it was brought home to him that he had been torn up by the lion, the king of animals. No animal dares to follow in its footsteps or step into the ring the lion draws with its tail. In the same manner Baering is king of all kings, for in his day no one was born whom he did not outshine. When Heinrek asked Lady Gertrud to spare his life, she responded:

"You shall now receive the same verdict as did my brother when you behaved so despicably to him in exchange for all the good that he had given you. On top of that you wanted to bring shame on me, when you seized my husband's lands and wanted to kill my only child. You shall now be deservedly avenged for your misdeeds." Heinrek's neck was broken and that is how he died. But Geirard was spared, and he left to meet with Baering.

Lady Gertrud then received a letter, graciously asking her to visit Baering, because he was now going to celebrate his wedding to Vindemia in the capital city of Venice. There came many rulers from various countries. Among all who were there, Baering was the tallest. His face was like the color of a red rose laid on a snow-white lily, and his eyes shone like carbuncles; not a single blemish was found on his body. No one was his equal in vigorous bravery, excepting Hector, the son of King Priam. Vindemia was similarly fair and wore splendid garments. They were now married in accordance with both divine and human law. Then

THE ROMANCE EPIC OF BAERING • 245

they went into the palace for the feast, and a magnificent wedding celebration took place, accompanied by appropriate merriment and all kinds of entertainment. Vindemia bestowed ninety pieces of costly stuff and material on the guests, and she bestowed many other riches on Baering's knights and men. To Lady Gertrud she gave a garment of costly material, worth much gold, as well as large gold rings and golden goblets. For his part, Baering gave lands and kingdoms to earls, barons, and the city's knights. Not a single person was there who did not receive a good garment. At the conclusion of the wedding festivities, all returned home and thanked the emperor and his queen for the splendid gifts. The emperor's domain was secure and legitimate: his franklins enjoyed peace and calm and freedom, but he punished severely those who plundered and conducted themselves immorally. The law was not broken in his realm.

Whoever arouses hatred and dissension, and sustains quarrels and unjust meddling will suffer revenge, though it may be slow in coming, because no one enjoys a good reputation from evil conduct. But whoever is righteous, believes in God, and keeps his commandments will have everlasting joy, and will be esteemed and honored, as was Baering, about whom this saga has been told.

The saga has now come to an end, and we are sent to Christ, as it were, in this world for our fate and fortune, and for the joy of the other world, which Almighty God has prepared for his beloved friends at the end of time in this world and in eternal glory without end *per omnia saecula saeculorum. Amen.*

Bibliography

Icelandic names are alphabetized by given name, not patronymic.

Primary Sources

Bærings saga. In *Fornsögur Suðrlanda*, ed. Gustaf Cederschiöld, 85–123. Lund: Berlings Boktryckeri, 1884.

Bevers saga. In *Riddarasögur*, ed. Bjarni Vilhjálmsson, 1: 283–398.

Bevers saga. In *Fornsögur Suðrlanda*, ed. Gustaf Cederschiöld, 209–67. Lund: Berlings Boktryckeri, 1884.

Bevers saga: With the Text of the Anglo-Norman Boeve de Haumtone. Ed. Christopher Sanders. Reykjavík: Stofnun Árna Magnússonar á Íslandi, 2001.

Bjarni Vilhjálmsson, ed. *Riddarasögur*. 6 vols. [Reykjavík]: Íslendingasagnaútgáfan, Haukadalsútgáfan, 1954–62.

Boeve de Haumtone and Gui de Warewic: Two Anglo-Norman Romances. Trans. Judith Weiss. Tempe, AZ: ACMRS, 2008.

Chrétien de Troyes. *Erec and Enide*. In Chrétien de Troyes, *The Complete Romances of Chrétien de Troyes*, trans. David Staines, 1–86. Bloomington: Indiana University Press, 1993.

—. *The Knight with the Lion*. In Chrétien de Troyes, *The Complete Romances of Chrétien de Troyes*, trans. David Staines, 257–338. Bloomington: Indiana University Press, 1993.

—. *Der Löwenritter Yvain von Chrétien de Troyes*. Ed. Wendelin Foerster. Amsterdam: Rodopi, 1965.

Der anglonormannische Boeve de Haumtone. Ed. Albert Stimming. Halle: Max Niemeyer, 1899.

Élie de Saint-Gilles: Nouvelle édition par Bernard Guidot d'après le manuscrit BnF n°·25516. Ed. Bernard Guidot. Paris: Honoré Champion Éditeur, 2013.

Elis saga ok Rósamundu. In *Riddarasögur*, ed. Bjarni Vilhjálmsson, 4: 1–135.

Elis saga ok Rósamundu. Ed. Eugen Kölbing. Heilbronn: Gebrüder Henninger, 1881.

Elis saga, Strengleikar and Other Texts: Uppsala University Library Delagardieska samlingen Nos. 4–7 folio and AM 666b quarto. Corpus Codicum Norvegicorum Medii Ævi: Quarto Serie 4. Oslo: Selskapet til utgivelse af gamle norske håndskrifter, 1972.

Elye of Saint-Gilles: A Chanson de Geste. Ed. and trans. A. Richard Hartman and Sandra C. Malicote. New York: Italica Press, 2011.

Bibliography • 247

Floovant: Chanson de geste du XIIe siècle. Ed. Sven Andolf. Uppsala: Almqvist & Wiksell, 1941.

Flóvents saga I. In *Fornsögur Suðrlanda*, ed. Gustaf Cederschiöld, 124–67. Lund: Berlings Bocktryckeri, 1884.

Flóvents saga II. In *Fornsögur Suðrlanda*, ed. Gustaf Cederschiöld, 168–208. Lund: Berlings Bocktryckeri, 1884.

Fornsögur Suðrlanda. Ed. Gustaf Cederschiöld. Lund: Berlings Bocktryckeri, 1884.

Gottfried von Strassburg. *Tristan: With the 'Tristran' of Thomas*. Trans. A.T. Hatto. London: Penguin, 1967.

"Gunnlaugs saga Ormstungu." In *Borgfirðingar sögur*, ed. Sigurður Nordal and Guðni Jónsson. Reykjavík: Hið íslenzka Fornrítafélag, 1938.

Hærra Ivan. Ed. Henrik Williams and Karin Palmgren. In *Norse Romance*, ed. Marianne Kalinke, vol. 3. Cambridge: D.S. Brewer, 1999.

Islendzk Æventyri: Isländische Legenden, Novellen und Märchen, Ed. Hugo Gering. 2 vols. Halle a.S.: Buchhandlung des Waisenhauses, 1882–83.

Ívens saga. Ed. and trans. Marianne Kalinke. In *Norse Romance*, ed. Marianne Kalinke, vol. 2: *The Knights of the Round Table*, 38–102. Arthurian Archives 4. Cambridge: D.S. Brewer, 1999.

Karlamagnus saga ok kappa hans: Fortællinger om Keiser Karl Magnus og hans Jævninger. Ed. C.R. Unger. Kristiania [Oslo]: H.J. Jensen, 1860.

Konraðs saga. In *Fornsögur Suðrlanda*, ed. Gustaf Cederschiöld, 43–84. Lund: Berlings Boktryckeri, 1884.

Konráðs saga keisarasonar. In *Riddarasögur*, ed. Bjarni Vilhjálmsson, 3: 269–344.

Layamon. *Layamon's Brut: A History of the Britons*. Trans. Donald G. Bzdyl. Medieval Texts & Studies 65. Binghamton: State University of New York, 1989.

"Il Libro delle Storie di Fioravante." Ed. Pio Rajna. In *I Reali di Francia: Ricerche intorno Ai Reali di Francia*, vol. 1, ed. Pio Rajna, 333–490. Bologna: Presso Gaetano Romagnoli, 1872.

Marie de France. *The Lais of Marie de France*. Ed. and trans. Glyn S. Burgess and Keith Busby. 2nd ed. London: Penguin Group, 1999.

—. *Lanval*. In *The Lais of Marie de France*, trans. Robert Hanning and Joan Ferrante, 105–25. New York: E.P. Dutton, 1978.

The Saga of Gunnlaug Serpent-Tongue. Trans. Katrina C. Attwood. In *Sagas of Warrior-Poets*, ed. Diana Whaley, 109–49. London: Penguin, 2002.

Strengleikar: An Old Norse Translation of Twenty-one Old French Lais. Ed. and trans. Robert Cook and Mattias Tveitane. Oslo: Norsk Historisk Kjeldeskrift-Institutt, 1979.

Thomas's Tristran. Ed. and trans. Stewart Gregory. In *Early French Tristan Poems*, ed. Norris J. Lacy, 2: 4–172. Cambridge: D.S. Brewer, 1998.

Tristrams saga ok Ísöndar. Ed. and trans. Peter Jorgensen. In Marianne Kalinke, ed., *Norse Romance*, vol. 1: *The Tristan Legend*, 23–226. Cambridge: D.S. Brewer, 1999.

Viktors saga ok Blávus. Ed. Jónas Kristjánsson. Reykjavík: Handritastofnun Íslands, 1964.

248 • Bibliography

Secondary Literature

Ailes, Marianne. "The Anglo-Norman *Boeve de Haumtone* as a *chanson de geste*." In *Sir Bevis of Hampton in Literary Tradition*, ed. Jennifer Fellows and Ivana Djordjevic, 9–24. Cambridge: D.S. Brewer, 2008.

Álfrún Gunnlaugsdóttir. *Tristán en el Norte*. Reykjavík: Stofnun Árna Magnússonar, 1978.

Bagerius, Henric. *Mandom och mödom: Sexualitet, homosocialitet och aristokratisk identitet på det senmedeltida Island*. Göteborg: Göteborgs Universitet, 2009.

Bampi, Massimiliano, Caroline Larrington, and Sif Rikhardsdottir, eds. *A Critical Companion to Old Norse Literary Genre*. Cambridge: D.S. Brewer, 2020.

Barnes, Geraldine. *The Bookish Riddarasögur: Writing Romance in Late Medieval Iceland*. Odense: University Press of Southern Denmark, 2014.

Bruckner, Matilda Tomaryn, and Glyn S. Burgess. "Arthur in the Narrative Lay." In *The Arthur of the French: The Arthurian Legend in Medieval French and Occitan Literature*, ed. Glyn S. Burgess and Karen Pratt, 186–214. Cardiff: University of Wales Press, 2006.

Budal, Ingvil Brügger. "A Translation and Its Continuation: The Use of the Present Participle in *Elíss saga ok Rósamundar*." In *Opuscula* 16, ed. Annette Lassen and Philip Lavender, 63–89. Bibliotheca Arnamagnaeana 50. Copenhagen: Museum Tusculanum Press, 2018.

Busby, Keith, and Leah Tether. "'*Que nus contes de ce n'amende*': Chrétien de Troyes and the Assertion of Copyright." *Journal of the International Arthurian Society* 11 (2023): 1–18.

Crosland, Jessie. *The Old French Epic*. Ktēmata 8. New York: Haskell House Publishers, 1971.

Darmesteter, Arsène. *De Floovante vetustiore gallico poemate et de merovingo cyclo*. Thesis, Paris, 1877.

De Vries, Jan. *Altnordische Literaturgeschichte*. 2nd ed. Berlin: de Gruyter, 1967.

Eriksen, Stefka Georgieva. *Writing and Reading in Medieval Manuscript Culture: The Translation and Transmission of the Story of Elye in Old French and Old Norse Literary Contexts*. Turnhout: Brepols, 2014.

Etheridge, Christian. "Canon, Dominican and Brother: The Life and Times of Jón Halldórsson in Bergen." In *Dominican Resonances in Medieval Iceland: The Legacy of Bishop Jón Halldórsson of Skálholt*, ed. Gunnar Harðarson and K.G. Johansson, 7–40. Leiden and Boston: Brill, 2021.

Farmer, David Hugh. *The Oxford Dictionary of Saints*. 3rd ed. Oxford: Oxford University Press, 2011.

—. "Giles (Aegidius)." In *The Oxford Dictionary of Saints*, 205–6. 3rd ed. Oxford: Oxford University Press, 2011.

Fendel, Sophie Charlotte Maria. *Tierische Wege gen Norden: Zur Physiologus- und Bestiarienrezeption in Nordeuropa*. Munich: Ludwig-Maximilians-Universität, 2023.

Finnur Jónsson. *Den oldnorske og oldislandske Litteraturs Historie*. 3 vols. Copenhagen: Gads Forlag, 1920–24.

Gaunt, Simon. "Romance and Other Genres." In *The Cambridge Companion to Medieval Romance*, ed. Roberta L. Kruger, 45–59. Cambridge: Cambridge University Press, 2000.

Glauser, Jürg. "Bærings saga." In *Medieval Scandinavia: An Encyclopedia*, ed. Phillip Pulsiano and Kirsten Wolf, 60. New York & London: Garland Publishing, 1993.

—. *Isländische Märchensagas: Studien Zur Prosaliteratur im spätmittelalterlichen Island*. Basel and Frankfurt: Helbing & Lichtenhahn, 1983.

—. "Romance – A Case Study." In *A Critical Companion to Old Norse Literary Genre*, ed. Massimiliano Bampi, Carolyne Larrington, and Sif Rikhardsdottir, 299–311. Cambridge: D.S. Brewer, 2020.

—. "Romance (Translated *riddarasögur*)." In *A Companion to Old Norse–Icelandic Literature*, ed. Rory McTurk, 372–87. Oxford: Blackwell Publishing, 2007.

Glauser, Jürg, and Susanne Kramarz-Bein. *Rittersagas: Übersetzung, Überlieferung, Transmission*. Tübingen: A. Francke, 2014.

Guðrún Nordal. "Learned Literature." In *The Cambridge History of Old Norse–Icelandic Literature*, ed. Heather O'Donoghue and Eleanor Parker, 518–36. Cambridge: Cambridge University Press, 2024.

Gunnar Karlsson. *Iceland's 1100 Years: The History of a Marginal Society*. Reykjavík: Mál og menning, 2000.

Heng, Geraldine. *The Invention of Race in the European Middle Ages*. Cambridge: Cambridge University Press, 2018.

Hughes, Shaun F.D. "Klári saga as an Indigenous Romance." In *Romance and Love in Late Medieval and Early Modern Iceland*, ed. Kirsten Wolf and Johanna Denzin, 135–63. Islandica LIV. Ithaca: Cornell University Library, 2008.

Jensson, Gottskálk. "Bishop Jón Halldórsson and 14th-Century Innovations in Saga Narrative: The Case of *Egils saga einhenda ok Ásmundar berserkjabana*." In *Dominican Resonances in Medieval Iceland: The Legacy of Bishop Jón Halldórsson of Skálholt*, ed. Gunnar Harðarson and K.G. Johansson, 59–78. Leiden and Boston: Brill, 2021.

Jochens, Jenny. *Women in Old Norse Society*. Ithaca and London: Cornell University Press, 1995.

Jóhanna Katrín Friðriksdóttir. "Brothers in Arms." In *Manuscripts from the Arnamagnæan Collection*, ed. Matthew James Driscoll and Svanhildur Óskarsdóttir, 80–81. Copenhagen: Tusculanum Press, 2015.

Kalinke, Marianne. "Arthurian Echoes in Indigenous Icelandic Sagas." In *The Arthur of the North: The Arthurian Legend in the Norse and Rus' Realms*, ed. Marianne E. Kalinke, 145–59. Cardiff: University of Wales Press, 2011.

—. *King Arthur, North-by-Northwest: The* matière de Bretagne *in Old Norse–Icelandic Romances*. Bibliotheca Arnamagnæana 37. Copenhagen: C.A. Reitzels Boghandel, 1981.

—. "Norse Romance (*Riddarasögur*)." In *Old Norse–Icelandic Literature: A Critical Guide*, ed. Carol J. Clover and John Lindow, 316–63. Toronto: University of Toronto Press, 1985.

250 • *Bibliography*

—. "Scribes, Editors, and the *riddarasögur*." *Arkiv för Nordisk Filologi* 97 (1982): 36–51.

—. "*Skikkjurímur*: We shall find ourselves better women." *Journal of English and Germanic Philology* 120 (2021): 1–17.

—. "Sources, Translations, Redactions, Manuscript Transmission." In *The Arthur of the North: The Arthurian Legend in the Norse and Rus' Realms,* ed. Marianne Kalinke, 22–47. Cardiff: University of Wales Press, 2011.

—. *Stories Set Forth with Fair Words: The Evolution of Medieval Romance in Iceland.* Cardiff: University of Wales Press, 2017.

—. "Table Decorum and the Quest for a Bride in *Clári saga*." In *At the Table: Metaphorical and Material Culture of Food in Medieval and Early Modern Europe,* ed. Timothy J. Tomasik and Juliann M. Vitullo, 51–72. Turnhout: Brepols, 2007.

—. "The Genesis of Courtly Romance in Iceland." *Journal of English and Germanic Philology* 123 (2024): 271–94.

—. "Romances (East and West Norse)." In *Oxford Bibliographies in Medieval Studies,* ed. Christopher Kleinhenz. New York: Oxford University Press, 2022.

Kalinke, Marianne, and Kirsten Wolf. *Pious Fictions and Pseudo-Saints in the Late Middle Ages: Selected Legends from an Icelandic Legendary.* Toronto: Pontifical Institute of Mediaeval Studies, 2023.

Kalinke, Marianne, and P.M. Mitchell, eds. *Bibliography of Old Norse–Icelandic Romances.* Ithaca and London: Cornell University Press, 1985.

Keller, Hans-Erich. *Autour de Roland: Recherches sur la chanson de geste.* Paris: Librairie Honoré Champion, 1989.

Kölbing, Eugen. "Die nordische Elissaga und Rosamundu und ihre Quelle." In *Beiträge zur vergleichenden Geschichte der romantischen Poesie und Prosa des Mittelalters,* 92–136. Breslau: Wilhelm Koebner, 1876.

Kraeger, Adèle. "Lapidaries and *lyfsteinar*: Health, Enhancement and Human-Lithic Relations in Medieval Iceland." *Gripla* 33 (2022): 115–55.

Krauß, Henning. "Romanische Heldenepik." In *Europäisches Hochmittelalter,* ed. Henning Krauß, 145–71. Neues Handbuch der Literaturwissenschaft 7. Wiesbaden: Akademische Verlagsgesellschaft Athenaion, 1981.

Lacy, Norris J. "Chrétien de Troyes." In *The New Arthurian Encyclopedia,* ed. Norris J. Lacy, 88–91. Garland Reference Library of the Humanities. New York & London: Garland Publishing, 1996.

Leach, Henry Goddard. *Angevin Britain and Scandinavia.* Cambridge: Harvard University Press, 1921.

Lodén, Sofia. *French Romance, Medieval Sweden and the Europeanisation of Culture.* Cambridge: D.S. Brewer, 2021.

—. "Laudine and Lunete Moving North." In *Medieval Romances across European Borders,* ed. Miriam Edlich-Muth, 95–106. Turnhout: Brepols, 2018.

Lodén, Sofia, and Leah Tether. "Translating Copyright: Herr Ivan and the Impediment of Chrétien de Troyes." In *Authorial Publishing in the Middle Ages from Late Antiq-*

uity to the Renaissance, ed. Samu Niskanen and Valentina Rovere. Turnhout: Brepols, forthcoming.

Meissner, Rudolf. *Die Strengleikar: Ein Beitrag zur Geschichte der altnordischen Prosaliteratur.* Halle a. S.: Max Niemeyer, 1902.

Olsen, Thorkil Damsgaard. "Den høviske litteratur." In *Norrøn Fortællekunst: Kapitler af den norsk-islandske middelalderlitteraturs historie,* ed. Hans Bekker-Nielsen, Thorkil Damsgaard Olsen, and Ole Widding, 92–117. Copenhagen: Akademisk Forlag, 1965.

Rajna, Pio. *I Reali di Francia: Ricerche intorno Ai Reali di Francia,* vol. 1. Bologna: Presso Gaetano Romagnoli, 1872.

Sanders, Christopher. "A Typology of the Primary Texts of *Bevers saga.*" In *Rittersagas: Übersetzung, Überlieferung, Transmission,* ed. Jürg Glauser and Susanne Kramarz-Bein, 133–51. Tübingen: A. Francke, 2014.

Schach, Paul. "Some Observations on the Translations of Brother Róbert." In *Les relations littéraires Franco-Scandinaves au Moyen Âge: Actes du Colloque de Liège (avril 1972),* 117–33. Liège: Université de Liège, 1975.

Schlauch, Margaret. *Romance in Iceland.* Princeton, NJ: Princeton University Press; New York: The American-Scandinavian Foundation, 1934.

Sif Rikhardsdottir. *Medieval Translations and Cultural Discourse: The Movement of Texts in England, France and Scandinavia.* Cambridge: D.S. Brewer, 2012.

—. "The Phantom of Romance: Traces of Romance Transmission and the Question of Originality." In *Medieval Romances Across European Borders,* ed. Miriam Edlich-Muth, 133–151. Turnhout: Brepols, 2018.

—. "Riddarasögur." In *The Cambridge History of Old Norse–Icelandic Literature,* ed. Heather O'Donoghue and Eleanor Parker, 435–51. Cambridge: Cambridge University Press, 2024.

Taylor, Jane H.M. (ed.), Peter F. Ainsworth, Norris J. Lacy, Edward Donald Kennedy, and William W. Kibler. "Late Medieval Arthurian Literature." In *The Arthur of the French: The Arthurian Legend in Medieval French and Occitan Literature,* ed. Glyn S. Burgess and Karen Pratt, 488–527. Cardiff: University of Wales Press, 2006.

Turville-Petre, Gabriel. *Origins of Icelandic Literature.* London: Oxford University Press, 1967.

Wellendorf, Jonas. "Homilies and Christian Instruction." In *The Cambridge History of Old Norse–Icelandic Literature,* ed. Heather O'Donoghue and Eleanor Parker, 354–71. Cambridge: Cambridge University Press, 2024.

Index

Works by known authors are listed under their names; anonymous works are listed under their titles. Icelandic names are alphabetized by given name, not patronymic. Readers may find the cross-references under "sagas" to be useful.

Af fru Olif ok Landres syni hennar 110 n1
Af Jorsalaferð 171 n2. See also *Pèlerinage de Charlemagne*
Ailes, Marianne 35
Alexander the Great 101, 147 with n20
Aliscans 17. See also *chansons de geste*
Althing 1
Andolf, Sven 8 n45
Andrea da Barberino: *I Reali di Francia* 29
anonymity: of authors of the *chansons de geste* 2; of copyists of chivalric romances 2
Arthur, king 219 n6
Asalabia, name of an animal 241 with n22

Bærings saga 11–12, 42–44, 49, 51; as medieval *Baedeker* 11; as medieval *Bildungsroman* 45; Baering given the cognomen Fair Knight (*inn fagri riddari*) in 43
baptism: of Élie in *Élie de Saint-Gilles* 27; of the giant Eskopart in *Bevers saga* 40, 184 with n7
Barnes, Geraldine 46 n202
Bevers saga 4, 6, 8, 10–13, 35–37, 41–42, 49–50, 222 n11; oldest manuscript of 37
Bible: Daniel 3, 6, and 13 133 n15; Luke 11:27 223 n13; Matthew 7:17 111 n3;

Proverbs 23:25 223 n13; Revelation 131; Revelation 21:19–20 33
Bjarni Vilhjálmsson 35, 46, 50
Björn Þorleifsson 28 n131
Bodel, Jean 1, 2, 9; and the matter of Britain, France, and Rome 1
Boeve de Haumtone 4–6, 9, 13, 35, 38, 41–42, 50, 184 n7, 190 n9, 194 n11, 195 n12
Book of Lais 4
Breton lays 3

canonical hours: in *Bærings saga* 211 n4, 215; in *Elis saga* 108; in *Flóvents saga* 119 n7
Cederschiöld, Gustaf 28, 35, 47–48
Chanson d'Aspremont 6
chanson d'aventure 38
Chanson de Roland 1–2, 6, 14; Roland in 9
La chanson de Saisnes 1
chansons de geste 1–6, 8–10, 12–15, 16–18, 28, 35, 42–43, 50–51; Franco-Italian 29, 51. See also *Aliscans; Chanson d'Aspremont; La chanson de Saisnes; Guillaume cycle; Moniage de Guillaume; Otinel; Pèlerinage de Charlemagne*
Charlemagne, king and emperor 2, 6, 9–10, 51, 53, 99, 171 n2

chivalric, courtly romances (*roman courtois*) 2

chivalric romances, sagas (Old Norse–Icelandic *riddarasögur*) 7, 10, 42

Chrétien de Troyes 2–3, 7, 9–10, 14, 32, 43, 123 n14, 180 n5, 182 n6, 219 n6; *Erec et Enide* 3, 32; *Perceval* 3; *Yvain* (*Le Chevalier au Lion*) 3, 7, 9, 14, 38, 132 n14, 180 n5, 186 n6

Christianization: of Iceland, book learning, translation of homilies, and saints' lives 1, 10, 12. *See also under* motifs

chronicle(s) 2; *Kaiserchronik* 2

cities: Abbaport 41, 193, 198–99, 201–2, 204; Anguriss 236; Babylon 199; Bardwick 210, 239–40; Bern 230, 233; Biterna 91 n16; Bononia 217 with n5, 227; Bozen 231, 233–34, 236; Braunschweig 213, 240, 242; Bremen 240; Carthage 177; Civile 193, 199; Cologne 159–60, 183–86; Constantinople 223, 243; Damascus 165, 170–71, 175; Eutin 210–11, 239–40; Florence 243; Hampton 159–60, 164, 171, 177, 184–86, 189, 191, 207–8; Hildesheim 240, 242; Jerusalem 177, 202, 209; Kiev 242; London 208, 212, 215; Lübeck 238–39; Munbrak 40–41, 173, 177, 191, 200–202, 204, 206–7, 209; Mylnar 237; Orleans 192; Paris 153–57, 218, 212; Rome 209, 242; Sion 29 n137; St Gilles-du-Gard 192 n10; Trento 233; Venice 227, 234, 243–44; Vicilior 237; Yarmouth 216

Clovis, king of France 29–30

Conrad III, emperor 2

Constantine the Great, emperor 29, 33–34, 110 n2, 120 n9

Constantinople (*Miklagarðr*) 12, 171 n2, 222 n10

continuation, Icelandic, of French epics: see under *Elis saga ok Rósamundu*

copyists: anonymous, of chivalric

romance 2; of oldest manuscript of *Bevers saga* 37; chapter titles in manuscript of *Flóvents saga* composed by 47; errors made by in Chrétien's *Yvain* 9

countries and regions: Denmark 238, 242; Egypt 163, 177, 184–85, 190–91; England 159–60, 177, 184–85, 190–91, 201, 207, 212, 238, 242; Finland 153; Flanders 209; France 11, 153–58, 242; Frisia 213, 238–39, 242; Germany 11, 159, 187; Greece 11, 192, 221, 223, 227, 238, 243; Holstein 211, 214, 238–39, 242; Italy 1; Lombardy 242, 244; Normandy 153–54, 158; Norway 1, 3–5, 8 n44, 13, 27, 35, 210; Nubia 153; Saxony 210, 242, 244; Scotland 187, 215; Sweden 210; Vlieland 238 with n20; Westphalia 242

courtly romances: *see* chivalric, courtly romances

Darmesteter, Arsène 29

de Vries, Jan 12

Dominicans, Dominican Order 5–6. *See also* Jón Halldórsson

Élie de Saint-Gilles 4, 8–10, 13–16, 18–21, 23, 28, 46, 51

Elis saga ok Rósamundu 4, 8–10, 13–22, 28, 32, 36, 42, 46–47, 49, 51; Icelandic continuation 23–27, 46, 49, 50; place names in 51; plagiarism in continuation 26

epic(s), heroic 1–2. *See also* romance epic(s)

Eufemia, queen of Norway 4

Finnur Jónsson 11

Floovant 4–6, 8–10, 13, 28, 30, 115 n5

Flóvents saga 4, 6, 8, 10–11, 13, 27–28, 30–32, 36, 39, 42, 47, 49, 51; *Flóvents saga I* 28–29, 33–34, 47–48; *Flóvents*

254 • *Index*

saga II 28, 33–35, 47; use of French proverbs in 28–29, 48–49, 153
Franks 30–31, 33–34; invasion 120 n9

Glauser, Jürg 14
Gottfried von Strassburg: *Tristan* 3
Guibourc, Saracen princess and wife of William of Orange 17
Guidot, Bernard 20
Guillaume cycle 14
Gunnlaugs saga ormstungu 12, 221 n9

Hærra Ivan 4
Hákon Hákonarson, king of Norway 3–5, 7, 9, 23, 47 n204, 97 n17
Hartman, A. Richard 15, 51
Hartmann von Aue: *Erek* and *Iwein* 3
hásæti: see under motifs
Heinrich III, the Lion, duke of Saxony and Bavaria 2–3
Hlöðvir konungr 50. *See also* Louis the Pious
Holy Spirit 31, 139, 158, 160, 163, 164, 240
Hugon, king 171 n2

Íslendingasögur (Sagas of Icelanders) 8, 34, 50
Ívens saga 3–4, 7

Jensson, Gottskálk 5
jongleurs 1, 6, 8–9, 19, 42
Jón Halldórsson, bishop of Skálholt and Dominican friar 5–6; translation of Latin *exempla* 6 with n26
Jorgensen, Peter 25
Jorsalaferð 171 n2
Judas 77

Karlamagnús saga 6–7, 9, 51, 110 n1, 171 n2
Klári saga 6
Knittelvers 4

Kölbing, Eugen 13, 26, 46
Konráðs saga keisarasonar 32
Kraeger, Adèle 131 n12

laisse(s) 15–16, 18–21, 35, 41–42
languages and language areas: Anglo-Norman 2, 5, 29, 35, 41–42, 50, 195 n12; East and West Norse 13–14; Franco-Italian 13, 29, 50; French 3–5; German 2–3; Latin 3; Norwegian 49; Old French 14; Old Icelandic 219 n6, 222; Old Norse 132 n14; Old Norse–Icelandic 5, 9, 14; Swedish 4
Layamon's Brut 31 n147
Lay du cort mantel 3, 7
lays, *lais* 3–4
Leach, Henry Goddard 12–13
Leiðarvísir 11 n58
literature: Middle High German 2; Old Icelandic and Old French 1–15; oral 1, 2, 12, 19; sacred and secular 1. *See also* anonymity; copyists; style; translation
Lodén, Sofia 14
Louis the Pious, king 15, 51, 53, 71, 99. *See also* Hlöðvir konungr

Mahomet: *see under* pagan gods, idols, and heroes
Malicote, Sandra C. 15, 51
manuscript(s): Copenhagen, Den Arnamagnæanske Samling, AM 333 4o 103 n20; AM 567 II 4o 12, 97 n19; AM 580 4o 7, 11–12, 28–29, 42, 47–48; Montpellier, Bibliothèque de la Faculté de Médicine, nr. 441 28; Oslo, Riksarkivet, NRA 61 7; Oxford, Bodleian Library, Digby 23 2; Paris, Bibliothèque nationale de France no 25516 15; Stockholm, Kungliga biblioteket, Holm perg. 6 4o 15, 35, 47; Holm perg 7 fol. 103 n20; Uppsala, Uppsala universitetsbibliotek, De la Gardie 4–7 15
– depositories: Arnamagnæan Institute,

Copenhagen 7; Riksarkivet, Oslo 7; Royal Library, Stockholm 15, 28
Marie de France: *Lais* 13–14; *Lanval* 39
Mathilde, wife of Heinrich the Lion 3
Meissner, Rudolf 5 with n20
Miklagarðr: see Constantinople
Moniage de Guillaume 6. See also *chansons de geste*
motifs: ambiguous oath 7; angels 228–29, 233; animals 25, 82, 86, 131 (images of), 95 (Arabian horse), 241 with n22 (Asalabia), 160, 164–65 (boar), 45, 211, 231, 241–42 (dragons), 120–21 (hart), 181, 192, 211, 244 (lions), 242 (ox), 172, 241 n23, 242 (serpents, snakes, and toads); Arthurian 38, 219 n6 (Round Table); audience address 8, 19, 41, 64; author commentary 10; bridal quest 6; changelings 141 n17; chastity belt 36–37, 173 n4; Christianization 139, 157, 207; consanguinity 27; easily consoled widow 44 n197, 228; fairies 26–27; *fin' amor* 15; flyting 49; giants, giantesses 12, 37–38, 44–45, 176–77, 182, 222 with n11, 231, 239–40; hall of statues 7; *hásæti* (throne-table) 219 with n6, 221, 229; holmgang 45; humor 39–40; *inn fagri riddari* (the Fair Knight) 43, 219, 221, 225–26, 229, 238; *la bele Sarrasine* 10, 30, 39; light-radiating carbuncle 171 n2; love potion 8; magic rings 38, 132 n14; magic stones 38, 144 n18; male gaze, female gaze 43, 229; marriage 162 with n1, 221 with n8; music 4, 25, 99, 107–8, 221; narrator commentary "nú er at segja" (now there is to be told) 50; proverb 231; proxy wooing 8; purloined patrimony 10–12, 43, 226; refusal to identify oneself 218–19, 223–25; shapeshifters (including Skadevald) 12, 45, 231 n15, 239 with n21, 240–41, 242 n24; sorcery 44–45, 231, 240; witchcraft 231, 240–41
Möttuls saga 5, 7

Nikulás Bergsson, abbot 11 n58

Óláfr Tryggvason, king 1
Otinel 6. See also *chansons de geste*

pagan gods, idols, and heroes: Apollin 151; Apollo 51, 68–70; Hector, son of King Priam 244; Jove 151; Mahomet 22, 31, 37, 51, 64, 68–72, 74–75, 79–81, 83–84, 87–88, 91, 93–97, 118, 120, 125–29, 131–32, 134–35, 137–41, 146, 148, 150–53, 164–65, 172, 175, 198; Menelaus 91; Paris and Helen 91; Tervagant 22, 31 with n147, 37, 51, 69, 97, 118, 119, 135, 139–40, 151–52, 154, 172, 206
Pèlerinage de Charlemagne 6–7, 171 n2
Pfaffe Konrad 2

riddarasaga, riddarasögur 7, 10, 12–13, 42, 48, 110 n1, 132 n14, 144 n18
Robert, Abbot 3–4, 10, 13, 15, 22–25, 46–47, 49, 97 nn17 and 18; presumed to be Brother Robert 4
Robert, Brother 3–4, 8
Rolandslied 2
romance(s): Arthurian 2–3 with n13, 6, 9, 180 n5, 219 n6; bridal-quest 6; chivalric 11; courtly (*roman courtois, romans* and *estoires*) 2, 3, 4–5, 6; epic(s) 4, 6, 43
romance epic(s) 4, 6, 8, 11, 12, 19, 42, 43, 51
Roncevaux Pass 1

sagas: of ancient heroes 1; of Icelanders 1; of Icelandic poets 12; of kings 1; *Bærings saga* 42–46; *Bevers saga* 35–42, 50–51; *Elis saga ok Rósamundu* 14–27,

54 n6, 97 n18; *Flóvents saga* 27–35. *See also* cities; countries and regions; motifs; pagan gods, idols, and heroes; saints; style

saints: Dennis (bishop) 58 n10; Dyonisius 52; Egidius (St Giles) 16, 17, 41, 51–52 with n1, 56, 71, 97, 108, 192 n10; Hilary (bishop) 53 with n3; James the Great (apostle) 51; John, Ioan postoli (the Evangelist) 51; John the Baptist 238 with n19; Mark (pope) 157 with n22; Martin (bishop) 57 with n7, 69; Mary, Virgin 126, 157 with n23 (Annunciation, feast of), 164, 240, 243 with n25 (Assumption); Peter (apostle) 54 n6, 55, 111; Santiago de Compostela 51, 53 n5; Sylvester (pope) 33, 110 n2, 114 with n4

Sanders, Christopher 35

Saracen(s) 10, 11, 12, 15, 17, 18, 22–23, 25, 27, 30–31, 33, 35, 36–37, 39–40, 43, 49, 116 n6, 222 n11; gods and idols 18, 22, 31–32, 36–37, 39, 45, 51; translation of term 51. *See also* pagan gods, idols, and heroes

Saxons 30–31, 33–34

Schlauch, Margaret 29–30

Sif Rikhardsdottir 5, 13–14

Skikkjurímur 219 n6

Song of Roland 2

Stimming, Albert 194 n11

Storie di Fioravante 29, 119 n8

Strengleikar 4

style: adverb *nú* 50; alliterating prose 10, 22–23, 46; assonanced stanzas 16;

audience address 8, 19, 41; courtly style 21; hypotaxis and parataxis 24, 49, 50; narrative past 24, 49, 50; narrator commentary 10, 23, 25, 34; participial constructions 23–24, 46; rhetorical devices 29; *teichoscopy* 145 n19; tense shifting 50

Tervagant: *see under* pagan gods, idols, and heroes

Thomas d'Angleterre: *Tristran* 2–3, 5, 7–8

throne-table (*hásæti*): *see under* motifs

translation: adaptations 12–13; of *chansons de geste* 4, 6–10, 14, 49; of courtly romances 3–4, 6–8, 10–11, 14–15, 132 n14, 144 n18, 173 n3, 180 n5; of epic poems 2–4, 13–14; of homilies and saints' lives 1; of lays 3–4, 7, 14; into Old Icelandic 13; into Old Norse 13, 132 n14; and *riddarasögur* 7–9, 11–14; of romance epics 11–12; variant versions 9–10, 13, 15–18, 20–22. See also *Elis saga ok Rósamundu*: Icelandic continuation; literature

Tristrams saga ok Ísoddar 7, 173 n3

Tristrams saga ok Ísöndar 3 with n13, 7–8, 15

Weiss, Judith 35, 50, 190 n9, 192 n10, 194 n11, 196 n13, 206 n14

William, count of Toulouse 14; *Vita sancti Willelmi* 14

William of Orange 9, 14 with n77, 15, 17, 22, 59, 60, 66, 67, 97

Wolfram von Eschenbach: *Parzival* 3